MEDIA

AN
INTRODUCTORY ANALYSIS
OF
AMERICAN
MASS COMMUNICATIONS

Peter M. Sandman
The University of Michigan

David M. Rubin
New York University
at Washington Square

David B. Sachsman
Rutgers—The State University
Livingston College

PRENTICE-HALL INC., ENGLEWOOD CLIFFS, N.J.

To Suzy, Tina, and Judy, our wives
And to William L. Rivers, our teacher

ISBN: 0–13–572420–1
Library of Congress Card Number: 72–39315

10 9 8 7 6

Printed in the United States of America

PRENTICE-HALL INTERNATIONAL, INC., London
PRENTICE-HALL OF AUSTRALIA, PTY. LTD., Sydney
PRENTICE-HALL OF CANADA, LTD., Toronto
PRENTICE-HALL OF INDIA PRIVATE LIMITED, New Delhi
PRENTICE-HALL OF JAPAN, INC., Tokyo

Contents

Newspaper Chains. Wire Services. The
Muckrakers. New Media. Old Media.
Depression and After. TV Develops.
The Old Media Respond. Notes.
Suggested Readings.

PART TWO

RESPONSIBILITY, 79

2   Self-Control [Ethics], 82

Media Codes. The Right to Privacy. The
Reporter as Part of the Story. Conflict of
Interest. The Junket. Paying for the
News. Dishonesty and the News.
Notes. Suggested Readings.

3   Internal Control [Gatekeeping], 95

Policy. Social Control. Unanimity.
Gatekeepers. The Telegraph Editor.
Other Media Gatekeepers. Unanimity
Again. Notes. Suggested Readings.

4   Monopoly Control, 112

Chains and Networks. Cross-Media
Ownership. Joint Operating
Agreements. Conglomerates. An
Overview. Abuses of Concentration.
Competition. Government Regulation.
Choosing among Evils. Notes.
Suggested Readings.

5   Advertiser Control, 130

Who Pays the Piper. Ideology Versus
Business. Patterns of Advertiser Control.
Threats, Bribes, and Understandings.
Broadcasting: A Special Case. Notes.
Suggested Readings.

PART FOUR

COVERAGE, 333

Foreword

Trying to avoid the products of the mass media is like trying to avoid daylight: You can do it, but only with an effort so demanding that it reaches the point of absurdity. Except for those who plan to enter monasteries, all college students will be immersed in the media for the rest of their lives. It follows that all—not just those who will become newspaper reporters, television producers, and film-makers, but also those who will be lawyers and stockbrokers and morticians—should learn about the strengths and the flaws of mass communication, what it can do for them, and what it can do *to* them.

Not so long ago schools and departments of journalism and communication were content to deal only with prospective reporters, advertising salesmen, film-makers, and others who were trying to learn to work in the media. The skills and techniques courses that make up the bulk of the curricula of that time were designed to *train* rather than to educate. There was precious little in those journalism programs that appealed to students who wanted a career outside the mass media. Now, however, programs almost everywhere offer at least a few courses—some offer a great many—that teach all comers *about* the world of mass communication. The result is surely better-informed practitioners and more knowledgeable laymen.

This book is completely in tune with the trend to broad-gauge journalism education. The authors are not at all concerned here with teach-

Introduction

The history of civilization is the history of a shrinking world. The spoken and written word, the wheel, the printing press, the railroad, the airplane, and the vacuum tube have all had the same basic effect on mankind: they bring us closer together. Marshall McLuhan sees all such extensions of man as media of communication, and strictly speaking he is right. A beard, a button-down shirt, or a wry smile communicates information in much the same way as a newspaper or a television program.

COMMUNICATION

Communication is the process of transmitting a message from a source to an audience via a channel. Consider, for example, a conversation, the most common kind of communication. The person who speaks is the source. The person who listens is the audience. What is transmitted is the message. And the spoken voice (involving vocal cords, air vibrations, ear drums, etc.) is the channel.

Now consider a more complicated example, an article in a newspaper. The message is everything the article says, everything it implies, and everything a reader might infer from it. The audience is everybody who reads the article or even glances at it. The source is everybody who contributes in one way or another to the article; this includes the newsmakers who are quoted, the reporter, the editor, and even the proofreaders and printers. The channel is, of course, the printed word, the newspaper itself.

What is a communication *medium?* Strictly speaking, a medium is a channel—the spoken word, the printed word, or whatever. But the term is often used to mean both the channel and the source, and sometimes even the message. It includes everything that reaches the audience. When we speak of the "mass media," for example, we usually mean not only the channels of mass communication, but also the content of those channels and the behavior of the people who work for them.

Wilbur Schramm thinks of communication as a sharing process. He puts it this way:

> *Communication* comes from the Latin *communis,* common. When we communicate we are trying to establish a "commonness" with some-one. That is, we are trying to share information, an idea, or an attitude. At this moment I am trying to communicate to you the idea that the essence of communication is getting the receiver and the sender "tuned" together for a particular message.[1]

Effective communication, then, is communication that succeeds in establishing Schramm's "commonness" between the source and the audience. Communication is perfectly effective when the audience receives precisely what the source intended it to receive.

Anything that interferes with effective communication can be called "noise." This bit of jargon is borrowed from electrical engineering, where "noise" refers literally to the static in an electrical system that lessens the precision of the transmission. A misspelled word, a fuzzy TV picture, and an ink splotch are all examples of noise in a communications channel.

Channel noise is usually a minor problem for the mass media, but other kinds of noise are not. Often the source of the communication produces his own noise. A public speaker may mumble or mispronounce a word; he may speak in a foreign language or use language that his audience doesn't understand. These are all examples of "source noise," or as it is more commonly called, "semantic noise."

The bulk of the noise in a communication system is contributed by neither the source nor the channel, but rather by the audience. People are enormously proficient at ignoring, misinterpreting, and misremembering communications that for one reason or another don't appeal to them. There are three psychological strategies that are relevant here:

   * *Selective attention.* People expose themselves primarily to communications they like. If you are not interested in buying a car, you will read very few automobile advertisements. If you are interested, you'll

probably read all the ads you can.   But once you settle on a Plymouth, you are likely to read only the Plymouth ads.

* *Selective perception.*   Once exposed to a communication, people tend to interpret it so as to coincide with their own preconceptions.   If you show a middle-class audience a drawing of a white man brandishing a razor in the face of a Negro, many will "see" the razor in the hand of the Negro instead.

* *Selective retention.*   Even if they understand a communication, people tend to remember only what they want to remember.   After reading a balanced discussion of Soviet Communism, anti-Communist students recall mostly the drawbacks of the system, while pro-Communist students tend to remember mostly its advantages.

Most communications are controlled by the source.   When a teacher lectures to a class, it is the teacher, not the class, who decides what will be said.   Selective attention, selective perception, and selective retention are the principal methods open to the audience for controlling the message.   If a student is bored or offended by what the teacher is saying, he may tune him out and think about something else.   Or he may unconsciously misinterpret the lecture, perhaps "hearing" that there will be one term paper when the teacher has said there will be two.   Or he may simply forget those parts of the message that appeal to him least, such as the reading assignment.   The teacher is likely to take a dim view of these lapses, but he is just as guilty as his students.   In grading papers, for example, he tends to "see" the right answers in the papers of students whose work he admires.

Selective attention, selective perception, and selective retention are universal.   They add a tremendous amount of noise to nearly every communication.   The source can easily control what he says, but he cannot control what the audience hears, or thinks it hears.

Audience noise is most potent when the message is controversial; simple and unthreatening messages, on the other hand, tend to be received relatively "clear."   As a result, it is next to impossible for any communication to convert an audience from one viewpoint to another.   It is much easier to create a new viewpoint where none existed before.   And it is easier still to communicate information that tends to support the established viewpoint of the audience.   All communicators—advertisers, politicians, newsmen, even teachers—must work within these constraints.

So far we have talked about communication as if it were a one-way street; the message moves in a straight line from the source to the channel to the audience.   In reality, every good communications system must work both ways.   The mechanisms for transmitting messages backward from audience to channel, from audience to source, or from channel to source are known as "feedback loops."   When a television performer checks the monitor to see how he looks on the screen, he is getting feedback from the channel. When he reads his fan mail, he is getting feed-back from the audience. And when the broadcaster looks over the show's ratings, he too is getting feedback from the audience.

The technical vocabulary of communications will be used sparingly in this book. Of course we'll be talking a lot about sources and audiences, but very little about channels, and even less about "noise," "selective attention," "feedback loops," and the like. Nevertheless, these are vitally important concepts to bear in mind. When we speak later about the influence of news bias, we will be describing a kind of noise. When we discuss the ineffectiveness of editorials, we will be referring to a special case of selective attention. And when we complain about the problem of public control of the media, we will be noting the absence of sufficient provision for feedback.

MASS COMMUNICATION

Interpersonal communication is the process of transmitting information, ideas, and attitudes from one person to another. Mass communication is the process of transmitting information, ideas, and attitudes to many people, usually through a machine. There are several important differences between the two.

First, the source of a mass communication has great difficulty gearing his message to his audience. He may know the demographic statistics of the audience—its average age, its average socioeconomic status, etc.—but he cannot know the individual quirks of each individual reader, listener, and viewer.

Second, mass communication systems typically include much weaker feedback loops than interpersonal communication systems. When you talk to somebody, you can usually tell whether he is listening, whether he understands, whether he agrees or disagrees, and so forth. All this is impossible in mass communication.

Third, the audience of a mass communication is much more likely than the audience of an interpersonal communication to twist the message through selective attention, perception, and retention. People turn off the TV (literally or figuratively) if they don't like what it's saying. It's a lot harder—though still possible—to turn off someone talking to you.

Fourth, and perhaps most important, mass communication systems are a lot more complicated than interpersonal communication systems. Each message (an article in a newspaper, for example) may have as many as a dozen sources, with different points of view and different goals for the communication. The channel, too, is typically a complex organization (such as a newspaper), composed of many individuals, whose viewpoints and goals may vary widely. Every mass communication is in a sense a committee product.

All four of these factors tend to lessen the effect of a mass communication on its audience. The power of the mass media is based on the size of their audience, on their ability to reach millions of people in one shot. But in dealing with any individual member of that audience, you'd be a lot more effective if you sat down and chatted with him.

When people sit down and chat, however, the things they talk about and the attitudes they express are often derived from the mass media. In 1940, Paul Lazarsfeld and his colleagues studied the voting behavior of a group of citizens in Erie County, Ohio. They discovered, to their surprise, that very few people decided how to vote on the basis of information learned directly from the mass media. Most voters made up their minds as a result of interpersonal communications—conversations with a friend, a neighbor, a union leader, a spouse.

Only a minority of Erie County's citizens made significant use of the media for voting information. Members of this minority then sat down with their friends and neighbors and transmitted the message of the media through interpersonal communication. Lazarsfeld called these minority members "opinion leaders." He concluded that "ideas often flow from radio and print to opinion leaders and from these to the less active sections of the population."[2] This is known as the "two-step flow" theory of mass-media influence.

More recent research has shown that even the two-step flow theory is oversimplified. A more accurate term might be "multi-step flow." For every field of interest (politics, fashion, economics, moviegoing, etc.) there are apparently certain people who make great use of the media for information and guidance. These opinion leaders then communicate with each other, crystalizing their views into a consistent stance. Later they transmit this attitude to lesser opinion leaders, who also make use of the mass media but not so much. The recipients compare what they get from the media with what they get from their opinion leaders, then pass the combination on down the line. Eventually the message reaches that large segment of the population which makes little or no direct use of the media.

In the field of labor relations, for example, the chain might run something like this: A group of union leaders, all inveterate newspaper readers, agree that they are opposed to the President's plan for wage and price controls. They pass this information on to the shop stewards, who have followed the issue casually on television. The shop stewards pass it on to the rank-and-file, who have a hazy understanding of the problem. And the rank-and-file pass it on to their wives.

The information chain for, say, cooking news would be quite different. A union leader is unlikely to read about a new recipe for veal and pass it along to his shop stewards. He is far more likely to hear about it from his wife, who heard about it from someone else's wife, who read about it in the paper. The principle, however, is the same. The direct effect of the mass media on labor relations and veal recipes is comparatively minor. But the indirect impact is huge.

AMERICAN MASS COMMUNICATION

The American system of mass communication has three characteristics that distinguish it from other systems:

1. Pervasive influence.
2. Freedom of the press.
3. Big-business journalism.

None of these characteristics is unique. There are other countries with powerful media, other countries with free media, other countries with profit-oriented media. But the United States embodies all three traits to an extent unmatched in the rest of the world.

A fish could no more tell you what it is like to live out of water than an American could tell you what it is like to live without mass communication. As soon as an American child is old enough to distinguish between two different makes of midget racing cars or fruit-flavored brands of toothpaste, he is bathed in a constant stream of messages from radio and television. He approaches the daily newspaper through the comics or sports section; these lead him to comic books and sporting magazines, and then perhaps to more serious books and magazines.

By the time he enters kindergarten, the average American child has already been exposed to hundreds, perhaps thousands of hours of radio and television. He has attended dozens of movies and browsed through scores of children's books. He has cut pictures out of magazines and scowled at the newspaper in unconscious imitation of his daddy. All these experiences have taught him something—something about literacy, perhaps, something about violence, something about America. He is in a real sense a child of the mass media.

For most adults, meanwhile, the mass media constitute the only advanced education they receive after high school or college. It is obvious that the media offer every American a continuous course in modern world history. But it is not so obvious, perhaps, that the very basics of community living come to us through the media: births, weddings, deaths, weather reports, traffic accidents, crimes, sales, elections.

It is hard to imagine an efficient system of democratic government without an equally efficient system of mass communications. Citizens would learn of new legislation only after it passed, and then only if they visited their representative in Washington. Incumbents would probably serve for life, because no challenger could make himself known to the electorate. Corruption would go largely unchecked. News of foreign affairs would remain the monopoly of the President and his State Department. And on the local level, mayors would be free to run their cities as personal fiefdoms. Political information is political power. Without the mass media to transmit such information, the American people would be powerless.

Dwarfing even the educational and political roles of the American media is their entertainment function. Television offers a seemingly unending stream of westerns, thrillers, comedies, and star-studded specials. Radio spins records and conversation. Newspapers lighten the weight of the news with puzzles, advice to the lovelorn, comics, sports, and back-fence gossip. Books, magazines, and films supply entertainment packages for more specialized audiences. The Number One source of recreational activity of almost every American is the mass media.

Of course the media are pervasive in other countries as well. Transistor radios are always among the first manufactured products to be imported into any underdeveloped area of the world. Newspapers and government-sponsored radio and TV stations follow soon afterward. Nevertheless, few observers would dispute that Americans are more a product of their media than any other people in the world.

The American government was founded on a radical political theory: representative democracy. According to this strange notion, the people of a nation should control the government by electing officials to carry out their will. The mass media necessarily play a central role in representative democracy. It is through the media that the people get the information they need to decide what they want their officials to do. And it is through the media that the people find out if their officials are doing it.

For this reason the First Amendment to the U.S. Constitution forbids the government to make any laws "abridging the freedom of the press." When it was first written, this provision was unprecedented. Other governments had assumed the right of the king to put a stop to any publication he deemed damaging to the nation. The American Constitution denied Congress and the President this fundamental right. The only thing that can damage a democracy, so the argument went, is a mass media system in chains. As long as every publisher (though not necessarily every reporter) is free to print whatever he wants to print, the truth will make itself clear, the people will be informed, and the democracy will flourish.

Today, many foreign governments have copied our First Amendment into their Constitutions, and some even practice the freedom they preach. The American government, meanwhile, restrains its media with the laws of libel, obscenity, and privacy, the licensing of broadcast stations, the postal regulations, and so forth.

Despite these limitations, there is no mass media system in the world today that is more free from government interference than the American system. In recent years, a number of very high officials have attacked the media for "irresponsible" opposition to government policy. Some have interpreted these attacks as attempts to control the press, and so they may be. But it is a testimonial to the almost incredible freedom of the American media that the attacks are limited to speeches and denunciations. The government can *do* little or nothing. The reader need only consult the latest issue of his favorite underground newspaper for fresh evidence of America's freedom of the press.

The purpose of a free press, you will remember, is to ensure that the people will be well-informed. Well, we have a free press. Do we have an informed population? Pollster George Gallup often quotes a survey of college graduates which found that only four in ten could name the two senators from their own state; only half could cite a single advantage of capitalism over socialism; only half had an accurate idea of the population of the United States; and only one in three could list five of the Soviet Union's satellite countries in Eastern Europe.[3]

The notion that freedom of the press is all that's needed for an informed population is known as the Libertarian Theory. The authors of the First Amendment firmly believed that if every publisher were free to print precisely what he wanted to print, somehow truth would emerge victorious. The only responsibility of the publisher was to tell it the way he saw it. The only responsibility of the government was to leave the publisher alone.

In recent years, many observers have begun to question the Libertarian Theory. In its place they have proposed a Social Responsibility Theory of the press. That is, they argue that the American mass media must recognize their obligation to serve the public—to be truthful, accurate, and complete; to act as a forum for conflicting viewpoints; to provide meaningful background to the daily news; etc. Social Responsibility theorists claim that if the media do not voluntarily live up to their obligations, then they must be forced to do so by the government.

Though the Social Responsibility Theory is gaining in popularity and influence, it is not yet established. The American mass media today are free—free to serve the public or not as they choose.

Perhaps the strongest weapon in the arsenal of the social responsibility theorists is the Big Business emphasis in the modern American media. The United States is one of the few countries in the world whose major media are all privately owned. Like General Motors and U.S. Steel, American newspapers, magazines, and broadcast stations spend much of their time worrying about stockholders, dividends, and profits. They may have too little time left for worrying about service to the public.

Like every business, the mass media have a product to sell. In the case of the book and film industries, the product is the medium itself; part of the price of a book or movie ticket is the manufacturer's profit. For the rest of the mass media, the product is you.   Newspapers, magazines, and broadcast stations earn their considerable profits by selling your presence and your attention to advertisers.   Articles and programs are just a device to keep you corralled, a come-on for the all-important ads.

The inexorable trend in American business is toward monopoly—toward bigness and fewness.   The mass media are no exception.   Chains dominate the newspaper and magazine industries.   The three networks have an iron grip on television programming.   The book business is controlled by a few giant companies on the East Coast, the movie business by a few giant companies on the West Coast.   Competing with the biggies in any of these fields is incredibly costly and hazardous.

Several conclusions follow from these facts.   First, since the American media are businesses first and foremost, they are likely to choose profit over public service when the two come into conflict.   Second, since the media are owned by big businessmen, they are likely to reflect a businessman's notion of what's good for the public—which may not be everybody's notion.   Third, since the media are close to monopolies, they are likely to offer the audience only a single viewpoint on public affairs, instead of the rich conflict of viewpoints envisioned by the Founding Fathers.   And fourth, since the media make competition extremely difficult, they are likely to "black out" positions and groups of which they disapprove.

Pervasive influence, freedom of the press, and the profit motive—this is the combination that makes the American mass media unique.   Nowhere else is such a powerful social force so little controlled by government, so much controlled by self-interest.

THE FOUR FUNCTIONS

The mass media in general, and the American mass media in particular, have four basic functions to perform.   They are:

1. To entertain.
2. To inform.
3. To influence.
4. To make money.

We will consider each in turn.

1. To Entertain.   Entertainment is by far the biggest service of the American mass media.   This is especially true from the viewpoint of the audience.   Political scientists may evaluate a television program in terms of how much information it imparts.   Advertisers may ask what kind of climate for persuasion it offers.   Station owners may wonder how much profit it brings in. But with rare exceptions, viewers want to know only how entertaining it is.

According to the Nielsen ratings, the following were the most popular TV shows for the week ending March 7, 1971:

1. Marcus Welby, M.D. (ABC)
2. Hawaii Five-O (CBS)
3. "Yuma" (ABC) [movie]
4. Medical Center (CBS)
5. Adam 12 (NBC)
6. Flip Wilson (NBC)
7. Mod Squad (ABC)
8. FBI (ABC)
9. Bonanza (NBC)
10. Here's Lucy (CBS)

Every show on the list is almost pure entertainment.

Television is undoubtedly the nation's Number One entertainment medium, but film and radio are not far behind. When the movie "Love Story" opened in December of 1970, it broke the house record in 159 of the 165 theaters in which it was shown. The film grossed over $2,400,000 in its first three days, and by the time this book is published its earnings will have topped $100,000,000. As for radio, the average American family owns at least two receivers in the home and a third in the car. Why do people go to movies and switch on the radio: to be entertained.

Even the print media succeed or fail largely in terms of their entertainment value. The best-seller lists for hardback and paperback books usually include a few works of significance and value. But the bulk of every list is always pure entertainment, and even the "important" books must be entertaining to succeed. Magazines, too, must season their informational content with a heavy dose of fun and games. The least entertaining of the mass media is undoubtedly newspapers. Yet even they offer the reader dozens of comics, humor and gossip columns, and human-interest features in every issue.

Because the public demands entertainment from its media, the media owner who wants to succeed has no choice but to try to be entertaining. Many critics have deplored this fact, complaining that mere entertainment was a waste and a degradation of media potential. Such an attitude ignores the important social role played by entertainment—the transmission of culture, the enlargement of perspectives, the encouragement of imagination, etc. And even the most virulent opponents of media entertainment must admit that the opportunity to relax and unwind is vital. Entertainment is not merely an economic necessity for media owners; it is an integral, essential function of the media.

But that is far from the whole story. The media have other functions besides entertainment. Moreover, the media *choose* the kinds of entertainment they wish to use. They are subject to criticism for their choices.

It is extremely difficult to come up with a clear-cut standard for distinguishing between "good" entertainment and "bad" entertainment. Nonetheless, most observers will agree that in some sense *Harper's* is better than *True Romances*, "Sesame Street" is better than "Bugs Bunny," and Hemingway is better than Erle Stanley Gardner. The media must cater to public tastes, but they also help to mold public tastes. If they choose violence, or pornography, or the lowest of lowbrow culture, then they must take responsibility for the choice.

2. To Inform. Entertainment may be what the public wants from its mass media, but information is probably their most important function. No doubt many people read *Time* and *Newsweek*, say, because they find them entertaining; and certainly the newsmagazines try to entertain their readers. But the best newsmagazine is not necessarily the most entertaining one. It is the one that successfully conveys the most information.

The power of the mass media to inform is almost incredible. On November 22, 1963, at 12:30 in the afternoon, President John F. Kennedy was assassinated. Within half an hour, two-thirds of all Americans knew of the event. Ninety percent knew within an hour, and 99.8 percent had heard the story by early evening.[4] Very few, of course, got the news directly from the mass media; most were told by family, friends, or strangers on the street. This is the "multi-step flow" all over again. A certain number of persons heard the news over the air. Everyone else heard the news from them.

There was an immediate rush to radio and television for more detail. During the days that followed, 166 million Americans tuned in to the assassination story on television. The average TV set was on for roughly eight hours a day.[5]

Most of the news supplied by the mass media is more routine than a Presidential assassination. Weather reports, stock listings, and movie timetables are among the best-read features in your daily newspaper—and among the most informative. We tend to dismiss these services not because they are unimportant, but because they are easy to prepare. Similarly, news reports of natural disasters, crimes, accidents, and the like are genuinely useful. Since they are standard fare for the media and difficult to handle poorly, scholars pay them very little attention—perhaps less attention than they deserve.

The more difficult a story is to cover, the less likely the media are to cover it well. The informational problems of the media are many and varied. Is a story so complicated that no reporter can understand it, much less repeat it? Is it so technical that few readers are likely to enjoy it or finish it? Does it require days of hard-nosed investigative digging among sources who would much rather keep their mouths shut? Might it insult or embarrass an advertiser, an important newsmaker, a friend of the publisher, or even a reader? Such stories may or may not be more important than the easier ones. But because they are difficult to cover, the way they are handled is a good measure of the media's responsibility to their informing function.

Perhaps the most important information of all is information about the government. The purpose of the First Amendment, after all, is to insure that the media will be free to report and criticize the actions of government officials, free to inform the public about public affairs. When a television station carries live the speech of a President, it is performing a valuable public service. When it offers intelligent commentary on the content and meaning of that speech, it is performing a much *more* valuable public service.

It is worth mentioning that everything in the mass media is in some sense informative, whether or not it is intended that way. Even a soap opera tells us something (true or false) about how people live, how they dress and talk and solve problems.

For centuries, Italy was a country with two different populations: the wealthy, cosmopolitan North and the poor, rural South. The two were so different they even spoke different dialects, and were almost completely unable to understand one another. Then, in 1954, nation-wide Italian television was introduced. In a few scant years, television began to unify the country.

A university professor comments: "Some intellectuals call television the 'opium of the people.' That may be so in a city like Milan or Turin. But can you imagine a modern bathroom appearing on TV screens from Naples southward." And a historian adds: "There's been more change in Italy's linguistic situation in the past fifteen years than in the century since Rome became the capital."[6]

The bulk of this book is devoted to an assessment and explanation of the informational performance of the American mass media. This is not because media owners, or advertisers, or audiences consider information the most important role of the media. They don't. We do.

3. To Influence. The power of the mass media to change people's minds directly is very limited. People don't like to have their minds changed, and so they ignore or misinterpret attempts to do so—usually successfully. If influence were limited to changing people's minds directly, the media would not be particularly influential.

But influence is more subtle than that. When William Randolph Hearst's New York *Journal* championed the war against Spain in 1898, he didn't achieve very many conversions. But through slanted news coverage and sensational writing, the *Journal* did manage to help create a climate of war fever. No doubt most readers viewed Hearst's style of journalism as entertainment and information, not influence. Yet he helped make them go to war.

More than a century before Hearst, Thomas Paine wrote a political pamphlet called *Common Sense,* urging an American Revolution. And nearly a century after Hearst, Richard Nixon engineered a series of television advertisements, urging his election as President. Paine didn't convert many Tories, and Nixon didn't win over many Democrats. But Paine did succeed in crystalizing the incoherent resentments of many colonists into a consistent revolutionary ideology. And Nixon succeeded in crystalizing the incoherent frustrations of many Americans into a Republican vote. So Paine got his revolution, and Nixon got the White House. The mass media played a vital role in the success of both men.

The most obvious and prevalent example of mass media influence is advertising. Media ad campaigns have a lot going for them. Through careful intermixture with entertainment and informational content, they gain a captive audience. Through bold colors and imaginative graphics, they make you pay attention. Through catchy slogans and constant repetition, they make you remember. Through irrelevant appeals to sex, snobbism, and the good life, they make you buy.

The very existence of newspapers, magazines, radio, and television testifies to the persuasive power of advertising. For if the ads were unsuccessful, there would be no ads. And if there were no ads, there would be no newspapers, magazines, radio, and television in the form we know them.

Not every media attempt to influence the public is successful, of course. Politicians and manufacturers may spend millions on the media and still lose out to the competition. Editorialists and polemicists may devote page after page to an urgent plea for action, and get no action. Not every revolutionary book foments a revolution; not every TV appeal to voters captures the White House. But it is nearly impossible to foment a revolution without a book, to win the White House without a TV appeal. The persuasive power of the mass media, though limited, is undeniable.

The most effective media influences are those that are unrecognizable as such. Often they are unintentional. Television soap operas are designed purely as entertainment, yet many viewers use them for guidance in deciding how to handle their own interpersonal problems. It is doubtful that a televised lecture on the subject would be followed so closely or obeyed so literally.

If intentional, a persuasive message should be as subtle as possible. For many years, most Americans neglected to use the seat belts on their cars, despite an extensive public-service advertising campaign. Then the National Association of Broadcasters passed a regulation forbidding advertisers and producers to show cars in use without seat belts. After a few years of constant exposure to this subtle influence, TV viewers will learn to use their seat belts.

4. To Make Money.   What can we say about the power of the mass media to make money that is not obvious before we begin? If the media didn't make money for advertisers, there would be no advertising. If they didn't make money for their owners, there would be no media.

It is possible to conceive of a mass media system not dedicated to profit. Such systems exist, in fact, in many countries. The British Broadcasting Company (BBC), to give but one example, is financed by a special tax on radio and television sets. It accepts no ads and earns no profits. Even in this country there are nonprofit TV stations, radio stations, magazines, newspapers, movie producers, and book publishers. Not many, but a few.

But the American system of mass media is overwhelmingly profit-oriented. And it is overwhelmingly successful at earning profits. To remain successful, the media must do a good job of influencing people, thus attracting advertisers. And they must do a good job of entertaining people, thus attracting audiences. Only one of the four functions of the media is inessential: to inform. It is to that superfluous and often neglected function that this book is largely devoted, and whole-heartedly dedicated.

NOTES

[1] Wilbur Schramm, "How Communication Works," *The Process and Effects of Mass Communication,* ed. Wilbur Schramm (Urbana, Ill.: University of Illinois Press, 1954), p. 3.

[2] Paul F. Lazarsfeld, Bernard Berelson, and Hazel Gaudet, *The People's Choice* 2nd ed. (New York: Columbia University Press, 1948), p. 151.

[3] George Gallup, "The Importance of Opinion News," *Journalism Educator,* Fall, 1966, p. 113.

[4] Wilbur Schramm, "Communication in Crisis," in *The Kennedy Assassination and the American Public: Social Communication in Crisis,* ed. Bradley S. Greenberg and Edwin B. Parker (Stanford, Calif.: Stanford University Press, 1965), pp. 14–15.

[5] A.C. Nielsen Co. [Pamphlet], "TV Responses to the Death of the President" (New York, 1963).

[6] "Talking Like a Native," *Newsweek,* March 9, 1970, p. 57.

SUGGESTED READINGS

SCHRAMM, WILBUR, ed., *The Process and Effects of Mass Communication* (Urbana, Ill.: University of Illinois Press, 1954).

———, ed., *Mass Communications,* 2nd ed. (Urbana, Ill.: University of Illinois Press, 1960).

PART ONE

DEVELOPMENT

The trouble with history is that you have to know a lot about the present before the past seems useful or relevant. And yet you can't really understand the way things are until after you have discovered how they got that way. Ideally, then, everyone would read this chapter twice—once now, to get a feel for the development of the media; and again after finishing the rest of the book, to get the background of the problems that will be discussed later.

If you haven't read the rest of the book yet, the best you can do is to try to keep your own catalogue of important issues and how they grew. There are dozens of them, all discussed some place later on, but let us suggest a few of the most crucial ones here:

1. *Trends in government control.* For many centuries, all governments maintained strict control over the media. Then they began to loosen the reins, allowing greater and greater measures of freedom of the press. How and why did this happen? Was it entirely a good thing? How has it affected the nature of the media today?

2. *Trends in individuality.* Throughout most of their history, the media have been very much the tools of individual writers and editors, who disagreed violently with each other and competed viciously for the allegiance of the public. This is much less true today. What caused the change? How has it affected the tone and function of the media? What can be done about it?

3. *Trends in the audience.* The mass media audience in the Seventeenth Century was limited to the literate upper class. Slowly it expanded to include merchants, factory workers, immigrants, farmers. How have the media adapted to these new audiences? Which ones have tried to reach all the public, and which have specialized in certain classes or groups? What implications does this have for democratic processes?

4. *Trends in technology.* Books were the first mass medium, followed by newspapers, then magazines, then film and radio, and finally television. Along the way came such revolutionary technological advances as the high-speed press and the telegraph. How has each new medium affected the older ones? Have the media made use of technology, or merely succumbed to it? How can they be expected to respond to future developments?

5. *Trends in influence.* At various points in history, the mass media have influenced the course of social change in many different ways—and have, in turn, been influenced by social change. What determines the power and influence of the media? Are they aware of their power? Do they use it wisely?

6. *Trends in news definition.* How the media define the word "news" determines the topics they cover and the way they cover them. How has this definition changed over time? What caused the changes? Which is the "right" definition?

7. *Trends in partisanship.* The principal function of the mass media has varied greatly throughout their history. Sometimes it has been to inform, sometimes to entertain, sometimes to persuade, and sometimes merely to make money. How did these variations come about? What effects did they have on the content of the media? What should be the main function of the media?

8. *Trends in professionalism.* Media owners once viewed themselves as professional advocates; today they are merely businessmen. Reporters and editors, on the other hand, were once mere employees; today they see themselves as professionals. Why did this turnabout take place? In what ways has it affected the structure and content of the media? How, if at all, is the conflict resolved?

This is only a partial list. Make your own as you go along. Above all, bear in mind the three basic questions of any historical survey: How did things get to where they are? How else might they have turned out? And where are they likely to go in the future?

1 Development

Today's mass media, like all complex social institutions, have developed over a period of centuries. The events of each century had a lasting effect on the structure and performance of the media. To understand the modern media in the United States, then, it is necessary to examine their roots in medieval Europe, Elizabethan England, and colonial America.

Medieval Europe was a land-based society. The fundamental economic and social unit was not the city or the country, but the feudal manor. Each manor was entirely self-sufficient; it produced its own food, employed its own artisans, and dispensed its own law.

Travel from one manor to another was extremely difficult. Except for churchmen, soldiers, and cutthroats, it was also pretty pointless. Literacy was equally irrelevant. Why bother to travel or read when the manor down the road was just like home? The local serf tilled his land. The local lord managed his serfs. The local priest memorized and recited his prayers. Neither serf nor lord nor priest had any reason to be interested in events beyond the horizon.

Throughout the Middle Ages, the monasteries had a virtual monopoly on literacy. Dutifully the monks hand-copied and hand-illustrated their meager supply of books. Some of the most beautiful were sold to the secular elite, who used them as decorations and status symbols. But it was an unusual nobleman who could do more than admire the colorful designs of his Bible.

CHRONOLOGY

1476	William Caxton establishes the first printing press in England.
1513	The first English "newsbook" is published.
1529–1530	Henry VIII forbids the publication of certain books, and requires all English printers to obtain royal licenses. This is the start of authoritarian control over the press. Other elements soon to develop include precensorship and seditious libel.
1550	The major trading companies of Europe circulate handwritten commercial newsletters among their employees and customers.
1609	The first primitive weekly newspaper appears in Germany, followed soon by weeklies in Holland and Belgium.
1620	Nathaniel Butter imports Dutch newspapers and distributes them in England. Called "corantos," the papers specialize in foreign news.
1621	Butter and Thomas Archer print the first English coranto, which soon meets with government repression. Nicholas Bourne joins the team, and government permission is obtained for *The Continuation of Our Weekly Newes,* the first regular newspaper in England.
1644	English poet John Milton publishes *Areopagitica,* advocating a free marketplace of ideas and urging an end to press licensing.
1694	England abandons licensing of the press.
1702	The first English language daily newspaper, the *Daily Courant,* appears in London.
1709	The first modern copyright law is enacted in England.
1712	England adopts the Stamp Tax, a heavy tax on newspapers and other publications.
1709–1720	Richard Steele, Joseph Addison, and Daniel Defoe produce the *Tatler,* the *Spectator,* and *Mist's Journal,* collections of magazine-type essays in newspaper format.

the winner. It celebrated and consolidated its power by granting increased civil and religious liberties to the nation, including a relaxation of press censorship. Poet John Milton was among those whose voices were raised in favor of freedom of the press. In his monumental *Areopagitica,* Milton argued:

> Truth and understanding are not such wares as to be monopolized and traded in by tickets and statutes and standards. We must not think

to make a staple commodity of all knowledge in the land, to mark and license it like our broadcloth. . . . Give me the liberty to know, to utter, and to argue freely according to conscience, above all liberties. . . . And though all the winds of doctrine were let loose to play upon the earth, so Truth be in the field, we do injuriously, by licensing and prohibiting, to misdoubt her strength. Let her and Falsehood grapple; who ever knew Truth put to the worse, in a free and open encounter.[1]

Spurred on by the new permissiveness, a series of daily reports called "diurnals" developed throughout England. They chronicled the tail end of the conflict between Parliament and Crown. That conflict ended in the mid-1640s with the Puritan Revolution. A victory for Parliament, the revolution soon proved a defeat for freedom of the press. Its leader, Oliver Cromwell, quickly established himself as a virtual dictator of England. Unlicensed printers were harshly dealt with, while licensed printers were subjected to incessant censorship. Ironically enough, it was John Milton himself who became the nation's chief censor under the Puritan regime.

The restoration of the monarchy under Charles II brought no immediate improvement for the press. But the power of the king was on the wane, and libertarianism was in the air. Instances of censorship were rare throughout the 1670s and the 1680s, and in 1694 licensing of the press was abandoned completely. By the time the *Daily Courant*, England's first daily newspaper, was founded in 1702, the English press was more or less free to write what it pleased, so long as it avoided seditious libel. The journalism of England in the early Eighteenth Century was to serve as a model for the young printers who introduced newspapers to the American colonies.

COLONIAL AMERICA

Two of the Pilgrims who landed in Plymouth in 1620 were skilled printers. They had published illegal Protestant tracts in England, and watched the production of primitive newspapers in Holland. But they brought no press with them to the New World. They realized that their tiny outpost in the wilderness would have neither the time nor the need for newspapers.

The Massachusetts Bay Colony, which settled Boston in 1630, was larger, wealthier, and better educated than Plymouth. All Puritan children were taught to read, and the brightest boys were sent to Harvard College to prepare for the ministry. In 1638 the first printing press in the New World was established at Harvard to produce religious texts.

In England the Puritans had been revolutionaries; in Massachusetts Bay they were the Establishment. Like other Establishments of the time, they feared that a free press might threaten the government and promote religious heresies. Printing was therefore strictly controlled. By the mid-1600s, various presses in Massachusetts had published lawbooks, volumes of sermons, poetry, and a history of the colony. But it was not until the last decade of the century that a printer dared to produce anything resembling a newspaper.

Benjamin Harris had come to Boston in 1686, after publishing a number of seditious pamphlets in England. In 1690 he printed the first issue of *Publick Occurrences,* a three-page newspaper roughly 6 x 9 inches in size. Featury by today's standards, the paper included the following item of special interest:

> The Christianized *Indians* in some parts of *Plimouth* have newly appointed a day of Thanksgiving to God for his Mercy in supplying their extream and pinching Necessities under their late want of Corn, & for His giving them now a prospect of a very *Comfortable Harvest.* Their Example may be worth Mentioning.[2]

The paper also gossiped about the presumed immorality of the King of France, and complained that the Indian allies of the British had mistreated French prisoners. These were bold topics—perhaps too bold. The colonial governor and the Puritan elders immediately ordered the paper suppressed. *Publick Occurrences,* America's first newspaper, died after one issue.

By 1700, the thriving commercial city of Boston was ripe for a second try. John Campbell, the local postmaster, met the need for news with a handwritten newsletter, which he distributed to shippers, farmers, merchants, and government officials throughout the colonies. Campbell was in an ideal position to run a newspaper. As postmaster, he was the first one to get a look at the English and European papers. Moreover, his postage-free "franking privilege" enabled him to send his newsletters through the mail without charge. Throughout the colonial period, the job of postmaster was closely linked to that of publisher.

In 1704 Campbell began printing his newsletter. Aptly called the *Boston News-Letter,* it was precensored by the governor and "Published by Authority." The single-page paper, printed on both sides, was sold by subscription only. By 1715 Campbell had perhaps 300 regular readers.

The *Boston News-Letter* was strictly a commercial newspaper. It emphasized local financial news and foreign political developments, the latter pirated directly from English papers. A smattering of births, deaths, and social events made Campbell's paper even more appealing to the economic elite of the colonies—but it was not a publication for the average citizen or the intellectual. As a commercial paper, the *News-Letter* was an obvious candidate for advertising. The very first issue carried this notice:

> This News-Letter is to be continued Weekly, and all Persons who have Houses, Lands, Tenements, Farms, Ships, Vessels, Goods, Wares or

Merchandise, &c to be Sold or Let; or Servants Run-away, or Goods Stole
or Lost; may have the same inserted at a Reasonable Rate, from *Twelve
Pence* to *Five Shillings.* . . .[3]

Before long, Campbell was earning a considerable profit from ads.

After losing the postmaster job in 1719, Campbell decided to continue
printing his newspaper without the franking privilege. The new postmaster, William Brooker, hired printer James Franklin to publish his own
paper, the *Boston Gazette.* Competition had come to the colonies, and
both papers were livelier as a result.

Two years later Franklin left the *Gazette* and established a third newspaper, the *New England Courant.* Franklin was an intellectual of sorts.
His interests were secular and political, not religious or commercial. The
articles and essays in the *Courant,* often written under pseudonyms, viciously attacked the Puritan clergy and its control over the Boston government. The third regular newspaper in Massachusetts was anti-Establishment.

Among the staff of the *Courant* was Franklin's younger brother Benjamin, an apprentice printer. Apparently without his brother's knowledge,
Ben Franklin was also the author of several satirical essays in the paper,
run under the byline "Silence Dogood." In 1722 James Franklin was jailed
for three weeks for his attacks on the government, and "Silence Dogood"
came out with an eloquent plea for freedom of the press. James soon got
out of jail, discovered the identity of "Dogood," and jealously ordered his
teenage brother to stick to the printing end of the business.

The *Courant* kept up its attacks on church and state, and in 1723
Franklin was ordered to submit his paper for precensorship. He got
around the command by making Ben titular publisher, a tactic that en-
raged the religious leadership of the colony but amused its citizens. This
was, in fact, Franklin's constant strategy for avoiding serious trouble—he
mocked the religious hierarchy, but was always careful to keep the business establishment on his side. Franklin was arrested for contempt of the
censorship order, but he was so popular that the government (headed by
Increase Mather and his son Cotton) didn't dare to try him. He was soon
released and resumed control of the newspaper. Precensorship had failed
in Massachusetts; it would never again succeed.

The American colonists were, by and large, an independent lot. They
boasted a higher literacy rate than any other frontier population in the
world. Schooled in religious dissent, they took naturally to political dissent as well. They read and reread Milton's *Areopagitica,* and hungrily
devoured the essay papers of Defoe, Addison, and Steele. The very at-
mosphere of the New World encouraged libertarian thought. At the end
of the first quarter of the Eighteenth Century, most colonial governments
still had licensing and precensorship laws on the books. But they were

seldom invoked, and almost never invoked with success. The *New England Courant* was the first outspoken anti-Establishment newspaper in
America—but it was by no means the last.

The first American printing press outside Massachusetts was brought
to Philadelphia by William Bradford in 1685. A book publisher, Bradford found the censorship laws in that Quaker city too stiff for comfort.
So in 1693 he moved his press to New York. Bradford's son Andrew soon
returned to Philadelphia, and in 1719 he established the *American Weekly
Mercury.* The *Mercury* was the first American newspaper outside Boston,
and the third regularly published paper in the colonies.

Never as outspoken as Franklin's *Courant,* the *Mercury* was nevertheless in constant trouble with the government of Philadelphia. Bradford
was ordered "not to publish anything relating to or concerning the affairs
of this Government, or the Government of any other of His Majesty's
Colonies, without the permission of the Governor or Secretary of this
Province."[4] Bradford often disobeyed the order. Once, after an especially
damning satire, he was arrested. But by this time the spirit of liberty was
strong even in Quaker Philadelphia, and Bradford was never prosecuted.

Young Ben Franklin, meanwhile, was bored with working for his
brother in Boston. In 1723, shortly after James Franklin was released
from prison, Ben ran away to Philadelphia. Six years later he founded
the weekly *Pennsylvania Gazette.* A shrewd politician, Franklin managed to publish the brightest and wittiest paper in the colonies without
government interference.

In 1741, Franklin inaugurated his *General Magazine;* not to be outdone, Andrew Bradford began the *American Magazine* in the same year.
Neither was successful. The American public was not yet ready for such
heavy doses of philosophical and literary commentary.

When Andrew Bradford left New York for Philadelphia, William
Bradford stayed behind. In 1725 he followed his son's example and
founded New York's first newspaper, the *New York Gazette.* The poorly
printed two-page paper carefully avoided antagonizing government officials. But stronger papers soon developed in New York: the *Weekly Post
Boy,* the *Evening-Post,* and the *New York Weekly Journal.* The latter
was edited by John Peter Zenger, one of the greatest heroes in the history
of American journalism.

By the end of the 1720s, a political power struggle was underway in
New York, between the rising middle class and the Tory Establishment,
headed by Governor William Cosby. In 1733 the leaders of the anti-
administration group decided that they needed a newspaper to champion
their cause. They founded the *New York Weekly Journal,* and asked
printer John Peter Zenger to be its editor.

Zenger immediately set about attacking Cosby and the aristocracy,
urging a more representative government for New York. Twice Cosby

CHRONOLOGY

1638   The Puritans establish the first printing press in America at Harvard College.

1685   William Bradford brings to Philadelphia, and later to New York, the first printing press in America outside Massachusetts.

1690   Benjamin Harris publishes the first American newspaper, *Publick Occurrences*. It is suppressed by Boston authorities after one issue.

1704   John Campbell's *Boston News-Letter* becomes the first regularly published newspaper in America.

1719   William Brooker and James Franklin found the *Boston Gazette;* Andrew Bradford establishes the *American Weekly Mercury* in Philadelphia.

1721   James Franklin emphasizes political and social criticism in his *New England Courant*. Despite government anger, he is allowed to continue publishing.

1725   William Bradford founds the *New York Gazette*, the first newspaper in New York.

1729   Benjamin Franklin begins publishing the *Pennsylvania Gazette* in Philadelphia.

1735   John Peter Zenger, publisher of the *New York Weekly Journal*, is acquitted on charges of seditious libel. After Zenger, colonial juries will refuse to convict journalists for printing the truth, however injurious to government.

1741   The *General Magazine* and *American Magazine* are founded in Philadelphia. Both are unsuccessful.

asked the grand jury to indict Zenger for seditous libel (criticizing the government), and twice the grand jury refused. Finally, Cosby's Council issued its own warrant for Zenger's arrest, and in November of 1734 the crusading editor was sent to jail. His *Journal* missed only one issue. Later editions were dictated to his wife through a "Hole of the Door of the Prison."5

The Zenger case came to trial in August, 1735. Andrew Hamilton, a famous lawyer nearly eighty years old, was brought in from Philadelphia to handle the defense.

Hamilton began by admitting that Zenger had, in fact, published the articles in question. Under existing law, that should have been the end of the case; criticism of the government, whether true or false, was illegal. As the prosecuting attorney explained: "I think the jury must find a verdict for the King; for supposing they [the libels] were true, the law says that they are not the less libelous for that; nay, indeed, the law says their being true is an aggravation of the crime."

It was precisely this point that Hamilton disputed. He argued what was then a novel legal contention: "The words themselves must be libelous, that is, *false, scandalous, and seditious* or else we are not guilty."

The judge sided with precedent and the prosecutor, ruling that truth was irrelevant. He refused even to let Hamilton try to prove Zenger's anti-government accusations. Hamilton then appealed directly to the jury:

> The question before the court and you, gentlemen of the jury, is not of small nor private concern, it is not the cause of a poor printer, nor of New York alone. . . . It is the cause of liberty . . . the liberty both of exposing and opposing arbitrary power (in these parts of the world, at least) by speaking and writing truth.[6]

The jury returned a verdict of not guilty, and Zenger was released.

The importance of the Zenger trial is not that it established a new legal principle. In fact, truth was not officially accepted as a defense in seditious libel cases until the Sedition Act of 1798. What the Zenger trial proved is that the average American colonist—in this case the jury—was unalterably opposed to authoritarian government. The trial recognized and solidified the role of the colonial press as critic of government and defender of liberty. It thus paved the way for the important part the press was to play in bringing about the American Revolution.

The American press in the last half of the Eighteenth Century was less interested in news than in comment—philosophical, social, literary, and political. Most colonial newspapers were quickly radicalized by the hated Stamp Act, and thereafter they led the cry for Independence. After the Revolution, the papers split into two camps: the elite Federalists and the populist Republicans. Each newspaper was read only by those who agreed with it; no newspaper tried to be objective in the modern sense. Political partisanship was to characterize the American press until well into the Nineteenth Century.

THE REVOLUTIONARY PERIOD

There were twelve newspapers in the American colonies in 1750, serving a population of just over one million. By 1775, the population would rise to 2.5 million, while the number of newspapers would jump to 48. Five successful magazines would be established during this period, and innumerable book publishers. The American mass media were thriving.

The typical newspaper of the times was a four-page weekly, 10 x 15 inches in size. The paper was rough foolscap imported from England; it was mottled and ugly, but surprisingly durable. Headlines were rare, and illustrations rarer still. A hand press was used to produce perhaps 400 copies of each issue.

The content of such a newspaper was composed mostly of philosophical-political essays. Even reports on specific local events were generally written in essay form—but most "articles" were not tied to an event at all. Libertarianism was the philosophy of the day. Every colonial newspaper devoted considerable space to reprints of English and French libertarian tracts, not to mention the wisdom of home-grown philosophers.

The English Stamp Act of 1765 provided a new focus for these libertarian essays: the evil of King George. The Stamp Act imposed a heavy tax on paper; it thus hit newspaper publishers harder than anyone else. Not that the tax itself was anything new. It was first levied against *English* newspapers in 1712, and had already been copied by the colonial legislatures of New York and Massachusetts. The English government argued with some justice that it was nearly bankrupt from fighting the French and Indian War and defending the American frontier. It seemed only fair that the colonists should bear part of the burden—and this the Stamp Act was designed to accomplish.

Still, never before had the English government imposed such a tax on American newspapers, and the colonial press was unanimous in its vehement opposition to this "taxation without representation." Several papers, including the *Maryland Gazette* and the *Pennsylvania Journal*, announced that they were suspending publication in protest. They later reappeared without nameplates, claiming that they were broadsides or handbills and thus exempt from the tax. Before long they resumed their original titles, but no colonial newspaper ever carried the required stamp or paid the required tax.

The Stamp Act was repealed in 1766—but it was too late. The experience of uniting in opposition to the established government is a heady one. From that experience the colonial press never recovered. After 1765, most American publishers were committed to Revolution in one form or another. Their newspapers were devoted to that cause.

The *Boston Gazette*, often edited by Samuel Adams, was typical of the militant papers of the day. With each new imposition of British rule, Adams and other radical writers throughout the colonies strove to stir up resistance. The following is the "lead" of the *Gazette*'s story on the "Boston Massacre" of 1770. It is thoughtful and contemplative, but hardly unbiased:

> The Town of Boston affords a recent and melancholy Demonstration
> of the destructive Consequences of quartering Troops among Citizens in
> a Time of Peace, under a Pretence of supporting the Laws and aiding

Civil Authority; every considerate and unprejudic'd Person among us was deeply imprest with the Apprehension of these Consequences when it was known that a Number of Regiments were ordered to this Town under such a Pretext, but in Reality to inforce oppressive Measures; to awe and controul the legislative as well as executive Power of the Province, and to quell a Spirit of Liberty, which however it may have been basely oppos'd and even ridicul'd by some, would do Honor to any Age or Country.[7]

To be sure, there were some moderates and even Royalists among American publishers. John Dickinson, for example, published his influential "Letters from a Farmer in Pennsylvania" in the *Pennsylvania Chronicle* of 1767–1768. A businessman, Dickinson resented English control over American foreign trade, and favored "home rule" for the colonies. But he was unalterably opposed to Revolution.

Yet men like Dickinson could do little to halt the effect of revolutionaries like Sam Adams—or Tom Paine, editor of the *Pennsylvania Magazine,* whose pamphlet "Common Sense" sold 120,000 copies in the spring of 1776.

By 1775, war had become inevitable. Publishers were forced to choose sides, becoming either radical Patriots or steadfast Loyalists; there was no middle ground left. Isaiah Thomas, editor of the *Massachusetts Spy,*

CHRONOLOGY

1765   Colonial newspapers refuse to pay the tax imposed by the English Stamp Act—thus taking a giant step toward radicalization.

1767   John Dickinson publishes the first of his moderate "Letters from a Farmer in Pennsylvania" in the *Pennsylvania Chronicle.*

1770   Boston publisher John Mein is attacked by Patriot leaders and forced to fold his Tory *Boston Chronicle*—a sign of growing polarization.

1772   Sam Adams, a regular contributor to the radical *Boston Gazette,* organizes the Committees of Correspondence, a network of agents "covering" events throughout the colonies on behalf of the Patriot press.

1773   James Rivington founds *Rivington's New York Gazetteer,* the most powerful Tory newspaper of the Revolution.

1776   Tom Paine's pamphlet, "Common Sense," is widely circulated throughout the colonies; the Declaration of Independence is carried on the front page of most colonial newspapers; the Revolution begins in earnest.

---

headlined his article on the Battle of Lexington: "The shot heard round the world." His lead paragraph left no doubt where he stood:

> Americans! forever bear in mind the BATTLE OF LEXINGTON!— where British troops, unmolested and unprovoked, wantonly and in a most inhuman manner, fired upon and killed a number of our country-men, then robbed, ransacked, and burnt their houses! nor could the tears of defenseless women, some of whom were in the pains of childbirth, the cries of helpless babes, nor the prayers of old age, confined to beds of sickness, appease their thirst for blood!—or divert them from their DE-SIGN of MURDER and ROBBERY![8]

At first, the war was hard on both Patriot and Tory newspapers. Neither were allowed to publish or circulate in territory controlled by the enemy. But as The Thirteen United States of America won victory after victory, the Loyalist press quickly disappeared. Wartime commerce, meanwhile, brought heavy loads of lucrative advertising to the pages of revolutionary newspapers. And public interest in the war itself gave some Patriot papers as many as 8,000 readers. The end of the Revolution left the American mass media—books, magazines, and newspapers—stronger and even somewhat unified than ever before. They had waged a battle, and they had won.

THE PARTISAN PRESS

The Revolutionary War had united rich and poor in the common cause of independence. But as soon as the war ended, this unity ended as well. Merchants, bankers, manufacturers, and large property owners— the "aristocracy" of America—urged the establishment of a strong central government. Small farmers and wage earners, on the other hand, feared the power of the monied interests; they supported a loose confederacy of local governments.

The agrarian-labor group was in control at the close of the war. The Articles of Confederation they passed in 1781 gave nearly all the power to the states. Without even the right of taxation, the new national government was too weak to cope with the postwar economic depression. Moreover, the propertied classes soon gained control of the various state legislatures. In 1787 they convened the Philadelphia Constitutional Convention to rewrite the Articles of Confederation and strengthen the federal government. The delegates to that Convention were nearly all propertied men, advocates of strong national government. The new Constitution reflected their aims and interests.

Once the Constitution was written, it was sent to the states for ratification. The battle was joined. The conservative, monied group now called itself the Federalists; the agrarian-labor bloc was known as the

Anti-Federalists or Republicans. Again, newspapers throughout the thirteen colonies (now the thirteen states) were forced to choose sides. One was either a Federalist or a Republican; once more, there was no middle ground.

Alexander Hamilton, James Madison, and John Jay wrote a total of 85 essays urging ratification of the Constitution. Collectively called *The Federalist,* these essays first appeared in the *New York Independent Journal.* They were carried by Federalist newspapers throughout the nation, and were circulated in pamphlet and book form as well. Anti-Federalist papers responded by publishing Richard Henry Lee's *Letters from the Federal Farmer,* which opposed the Constitution as a document of the propertied classes.

One bone of contention was the conspicuous absence in the new Constitution of specific guarantees of individual rights, including the right of freedom of the press. Nine of the thirteen states already provided for such freedom in their state constitutions, and the Federalists presumably felt that that was enough. The Federalists were not by nature sympathetic to press freedom; the Constitution itself was debated in strict secrecy. As Alexander Hamilton wrote:

> What is Liberty of the Press? Who can give it any definition which does not leave the utmost latitude for evasion? I hold it to be impracticable; and from this I infer, that its security, whatever fine declarations may be inserted in any Constitution respecting it, must altogether depend on public opinion, and on the general spirit of the people and of the Government.[9]

The Republicans, by contrast, believed freedom of the press to be crucial to the survival of American democracy. Thomas Jefferson, by birth an aristocrat but by choice a "friend of the common man," was the acknowledged leader of the Republicans. In a letter to a friend, Jefferson wrote:

> The basis of our government being the opinion of the people, the very first object should be to keep that right; and if it were left to me to decide whether we should have a government without newspapers, or newspapers without a government, I should not hesitate a moment to prefer the latter.[10]

In 1788, after a year of bitter strife, the Constitution was finally ratified. The Federalists easily dominated the first Congress of the new nation. In an effort to reunify the country, they proposed a Bill of Rights. It included what is now the First Amendment: "Congress shall make no law . . . abridging the freedom of speech or of the press." In 1791 the Bill of Rights was ratified by the states and became law.

The Bill of Rights did little to bridge the gap between the two factions.   General George Washington was the unanimous choice for President.   His Vice-President was John Adams, a Federalist.   His Secretary of the Treasury was Alexander Hamilton, also a Federalist.   His Secretary of State was Thomas Jefferson, leader of the Republicans.   Throughout the Washington administration, Federalists and Republicans were at each other's throats.

Not content with the support of independent publishers, both parties established "house organs" to serve as direct pipelines between political leaders and their followers.   Federalist funds were responsible for John Fenno's *Gazette of the United States* and Noah Webster's *American Minerva,* both in New York.   Hamilton personally set editorial policy for both papers.   Not to be outdone, Jefferson appointed Philip Freneau official translator for the State Department, in return for Freneau's agreement to publish a Republican party organ in Philadelphia.   Policy for Freneau's *National Gazette* was personally set by Jefferson.   Other publishers throughout the country looked to one or another of these newspapers for guidance on how to handle the news.

In 1796, Federalist John Adams was elected President; Jefferson, the loser, became Vice-President.   The most divisive issue of the moment was the war in Europe between France and England.   The Republicans, who had applauded the populist French Revolution several years earlier, supported France.   The Federalists, with control of both the Presidency and Congress, supported England.   The United States prepared to go to war against France.

With war fever at its highest, and rival journalists brawling in the streets, the Federalists made their move to squelch the opposition.   In 1798, Congress passed the Sedition Act.   Under the Act, it became a federal crime to publish any false or scurrilous criticism of the government or government officials.

The Sedition Act is remembered for two conflicting reasons.   On the one hand, it was the first seditious libel law that explicitly accepted truth as a defense; only *false* criticisms of the government were illegal.   On the other hand, it was also the most outstanding piece of repressive legislation in the early history of the United States.

The Federalists used the Sedition Act to purge the nation of anti-Federalist thought.   Federalist editors were allowed to continue their defamatory attacks on Jefferson and his supporters—but seven leading Republican editors were prosecuted and convicted for similar invective against the Federalist leadership.   The plan backfired.   In 1800, public resentment of the Sedition Act helped sweep Jefferson into the Presidency.   War preparations were immediately halted, and in 1801 the Sedition Act was allowed to lapse.   In later years, when individual states revived the Sedition Act on a local level, they invariably included the provision for truth as a defense.

The last quarter of the Eighteenth Century was the heyday of the Partisan Press. There were no words so insulting that Federalist and Republican editors were unwilling to use them to describe their enemies. Benjamin Franklin Bache (grandson of Ben Franklin) was publisher of the strictly Republican Philadelphia *Aurora*. In 1797, he celebrated the retirement of George Washington in the following terms:

> The man who is the source of all the misfortunes of our country is this day reduced to a level with his fellow-citizens, and is no longer possessed of power to multiply evils upon the United States. . . . Every heart in unison with the freedom and happiness of the people, ought to beat high with exultation that the name of Washington from this day ceased to give a currency to political iniquity and to legalized corruption.[11]

This was too much for William Cobbett, the Federalist editor of *Porcupine's Gazette*, also in Philadelphia. Putting aside politicians for the moment, Cobbett attacked Bache directly:

> He spent several years in hunting offices under the Federal Government, and being constantly rejected, he at last became its most bitter foe. Hence his abuse of general Washington, whom, at the time he was soliciting a place, he panegerized up to the third heaven. He was born for a hireling, and therefore when he found he could not obtain employ in one quarter, he sought it in another. . . . He is an ill-looking devil. His eyes never get above your knees.[12]

Neither of these quotations, by the way, comes from an "editorial." Throughout the Eighteenth Century and well into the Nineteenth, it was customary for newspapers to intersperse news and opinion, often within the same article. By 1800, a few papers, including the *Aurora*, had set aside page two as an editorial page of sorts—complete with the editorial "We." But opinions were to be found on the other pages as well. Objectivity in the modern sense simply wasn't a characteristic of the Partisan Press.

Almost without exception, the dedicated Federalist and Republican newspapers were weeklies. There was no need to hurry a vituperative essay into print; next week would do as well as tomorrow. Urban merchants, on the other hand, were desperate for daily reports on ship arrivals and other commercial news.

The first American daily newspaper was the *Pennsylvania Evening Post and Daily Advertiser*, founded in 1783. A year later the *Pennsylvania Packet and Daily Advertiser* appeared. It was a better newspaper than the *Post*, and despite its expensive price (fourpence), it soon forced the competition to fold. In 1785, two more dailies appeared—the *New York Morning Post and Daily Advertiser*, and the *New York Daily Advertiser*. By 1800, there were twenty daily newspapers in the United States.

As their names imply, the new daily papers depended heavily on advertising. Many were able to fill sixteen out of twenty columns with ads, leaving only four for news. This was all right with their readers, who often found the advertisements as useful as the editorial copy. They cheerfully paid as much as eight dollars a year (roughly the cost of a full barrel of flour) for subscriptions. The *New York Daily Advertiser* pioneered the use of half-inch-high headlines in its ads; large type would soon be used for news headlines as well.

The partisan weeklies flourished right along with the commercial dailies. By 1800, there were roughly 200 weeklies in operation, all but a few dozen of them founded after the end of the Revolution. Subscriptions averaged around $2.50 a year; the number of subscribers averaged 600–700. As much as half the space in a successful weekly might be made up of advertising.

Most of these weeklies served small cities and towns, pirating their news from the larger metropolitan papers. They were able to survive largely because of the Post Office Act of 1792, which set a low one-cent rate for the mailing of newspapers. The Act also provided that publishers could exchange their papers by mail without charge, enabling frontier papers to get all their news free. The government supported the newspaper industry in other ways as well. Perhaps the most important subsidy was the legal printing contract. Key newspapers in each state and territory were paid to reprint the texts of various laws. This plum was handed out strictly along party lines, as a form of political patronage. Scores of influential frontier papers could never have started without their government printing contracts.

Between 1800 and 1830, the American media prospered, but they changed very little in character. Some of the commercial dailies turned partisan, while some of the partisan weeklies went daily—and dozens of new weeklies were founded every year. By 1830, then, there were three kinds of newspapers in America: (1) A handful of strictly commercial dailies; (2) Roughly sixty partisan metropolitan dailies; and (3) Well over a thousand small-town and frontier weeklies, most of them partisan.

Improvements in printing (the iron press in 1798, the steam-driven press in 1811) enabled publishers to produce as many as 1100 impressions an hour. The extra capacity was seldom needed—the average daily still circulated only a thousand copies, and weekly circulation was lower still. The cost of the average newspaper rose to six cents an issue, the same price as a pint of whiskey. Headlines improved the appearance of the typical paper, while the use of part-time "correspondents" in Washington and elsewhere improved its quality. But the overall look of the page was still very gray, and most of the content was still essays and commentary.

The magazine and book industries also thrived. Most of the hundred-odd magazines in business in 1830 neglected politics and concentrated on literary and social comment. Typical were the *Port Folio* (founded in

1801), the *North American Review* (1815), and the *Saturday Evening Post* (1821). The *Post,* an immediate success, was made up of fiction and poems, essays, and regular columns on morals and religion. Although most books sold in the United States were still printed in England, by 1820 more than 40,000 titles written and published by Americans had appeared. Among the best-sellers were histories (John Marshall's *Life of Washington*), political commentaries (*The Federalist*), and novels (James Fenimore Cooper's *The Spy*).

The American mass media in 1830 were healthy and flourishing, but they were nevertheless the property of the privileged classes. Neither books, nor magazines, nor newspapers were designed to appeal to the common man. They were too expensive, for one thing. For another, they were too literate. What did a dock worker in New York care about the price of wheat on the Philadelphia commodity market or the latest antics of a famous novelist? The population of the United States in 1830

CHRONOLOGY

1783	The first American daily newspaper, the *Pennsylvania Evening Post and Daily Advertiser,* is published in Philadelphia.
1787	Federalist newspapers print *The Federalist,* a series of essays by Alexander Hamilton and others urging ratification of the Constitution. Republican papers respond with Richard Henry Lee's *Letters from a Federal Farmer.* The Federalist-Republican split will characterize the press for the next forty years.
1789	*The Triumph of Nature,* the first native American novel, is published.
1791	The First Amendment to the Constitution is ratified, guaranteeing freedom of the press from Congressional censorship.
1792	The Post Office Act grants newspapers special low mailing rates.
1798	The Federalist Congress enacts the Sedition Act in an effort to restrain Republican newspapers. The invention of the iron press permits printers to make as many as 250 impressions per hour.
1811	Fredrich Koenig of Germany invents a steam-driven cylinder press, capable of producing 1100 impressions per hour.
1821	The *Saturday Evening Post* is founded, the first successful magazine to appeal to women as well as men.
1822	A crude but permanent photograph is produced in France. By 1839 the process will be practical.
1827	The Washington Hand Press is invented; it will cross the continent and give the frontier nearly all its newspapers.

was twelve million. The total circulation of all the newspapers in the country was well under two million.

The times were ripe for a newspaper for the masses.

———

By 1830 the urban working class was the largest potential newspaper audience in America. The papers that emerged to meet the needs of that audience were cheap and readable, stressing human-interest features and objective news over political partisanship. These were the first genuinely mass media in the country, and they quickly became the most influential. Other kinds of newspapers survived (the partisan press, the frontier press, the elite press), but they were clearly secondary in importance.

THE PENNY PRESS

The Industrial Revolution began in America early in the Nineteenth Century. Thousands of farm boys and recent immigrants flooded the cities of the eastern seaboard in search of factory work. This new urban working class soon demanded—and received—the right to vote. The workers used their suffrage to institute tax-supported public schools, and by 1830 most of them knew how to read. But they couldn't afford the newspapers of the period, nor were they interested in shipping and commercial news.

On September 3, 1833, Benjamin Day published the first issue of the *New York Sun.* He greeted his audience with these words:

> The object of this paper is to lay before the public, at a price within the means of every one, ALL THE NEWS OF THE DAY, and at the same time afford an advantageous medium for advertising. . . .[13]

Day's definition of news was much broader than that of the commercial and political newspapers of his time. It included whatever might entertain the masses—especially human-interest features. The first issue of the *Sun* carried this story on Page One:

> *A Whistler.*—A boy in Vermont, accustomed to working alone, was so prone to whistling, that, as soon as he was by himself, he unconsciously commenced. When asleep, the muscles of his mouth, chest, and lungs were so completely concatenated in the association, he whistled with astonishing shrillness. A pale countenance, loss of appetite, and almost total prostration of strength, convinced his mother it would end in death, if not speedily overcome, which was accomplished by placing him in the society of another boy, who had orders to give him a blow as soon as he began to whistle.[14]

Everything in the *Sun* was designed with the urban masses in mind. Day chose a type face nearly twice as large as the opposition's. He cut the paper down to three columns per page, a far more readable format than the customary jumble of five or six columns per page. More important, Day filled the *Sun* with entertaining features. Perhaps the most entertaining was George Wisner's "Police Office," a daily round-up of local crime news. Wisner was the first police reporter in American journalism. He was one of the first reporters of any kind.

The key to the *Sun's* financial success was marketing. Recognizing that the urban masses could not afford six cents for a newspaper (nor an annual subscription at almost any price), Day sold the *Sun* on the street for a penny a copy. Newsboys bought the paper for 67 cents a hundred, then filled the downtown area with cries of crime and violence—on sale for only a penny. By 1836 the *Sun* had a daily circulation of more than 30,000.

The success of the *Sun* spawned dozens of imitators throughout the East. But the three most important ones were right in New York: the *New York Herald,* the *New York Tribune,* and the *New York Times.*

James Gordon Bennett founded the *Herald* in 1835. He matched the *Sun* crime for crime and sensation for sensation, and then some; in 1836 the *Herald* turned the murder of a local prostitute into a national issue. But Bennett was not content with just the working class audience. He challenged the middle-class press as well, with up-to-the-minute coverage of commercial, political, and foreign news. Bennett's private pony express carried first-hand reports from Washington and European news intercepted in Newfoundland. When Samuel Morse's telegraph proved itself effective in 1844, the *Herald* became one of its biggest customers.

Such newsgathering techniques were costly, and Bennett was forced to charge two cents for his paper. The public was apparently willing to pay the price. The *Herald's* extensive (and expensive) coverage of the Mexican War gave a giant boost to both circulation and advertising. By 1860 the *Herald* was the richest newspaper in America, selling 60,000 copies a day.

Horace Greeley's *New York Tribune,* founded in 1841, proved that a penny newspaper could succeed without sensationalism. Greeley's large editorial staff included correspondents in six American cities, plus Europe, Canada, Mexico, Central America, and Cuba. In place of scandal, the *Tribune* offered solid news coverage and a zesty editorial page. Greeley campaigned against slavery, whiskey, tobacco, debt, and numerous other evils both personal and political. A special weekly edition of the *Tribune* circulated nation-wide—200,000 copies a week by 1860.

The *New York Times* was a latecomer to the Penny Press, founded by Henry J. Raymond in 1851. Almost from the first, the *Times* was the most "elite" of the mass market newspapers. Its news was well-balanced and well-edited, and there was plenty of it—with special attention to foreign affairs. The *Times* was not yet the "paper of record" for the United States, but it was on its way.

The Penny Press began with sensationalism and human interest. By mid-century it was the "two penny" press. The human interest continued unabated, but the sensationalism began to disappear; it was replaced with hard national and international news.

In 1848 six New York newspapers banded together to share the cost of telegraphing national news from Washington and European news from Boston. The organization they formed, the Associated Press of New

---

CHRONOLOGY

1830	*Godey's Lady's Book* is founded, a monthly magazine especially for women.
1830–1833	Englishman David Napier perfects the Koenig steam press, producing thousands of impressions per hour.
1833	Benjamin Day publishes the *New York Sun,* the first of the penny newspapers, designed for the working class.
1835	James Gordon Bennett starts the *New York Herald* with $500. The two-cent paper will appeal to both the workers and the middle class.
1840	A German process for making paper from wood pulp permits truly mass-market publishing.
1841	Horace Greeley's *New York Tribune* stresses hard news and editorials instead of sensationalism.
1844	Samuel F. B. Morse perfects the telegraph.
1846	The rotary or "lightning" press is invented; it costs $25,000 —but can produce 20,000 impressions an hour.
1848	Six New York newspapers form the Associated Press of New York to pool telegraph costs. Other papers will soon tie onto the AP, forcing it to report the news objectively.
1850	*Harper's Monthly* is founded, with an emphasis on science and travel.
1851	Henry J. Raymond publishes the *New York Times,* with an initial investment of $100,000. The *Times* will emphasize hard news, especially from abroad. Paul Julius Reuter establishes the first commercial wire service in Europe.
1857	*Harper's Weekly* is founded, using dramatic engravings to report national news.
1860	The Government Printing Office is established; partisan newspapers lose the patronage of federal—but not local governmental—printing.

York, soon became a wire service for the entire nation. Newspapers throughout the country purchased the news reports that AP prepared in Washington and Boston. Since the member papers represented a variety of editorial viewpoints, AP could satisfy them all only by having no viewpoint of its own. Objectivity had come to American journalism.

Now it was left to each newspaper to add its own interpretation or bias to the AP story. Many did just that—but many more didn't bother. Before long, newspapers in Atlanta, Chicago, and New York were carrying identical, unbiased reports. The change was startling. The following wire article on the Supreme Court's Dred Scott decision was carried by the *New York Times* in 1857. It is impossible to tell from the article where the *Times* stood on slavery:

> The opinion of the Supreme Court in the DRED SCOTT case was delivered by Chief Justice TANEY. It was a full and elaborate statement of the views of the Court. They have decided the following important points:
> *First*—Negroes, whether slaves or free, that is, men of the African race, are not citizens of the United States by the Constitution. . . .[15]

The magazine and book industries, meanwhile, followed the same trends as newspapers—appealing to the mass market first through sensationalism and human interest, and later through solid news coverage. *Godey's Lady's Book* (founded in 1830) was the first of a host of monthlies on feminine manners and morals. *Graham's* (1840) did the same job for the special interests of men. *Harper's New Monthly Magazine* (1850) concentrated on science, travel, and current events, while the *Atlantic Monthly* (1857) had a more literary flavor. Weekly periodicals like *Gleason's Pictorial* (1851) and *Leslie's Illustrated Newspaper* (1855) attracted readers with woodblock illustrations of fires, railroad accidents, lynchings, and the like. *Harper's Weekly* (1857) added dramatic engravings of more important national events.

The fortunes of book publishing rose with the appearance of great American authors. Emerson, Thoreau, Poe, Cooper, and Whitman were read by "everyone." So were scores of sentimental novels—and Harriet Beecher Stowe's blockbuster, *Uncle Tom's Cabin*.

THE CIVIL WAR

The second third of the Nineteenth Century witnessed the development of several crucial journalistic trends—mass circulation newspapers and magazines, human-interest stories, and objectivity. But the Partisan Press was by no means dead during this period. It was kept alive first by the issue of Jacksonian Democracy, and later by the even more divisive issue of slavery.

As early as 1837, an abolitionist editor died for his views. He was Elijah Lovejoy, editor of the *St. Louis Observer,* a strident antislavery weekly. Lovejoy was forced by public pressure to move his presses across the river to Alton, Illinois. Three times his office was ransacked—but still he refused to moderate his words. Finally, the editor was murdered by an angry mob. The *Liberator,* a Boston abolitionist paper edited by William Lloyd Garrison, headlined the story:

Horrid Tragedy!
BLOOD CRIETH!
Riot and Murder at Alton.[16]

By the outbreak of hostilities in 1861, the American mass media were once more divided. Almost without exception, the Southern newspapers supported slavery and secession, while the Northern press was firmly opposed to both. Once again, there was no middle ground.

The Civil War was covered as no American war had ever been covered before. More than 150 newspaper and magazine reporters scoured the Northern front for news, while the well-organized Press Association of the Confederate States of America served Southern newspapers from the other side of the line.

The libertarian theory of the press makes no provisions for the exigencies of a Republic at war with itself. Civil War censorship was the rule rather than the exception. In 1861, Union officials discovered that Confederate spies were masquerading as Northern reporters, sending back military secrets in the form of "news" telegrams. The Union army quickly issued an order forbidding telegraph companies from sending reports on military activity without prior government approval. The rule was almost certainly unconstitutional, but this was wartime, and the Supreme Court declined to rule on the matter.

Military officials used their censorship powers not only to protect military secrets, but also to preserve their own reputations. The war between the generals and the reporters was nearly as violent as the war between the North and the South. In 1863, correspondent Thomas W. Knox described the Northern defeat at Vicksburg for the *New York Herald:*

> Throughout the battle the conduct of the general officers was excellent, with a few exceptions. General Sherman was so exceedingly erratic that the discussion of a twelvemonth ago with respect to his sanity was revived with much earnestness. . . . With another brain than that of General Sherman's, we will drop the disappointment at our reverse, and feel certain of victory in the future.[17]

Sherman immediately had Knox court-martialed as a spy. The reporter was found guilty only of ignoring the censorship regulations, and was handed a light sentence. But Sherman succeeded in having him banished from the front lines for the remainder of the conflict. The *Herald* had to find a new war correspondent.

In 1864, the *New York World* and the *Journal of Commerce* mistakenly published a forged Presidential proclamation, ordering the draft of 400,000 men. The government retaliated by closing down both papers for a two-day period. Consistently "Copperhead" (pro-Southern) newspapers, meanwhile, were stormed by mobs and forced to quit publishing. It was the same in the South. The *North Carolina Standard* argued that the war benefitted only the wealthy; its office was destroyed by a Georgia regiment. Freedom of the press, it seems, was a concept reserved for peacetime.

The Civil War brought about several major changes in American journalism. For one thing, Washington D.C. became the most important news center in the country—a role it still plays. Reporters had been covering the Capitol since 1822, and the *New York Herald* had established the first Washington bureau in 1841. But when war came the number of reporters in Washington more than doubled, and for the first time a man was assigned to cover the White House. From the Civil War on, more news came out of Washington than any other American city.

Reporters at the battle fronts, meanwhile, were suspicious of the new

---

CHRONOLOGY

1831	William Lloyd Garrison founds the *Liberator* in Boston, the most influential of the abolitionist newspapers.
1837	Abolitionist editor Elijah Lovejoy is killed by a proslavery mob in Alton, Illinois.
1850	Horace Greeley's *New York Tribune* adopts the cause of abolition, the first major daily to do so.
1851	Robert Barnwell Rhett, editor of the Charleston *Mercury,* is elected to the Senate. Rhett will lead the Southern fight for secession.
1852	Harriet Beecher Stowe's *Uncle Tom's Cabin,* formerly serialized in newspapers, becomes a best-selling book, arguing forcefully against slavery.
1861	The Civil War begins. Both sides immediately institute strict military censorship of war correspondents.
1862	The Press Association of the Confederate States of America is founded.

telegraph machine. Fearful that their entire dispatch might not get through, they made sure to put the most important information first, leaving details and "color" for later. The rambling, roughly chronological news style of the early 1800s gave way to this tighter structure, which we now call the "inverted pyramid" style.

Telegraph reports from the front were often transmitted in fits and spurts. Instead of waiting for the rest of the story, editors began setting these "bulletins" in headline type while the details were still being written. Such many-decked headlines became characteristic of the mid-Nineteenth Century press, and remain characteristic of some newspapers to this date.

A final result of the war was the development of the feature syndicate. Ansell Kellogg, publisher of a weekly in Baraboo, Wisconsin, was short of printing help in his backshop. So he arranged for the *Wisconsin State Journal* in Madison to send him sheets of war news, ready to fold into his own paper. One side was left blank so that Kellogg could add local copy or advertisements. Seeing a good thing, Kellogg later moved to Chicago and started his own syndicate service. By 1865 he had 53 clients.

Some of these trends can be seen in the following article from the *New York Times* of April 15, 1865, reported by Associated Press correspondent Lawrence A. Gobright:

AWFUL EVENT

President Lincoln Shot by an Assassin

The Deed Done at Ford's Theatre Last Night

THE ACT OF A DESPERATE REBEL

The President Still Alive at Last Accounts

No Hope Entertained of His Recovery

Attempted Assassination of Secretary Seward

DETAILS OF THE DREADFUL TRAGEDY

WASHINGTON, Friday, April 14—12:30 A.M.   The President was shot in a theatre tonight and is, perhaps, mortally wounded. . . .[18]

TRANSITION

In a sense, the history of the United States starts over again at the end of the Civil War.   The last third of the Nineteenth Century was characterized by three vitally important trends: industrialization, immigration, and urbanization.

Between 1865 and 1900, the national wealth of the country quadrupled, while manufacturing production increased sevenfold.   This was the age of steel, oil, railroads, and electricity; the age of expanding factories and a growing labor movement.   Meanwhile, the population more than doubled, from 35 million in 1865 to 76 million in 1900.   Much of the growth was due to immigration, averaging as many as half a million new residents a year.   Most of the immigrants, naturally, remained in the large cities on the East Coast, where jobs were plentiful for the unskilled.   In the generation from 1860 to 1900, the population of New York City alone grew from slightly over a million to 3.4 million.

Inevitably, the American mass media changed with these conditions.   By 1900, there were 2,326 daily newspapers in the country, roughly six times the number in 1865.   More important, newspapers geared themselves more and more for the blue-collar reader, especially the urban immigrant.   They were cheap and easy to read, filled with bold headlines, exciting artwork, human-interest stories, and editorials that championed the rights of the working classes.   These developments were to culminate in the turn-of-the-century "New Journalism" of Joseph Pulitzer, William Randolph Hearst, and E. W. Scripps.

Of course not all American publishers were busy cultivating the urban mass market.   The frontier press, for example, had no mass market to cultivate.   Many Western weeklies survived on circulations of only a few hundred.   Located in tiny frontier towns, they played a vital role in the growth of their communities and territories.   A few such papers were lucky enough to attract superlative journalists.   Mark Twain, for instance, worked for several years as a reporter for the *Territorial Enterprise* of Virginia City, Nevada.   But most frontier newspapers made do with more ordinary talent.   Their pages were dominated by government proclamations (paid legal advertising) and reports on the activities of local civic groups.

The elite press, meanwhile, pursued the specialized interests of its readers with little regard for national trends. Every large city supported at least one newspaper devoted to commercial and financial news, plus a second paper which stressed the conservative, "businessman's" attitude toward the events of the day. Intellectuals could subscribe to any of hundreds of literary magazines. For political and social commentary they might read *The Nation*, a weekly magazine founded by E. L. Godkin in 1865. *The Nation* consistently lost money (in more than a hundred years of continuous publication, it has never once earned a profit), but it was (and is) a highly influential vehicle for liberal political philosophy.

The elite press and the frontier press were important, but it was the mass-circulation newspaper that was to change the course of American journalism. Industrialization, immigration, and urbanization created the mass market. Publishers did their best to capture it.

They could never have succeeded without the help of dozens of inventors and engineers. The following technological developments all took place between 1860 and 1900, making possible a truly mass-circulation newspaper:

1. The first trans-Atlantic cable is completed, permitting up-to-the-minute news reports from overseas.
2. The telephone is invented, speeding the flow of information from news source to newsroom.
3. The web perfecting press is developed, capable of simultaneously printing both sides of a continuous roll of paper.
4. The electric press and the color press are introduced, increasing production speed to 48,000 12-page papers per hour.
5. Improved paper-making techniques reduce the price of newsprint from $246 a ton in 1870 to $42 a ton in 1900.
6. The development of the electric light bulb makes after-dinner reading possible, stimulating an upsurge in evening newspapers.
7. The typewriter is invented and adopted by the Associated Press and many large newspapers.
8. The linotype machine is patented, immediately tripling the speed of typesetting.
9. Halftone photoengraving is perfected, enabling newspapers and magazines to print photographs in addition to drawings and woodcuts.

All this newfangled equipment cost money—a lot of money. A single high-speed press might cost as much as $80,000; linotype machines, photoengravers, and even typewriters added to the bill. In 1835, James Gordon Bennett had started the New York *Herald* with a capital investment of $500. In 1895, William Randolph Hearst paid $180,000 for the printing plant of the New York *Journal*. And in 1901, *Editor and Publisher* magazine estimated that it would take at least a million dollars to launch a daily newspaper in New York. In order to run a "modern" newspaper, then, the turn-of-the-century publisher *had* to attract a mass audience. A high-speed press is simply too expensive to stand idle; it must be used to capacity, or it loses money.

Metropolitan newspapers need a mass audience to survive, but they seldom earn their profits directly from that audience. The profits come from advertising. It is doubtful that mass circulation newspapers would have been possible without the invention of the department store.

Until the 1860s, newspaper advertising was mostly of the "classified" variety—brief, solid-type notices of products for sale. Then department stores began to replace neighborhood merchants as the chief source of goods. Besides the convenience of buying everything in one place, they offered fixed prices, credit, and free delivery. They also offered the first standardized, uniform-quality merchandise—the same hat or tin of flour in Boston as in Chicago. Suddenly newspapers were inundated with two new kinds of advertising: ads from the department stores (special on soap flakes at John Wanamaker's), and ads from the manufacturers whose brand names the stores carried (our chewing tobacco is better than their chewing tobacco). By 1880, advertising accounted for nearly half of newspaper gross revenue. By 1910, the figure would be two-thirds.

Most of this advertising was aimed at women—then as now the main customers for consumer goods. This was a boon for the women's magazines of the period (*Ladies' Home Journal, Woman's Home Companion, McCall's*). It also forced the daily newspapers to supply more material of special interest to women: fashion, cooking, society, etc. This was not the last time that the American mass media would tailor their content to the needs of advertisers.

Once a publisher has sunk a few hundred thousand dollars into a printing plant, he wants to get as much use out of it as he can. Morning newspapers thus began printing afternoon editions as well. With improvements in home lighting in the 1870s, these became evening editions, serving both the homeward-bound commuter and his wife, eager to check out the ads and plan her next day's shopping. By 1890, evening newspapers outnumbered morning ones two-to-one.

The same logic led to the development of the Sunday edition. Publishers were happy to have another use for their presses, while retailers were eager to reach the reader on a no-work day. Since there was little real news over the weekend, the Sunday papers were filled with features, short fiction, comics, and the like. They soon outstripped their parent dailies in size, circulation—and profit.

By the mid-1880s, industrialization, immigration, and urbanization had progressed to the point where, for the first time, a truly mass market existed for newspapers. By the mid-1880s, also, technological improvements and retail display advertising had developed sufficiently to permit publishers to exploit that market. It was the era of Big Business in American history. And the mass media were about to become a big business themselves.

The period from 1880 to 1910 produced a revolution in American journalism. Joseph Pulitzer and William Randolph Hearst created the nation's first truly mass-circulation newspapers, reaching heights of sensationalism never matched before or since. E. W. Scripps founded the first of the great newspaper chains, helping to transform journalism into a Big Business. Powerful wire services introduced standardization in newspaper content, while magazines like McClure's offered readers their first and finest taste of persistent full-length muckraking.

JOSEPH PULITZER

Joseph Pulitzer came to America from Hungary to fight in the Union army. Instead, he wound up as a newspaper reporter in St. Louis. He soon became active in Republican politics, fighting graft as both a state legislator and a local columnist. In 1878, he founded the St. Louis *Post-Dispatch*. The paper was an immediate success, and by 1883 Pulitzer had saved enough money to try the Big Time. He moved to New York and bought the *World*—a sober, businessman's paper with a circulation of 20,000.

In his very first issue, Pulitzer announced that the *World* would be sober no longer:

> There is room in this great and growing city for a journal that is not only cheap but bright, not only bright but large, not only large but truly democratic—dedicated to the cause of the people rather than to that of the purse potentates—devoted more to the news of the New than the Old World—that will expose all fraud and sham, fight all public evils and abuses—that will battle for the people with earnest sincerity.[19]

Two weeks later Pulitzer began to fulfill his promise. The Brooklyn Bridge was dedicated, and the *World* launched its first crusade: no tolls. In the months that followed, the paper exposed and denounced the New York Central Railroad, the Standard Oil and Bell Telephone monopolies, white slavery, political bribery, tenement housing conditions, inheritance tax loopholes, vote-buying, and civil service corruption—all on the front page.

CHRONOLOGY

1863	William Bullock introduces the web perfecting press, which prints both sides of a continuous roll of paper.
1865	E. L. Godkin founds *The Nation,* an elite weekly opinion magazine. Godkin will later become editor of the New York *Evening Post.*
1866	The first successful trans-Atlantic cable is completed.
1868	Charles A. Dana buys the New York *Sun,* and turns it into a lively combination of political activism and feature writing.
1869	The N. W. Ayer & Son advertising agency is founded to help advertisers buy newspaper space.
1871	The New York *Times* and *Harper's Weekly* (through cartoonist Thomas Nast) break the story of Tammany Hall corruption in New York government—an early example of muckraking journalism.
1876	Alexander Graham Bell invents the telephone.
1878	Thomas A. Edison develops the first phonograph. Frederick E. Ives introduces a practical method for halftone photoengraving; the technique will not be widely used for newspaper photography for another twenty years.
1879	Edison invents the incandescent bulb (electric light). John Wanamaker of Philadelphia buys the first full-page newspaper advertisement for his department store.
1885	Ottmar Mergenthaler files a patent for the first linotype machine.

Pulitzer's *World* also offered solid news coverage of the city, the country, and the world—but so did many other newspapers. What was special about the *World* was its exposés, its human-interest stories, and its stunts.

Averaging sixteen pages an issue, the paper was filled with gossip, scandal, and sensational tidbits of all sorts. Headlines were lively, and illustrations were plentiful: crime scenes (X marked the spot), disaster drawings, political cartoons, etc. The *World* promoted itself in every issue, using coupons, contests, and assorted other gimmicks. Pulitzer led the drive to build a pedestal for the Statue of Liberty, and sent an expedition to rescue a pioneer girl from Indian captors. He designed and executed some of the first public opinion polls. He invented the man-in-the-street interview. He sent columnist "Nellie Bly" (Elizabeth Cochran) to improve on Jules Verne by circling the globe in only 72 days. All to build circulation.

In 1884, one year after Pulitzer took over, the *World's* circulation hit 100,000. Ten years later the figure, including both morning and evening editions, topped 400,000. Pulitzer's formula (news + human interest +

stunts + editorial crusades) was a resounding success. It would be widely imitated.

WILLIAM RANDOLPH HEARST

While a student at Harvard, William Randolph Hearst was fascinated by the sensationalism of Pulitzer's *World*. He begged his father, owner of the San Francisco *Examiner,* to let him try the same trick. Daddy went along, and the *Examiner* had a new, twenty-four-year-old publisher.

"Wasteful Willie" spent a small fortune transforming the paper into an exciting medium for the masses. He used special trains to get his reporters to the scene first, and hired the finest and most sensational writers he could find, whatever the cost. News for Hearst was defined as anything that made the reader say "Gee whiz"—and the columns of satirist Ambrose Bierce and sob-sister "Annie Laurie" (Winifred Black Bonfils) more than filled the bill. Within a year the *Examiner* had doubled its circulation. In 1893 it overtook the staid San Francisco *Chronicle* to become the most successful newspaper in the West.

Young Hearst was eager to battle Pulitzer on the *World*'s home turf. Financed by the family fortune, he purchased the New York *Morning Journal* in 1895. Scandal, gossip, sex, and pseudoscience immediately began to fill the pages of the *Journal*. Hearst spent wildly to acquire an all-star line-up, hiring, among others, the entire staff of the *World*'s Sunday edition. The *Journal*'s circulation rose to 150,000, and several advertisers dropped Pulitzer to take advantage of Hearst's cheaper ad rates.

A few years before, Pulitzer had hired R. F. Outcault to draw the first cartoon comic, "The Yellow Kid of Hogan's Alley," for his Sunday edition. Printed in color, the strip was wildly successful. When Hearst stole Outcault from the *World,* Pulitzer hired himself another artist. Both newspapers now carried "The Yellow Kid." The competition between the two comics came to symbolize the entire Hearst-Pulitzer circulation war, and gave that war a name: yellow journalism.

By 1897, both the *World* and the *Journal* were publishing morning, evening, and Sunday editions. Hearst's daily circulation matched Pulitzer's at 700,000; his Sunday circulation of 600,000 was coming close. In the struggle for readers, no feature was too silly to run. A typical article from the Sunday *World* was headlined "Does Tight Lacing Develop Cruelty?" The story began:

> The wearing of tight corsets will lower the moral character of the most refined woman. It will make her cruel. It will lead to morbid impulses—perhaps to crime. It will wholly destroy in her the naturally gentle and humane impulses of the feminine character.
>
> Tight lacing, we are told, compresses the solar plexus. . . . By reflex

action the compression of the corset disturbs the entire nervous system—
and the victim proceeds to descend from her lofty mental heights and to
grovel in the depths of nervous depression.[20]

Yellow journalism reached its high point as the *World* and the *Journal*
(and dozens of imitators across the country) covered the Cuban struggle
against Spanish colonial rule. Hearst, in particular, intentionally built up
war fever in order to build up circulation—and his competitors undertook
to play the same game. It is probably unfair to claim that the *Journal*
single-handedly started the Spanish-American War, but certainly Hearst
did his share.

In 1897, Hearst sent writer Richard Harding Davis and artist Frederic
Remington (both nationally famous) to cover the Cuban story first-hand.
Nothing much was happening, and Remington cabled Hearst for permission to come home. The publisher is supposed to have replied: "Please
remain. You furnish the pictures and I'll furnish the war." And so he
did. One issue of the *Journal* carried a Remington sketch of a naked
Cuban girl surrounded by leering Spanish officers, supposedly searching
her clothes while on board an American ship. The banner headline read:
"Does Our Flag Protect Women?" The *World* piously revealed that no
such incident had ever happened—and then went out in search of its own
atrocity stories.

When the battleship Maine exploded mysteriously in Havana harbor,
both papers pulled out all the stops. The *Journal* devoted its whole front
page to the story. "Destruction of the war ship Maine was the work of
an enemy," it announced—and then went on to offer a $50,000 reward for
proof of the claim. The *World* discovered "evidence" that a Spanish
mine was responsible. Both newspapers passed the one-million circulation mark. Weeks later the war began.

NEWSPAPER CHAINS

In 1873, James E. and George H. Scripps founded the Detroit *News*.
In 1878 Edward Wyllis Scripps started the Cleveland *Press*. During the
next twelve years, the three brothers added the Buffalo *Evening Telegraph*, the St. Louis *Chronicle*, the Cincinnati *Post*, and the Kentucky
Post. The first modern newspaper chain was born.

E. W. Scripps quickly proved the most talented of the three brothers.
His formula was simple. Find a city with weak newspapers and an editor
with strong ideas. Start a new paper from scratch, emphasizing human-
interest stories and an occasional crusade, always on behalf of the working man. Pay your top editor $25 a week until the paper shows a profit,
then give him a huge block of stock. And sit back and wait.

Not every Scripps paper succeeded, but the successes far outweighed the losers. By 1914, the Scripps-McRae League was publisher of 23 newspapers across the country, most of them small-city afternoon mass-market dailies. Scripps himself wrote the editorials for all his papers. The chain was further unified by the United Press Association (a wire service), plus a feature syndicate and a science service. Readers of Scripps papers from coast to coast were offered identical national news and editorials.

E. W. Scripps was not primarily a businessman. He was sincerely dedicated to his crusades for the common man, and so hated pressure from advertisers that he twice experimented with adless papers. Nevertheless, Scripps proved that a large chain of newspapers, run from afar, could earn immense profits for its owner. Later chain publishers were often more interested in the profits than news and editorial influence.

Until 1900, William Randolph Hearst owned only two newspapers, the San Francisco *Examiner* and the New York *Journal*. Then, obviously observant of Scripps' success, he began to make up for lost time. First came papers in Chicago, Boston, and Atlanta, then two new ones in San Francisco—all before 1917. Between 1917 and 1921, the Hearst chain acquired six properties. Seven more were added in 1922, and sixteen more by 1934.

Hearst ran his papers with an iron hand. They were as fanatically antiwar and anti-Ally in 1916 as they had been prowar and pro-Cuban in 1897. Hearst personally directed local crusades for his member papers, and led them on the first great "red hunt" after the Russian Revolution. The chain was united by two wire services—International News Service and Universal Service. Other Hearst subsidiaries included King Features (now the largest feature syndicate in America) and *American Weekly,* a Sunday supplement which was stuffed into every Hearst paper.

Hearst rule was healthy for some newspapers, deadly for others. In search of top-flight staffs and no competition, Hearst often bought out and merged or folded the opposition papers. In Chicago, the *Herald* and *Examiner* became the *Herald-Examiner;* in Boston, the *Daily Advertiser* was merged into Hearst's *Record*. Came the Depression of the 1930s, the Hearst chain found that it had overextended its financial reach, and began killing its own papers in a frantic economy drive. At one time or another, Hearst owned 42 newspapers. By the time he went into semi-retirement in 1940, the chain was down to 17. Seven of the others had been sold. The remaining 18 were dead.

WIRE SERVICES

The development of mass-circulation daily newspapers greatly increased the importance of the wire service—how else could a paper get the news of the world quickly and cheaply? For 34 years after its founding in 1848, the Associated Press was the only wire service in America (aside from the short-lived Confederate group during the Civil War). A loose co-operative of regional services (New England AP, Western AP, etc.), the Associated Press was actually run by the New York AP. The New York group had economic ties with Western Union, as well as agreements with the Reuters service in England and Havas in France. It used its power to set rates and news policies that favored the needs of New York newspapers. It also enforced a rule whereby any member newspaper could blackball a competitor from AP membership.

By 1882 the need for a second wire service was obvious. A new group, calling itself the United Press, was organized to meet that need. Soon it had enrolled non-AP papers in nearly every major city. But this was the age of monopoly. Instead of competing with the new service, the Associated Press decided to make a deal. A secret agreement was negotiated; UP promised not to encourage any new papers in AP cities, and both services agreed to share their news reports.

Word of the agreement eventually leaked out to the Western AP members (already unhappy with New York's management), and in 1890 a government investigation was launched. Embarrassed, the New York group bolted to the United Press, leaving the Westerners in charge of the AP. They quickly incorporated as the Associated Press of Illinois.

Melville E. Stone was drafted as general manager of the newly organized AP. Stone managed to work out exclusive news-exchange contracts with the European press services, severely hampering the UP operation. In 1897 the United Press was forced into bankruptcy. Again the country was left with only one national wire service.

In 1900 the Illinois Supreme Court ruled that the AP was not entitled to blackball would-be members. In response, the company left Illinois and incorporated in New York. The membership protest right (blackball) survived until 1945, when the U.S. Supreme Court finally outlawed it.

In the meantime, a newspaper without an AP membership had only two alternatives. It could buy out a member paper, or it could start its own wire service. In 1907, E. W. Scripps founded the United Press Association, and Hearst followed in 1909 with the International News Service. Instead of issuing memberships, these services sold their reports to subscribers. In 1958 they merged. The resulting United Press International had little trouble competing successfully with the Associated Press.

THE MUCKRAKERS

In October of 1902, *McClure's* magazine printed the first of a nineteen-part series on "The Rise of the Standard Oil Company." Written by Ida Tarbell, the series revealed a number of secret agreements—kickbacks, rebates, and the like—between Standard Oil and the railroads. The pub-

1895	Hearst buys the New York *Journal* to compete directly with Pulitzer.
1896	Adolph S. Ochs takes over the undistinguished New York *Times;* he will buck the trend by stressing accuracy, objectivity, and depth.
1897	The United Press goes into bankruptcy.
1897–1898	Competition between Pulitzer and Hearst leads to sensational "yellow journalism," culminating in coverage of the Cuban insurrection and the Spanish-American War.
1902	*McClure's* magazine presents the first great magazine exposé, a 19-month attack on Standard Oil. E. W. Scripps founds the first national feature syndicate, the Newspaper Enterprise Association.
1904	Ivy Lee founds the first modern public-relations firm in New York.
1907	Scripps organizes the United Press Association to compete with the Associated Press; two years later Hearst will add a third wire service, the International News Service.
1911	Will Irwin begins a 15-part muckraking series in *Collier's* on "The American Newspaper."
1914	Hearst forms the King Feature Syndicate.

responsible, and immensely profitable. The most prestigious newspaper in the country was, again, not the *World* or the *Journal*, but Adolph S. Ochs' New York *Times*—accurate, voluminous and dull.

Historians Harry J. Carman and Harold C. Syrett summarize the period this way:

> As the circulation of the large urban dailies reached unprecedented figures, many of them became huge enterprises that in all essential features were similar to the large corporations of industry and transportation. . . . Despite important exceptions, the increasing financial success of the larger papers often resulted in a corresponding growth of a conservative outlook in their editorial columns. This view was succinctly expressed by Arthur Brisbane, a Hearst employee: "Journalistic success brings money. The editor has become a money man. 'Where your treasure is, there your heart will be also.'" As journalism became more and more a big business, there was also a noticeable development toward standardization. The press services supplied the same news to all their customers, and syndicates furnished many papers with the same cartoons, comic strips, photographs, and feature stories. Equally striking evidence of the trend toward standardization was the formation of several newspaper chains that had papers in several cities under a single management. . . .[21]

The era of yellow journalism left a legacy of many characteristics still to be found in today's newspapers: large headlines and pictures, Sunday comics, human-interest features, public-service crusades. It also left a tradition of stunts and sensationalism that still influences many editors. But the greatest effect of the yellow journalists was paradoxical: They produced the first Big Newspapers, and thus inevitably turned newspapering into a Big Business. Pulitzer, Hearst, and Scripps might best be described as "crusading press barons." Today we have press barons galore, but few crusaders.

The history of the mass media before the Twentieth Century is the history of printing—newspapers, magazines, and books. Then came the new media: first film, next radio, and finally television. These upstarts quickly began to compete with the established media, forcing them to change their character in order to retain their influence. Broadcasting, in particular, had a tremendous effect on the other media, an effect that is only now being felt full-force.

NEW MEDIA

The existence of the motion picture rests on the 1824 discovery that the human eye retains an image for a fraction of a second longer than the picture actually appears. If a second, slightly different picture is substituted during this brief interval, the illusion of motion results.

In 1903, almost 80 years later, Edwin S. Porter produced the first American commercial film with a plot. "The Great Train Robbery" was eight thrilling minutes of stunt-riding and gunfighting. Suddenly film was a realistic medium, a worthy competitor of the legitimate theater.

Until 1912, no American film ran longer than fifteen minutes. This was the decision of the Motion Picture Patents Company, an industry association which apparently felt there was no market for films of more than one reel. The Patents Company also ruled that film actors should not be identified—since a well-known performer might demand higher wages. And it established the National Board of Censorship to insure that member producers did nothing to offend the moviegoer.

Then, in 1912, Adolf Zukor purchased the American rights to a four-reel production of "Queen Elizabeth," starring Sarah Bernhardt. The Patents Company refused to distribute the film through normal channels (nickelodeons and store shows), so Zukor persuaded the Lyceum Theatre in New York to run it. The movie later toured the country, and Zukor founded Paramount Pictures with the profits.

Three years later, D. W. Griffith produced "The Birth of a Nation," incorporating a sympathetic approach to the Ku Klux Klan. It ran twelve reels (nearly three hours), and had a special score performed by a symphony orchestra. Griffith's film gripped its audience as no movie had before, and as few have since. Race riots followed its presentation in several cities; Woodrow Wilson called it "like writing history in lightning."[22] Film was now a force to be reckoned with.

During the next decade, the movie industry moved West to Hollywood, where it found lower taxes and better shooting weather. The Patents Company weakened and dissolved. The feature film replaced the one-reeler, and the "first run" movie theater replaced the nickelodeon. Moviegoers came to idolize certain performers—Mary Pickford, Lillian and Dorothy Gish, Lionel Barrymore, William S. Hart, Fatty Arbuckle, Douglas Fairbanks, Charlie Chaplin. The appearance of any of these stars guaranteed a box-office hit.

By the mid-1920s, movies were Big Business—slick, commercial, and very profitable. But a new competitor was already on the scene: radio.

Radio owes its existence to the "wireless telegraph," invented by Gugliemo Marconi in 1895. The wireless was fine for dots and dashes, but voice transmission was impossible until 1906, when Lee De Forest perfected the vacuum tube. Four years later, De Forest dramatically broadcast the voice of Enrico Caruso from the stage of New York's Metropolitan Opera House.

Experimentation continued during World War One, and in 1919 Westinghouse engineer Frank Conrad began broadcasting music throughout the Pittsburgh area. Listener response was enthusiastic; Westinghouse immediately started advertising its crystal sets "to hear Dr. Conrad's popular broadcasts." In 1920, the station was christened KDKA.

The *Detroit News*, meanwhile, was running what was to become radio station WWJ in order to gain goodwill and help sell newspapers. Publishers in Kansas City, Milwaukee, Chicago, Los Angeles, Louisville, Atlanta, Des Moines, and Dallas soon followed suit. Department stores ran radio stations to promote their goods. So did manufacturers like AT&T, General Electric, and of course Westinghouse.

From the very beginning, news was an important part of broadcasting. KDKA's first transmission was the 1920 election returns. In 1922, the Associated Press decided that radio might soon constitute a major threat to the newspaper business, so it ruled that AP reports could not be carried on radio. Station-owning publishers rebelled against the rule, complaining that their competitors would use the UP or INS reports anyhow. Although AP tried to reserve its 1924 election returns for the print media only, some three million families learned of the victory of Calvin Coolidge via radio. AP soon joined the other wire services in supplying news to broadcast stations.

Meanwhile, New York station WEAF was discovering, rather to its surprise, that radio could earn money. In 1922 the station's owner, AT&T, began selling time to advertisers. Word spread quickly, and the race for broadcast licenses was on. Plans to develop radio as a non-profit public-service institution were abandoned. In 1921 there had been only 30 commercial radio stations; by 1923 there were more than 500.

Radio networks developed to meet the needs of national advertisers. By 1925, AT&T already owned a chain of 26 stations, stretching from New York to Kansas City. RCA, Westinghouse, and General Electric (all radio manufacturers) were working together to organize a competing network. In 1926, AT&T agreed to sell out to its rivals in return for a monopoly over all network relays, the lines that connect member stations. The National Broadcasting Company was founded as an RCA subsidiary to run the new operation. The old AT&T network became the NBC "red network," while the original Westinghouse-RCA-GE network was called the "blue network." Coast-to-coast programming began in 1927, under the leadership of NBC head David Sarnoff. Three years later, Westinghouse and GE were forced out of network operation by an antitrust suit, and Sarnoff took over control of RCA.

The competing Columbia Broadcasting System was founded in 1927 by the Columbia phonograph record company. William S. Paley soon became its president, and by 1929 CBS was making money.

In 1927 there were 733 stations in the nation. Many of them found it necessary to skip around from frequency to frequency, searching for a clear one where they could broadcast without interference. Inevitably, the more powerful stations were smothering their weaker rivals. The radio industry and the listening public asked the federal government to clear up the interference problem by assigning each station its own frequency. Congress accepted the responsibility. The Radio Act of 1927 gave a five-man Federal Radio Commission the power to regulate all broadcast transmissions.

CHRONOLOGY

1824   Peter Mark Roget discovers the principle of motion pictures—that the human eye retains an image briefly after the picture is gone.

1839   Louis Daguerre and Joseph Niepce develop a practical photographic process.

1877   Eadweard Muybridge and John D. Issacs use 24 cameras in sequence to photograph a race horse in action.

1878   Edison invents the phonograph.

1884   George Eastman introduces roll film, leading to the easy-to-operate Kodak camera.

1889	Edison and William K. L. Dickson develop a sprocket system for motion pictures.
1895	Systems for projecting motion pictures on a screen are developed simultaneously in several countries. Gugliemo Marconi transmits wireless telegraph signals for one mile.
1901	Marconi sends wireless signals across the Atlantic.
1903	"The Great Train Robbery" becomes the first American movie with a plot.
1906	Lee De Forest perfects the vacuum tube, making possible radio voice transmissions.
1912	Adolf Zukor presents the four-reel movie "Queen Elizabeth," starring Sarah Bernhardt. Congress passes the Radio Act of 1912 to prevent individual ham operators from interfering with government transmissions.
1915	D. W. Griffith produces "The Birth of a Nation," the longest and most powerful film to date.
1919	Westinghouse engineer Frank Conrad begins broadcasting music throughout the Pittsburgh area.
1920	Westinghouse obtains a license for station KDKA in Pittsburgh.
1922	New York station WEAF begins selling airtime to advertisers. The Associated Press refuses to allow the broadcasting of AP reports. In an effort to avoid government censorship, the movie industry establishes a Production Code and self-censorship procedures.
1923	The Eveready Battery Company prepares and sponsors its own hour-long show on WEAF; a year later it will produce the show on a national network.
1926	AT&T turns its radio network over to a joint RCA-Westinghouse-GE consortium, leading to the development of the RCA-controlled National Broadcasting Company.
1927	The Columbia Broadcasting System is organized to compete with the NBC network. The Radio Act of 1927 establishes a five-man Federal Radio Commission to license broadcasters and prevent signal interference.

The job of the FRC was to grant licenses for the use of specific frequencies, renewable every three years. Licensees were expected to provide "fair, efficient, and equitable service," and to act "in the public interest, convenience, or necessity."[23] The implicit power of censorship through license renewal expressed in these standards has been used only rarely (and very hesitantly) by the Commission.

In order to put a stop to signal interference, the FRC eliminated more than a hundred stations, leaving the total number at roughly 600. "Clear channels" were established to allow selected urban stations to reach distant rural areas with no stations of their own. Most of these highly lucrative channels soon fell into network hands.

The film and radio industries both experienced a surge of tremendous growth in the 1920s. What were the print media doing during that decade?

OLD MEDIA

America may have entered World War One reluctantly, but American newspapers entered with enthusiasm. Even the isolationist Hearst chain abandoned its campaign for neutrality after the 1917 declaration of war. Throughout the 19 months of fighting, anti-German propaganda dominated the press.

The government did what it could to ensure that dominance. President Wilson appointed former newsman George Creel to head the Committee on Public Information. The C.P.I. issued over 6,000 patriotic press releases during the course of the war, most of which were faithfully carried by the nation's press. The Creel Committee also established "guidelines for voluntary censorship" on touchy subjects such as troop movements.

In addition, Congress passed a series of laws aimed at putting a stop to "treasonous" publications. These laws culminated in the Espionage Act of 1917 and the Sedition Act of 1918. The latter outlawed, among other things, "any disloyal, profane, scurrilous, or abusive language about the form of government of the United States, or the Constitution, military or naval forces, flag, or the uniform of the army or navy of the United States."[24] No attempt was made to invoke the Sedition Act against mainstream publishers; it was used instead to stifle the socialist and German-language press. Mainstream publishers, after all, minded their manners. When the war was over, the *Nation* magazine was moved to comment:

> During the past two years, we have seen what is practically an official control of the press, not merely by Messrs. Burleson and Gregory [heads of the Post Office and Justice Department] but by the logic of events and the patriotic desire of the press to support the government.[25]

The end of World War One was the start of the Roaring Twenties. It was a sensational decade—jazz and flappers; Prohibition, speakeasies, and gangsters; Mary Pickford and Douglas Fairbanks; Charles Lindbergh and the Prince of Wales; Jack Dempsey, Red Grange, and Babe Ruth; Leopold and Loeb; Sacco and Vanzetti. The Roaring Twenties virtually cried out for a Renaissance in yellow journalism.

The cry was answered with a new kind of newspaper: the tabloid. Tabloids may be recognized by their small size (easy to carry on the subway), their small number of columns (seldom more than five), and their extensive use of photography (often the whole front page). The first modern American tabloid was the New York *Daily News*, founded by Joseph M. Patterson in 1919. The *News* offered its readers a steady diet of sex and crime, luridly illustrated and simply written. By 1924 it had the largest daily circulation of any newspaper in America.

Typical of the *News* approach to news was the paper's 1928 front-page photo of the execution of convicted murderess Ruth Snyder. The heavily retouched picture filled the entire page, with the following caption:

> WHEN RUTH PAID HER DEBT TO THE STATE!—The only unofficial photo ever taken within the death chamber, this most remarkable, exclusive picture shows closeup of Ruth Snyder in death chair at Sing Sing as lethal current surged through her body at 11:06 Thursday night. . . . *Story and another electrocution picture on page 3.*[26]

Dozens of tabloids appeared in major cities throughout the country in the 1920s, modeled on the *News* formula of sex and violence. Some died off, but many survive to this day, often with very healthy circulation figures. Though tabloids obviously exert great influence on their readers, they are viewed by journalists and students of journalism almost as a quirk, quite separate from the mainstream of American publishing. The New York *Daily News* still has the highest newspaper readership in the United States, and as a *news*paper it has greatly improved since the 1920s —but not one university in a hundred receives and microfilms the paper.

Like the Penny Press and the Yellow Press, the Tabloid Press built its circulation on people who had not regularly read a daily newspaper— immigrants and blue-collar workers. Mainstream newspapers ignored the tabloids, sticking firmly to the standards of accuracy, objectivity, and responsibility established before the war. The finest example of this tradition was the New York *Times*, published by Adolph S. Ochs and edited by Carr V. Van Anda.

The *Times* strove in every issue to be a "newspaper of record," correct, careful, and complete. Its motto was "All the News That's Fit to Print." An unwritten corrolary was "and not a *word* of interpretation." According to the *Times* ethic, interpretation was like bias, unworthy of a newspaper that prided itself on straight reporting.

Not every newspaper in the 1920s was a miniature New York *Times*, but except for the tabloids nearly every newspaper secretly wished it was. The wire services helped to point the way. In an effort to please publishers with all sorts of viewpoints, AP, UP, and INS tried to write without any viewpoint. The wire story—an assortment of accurate but uninterpreted facts—became the epitome of good newspaper journalism. Occasionally every paper would lapse into sensationalism or bias or interpretation, and some papers lapsed more than others. But every paper (tabloids aside) tried to lapse as little as possible, to stick as best it could to the straight and narrow path of objectivity.

American journalists now considered themselves members of a full-fledged profession. In 1922, the editors of the major daily newspapers organized the American Society of Newspaper Editors. The group had its first annual meeting in 1923, and immediately adopted a seven-point code of ethics, known as the "Canons of Journalism." The Canons stressed sincerity, truthfulness, accuracy, impartiality, fair play, decency, independence, and fidelity to the public interest. They were extremely general and strictly voluntary. The Canons were an expression, not of what newspapers were, but rather of what newspapers thought they ought to be. They were thus indicative of a major transition in American journalism, from the free-wheeling libertarian theory of the Nineteenth Century to the more sober "social responsibility" theory of the Twentieth.

But the social responsibility of the press, according to the Canons of Journalism, was limited to telling the truth about the news. Nothing was said about interpreting the news, giving it meaning, or making sense of it for the reader. Editors and publishers would soon discover that this limited notion of responsibility was not enough.

As newspapers grew more "responsible," they also diminished in number. Competition and economic pressures caused the death of many papers. Intentional consolidation at the hands of media barons killed others.

CHRONOLOGY

1917   World War One begins, and American newspapers willingly accept "voluntary" censorship at the hands of the Creel Committee.

1918   Congress passes the Sedition Act and other laws which were used to stifle the socialist and German-language press.

1919   The war ends, and Joseph M. Patterson founds the New York *Daily News,* the first of the sex-and-violence tabloids.

1922   DeWitt Wallace begins publishing *The Reader's Digest,* destined to become the largest general-interest magazine in the world.

1923   The American Society of Newspaper Editors adopts the Canons of Journalism, an expression of the "social responsibility" of the press. Henry R. Luce and Briton Hadden found *Time* magazine, the first of the weekly newsmagazines.

1924   H. L. Mencken establishes the *American Mercury,* an outspoken and frequently obstreperous magazine of opinion.

Still others died simply because there was no longer any need for them; as newspaper content became more and more standardized, readers cared less and less which paper they read. In 1910, there were 2,200 English-language dailies in the United States, serving 1,207 cities. By 1930 there were only 1,942 dailies serving 1,002 cities. During the same period, the number of American cities with competing daily newspapers plummeted from 689 to 288. These trends would continue in the decades ahead. By 1960, the number of daily newspapers would be down to 1,763; the number of cities with competing dailies would be down to a mere 61.

The magazine industry, meanwhile, grew less and less concerned with news and public affairs. The muckraking magazines of the turn of the century either folded or reverted to features and fiction. So did most of the serious magazines of opinion that had flourished before the war. They were replaced for a while by H. L. Mencken's *American Mercury*. Founded in 1924, the *Mercury* was outspoken and sensational, the magazine equivalent of a tabloid. Other new entries of the 1920s included the *Reader's Digest* (1922), the *Saturday Review of Literature* (1924), and the *New Yorker* (1925).

The major exception to the retreat of magazines from the real world was *Time*, founded by Henry R. Luce and Briton Hadden in 1923. Both were young men in their twenties; both wanted to publish a weekly magazine that would make sense of the news. "People are uninformed," they argued, "because no publication has adapted itself to the time which busy men are able to spend on simply keeping informed."[27] *Time's* interpretations of the news were slick, facile, and often misleading—but it *did* interpret the news. It thus satisfied a need that would become increasingly acute in the years to come.

DEPRESSION AND AFTER

On October 29, 1929, the New York stock market crashed—heralding the Great Depression, the New Deal, and a revolution in American life. Every institution was significantly changed by the events of the 1930s, and the mass media were no exception.

The Depression cut heavily into newspaper revenue, but radio continued to grow and prosper. In 1932, the American Newspaper Publishers Association voted to combat the electronic competition by cutting off its supply of news. ANPA asked the wire services to stop selling news to radio stations, except for brief announcements that would stimulate the sale of newspapers. It also recommended that member papers start treating their radio logs as advertising. The wire services and most major newspapers supported the boycott, and radio was on its own.

CBS immediately set up news bureaus in New York, Washington, Chicago, Los Angeles, and London. Within a few months, daily newscasts by H. V. Kaltenborn and Boake Carter were supplying CBS affiliates with an adequate replacement for the wires. The NBC news service wasn't nearly as good, but many local stations didn't really care—they simply stole their news reports out of the early editions of local newspapers. Several lawsuits by the Associated Press clearly established the illegality of this practice. But AP couldn't afford to sue half the radio stations in the country.

The boycott was a failure. A compromise Press-Radio Plan was worked out in 1934, granting stations the right to ten minutes of wire news a day. It wasn't enough. Radio wanted more, and was willing to pay for it. In 1935, UP and INS agreed to sell complete news reports to stations. AP soon followed suit. Today, both major services have special radio wires. AP services 3,100 broadcast clients (and only 1,750 publications), while the UPI wire goes to 2,300 stations (and only 1,600 publications).

Radio soon became *the* mass medium for spot news. The vacuum tube has a tremendous advantage over the printing press: speed. It warms up faster; it requires no typesetters and no delivery boys. Radio can have a story on the air minutes after the event; newspapers take hours. By the end of the 1930s, it was obvious to editors that the "scoop" and the "extra" were obsolete. Newspapers could still serve the public by supplying the details of the news, or the significance of the news—but radio was bound to get there first with the news itself.

Thus interpretive journalism was born. It was pioneered in the 1910s and 1920s by columnists like David Lawrence (New York *Evening Post*), Mark Sullivan (New York *Herald Tribune*), and Frank R. Kent (Baltimore *Sun*). It was picked up by the feature syndicates in the early 1930s, making national figures of such pundits as Walter Lippmann, Heywood Broun, and Drew Pearson. All these men did their best to tell newspaper readers "the news behind the news."

Interpretive journalism made it to the front page in 1933, when the United States went off the gold standard. This was far too complex a subject to report "straight." President Roosevelt sent a group of White House economic advisers over to the press room to help reporters understand the meaning of the move. The reporters were grateful, and interpretive news articles (with or without the help of Presidential advisers) soon became commonplace.

Consider, for example, this "news lead" from a 1935 issue of the Buffalo (N.Y.) *Evening News:*

> WASHINGTON, Aug. 15.—A scratch of a pen by the Chief Executive Wednesday extended to approximately a fourth of America's population some measure of federal protection from the vicissitudes of life.

It was the signing by President Roosevelt of the nation's first social security legislation, regarded by the President more than any other action taken during his administration as the heart of the New Deal.[28]

A sidebar to the story began: "Here are some examples of how the new social security program will operate. . . ." This was the kind of reporting that radio couldn't do.

What radio *could* do was offer the country a varied diet of news and entertainment. Performers like Amos 'n' Andy, Jack Benny, Rudy Vallee, and Kate Smith entertained millions of Americans throughout the Depression. Kaltenborn's news broadcasts and President Roosevelt's "fireside chats" proved the medium's potential for more than pap. So did live coverage of the Spanish Civil War, and of innumerable sporting events. By the end of the decade, William L. Shirer in London and Edward R. Murrow in Vienna (later in London as well) were reporting the rise of Nazism *as it happened,* to a public that had learned to expect its news instantly.

As radio thrived and newspapers turned more interpretive, the film industry discovered sound. The first full-length talking picture, "The Jazz Singer" starring Al Jolson, was produced by Warner Brothers in 1927. It was an instant success. Sound movies single-handedly rescued the film industry from the doldrums caused by radio competition. By 1929, nearly half of the nation's 20,000 movie theaters were equipped to handle sound. Paid admissions rose from 60 million a week in 1927 to 110 million a week in 1929. By the early 1930s, the silent film was dead.

Movie magnates had other problems to worry about. Censorship was by far the biggest. The public outcry against "dirty movies" was fed as much by stories of corruption and immorality in Hollywood as it was by the films themselves. In 1922 the major studios had founded the Motion Picture Producers and Distributors of America, headed by Will H. Hays. The "Hays Office" did its best to forestall government censorship by instituting self-censorship instead. The tactic was only partially successful. It stopped the government (by and large), but it didn't stop the Legion of Decency, established by a group of Catholic laymen in 1934. It wasn't until the late 1950s that movie producers discovered that the public would support a good film (and sometimes a bad film) even if it lacked the Legion's seal of approval.

Newsreels were standard movie theater fare throughout the 1920s and 1930s. Though newsreel news was often two or three weeks old, it had the tremendous advantage of including both pictures and sound. Newsreels remained popular until the advent of television.

The motion picture industry of the 1930s produced movies in waves— musicals, then prison pictures, then screwball comedies, then biographies, etc. As World War Two drew near, Hollywood went to war. From the beginning, the Nazis were the villains. When the United States entered the conflict in 1942, war movies were turned into frank propaganda for the Allies.

World War Two was radio's "finest hour." Kaltenborn left CBS to head the NBC news team in Europe, but no one at NBC could match

CHRONOLOGY

1922	The Motion Picture Producers and Distributors of America is founded. Called the "Hays Office," the group will impose self-censorship on the movie industry in order to avoid government censorship.
1927	Warner Brothers produces the first sound movie, "The Jazz Singer" starring Al Jolson.
1929	The stock market crashes and the Depression begins.
1931	Political columnist Walter Lippmann begins publishing in the New York *Herald Tribune;* his column was soon syndicated throughout the country.
1932	The American Newspaper Publishers Association and the wire services refuse to sell news to radio. Drew Pearson and Robert S. Allen begin their free-wheeling syndicated political column, "Washington Merry-Go-Round."
1933	The U.S. goes off the gold standard, and reporters turn to interpretive journalism in order to make sense of the event. The American Newspaper Guild, the first union for newsmen, is founded in Cleveland.
1934	Congress passes the Communications Act, establishing a seven-man Federal Communications Commission to oversee the electronic media. The Legion of Decency is organized to fight dirty movies.
1935	UP and INS agree to sell news to radio stations. Time, Inc. introduces "The March of Time," a superior newsreel series that includes analysis and interpretation.
1940	The Associated Press establishes a special radio wire. Edward R. Murrow describes the Nazi blitz of London on CBS radio.
1942	The United States enters the war, and issues a voluntary-but-detailed Code of Wartime Practices for the American Press.
1943	Under pressure from the FCC, NBC sells its "blue chain" to Lifesaver king Edward J. Nobel; it is renamed the American Broadcasting Company and becomes the nation's third network.

the impact of Edward R. Murrow, broadcasting from London for CBS. "Neutral" Americans listened in awe as Murrow narrated, blow by blow, the Battle of Britain. For newspapers, meanwhile, the war was a repeat of World War One: massive reporting of battles, scant reporting of issues, and voluntary self-censorship of military details.

This, then, is how the American mass media stood at the end of World War Two. Radio was fat and sassy, with both the number of stations and the amount of advertising expanding rapidly. It offered listeners a potpourri of news, culture, sports, and lowbrow entertainment. Newspapers were also doing well, the beneficiaries of consolidation, monopoly ownership, and the postwar boom. Most combined their straight news with interpretive stories, features, backgrounders, syndicated columns, and editorials. Magazines were slick and profitable, geared for entertaining the mass market and little more. So were movies. And even the book industry was earning money, especially with its paperback and textbook lines.

Then came television.

Television had its start in the 1920s, but it didn't begin to develop seriously until after the war. Then, in just a few years, it transformed itself from an experiment into a way of life. In revenue, in circulation, and in the devotion of its audience, television quickly became the mass medium of the mid-Twentieth Century. All other media have been forced into subordinate roles.

TV DEVELOPS

In 1923, Vladimir Zworykin invented the iconoscope and the kinescope, the basis for television transmission and reception respectively. Philo Farnsworth added the electronic camera, and Allen B. Dumont contributed the receiving tube. General Electric put them all together, and in 1928 founded the first regular television station, WGY, in Schenectady, New York. By 1937, there were 17 such experimental stations on the air.

The development of the coaxial cable in 1935 enabled these early TV stations to hook up into a primitive "network" in order to broadcast special events. They did so for the opening of the New York World's Fair, for the 1940 nominating conventions, for several football and baseball games, and for at least one speech by President Roosevelt.

In 1939 the Milwaukee *Journal* applied for a commercial TV license. The Federal Communications Commission pondered the notion of commercial television for a few years, finally approving the license in 1941. Ten commercial stations, including the *Journal's*, appeared within a year, and immediately began soliciting ads. When war broke out in 1942, the FCC put a "freeze" on TV development: no new licenses, no new receivers to be manufactured, and a limited schedule for stations already on the air. Only six of the ten 1941 pioneers lasted through the war.

The influence of government over broadcasting was becoming increasingly important. In 1934 Congress had replaced the five-man Federal Radio Commission with a seven-man Federal Communications Commission, responsible for television, telephone, and telegraph as well as radio. Like the FRC before it, the FCC viewed its job as a maintenance function: dividing up the spectrum and preventing interference. But there were more applicants for radio licenses than there was space on the radio band. The Commission was forced to choose between applicants, to decide which would best serve "the public interest, convenience, and necessity."

It simply wasn't possible for the FCC to confine its duties to technical matters. In 1939, for example, the Mayflower Broadcasting Corporation applied for the license of radio station WAAB, arguing that the frequent editorials of the current WAAB licensee were not in the public interest. After much thought, the Commission agreed. Mayflower was denied the license on other grounds, but WAAB was ordered to stop editorializing. This 1941 "Mayflower decision" outlawing broadcast editorials stood until 1949, when the Commission changed its mind and reversed the ruling. The so-called "fairness doctrine," requiring broadcasters to give fair treatment to all sides in a controversy, developed out of the Mayflower confusion.

Even when it confined itself to technology, the FCC had a vast impact on the future of broadcasting. The Commission spent the war trying to decide what to do about two new media—television and frequency modulation (FM) radio. FM had been invented by Edwin H. Armstrong in 1933; Armstrong's experimental station was on the air in Alpine, N.J., by 1939. Like television, FM boomed in the early 1940s. Like television, it was "frozen" by the FCC during the war.

In 1945 the Commission made its crucial decision. It moved FM "upstairs" to another part of the spectrum (making all existing FM receivers obsolete), and opened up more space for 13 commercial television channels instead. The move set FM back nearly twenty years. NBC, which had encouraged its affiliates to apply for TV licenses, was elated. CBS was badly hurt; it had put its money on FM instead.

Once a favorable decision had been made, television growth was fast and furious. In 1948 the FCC reassigned Channel 1 for nonbroadcast services, and again ordered a freeze on channel allocations, this time to study the interference problem and the possibility of color television. The Korean War prolonged the freeze until 1952. Nevertheless, some 15 million families purchased TV sets during the freeze in order to watch the

108 stations then on the air. They saw Milton Berle's debut in 1948 on a 13-station NBC network. They saw Ed Sullivan on CBS for the first time that same year. They saw baseball's World Series as it happened. They saw news and public affairs broadcasting, too, notably the Kefauver Committee investigation into organized crime. And they saw some fine theater—*Philco Playhouse, Goodyear Playhouse,* Gian-Carlo Minotti's opera *Amahl and the Night Visitors.* But mostly they saw *I Love Lucy* and *Your Show of Shows; Arthur Godfrey's Talent Scouts* and *Kukla, Fran, and Ollie; The Web, The Front Page, The Big Story,* and *The Cisco Kid.*

And they saw ads—hour after hour of ads—for cars and appliances, for cigarettes and detergents, for banks and insurance companies, for Presidential aspirants Eisenhower and Stevenson.

When the freeze was lifted in 1952, television grew quickly. The development of microwave relays made coast-to-coast hook-ups practical for the first time, and the networks were quickly to employ them. By 1961 there were 548 television stations in the country, broadcasting to 60 million receiving sets (in 89 percent of all American homes). Of these stations, 205 were affiliated with CBS, 187 with NBC, and 127 with ABC; only 29 stations had no connections with any network. The average TV station in 1961 earned a profit of fifteen percent. The average TV set was left running for at least five hours a day, 365 days a year.

Television changed little in the 1960s. It grew, of course. By 1970 more than 59 million U.S. homes (97 percent) had one or more of the nation's 84 million TV sets. And the 1959 quiz show scandals forced the three networks to produce most of their own programs, instead of letting the advertisers do it for them. But aside from that, TV content in 1970 was much the same as TV content in 1960 and 1950: one-tenth news and public affairs, one-tenth drama and culture, and four-fifths ads and light entertainment.

To the extent that TV changed at all in the 1960s and early 1970s, it changed at the hands of the Federal Communications Commission. In 1970, for example, the FCC adopted a series of rules requiring local stations to carry something other than network programming in prime time. The Commission also proposed a restriction on the number of media outlets any broadcaster could own in a single market. The rules were designed to alleviate the two biggest problems of American television today: the social and esthetic evil of bland homogeneity, and the economic and political danger of monopoly.

Meanwhile, the FCC continued to arbitrate the demands of technological innovations that could (at least potentially) revolutionize the broadcast industry. The RCA system for color television got the final go-ahead in 1953; by 1970, 40 percent of all American homes had a color TV set. A huge slice of the spectrum was set aside in 1952 for ultrahigh frequency (UHF) television. UHF developed slowly until 1962, when the

CHRONOLOGY

1923   Vladimir Zworykin invents the iconoscope and the kinescope, the basis for television.

1928   The first experimental TV station, WGY, begins operation in Schenectady, New York.

1933   Edwin H. Armstrong invents FM radio.

1934   Congress passes the Communications Act, establishing a Federal Communications Commission with authority over television as well as radio.

1935   The first coaxial cable is built between New York and Philadelphia, making TV hook-ups possible.

1939   Armstrong begins operating his experimental FM radio station in Alpine, New Jersey.

1941   The FCC issues the first ten commercial TV licenses.   The Mayflower decision outlaws broadcast editorials.

1942   The FCC puts a wartime freeze on TV and FM development.

1945   The freeze ends; the FCC decides to encourage television and downgrade FM radio.

1946   The FCC "Blue Book" obligates broadcasters to include some public affairs programming.

1948   Once again the FCC freezes TV development; this time the delay will last until 1952.

1949   The FCC reverses the Mayflower decision; broadcasters may "editorialize with fairness."

1950   The first commercial cable TV system begins serving the mountainous community of Lansford, Pa.   The FCC authorizes experimental "pay TV" and approves the CBS system for color television.

1951   The first transcontinental microwave relay connects TV stations in New York and San Francisco.

1952   The FCC provides for the future development of 70 ultrahigh frequency (UHF) television channels, reserving many of them for nonprofit and educational use.

1953   Reversing its earlier decisions, the FCC approves the RCA (NBC) color TV system, because it permits noncolor sets to receive color programming in black-and-white.

1959   The quiz show scandals force the networks to forbid advertisers to produce their own shows.

1962   The Telstar satellite makes live international broadcasting possible. A prolonged and inconclusive experiment with pay TV is begun in Hartford, Conn.   At the FCC's request, Congress requires UHF receivers on all new television sets, starting in 1964.

1966 The FCC asserts control over cable television and passes restrictive regulations designed to encourage UHF at the expense of cable.

1968 The FCC authorizes commercial pay TV.

1970 The FCC proposes rules to curb multiple ownership of the media, to encourage local programming, and to aid the growth of cable TV.

FCC asked Congress to require all new TV sets to include UHF receivers. Then it grew quickly; by 1970, 287 out of a total of 872 television stations were UHF. Educational television was also given a boost by the Commission, which set aside special channels for noncommercial use. There were 182 such stations in operation by 1970.

Color, UHF, and educational TV are practical and important—but the greatest potential for change is in cable and satellite television. The first commercial cable TV system was authorized in 1950, bringing television to Lansford, Pennsylvania. Satellite transmission began twelve years later, with the launching of Telstar in 1962. At the moment, cable is used mainly to improve TV reception in hilly regions and skyscraper cities. Satellites are used for international viewing of funerals, world figures, inaugurations, and Olympic Games.

Either one could revolutionize broadcasting—cable by permitting the growth of thousands of local channels, satellites by replacing local channels with dozens of national networks. But cable systems are controlled largely by existing television stations, which are reluctant to see them prosper. And the satellite program is run by Comsat, which is controlled by AT&T, which also owns the existing land lines and has no interest in building competition for itself. And until recently the FCC has discouraged the growth of both cable and satellite TV, apparently in order to help build UHF.

The future of broadcasting in the 1970s and 1980s will depend largely on what the FCC does about cable TV and satellite TV in the next few years.

THE OLD MEDIA RESPOND

Television revolutionized American life. Naturally, it revolutionized the other mass media as well.

Part of the revolution was economic. In 1950, the infant TV industry received only three percent of all money spent on advertising. Newspapers got 36 percent; magazines, nine percent; and radio, 11 percent (the other 41 percent went to billboards, direct mailings, and the like).

In 1968, by contrast, TV received 18 percent of the advertising dollar. Newspapers were down to 29 percent; magazines to seven percent; radio to six percent.   If you eliminate local ads and billboards and the like, the figures are even more impressive.   In 1939, national media advertising was almost evenly divided: 38 percent for newspapers, 35 percent for magazines, and 27 percent for radio.   In 1968, this was the division: television, 49 percent; magazines, 25 percent; newspapers, 19 percent; radio, eight percent.   Television was rich.   Everyone else, at least comparatively, was hurting.

But economics are only half the story.   Television did (and does) a superlative job of satisfying the public's appetite for spot news and light entertainment.   No other medium could possibly compete with TV in those areas.   The older communications industries were forced to rebuild their formats along new lines.

Radio was the hardest hit.   Audio news programming could not help but suffer as the networks became more and more TV-oriented.   Edward R. Murrow's "Hear It Now" turned into "See It Now," and radio documentaries disappeared almost completely.   The networks continued to supply stations with hourly spot news reports, but the rest of the news operation was geared for TV and TV alone.   Moreover, the melodramas, soap operas, comedy shows, and variety programs that had comprised the bulk of radio time soon became standard fare on television instead.   The local station owner was left with hour after hour to fill on his own—on a dwindling budget and limited advertiser support.

For a while it seemed to some that commercial radio might die.   Instead, radio became the "low key" medium of the 1960s and 1970s, unspectacular but steady.   News, sports, and music were the winning combination for thousands of stations.   Others chose to specialize: all-rock, all-classical, all-news, or all-talk.   Still more specialized stations aimed their shows at one or another minority group—blacks or chicanos, hippies or commuters.   Whatever the format, it was always low-budget. An engineer, an ad salesman, and two or three disc jockeys were all the average station needed.

Radio never regained the "importance" it had had before television, but it did manage to retain its popularity.   Between 1950 and 1970, the number of AM radio stations in the country rose from 2,086 to 4,269. The number of radio sets reached an incredible 303 million—a radio and a half for every man, woman, and child.   No home, car, or beach blanket was without one.

Because it was less profitable to begin with, FM radio recognized the threat of television a little sooner than AM.   By 1950 it was already gearing itself for specialized audiences, offering high-quality reception and highbrow music.   During the 1960s the FCC did its best to promote the development of FM. It authorized stations to broadcast in multiplex stereo, and required them to originate some of their own programming. Aided by these policies, the number of FM stations grew from 753 in 1960 to 2,471 in 1970.

The movie industry had enough problems even before television. A 1949 Supreme Court decision forced film producers to sell off their chains of movie theaters. This solved the antitrust problem of combined production and distribution, but it also cut deeply into Hollywood revenues. The political purges and anti-Communist witch-hunts of the early 1950s added to Hollywood's headaches.

When television came along, the movie companies declared a fight to the finish. Film stars were not allowed to appear on TV, and the studios refused to sell their old films to the rival medium. But it was soon obvious that the public would no longer pay to see Grade B movies when equivalent fare was available on television. One by one, the great studios reversed their position. They sought windfall profits by selling their old movies to be shown on the tube, and urged their stars to trade TV appearances for plugs. Finally, the large companies agreed to produce programs specifically for the television screen. The major studios were now part of the electronic medium.

Because routine movies wouldn't sell any more, the film industry turned in desperation to giant wide screens, stereophonic sound, and multimillion-dollar epics. To save money, these pictures were often produced abroad. And still they lost money. In 1950, there were 474 actors, 147 writers, and 99 directors under contract to the major studios. By 1960 the figures were down to 139 actors, 48 writers, and 24 directors. Three studios (RKO, Republic, and Monogram) stopped production entirely, and some 6,000 movie theaters shut down. Hollywood sank into what can only be described as a slow death. The back lots of many once-prosperous studios are now apartment complexes.

Into the struggling movie market came the independent producers, Europeans as well as Americans. Their topical, low-budget films struck a responsive chord in the increasingly youthful theater-going public. They intentionally violated the industry's code of self-censorship, fighting (and winning) their case in court. Taboos about drugs, sex, violence, and language disappeared. While the large studios lost vast sums on spectaculars like *Cleopatra*, independent producers filled movies houses with low-budget films like *Easy Rider*.

Television hit the magazine business almost as hard as it hit radio and film. Magazines, after all, are largely dependent on national advertising, also the main support for network TV. Moreover, television tended to satisfy the public demand for light entertainment and illustrated news— the two main staples of magazine content.

The result: General-interest magazines began losing money. Some went out of business, including *Collier's, Coronet, American, Look,* and the *Saturday Evening Post.* Others, though not about to fold, faced serious trouble—*Life,* even the monumental *Reader's Digest.* Increased production costs and postal rates added to their difficulties. By 1970, many observers felt that the mass-circulation general-interest magazine was doomed.

Other kinds of magazines did better. Newsmagazines like *Time* and *Newsweek* offered background and interpretation as well as straight news, and thus survived the rise of television. The "quality" magazines (*National Geographic, New Yorker,* and the like) were little damaged by TV, and the same was true of the women's magazines (*Ladies' Home Journal, McCalls, Good Housekeeping*). All these publications seemed to prosper throughout the 1960s.

By and large, the most successful magazines were the most specialized; television was unable to steal either their audience or their advertisers. Leaders in the specialty fields range from *Playboy* to *Scientific American,* from *Business Week* to *Better Homes and Gardens,* from *Women's Wear Daily* to *Sports Illustrated,* from *Successful Farming* to *Rolling Stone.* Ironically, the most successful of all the specialized magazines was *TV Guide.*

Television's effect on the book industry was indirect, but powerful. As soon as the first TV station was erected in a city, public library use and bookstore sales began to decline. People simply weren't using as much leisure time for reading; they spent more time with the tube instead.

Broadly speaking, there are three kinds of books. Textbooks are sold directly to primary and secondary schools, or through college bookstores to students. Mass-market paperbacks are sold by the millions through drugstores, supermarkets, and the like. Trade books are sold through ordinary bookstores; they include the vast majority of the 30,000 new books published every year, both paperbacks and hardcovers, fiction and non-fiction.

Textbooks and mass-market paperbacks are immensely profitable. Trade books earn much less. Most Americans today read only two kinds of books: what they have to read in school, and the lightest of light fiction.

Surprisingly enough, the mass medium least affected by the rise of television was the newspaper. TV did cause a precipitous drop in the newspaper's share of national advertising, but this was more than balanced by an increase in local ad linage. The growth of "cold type" offset printing helped many smaller papers cut costs, while the larger ones turned to computerized typesetting and other labor-saving devices.

The 1950s and 1960s witnessed a tremendous explosion in suburban living, opening up new markets for new publishers. Suburban news-

papers like *Newsday* (on Long Island) built huge circulations almost overnight. Such papers were often among the most profitable in the country.
Residents depended on them for neighborhood news (which television
couldn't provide), and every new shopping center meant thousands of
dollars more in advertising.

The development of regional printing facilities, meanwhile, led to the
growth of the country's first truly national newspapers: the *Wall Street
Journal* and the *Christian Science Monitor*. The New York *Times* continued as a national paper of sorts. It was the nation's "newspaper of re-

CHRONOLOGY

1940	*Newsday* is founded in suburban Long Island; twenty years later it will soar to leadership in both circulation and advertising revenue.
1945	Bernard Kilgore takes over the *Wall Street Journal*; by 1965, under his guidance, the newspaper will have a national circulation of 800,000.
1948	Radio ad revenue reaches its peak and begins to decline.
1949	The Supreme Court forces movie companies to sell off their theater holdings. The film audience reaches a peak of 90 million tickets a week; by 1968 it will be down to 21 million a week.
1950	The Intertype Corporation comes out with its "fotosetter," making offset newspapers feasible.
1951	Edward R. Murrow's documentary "Hear It Now" leaves radio for television, becoming "See It Now."
1953	Twentieth Century Fox produces "The Robe," the first of the wide-screen Cinemascope spectaculars.
1955	The major film studios begin selling old movies to television; they will sell nearly 9,000 of them by 1958.
1956	*Collier's* becomes the first of the big mass-circulation, general-interest magazines to fold.
1958	United Press and International News Service merge to form United Press International; both UPI and AP begin moving interpretive articles.
1960	Editor John Denson of the New York *Herald Tribune* leads the trend toward magazine-style layout.
1961	The FCC approves multiplex stereo for FM radio.
1963	Several metropolitan daily newspapers begin setting type by computer.
1964	The FCC rules that AM-FM radio combinations must run different programs on the two stations at least half the time.

cord"—and no legislator, public library, or university could do without it.

In the face of these trends, the metropolitan daily suffered but survived. There were still enough readers and advertisers in the inner city to support at least one morning and one evening paper—and by the mid-1960s very few cities had more than that number.

The existence of television news forced some changes in newspaper content, but they were little more than the continuation of changes already begun in the face of radio news. Now it was television as well as radio that could reach the public with a bulletin before any newspaper had a chance. All the more reason for newspapers to go the way they were already going—interpretive and featury, the details of the news and the news behind the news. The trend simply intensified. In keeping with their content, many papers followed the lead of the New York *Herald Tribune* and moved to a simplified, uncluttered, magazine-style layout. And even the wire services abandoned the who/what/where/when concept of journalism and began moving interpretive stories. The typical American newspaper is still far from a daily edition of *Time* magazine, but it appears to be moving in that direction.

Though the content of newspapers changed little because of television, their impact may have changed greatly. Researchers have found that the most widely read items in today's newspapers have nothing to do with "news." They are the weather report, the advice column, the movie listings, the stock market report, the TV log, the sports results, and the ads. Most of the hard news available to Americans every day is published in newspapers, not broadcast on TV. But the average American never sees it. He gets most of his news from television.

This, then, is how the American mass media stand as of 1970. Newspapers are profitable little monopolies, moving toward interpretive news but read mostly for their ads and service items. Books have failed to attract a mass audience, except for light paperbacks and required school texts. Magazines are becoming more and more specialized, while those that can't make the switch are losing money. Movies are torn between spectacular blockbuster gambles and safer, low-budget topical productions; many are planned with TV in mind. Radio has settled on a low-key, background approach that earns steady if unimpressive profits. And television, television is for viewers a way of life, and for owners a license to print money.

1980? Who knows?

NOTES

[1] John Milton, *Paradise Lost and Selected Poetry and Prose,* ed. Northrop Frye (New York: Rinehart & Co., 1951), pp. 486–500.

[2] Edwin Emery, ed., *The Story of America* (New York: Simon and Schuster, Inc., 1965), p. 3.

3 James Playsted Wood, *The Story of Advertising* (New York: The Ronald Press Co., 1958), p. 45.

4 Frank Luther Mott, *American Journalism,* 3rd ed., (New York: The Macmillan Co., 1962), p. 25.

5 Emery, *Story of America,* p. 5.

6 Louis L. Snyder, and Robert B. Morris, *A Treasury of Great Reporting* (New York: Simon and Schuster, Inc., 1949), pp. 21–24.

7 Emery, *Story of America,* p. 10.

8 Snyder and Morris, *Treasury of Great Reporting,* pp. 29–30.

9 *The Federalist,* LXXXIV, in Mott, *American Journalism,* p. 145.

10 Paul L. Ford, ed., *The Writings of Thomas Jefferson* (New York: G. P. Putnam's Sons, 1892–99), II, p. 69.

11 *Aurora,* March 6, 1797, in Frederick Hudson, *Journalism in the United States* (New York: Harper & Brothers, 1873), pp. 210–11.

12 Emery, *Story of America,* p. 27.

13 *Ibid.,* p. 44.

14 *Ibid.,* p. 44.

15 *Ibid.,* p. 61.

16 *Ibid.,* p. 48.

17 Thomas H. Guback, "General Sherman's War on the Press," *Journalism Quarterly,* Spring, 1959, pp. 172–73.

18 Emery, *Story of America,* p. 80.

19 *The World,* May 11, 1883, in Mott, *American Journalism,* p. 434.

20 Emery, *Story of America,* p. 107.

21 Harry J. Carman and Harold C. Syrett, *A History of the American People,* (New York: Alfred A. Knopf, Inc., 1958), II, p. 228.

22 Arthur Knight, *The Liveliest Art* (New York: Mentor Books, 1957), p. 35.

23 Radio Act of 1927.

24 Mott, *American Journalism,* pp. 623–24.

25 *Ibid.,* p. 625.

26 Emery, *Story of America,* p. 184.

27 Edwin Emery, *The Press in America,* 2nd ed. (Englewood Cliffs, N.J.: Prentice-Hall, Inc., 1962), p. 645.

28 Emery, *Story of America,* p. 203.

SUGGESTED READINGS

BARNOUW, ERIK, *A Tower in Babel* (Vol. I—to 1933). New York: Oxford University Press, Inc., 1966.

———, *The Golden Web* (Vol. II—1933–1953). New York: Oxford University Press, Inc., 1968.

———, *The Image Empire* (Vol. III—from 1953). New York: Oxford University Press, Inc., 1970.

EMERY, EDWIN, *The Press in America* (2nd ed.). Englewood Cliffs, N.J.: Prentice-Hall, Inc., 1962.

———, ed., *The Story of America.* New York: Simon and Schuster, Inc., 1965.

KNIGHT, ARTHUR, *The Liveliest Art.* New York: Mentor Books, 1957.

MOTT, FRANK LUTHER, *American Journalism* (3rd ed.). New York: The Macmillan Co., 1962.

SIEBERT, FRED S., THEODORE PETERSON, and WILBUR SCHRAMM, *Four Theories of the Press.* Urbana, Ill.: University of Illinois Press, 1956.

SNYDER, LOUIS L. and RICHARD B. MORRIS, eds., *A Treasury of Great Reporting.* New York: Simon and Schuster, Inc., 1949.

SWANBERG, W. A., *Citizen Hearst.* New York: Bantam Books, Inc., 1961.

TALESE, GAY, *The Kingdom and the Power.* New York: World Publishing Co., 1969.

PART TWO

RESPONSIBILITY

The first two sections of this book have dealt with the functions and history of the mass media. By this point it should be clear that, if nothing else, the media are important.

We turn now to the question of responsibility. Which individuals, groups, and institutions in this country determine the functions of the mass media? Which ones wield its enormous power? Which chart the course of its future history? If the media themselves are important, then these questions are also important.

In the next seven chapters we will examine the following sorts of control over the media:

1. *Self-control* through professional codes and ethical standards.
2. *Internal control* at various points in the media bureaucracies, from publisher and station manager down to reporter and assignment editor.
3. *Monopoly control* through chains, conglomerates, networks, and other forms of media monopoly.
4. *Advertiser control*, whether directly through pressure from individual advertisers or indirectly through media recognition of broad business needs.
5. *Source control* through secrecy, news management, and other tech-

niques for the manipulation of media content before it reaches the media.

6. *Government control,* including the massive influence of law and the even more massive influence of the federal regulatory agencies.

7. *Public control* through letters to the editor, ratings, and many less passive techniques.

It is the firm opinion of the authors that the first and the last items on this list—self-control and public control—are far too weak. The remaining five are too strong, or misapplied, or both. If we were forced to rank the seven forms of control from the most dangerous down to the least, we would tend toward the following order:

1. Too much monopoly control.
2. Too little public control.
3. Too much source control.
4. Misapplied government control.
5. Too little self-control.
6. Too much and misapplied internal control.
7. Too much advertiser control.

Others might propose a different order, but few would object to the general picture of media control outlined here. The American mass media today are run largely by giant monopolies, which impose homogeneity and greatly reduce the diversity of media content. Major sources of information, both private and governmental, possess tremendous power to control the news they make. Through courts, agencies, and informal policies, the federal government exercises considerable influence on the present conduct of the media, and almost total control over their future course. Well-placed employees within the media are in a position to make their weight felt in surprising ways. Advertisers are permitted to demand special favors as well as overall formats suitable to their needs. Ethical standards, meanwhile, exert little influence, and public opinion is almost totally powerless to affect the media.

Two vital point must be made with respect to the interplay of these seven factors. They are emphasized here because they will be largely ignored in the following chapters, as the forms of media control are treated one at a time.

1. *The dynamics of media control are an on-going process, and may change dramatically from decade to decade.* In the 1950s, for example, monopolies were a far less serious problem than they are today. Media tended to be somewhat more responsive to the public—but they were even more responsive to the demands of advertisers. The implications of government control over broadcasting were just beginning to be recognized —and so was the importance of professional and ethical standards. It is

difficult to guess what the patterns of media control will be like in the 1980s and 1990s, but it is unlikely that they will resemble too closely today's patterns.

2. *The various forms of media control are in conflict, not balance, and often help keep each other in check.* Consider, for example, the interplay of government and monopoly control. The television network is a dangerous monopoly, an incredible concentration of power in the hands of a few men. Yet only the networks are strong enough to defy the government when it demands—even more dangerously—that newscasters be kinder in their commentary on the war in Viet Nam. The power of the federal regulatory agencies, conversely, is frightening when applied to something so delicate as the First Amendment. Yet only the government has the necessary strength to forbid newspapers to own broadcast stations in the same city—perhaps an even more frightening First Amendment infraction.

Pluralism is central to a democracy. The goal of a social critic or policy maker should always be to equalize power, to play off one influence against another in the hope that freedom will be the winner. If all seven forms of media control on our list were equally powerful, there would be no danger. It is only when one or two of the seven usurp the power of the others and upset the dynamic tension that we need to worry.

2 Self-Control

Like other professions, journalism is greatly influenced by ethical standards. Unlike other professions, however, journalism has avoided codifying its ethics into clear and usable rules. The various professional codes of the mass media tend to concentrate on truisms and trivia, ignoring the real ethical problems faced by working journalists. There are no sure answers to these problems. But the "media establishment" has been inordinately slow to formulate even tentative answers.

Gabe Pressman, a television newsman for WNBC in New York, has said that: "As a group, reporters have really never formalized their ethics. Yet I think that the best of them have always followed the strictest code of ethics, a code that would compare with what the medical and legal professions have established. It's a dedication to uncovering the truth, to communicating the information to people . . . to reporting the news without prejudice."[1]

Pressman is right, of course, and yet he ignores the vital difference between journalism and other professions like medicine and law. Because they have formalized their ethics into codes, doctors and lawyers are able to enforce them; if necessary they can expel from their ranks an unethical member. An unethical journalist, on the other hand, can be fired only by his employer, not by his colleagues. Sociologists claim that two of the defining characteristics of a profession are a code of ethics and rules of enforcement. Journalism has neither.

Every mass media group has its code of ethics, including even the Comics Magazine Association of America. Almost without exception the codes are mere collections of platitudes.

The oldest, shortest, and broadest of the codes is the Canons of Journalism, adopted by the American Society of Newspaper Editors in 1923. The seven "canons" are entitled Responsibility; Freedom of the Press; Independence; Sincerity, Truthfulness, Accuracy; Impartiality; Fair Play; and Decency. The canons themselves are no more specific than their titles. "Responsibility," for example, reads as follows:

> The right of a newspaper to attract and hold readers is restricted by nothing but considerations of public welfare. The use a newspaper makes of the share of public attention it gains serves to determine its sense of responsibility, which it shares with every member of its staff. A journalist who uses his power for any selfish or otherwise unworthy purpose is faithless to a high trust.[2]

There is nothing in the Canons of Journalism that a publisher or editor need fear—but just to be on the safe side journalists are not required to subscribe to the Canons. And should a newspaper "violate" one —whatever that might mean—there is no punishment or means of enforcement.

The other four major media codes (for movies, radio, television, and comic books) were all developed in the face of public pressure and criticism. They were designed to forestall government regulation by substituting self-regulation instead. As a result, they are negative rather than positive, and more specific than the Canons of Journalism—but only a little.

Consider the Television Code, adopted by the National Association of Broadcasters in 1952. It starts with sections on "Advancement of Education and Culture," "Responsibility Toward Children," and "Community Responsibility"—all very broad and very trite. Then comes the meat of the code, a list of 35 "General Program Standards." These are almost exclusively concerned with guaranteeing that nobody is ever offended by anything on television. They include such items as:

> 6. Respect is mantained for the sanctity of marriage and the value of the home. Divorce is not treated casually as a solution for marital problems. . . .
> 9. Law enforcement shall be upheld and, except where essential to the program plot, officers of the law portrayed with respect and dignity. . . .
> 11. The use of animals both in the production of television programs and

as a part of television program content, shall at all times, be in conformity with accepted standards of humane treatment. . . .

18. Narcotic addiction shall not be presented except as a vicious habit. The administration of illegal drugs will not be displayed.[3]

After the General Program Standards comes another collection of platitudes, this time on the desirability of good news and religious programming. The final section is devoted to advertising standards. It contains the most specific and potentially the most valuable provisions of the code—items like: "Commercial material, including total station break time, in prime time shall not exceed 17.2% (10 minutes and 20 seconds) in any 60-minute period."[4]

Enforcement of the Television Code is almost nonexistent. The NAB has a Code Review Board which awards a Seal of Approval to any station that subscribes to the code and obeys it. The seal is customarily flashed, with a brief explanation, at sign-on and sign-off; farmers and insomniacs are thus able to get a quick look at it. The only penalty for a station that does not subscribe to the code or does not follow it is denial of permission to exhibit the seal.

Here's how it works. In 1957 the Code Review Board outlawed TV ads for hemorrhoid remedies and feminine hygiene products. When "enforcement" of the ban began in mid-1959, 148 stations were advertising Preparation H, a hemorrhoid remedy; 84 of them were code subscribers. After two weeks 17 stations resigned from the code rather than drop the ads, and 21 more continued the ads and lost the seal. Only 46 out of 148 stations agreed to conform to the code.[5]

TV broadcasters like their code the way it is—toothless. In the late 1950s, the FCC toyed with the idea of regulating the amount of time stations could devote to commercials. It proposed a rule that precisely duplicated the Television Code's own standards. The TV industry vehemently objected, and the Commission backed down. So the standards are still voluntary.

The radio, motion picture, and comic book codes are just as unenforced and unenforceable as the Television Code. They are, in fact, remarkably similar. All are designed to avoid offending the public, and thereby to avoid the threat of government regulation. None of them offers much help to the media owner or journalist with a real ethical problem on his hands.

A number of publishers and broadcasters have tried to fill the gap with their own in-house codes. Useful though these may be, they are not an adequate substitute for professional standards. In-house codes come in the form of instructions from the boss, not standards from the profession. Having your employer tell you what to do is not at all the same thing as having your peers tell you what ought to be done.

If we accept the sociological doctrine that every profession must have a clear code of ethics and a means of enforcing it, then journalism must be something other than a profession. For the "ethical codes" of the mass media are not clear, nor are they enforced, nor do they treat the real ethical problems of working journalists. Eventually, perhaps, all this will change, and journalism will attain equal status with the medical and legal professions. In the meantime, the reporter with a problem is very much on his own.

The remainder of this chapter is devoted to six ethical problems confronting the modern journalist:

1. The right to privacy.
2. The reporter as part of the story.
3. Conflict of interest.
4. The junket.
5. Paying for the news.
6. Dishonesty and the news.

These are by no means all the ethical problems around, but they are among the most important. As we shall see, none of them is easily solved.

THE RIGHT TO PRIVACY

The most common ethical problem facing every newsman is the likelihood that his story may in some way injure the people he writes about or those he gets his information from. In 1965, for example, a New York *Times* reporter discovered that a prominent member of the American Nazi Party was of Jewish ancestry. The man made it clear to the reporter that his "career" would be finished if this fact were revealed to the public. The *Times* ran the story anyhow, and the Jewish Nazi committed suicide.[6] Was this a valid intrusion on the man's private life, or was it unethical?

During a mid-1950s murder trial, a reporter discovered that one of the jurors had been convicted on a misdemeanor homosexuality charge eleven years before. The press rehashed the old story, and even went so far as to interview the man's wife. He soon asked to be excused from the jury. "I feel," he said, "I would be a subheadline as long as this trial goes on." Similarly, the year-old case of an army general court-martialled for accidentally revealing military secrets made headlines all over again when the general's son, a West Point cadet, died in a fire while on leave.[7] Are these two incidents less ethical than the Nazi example? If so, why?

In many European countries it is illegal even to mention the criminal record of a person who has paid his penalty and not been in trouble again. But in the United States this sort of rehash of old crimes is not only legal—it is extremely common.

Former criminals are not the only ones whose privacy is often invaded by the mass media. Broadcaster Robert Schulman recalls his cub reporter days, when he was often sent to the home of a recent widow to pick up a photo of her deceased husband. Once Schulman was the first to arrive, and had to tell the woman her husband was dead before asking for the picture.[8] WNBC's Gabe Pressman was in a New York airport when news arrived of a transoceanic plane crash. Pressman recalls how uncomfortable *he* was watching a TV reporter interview the shocked relatives—capitalizing on their sorrow for the sake of a "news" story.[9]

Privacy versus the public's right to know: That is the problem. Should press photographers accompanying a police raid on an abortion clinic have photographed the women who were waiting for the illegal operation? Should photographers have chased down a grand jury witness in a gambling probe when the man was avoiding publicity for fear of mob reprisals? Should reporters have printed the names of police doctors accused of brutality by a freshman coed arrested at a peace march?

On the other hand, should the world's foreign correspondents have agreed in 1963 to keep the secret that Pope John XXIII was dying of cancer? The Vatican reporters protected the Pontiff from a five-month orgy of premature mourning—but they also hid from their readers and viewers a news event of worldwide importance.

In 1954 the mass media of San Francisco blacked out a local kidnapping story for 61 hours, at the request of the police and the victim's parents. Only after the kidnappers were caught did they report the story. Commenting on the silence, the chief of police stated that "The press deserves a large share of credit for solving this crime." The San Francisco *Chronicle* was reluctant to accept the praise. "Supression of information," it editorialized, "is certainly not our business; it is the opposite of the proper function of a free press." [10] Had the victim been killed or the kidnappers escaped, the media might well have been criticized for their failure to inform the public. And if the kidnappers had added a second victim during the blackout, the criticism of the media would have been overwhelming. Was this an occasion when the media should have protected the privacy of their sources, or should they have warned the public of a kidnapper on the loose?

THE REPORTER AS PART OF THE STORY

One day in 1957, a Pittsburgh reporter heard over the radio that the police were engaged in a shootout with a man trapped inside a house. The reporter telephoned the gunman, and after three calls convinced him to give himself up.[11]   Question: Was this reporter acting as a journalist, or as a kind of assistant policeman?

The ethical problem of a reporter who gets involved in his own story is often a serious one. In the late 1960s Sanford Watzman was Washington correspondent for the Cleveland *Plain Dealer*. Watzman wrote a ten-part series for his paper on overcharging in defense contracts. Except for the Cleveland area, the series was ignored, so Watzman asked Ohio Senator Stephen Young to insert it into the Congressional Record. He also drafted a speech on the subject for Young, and sent a copy of the series to each member of Ohio's 26-man Congressional delegation. Finally, Watzman proposed corrective legislation to Wisconsin Senator William Proxmire and Ohio Representative William Minshall. Several months later "Watzman's bill" became a law.

Watzman apparently saw no conflict in the fact that he was a participant in the events he covered. "The test in my mind," he said, "is whether you do this on behalf of a special interest group or on behalf of the public." But Edward Barrett, former dean of the Columbia School of Journalism, is not so sanguine. He finds the reporter's dual role "very disturbing," though he "wouldn't put down a blanket prohibition against it." Barrett believes a reporter may be less objective under such circumstances, and therefore "has an obligation to disclose his involvement to his editors and probably to his readers."[12]   As we shall see in Chapter 15, it is by no means unusual for a Washington correspondent to become a newsmaker as well as a news reporter. Very few of them ever mention it in their stories.

Newsmen sometimes affect the news without intending to. After the assassination of President John F. Kennedy, hordes of reporters descended on the city of Dallas. Among other things, they demanded that suspect Lee Harvey Oswald be transferred from one jail to another in public, not in secret. The resulting confusion, many have charged,

---

REPORTER TURNS STATESMAN

In October, 1962, ABC diplomatic correspondent John Scali received a telephone call from the Russian embassy in Washington. The caller asked Scali to relay to the State Department a new proposal for defusing the Cuban missile crisis, which was threatening to blow up into a third world war. For the next three days Scali was the major U.S. spokesman to the Soviet Union. It was he who met Russian official Alexander Fromin in a deserted hotel ballroom and called the new proposal "a dirty, rotten, lousy, stinking double cross." When the crisis was over, President Kennedy asked Scali to keep his own role a secret, which he did until Kennedy was assassinated the following year.[13]

---

permitted Jack Ruby to slip by police and murder Oswald. This is a rare case. Much more common is the effect of reporters and cameramen on riots, demonstrations, and similar events. We will return to this problem when we discuss coverage of civil disturbances in Chapter 16.

CONFLICT OF INTEREST

Conflict of interest results from the fact that a newsman is also a private individual. Consider, for example, the financial editor of a daily newspaper. He hears business news in advance of the general public, and is thus in a good position to make timely investments. He may also slant his reporting in order to benefit his investments, and may even be offered free stock in return for favorable news treatment. In 1963 the Securities and Exchange Commission found evidence that all three unethical measures were being practiced.

In order to curb such profiteering, the Louisville *Courier-Journal*, for example, instructs employees that they "must never use their position to obtain an advantage over the general public should a situation arise in connection with stock transactions." The New Orleans *Times-Picayune* goes even further, requiring that "no member of the financial news staff own any interest in any stocks or bonds which are listed in our tables or otherwise figure in financial page coverage." But many newspapers have no such policy, letting each man police his own investment practices. Explained John J. Cleary of the Cleveland *Plain Dealer:* "We feel that formalized rules would not thwart an individual bent on shady practice."[14]

Not all conflict of interest cases are so obviously unethical. In 1968 newsman Chet Huntley twice editorialized on radio against the Federal Wholesome Meat Act of 1967, which set standards of cleanliness for meat packing plants. At the time, Huntley had a financial stake in Edmund Mayer, Inc., a New York City packing plant. The new law would have cost Mayer (and therefore Huntley) considerable sums of money. Should Huntley have revealed his financial holdings? Should he have been allowed to editorialize at all?

During the 1961 mayoral campaign in Los Angeles, conservative newscaster George Putnam made a series of personal appearances for candidate Sam Yorty. Nine years later, Washington educational TV station WETA dismissed newsman William Woestendiek for potential conflict of interest after his wife was hired as press secretary for Martha Mitchell, wife of the U.S. Attorney General. Must a reporter take no part in political and civic activities during his off hours? And if he does take part, how can he avoid conflicts of interest?

Because of low wages, newspapermen are often forced to "moonlight," taking a second job to help make ends meet. Since their major talent is writing, many reporters are hired as part-time publicity men for local companies. Others wind up working for charities, political groups, and the like. Some even run for public office. Many metropolitan newspapers forbid all kinds of moonlighting except magazine free-lance writing. Most smaller papers have no policy at all.

The potential for conflict of interest in all these situations is obvious. But the alternative seems to be requiring that off-duty newsmen not write for pay.

THE JUNKET

In the space of one recent year, Aileen Ryan of the Milwaukee *Journal* was offered free trips to Spain (to look at olive groves), to Switzerland (a soup company plant), to Colorado (sheep ranches), and to Idaho (potato farms). Miss Ryan refused them all—which is the most unusual thing about her story.

A junket is a free trip arranged by a publicity man for a reporter in the hope of reaping a complimentary article. Travel and business reporters get the most junket offers, but most newsmen receive at least a couple in the average year. As P.R. man J. E. Schoonover puts it, the story that results from a junket "carries a stamp of objectivity and credibility no paid advertisement can match."[15]

Reporters deal with junkets in a number of ways. Some, like Miss Ryan, never accept any at all. Many accept them only if the story is worth covering and cannot be covered in any other way; they try to put the generosity of the source out of their minds while writing the article. But some reporters accept just about every junket that comes their way, and as a matter of course repay their hosts by writing a favorable story.

Junketing has many close cousins—Christmas gifts, free movie tickets, dinners on the house, and so forth. A few of the better newspapers forbid employees to accept any favors of any sort from anybody. Some have open season on gifts and junkets, while most compromise somewhere in the middle.

The ethics of junketing is not as clear as most laymen imagine. The travel editor of a newspaper, for example, has far too low a budget to cover much of anything without some financial help from the travel industry. Very few papers can afford to send their sports reporters to away games unless the reporters can travel with the team at team expense. And only a purist would object to a war correspondent who hitches a ride with the army, or a film reviewer who declines to pay for

INTERVIEW ETIQUETTE

The following is taken from a radio interview with Senator Strom Thurmond, conducted in 1964 by newsman Robert Fargo. The Senator had just stated that there were Communists teaching in the nation's public schools.

FARGO: Will you name one? Will you name one? Will you name one teacher without your Congressional immunity. . . .

THURMOND: No, I'm not. . . .

FARGO: Name one teacher. . . . Name one school in the United States of America that has ever been indicted and convicted in a Federal grand jury of subversion, sedition, or anything else. Name one right here. I ask you, right now.

THURMOND: I. . . .

FARGO: That's my final question.

THURMOND: I could name . . . I could name . . . I could name. . . .

FARGO: Name one. . . . Name one right here.

THURMOND: Many of. . . .

FARGO: Name one, right here.

THURMOND: I am not indulging. . . .

FARGO: Name one.

THURMOND: You have asked your question. I'm now answering it if you'll. . . .

FARGO: Name one. Name one. I'm asking you to name. . . .

THURMOND: Keep quiet.

FARGO: I'm asking you to name one, right here and now, without Congressional immunity.

THURMOND: Are you now through asking your question? I'll attempt to answer it. My answer is that I am not indulging in personalities. . . .

FARGO: All right, I'll take your refusal right here.

THURMOND: I have not indulged. . . .

FARGO: What you have pointed out is very, very important.

THURMOND: If you'll wait until I get through. . . .

FARGO: A smear is very important. Name one.

THURMOND: Who do you represent? Who do you represent?

FARGO: Name one.

After the exchange, Senator Thurmond demanded, and received, an apology from the station's general manager. Most of the journalists present agreed that Fargo had acted unethically and inexcusably, trying to "get" the Senator rather than get the news. Said one: "This one shallow-minded tirade could undo months of dedicated work by the majority."[16]

his movie tickets. Yet even these relatively benign sorts of favors undoubtedly raise ethical problems for newsmen.

PAYING FOR THE NEWS

"News is like love," says Richard Salant, President of CBS News. "It's a lot better if you don't pay for it."[17]

Nevertheless, the media have been paying for news stories ever since the first circulation wars of the 1800s. In 1908, for example, explorers Robert E. Peary and Frederick A. Cook set out to reach the North Pole. The New York *Times* had its money on Peary; it had arranged for exclusive rights to his story. The rival New York *Herald* was backing Cook. When both explorers claimed to have discovered the North Pole, a lively battle erupted in the New York press, each paper supporting its own man. Peary turned out to be right—but it was not that victory that made the New York *Times* the fine newspaper it is today.

It is well known in the mass media that certain types of public figures give "better answers" in interviews if there's some money in it for them. Professional athletes are often paid for broadcast interviews, and as a matter of course most guests on pregame and postgame shows receive cash or gifts. Elvis Presley among show business personalities, and Madame Nhu among jet-set politicians, have also demanded money for interviews. NBC paid $4,000 to interview former Nazi Baldur Von Schirach when he was released from Spandau Prison. And escaped Chinese violinist Ma Szu-tsung told *Life* magazine all about his experiences in Communist China—for a price.

In 1967, *Life* set a disturbing precedent by offering every U.S. astronaut $6,200 a year for the "personal" story of his involvement in the manned space program. Since the astronauts receive all their training and experience at the taxpayer's expense, there is reason to question the ethics of their selling exclusive rights to their story—and reason also to question the ethics of *Life* in making the offer.

There are at least three dangers in paying for the news. First, the less wealthy media may not be able to compete. Second, the cost will inevitably be passed on to the consumer. Third and most important, news sources may be tempted to sensationalize their stories—perhaps even invent them—in order to earn a higher price. In the late 1960s, a group of self-proclaimed revolutionaries asked CBS for $30,000 for the rights to film their invasion of Haiti. It soon became clear to the network that the $30,000 would finance the invasion, or at least a landing on a strip of unpatrolled beach. No money, no invasion.[18] A Congressional committee later investigated the incident. Its conclusions were highly critical of CBS, but it did not recommend any official action.

Until recent years faked stories were reasonably common in the press. Back in 1905, a night editor desperate for a Monday morning lead invented a Mexican atrocity story, describing in infinite detail the torture and murder of a band of Americans at the hands of the Yaqui Indians. It was a popular article, so later that year he tried again. This time he reported that the Russian Navy had totally destroyed the Japanese fleet. Three day later the expected battle took place, and it was the Russian fleet that was destroyed—along with the editor's reputation.[19] Fakery on this scale is no longer accepted. But magazine writers still make up examples to illustrate their points, and newspapermen still invent man-in-the-street quotes out of whole cloth—apparently without any ethical qualms at all.

A more debatable question is whether or not reporters should ever disguise their identities to get information. It is argued with some justice that there is no other way to get an accurate report on groups like the John Birch Society or the Black Panthers. Many good stories have resulted from this sort of infiltration, but at a price: the eternal distrust of the source. Undercover newsmen, like undercover policemen, do not inspire confidence.

The late columnist Drew Pearson was never one to worry about how he got his information. The facts which led to the censure of Connecticut

---

REPORTER ON THE TAKE

For well over ten years, Harry J. Karafin was the ace investigative reporter of the Philadelphia *Inquirer*. He was also a crook. Karafin's technique was to gather incriminating evidence about a news source, then demand to be paid off. In the late 1950s, for example, he asked a fly-by-night home repair firm to hire him as a P.R. consultant. When the company refused, Karafin wrote an exposé for the *Inquirer*, describing how such operations worked and warning Philadelphians against them. Then he went back to the company and asked again. This time they signed him on for $3,000 a year.[20]

A few years later, Karafin wrote his way onto the payroll of a construction firm that was under attack for rigging its bids for city maintenance contracts. In return for defending the company in his columns, Karafin received something over $10,000 a year.[21]

In early 1967, these and other Karafin corruption stories were exposed in an article in *Philadelphia* magazine. It took the *Inquirer* six weeks to report the story—and the rival *Bulletin* and sister *News* never touched it.

Senator Thomas Dodd for campaign fund irregularities came from Pearson's column. Pearson bought them from the Senator's aides, who copied them from the Senator's private files. In 1969 a federal court ruled that this was not an illegal invasion of privacy on Pearson's part. But was it ethical?

In this chapter we have discussed six ethical problems of the mass media. If space permitted, we could as easily have discussed twenty-six or sixty-six.

There are three points worth emphasizing. First, none of the problems is obvious or easy to solve. Second, most newsmen do their best to solve them, to be as ethical as they know how. Third and most important, the working journalist receives little if any help from his peers in deciding and enforcing ethical standards. If journalism is a profession, it is the only profession without a meaningful code of ethics.

NOTES

[1] Gabe Pressman, Robert Lewis Shayon, and Robert Schulman, "The Responsible Reporter," *Television Quarterly*, Spring, 1964, p. 8.

[2] Canons of Journalism, in William L. Rivers and Wilbur Schramm, *Responsibility in Mass Communication*, revised ed. (New York: Harper & Row, 1969), p. 253.

[3] Television Code, in Rivers and Schramm, *Responsibility*, pp. 259–60.

[4] *Ibid.*, p. 268.

[5] Meyer Weinberg, *TV in America* (New York: Ballantine Books, 1962), p. 93.

[6] Gay Talese, *The Kingdom and the Power* (New York: Bantam Books, 1970), pp. 431–48.

[7] Ignaz Rothenberg, "Newspaper Sins Against Privacy," *Nieman Reports*, January, 1957, pp. 41–42.

[8] Pressman *et al.*, "The Responsible Reporter," p. 22.

[9] *Ibid.*, p. 10.

[10] Kenneth E. Wilson, "The Great Secrecy Case," *Nieman Reports*, April, 1954, pp. 3–6.

[11] Curtis D. MacDougall, *Reporters Report Reporters* (Ames, Iowa: Iowa State University Press, 1968), pp. 101–2.

[12] Noel Epstein, "Capital Newsmen Often Play a Role in Creating the Events They Cover," *Wall Street Journal*, September 11, 1968, pp. 1, 23.

[13] William L. Rivers, *The Opinionmakers* (Boston: Beacon Press, 1965), pp. 160–61.

[14] Blaine K. McKee, "Reporters as Insiders: Financial News and Stock Buying," *Columbia Journalism Review*, Spring, 1968, p. 41.

[15] Frederick C. Klein, "Junket Journalism," *Wall Street Journal*, February 14, 1966, pp. 1, 12.

[16] "Etiquette for Interviewers," *Columbia Journalism Review*, Winter, 1964, pp. 43–44.

[17] Frederick C. Klein, "Paying for the News," *The Quill*, July, 1967, p. 25.

[18] Bill Surface, "Should Reporters Buy News?" *Saturday Review*, May 13, 1967, p. 86.

[19] Albert F. Henning, *Ethics and Practices in Journalism* (New York: R. Long and R. R. Smith, Inc., 1932), pp. 114–15.

[20] "Harry the Muckraker," *Time*, April 21, 1967, p. 84.

[21] "How Did He Do It?" *Newsweek*, May 1, 1967, pp. 64–65.

SUGGESTED READINGS

KLEIN, FREDERICK C., "Junket Journalism," *Wall Street Journal*, February 14, 1966.

McKEE, BLAINE K., "Reporters as Insiders: Financial News and Stock Buying," *Columbia Journalism Review*, Spring, 1968.

PRESSMAN, GABE, ROBERT LEWIS SHAYON, and ROBERT SCHULMAN, "The Responsible Reporter," *Television Quarterly*, Spring, 1964.

SURFACE, BILL, "Should Reporters Buy News?" *Saturday Review*, May 13, 1967.

WILCOX, WALTER, "The Staged News Photograph and Professional Ethics," *Journalism Quarterly*, Autumn, 1961.

3   Internal Control

The main qualification for owning a newspaper, magazine, or broadcast station in this country is enough money to buy it. Besides cash, mass media owners have one other thing in common: power. By hiring and firing, rewarding and punishing, commanding and forbidding, an owner can control news content as much as he wishes. Many media owners use this power sparingly. Others resort to it freely; they view the media as convenient outlets for their own economic aims, personal whims, and ideological convictions.

Horace Greeley launched the New York *Tribune* in 1841. Greeley was greatly taken with the philosophy of French socialist Charles Fourier. For five years he preached Fourierism wherever he went—and so did the *Tribune*. Then he lost interest in the movement, and his paper never mentioned it again. Greeley was a teetotaler; the *Tribune* fought for prohibition. Greeley was opposed to capital punishment; the *Tribune* campaigned for its abolition. Greeley was a bitter enemy of slavery; so was the *Tribune*.

Joseph Medill bought into the Chicago *Tribune* in 1855, and by 1874 owned the majority of its stock. Medill was a firm believer in simplified spelling, so for years the *Tribune* used words like "infinit," "favorit," and "telegrafed." Medill also attributed all natural phenomena to sunspots—until one day he read of the existence of microbes, which he immediately adopted as his new explanation. Soon after, a *Tribune* editor wrote that a plague in Egypt had been caused by sunspots. Medill went through the copy and crossed out each reference to sunspots, substituting "microbes" instead.

Greeley and Medill are typical of Nineteenth Century publishers. They viewed their newspapers as extensions of themselves. Greeley knew that most New Yorkers are fond of alcohol—but he wasn't, so his paper wasn't either. Medill knew that most Chicagoans spell words the way the dictionary does—but he didn't, so his paper didn't either. Both men spent a great deal of time in their respective newsrooms, making sure that reporters and editors covered the news *their* way.

Today's metropolitan publisher belongs to a different breed. Whether he owns one newspaper or a chain of twenty, he is far more likely to be found in the "front office" than in the newsroom. He looks after the financial health of the company, and lets his professional employees look after the news.

Yet even today the mass media owner retains almost absolute power to control news coverage—and sometimes he uses it.

POLICY

In 1967 David Bowers surveyed hundreds of newspaper managing editors throughout the country, asking each to assess the influence of his publisher. Bowers found that the larger the paper, the smaller the role of the publisher in day-to-day news coverage. This is presumably because metropolitan publishers are too busy with corporate affairs to waste much time looking over a reporter's shoulder. Nearly a quarter of the editors told Bowers that their publishers never entered the newsroom.[1]

Still, that leaves three-quarters of the publishers who did find their way into the newsroom from time to time. And there are plenty of ways for a publisher to influence news coverage without ever leaving his office. Rodney Stark suggests some typical techniques: (1) The publisher can hire compliant reporters to start with. (2) He can fire those reporters whose articles he finds offensive. (3) He can demand that editors and reporters consult with him on potentially controversial stories. (4) He can personally write, edit, or rewrite copy to meet his specifications. (5) He can issue standing orders to downplay certain topics or people and emphasize others. (6) He can reward those reporters who go along by tolerating their absenteeism or alcoholism, by assigning them to "choice" stories, or by sending them on junkets.[2]

Publishers use these tactics to enforce "policy"—their notion of what the newspaper should and should not say. Though the evidence is mixed, most of the mass media appear to have some kind of owner-enforced policy.   Charles Swanson, for example, asked reporters whether they agreed with the statement: "I am not aware of any definite fixed news and editorial policies of this newspaper."   Only 24 percent agreed; the rest thought that such policies did in fact exist.   Furthermore, 32 percent of the reporters told Swanson that they had had stories "played down or killed for 'policy' reasons," and another 16 percent were unsure.[3]

There are three reasons why a mass media owner may wish to control news coverage, and each reason dictates its own sort of policy.   Thus:

1. The economic interests of the company dictate a "business policy."
2. The individual likes and dislikes of the owner dictate a "personal policy."
3. The ideological convictions of the owner dictate a "political policy."

We will discuss each in turn.

1. Business Policy.   Since modern media owners are most concerned with the financial health of their companies, it is scarcely surprising that more news is altered because of business policy than for any other reason. Even the most *laissez faire* publisher, Bowers found, is very interested in any article that might directly or indirectly affect newspaper revenue. Most such articles have to do with advertisers or potential advertisers. The daughter of a department store owner is charged with drunk driving —should the newspaper report it?   A new shopping center would like its grand opening covered on television in exchange for a healthy spot advertising contract—should the station accept?   A national magazine is asked to print a 12-page "news" supplement written by a corporation P.R. department—is it worth the money?   Such decisions are made every day, and usually by the owner or publisher.

Business policy is not a recent invention.   In 1911 *Collier's* magazine ran an anonymous article, "The Confessions of a Managing Editor," in which the author unburdened his conscience by revealing the tight policy control of his boss.   He told how caustic movie reviews were abandoned because they displeased a theater owner who advertised regularly; a harmless department store fire was reported so as to imply that the stock had been damaged, permitting the store to announce a "fire sale" in the next day's paper; a story on a local electric power monopoly was killed because the chairman of the power company was a major advertiser.[4]   If this 1911 article were reprinted in 1971, few informed readers would sense any incongruity—the same abuses are still taking place.

When business policy doesn't concern advertisers, it usually involves investors.   In the 1964 Presidential campaign, for example, the fiercely pro-Goldwater Manchester (N.H.) *Union-Leader* editorially rebuked its own candidate for criticizing Teamster boss James Hoffa, who was subsequently jailed for jury tampering.   The Teamsters, it seems, had a $2,000,000 investment in the paper, and Hoffa was to be treated nicely. Similarly, when Joseph Kennedy put $500,000 into the financially ailing Boston *Post*, the paper prudently switched its editorial endorsement to his son John.[5]

2. Personal Policy. Like everyone else mass media owners have friends, and like everyone else they do what they can to help their friends. In the case of the media, this means playing up stories that the friends are proud of (like a society wedding), and playing down or killing stories that the friends find embarrassing (like divorce or an arrest). The friends of mass media owners, by the way, tend to be leaders of the local business community. They are often in the news, so the owners have plenty of chances to do them favors.

Media owners are also subject to their own personal whims—and the privilege of indulging them. Walter Annenberg is a good example. Annenberg is owner of Triangle Publications, which publishes *TV Guide;* until 1970 he also owned the Philadelphia *Inquirer* and *News*. In addition, Annenberg is a man with strong likes and dislikes.

Veterans of the *Inquirer* newsroom recall Annenberg's "shit list," a collection of names never to be printed in the paper. Columnist Rose DeWolf once did an article on the Philadelphia-Baltimore Stock Exchange, quoting its president, Elkins Wetherkill, at length. Told that Wetherkill was on the list, she had to call him back and ask that all his quotes be attributed to an Exchange vice-president. The president of the University of Pennsylvania, Gaylord P. Harnwell, was also on Annenberg's list. Each year Harnwell awarded the prestigious Wharton School gold medal to a distinguished alumnus; each year the *Inquirer* ascribed the presentation to an unnamed "university official." Other names banned from all Annenberg publications included Imogene Coca, Zsa Zsa Gabor, and Dinah Shore—a constant challenge for the staff of *TV Guide*. Even the Philadelphia 76ers basketball team was in Annenberg's bad graces. He limited the team to two paragraphs after each win, one paragraph after each loss.[6]

The personal predilections of a publisher usually do the reader more harm than good, but sometimes the tables are turned. The Knowland family, owners of the Oakland (Calif.) *Tribune*, are fanatic conservationists. As a result, the *Tribune*—in many ways a mediocre newspaper—is well ahead of other California papers in its coverage of ecology. Neighboring publishers are reluctant to mention corporate polluters by name; the *Tribune* seldom hesitates.

3. Political Policy. Many Nineteenth Century publishers were ideologues; they purchased newspapers largely in order to advance a particular political or social philosophy. Most modern publishers, by contrast, are strictly businessmen; they purchase newspapers in order to make money, and they never mount the soapbox.

There are exceptions, of course. The Wilmington (Del.) *News* and *Journal*, for example, are owned by the Du Pont family. Their Board of Directors is highly conservative. After a straightforward news account of a Democratic rally, one board member (also on the Republican National Committee) wrote the executive editor of the papers: "This was a matter which, if properly handled, could, in my opinion, have been very useful to the Republican Party and their success at the polls in November." Another board member criticized an editorial praising President John Kennedy's Supreme Court nominations. He sent the executive editor a memo asking: "Why should we devote space to one who is an enemy of private enterprise and the capitalistic system?" The beleaguered editor finally quit when he was ordered to report to a new boss—an executive assistant in the public relations department at Du Pont.[7]

Political policy is not the sole property of Republicans. During the 1968 Democratic presidential primary in Indiana, publisher Eugene Pulliam of the Indianapolis *Star* and *News* was often seen in the newsroom. The primary was a three-way race between Governor Roger D. Branigin (standing in for Lyndon Johnson), Robert Kennedy, and Eugene McCarthy. Pulliam supported Branigin.

From March 28 to May 7, 1968, Branigin received 1,048 column inches in the *Star* and *News*. Kennedy got 712 inches, and McCarthy 584 inches. Kennedy, the favorite, was on the front page of the two papers 17 times; Branigin was front-paged a total of 31 times. Shortly before the primary, syndicated columnist Joseph Kraft wrote a piece praising Kennedy. The *Star* ran it with the following editor's note: "This article by Joseph Kraft, long-time columnist friend of the Kennedy family, ridiculing Indiana, is typical of the propaganda being turned out by pro-Kennedy writers to push the candidacy of Senator Robert F. Kennedy."[8]

We have detailed three ways that mass media owners control the news —business policy, personal policy, and political policy. The first is by far the most common. The third is probably the most dangerous. All three are important forms of media control.

SOCIAL CONTROL

In 1967, Lewis Donohew studied coverage of the Medicare issue in 17 Kentucky daily newspapers. He related coverage to three factors: community need for Medicare, community attitudes toward Medicare, and publisher attitudes toward Medicare. His findings were surprising. The correlation between the attitude of the publisher and the kind of coverage was 73 percent. The other two factors did not correlate significantly with coverage. In other words, newspapers whose publishers favored Medicare gave the issue favorable treatment and plenty of it—regardless

POLICY AT TIME

Newsmagazines are renowned for committee editing and the mammoth influence of policy on content. Much of this reputation stems from the record of *Time* magazine under the ownership of Henry R. Luce. In *Luce, His Time, Life, and Fortune,* author John Kobler paints the following picture of *Time's* coverage of Viet Nam in the early 1960s:

> Operating in the area of national and foreign affairs like a state within a state, *Time* was seldom content to print news as its correspondents filed it from the scene. Such stories had to be pondered at New York headquarters in the light of Lucean policy decisions. There would be weighty conferences and staff luncheons resembling a convocation of the National Security Council by the President of the United States. Frequently, editors and executives would take quick fact-finding trips like Congressmen. . . . During a visit home in 1963 *Time's* Hong Kong correspondent, Stanley Karnow, was repeatedly asked by the big brass, "What's the alternative to Diem?" They seemed to feel that they ought not to criticize the beleaguered ruler unless they could propose a successor. *Time* should confine itself to reporting the war, said Karnow, instead of trying to make policy. He cut no ice.[9]

Luce was an ardent opponent of Red China. In an article on the Chinese economy, Karnow wrote that its failures resulted from "successive years of mismanagement, confusion, natural calamities and population pressures— and perhaps the sheer unwieldiness of China itself." Luce noted in the margin of the manuscript: "Too many explanations. The simple answer is Communism." Where Karnow commented that China had "exaggerated" its claims of economic progress, Luce changed the word to "lied." For "official statements," Luce substituted "official lies."

The Luce bias affected the reporting of domestic affairs as well. The week before Roosevelt's easy second win in 1936, an editor asked Luce why *Time* didn't tell its readers that Roosevelt was winning. Luce answered: "Because it might help him win."[10]

---

of community attitudes or community needs. Papers with publishers opposed to Medicare, on the other hand, accorded it much less space and handled it much more critically.[11]

The important point here is that Donohew found almost no evidence of overt publisher influence on Medicare coverage. Apparently the Kentucky reporters and editors knew without being told what sort of news play would be most pleasing to their boss. And, without any direct orders, they gave it to him.

In a landmark essay on "Social Control in the Newsroom," written in 1955, sociologist Warren Breed reached essentially the same conclusion.

Newspapermen, Breed argued, learn "by osmosis" which stories involve policy and how they should be handled. It is seldom necessary—and considered rather gauche—for an owner to issue an explicit policy manifesto.[12]

This view is supported by a disturbing experiment conducted on journalism students in 1964. The students were instructed to write news articles (based on fact sheets) for imaginary newspapers. They were told in advance what the editorial policy of their paper was toward that particular issue. In the overwhelming majority of cases, the students voluntarily biased their articles in the direction of the paper's policy. Students whose own beliefs were farthest from policy made the greatest effort to go along. Those who agreed with the newspaper policy were actually more likely to be fair to the antipolicy view than those who were themselves antipolicy. On the other hand, business students with no training in journalism tended to be much less influenced by the policies of their imaginary publishers.[13]

The more you think about this study the more frightening it is. These were journalism students; today many of them are probably working journalists. Without the slightest hesitation, they slanted the news the way they thought their employer wanted it slanted. If most newsmen are like the subjects in this experiment, then there is really no need for owners to be crass about policy. All they have to do is let it be known how they like their news—and that's how they'll get it.

UNANIMITY

Suppose there are two independent newspapers in a city, and both publishers have a lot to say about how the news is covered. This is a bad enough situation even if the publishers are enemies. But suppose they're friends, suppose they play tennis together every weekend at the club, suppose they agree on almost every issue. Then the situation becomes much more dangerous.

It is a fact of life that mass media owners are businessmen. Most of the important ones are, by definition, big businessmen. Whether high-level corporate executives or self-made entrepreneurs, they inevitably share many of the same attitudes and opinions. To the extent that they influence news coverage, they are likely to influence it in the same direction.

Look at the three sorts of policies we have discussed—business, personal, and political. Media owners are all in the same business, dependent upon the same advertisers. So their business policies are similar. Media owners move in the same circles, with the same kinds of likes and dislikes and the same kinds of friends. So their personal policies are similar. Media owners share the same conservative, capitalistic political orientation. So their political policies are similar.

The influence of policy, in other words, may be a consistent bias in the media—not just in one newspaper here and another TV station there, but in nearly every newspaper and nearly every TV station everywhere. The phenomenon has sometimes been called "Country Club Journalism."

The arena in which this battle is customarily fought is politics. Many observers have charged that, while the country itself contains more Democrats than Republicans, the mass media are overwhelmingly Republican. In the 1952 Presidential campaign, for example, 67 percent of the nation's newspapers (with 80 percent of the circulation) supported Eisenhower. Only 15 percent of the papers (with 11 percent of the circulation) endorsed Stevenson.[14] The split in the popular vote, of course, was much closer.

The newspapers showed their bias in four ways, aside from the endorsements:

1. They gave larger headlines to the favored candidate.
2. They ran more lead stories on the favored candidate.
3. They gave more prominent position to articles on the favored candidate.
4. They printed more quotations from the favored candidate, and more remarks praising him.

Though the Democratic newspapers were just as biased in 1952 as the Republican ones, most of the papers were Republican.

Political reporting has improved since 1952. A study of 15 leading newspapers in 1960 and 1964, for example, revealed that the papers gave almost equal space to the Democratic and Republican Presidential candidates. The Democrats got slightly more column inches, while the Republicans received slightly better placement.[15] The furor that followed the 1968 Indianapolis incident (see Page 99) indicates how unacceptable slanted political coverage is to today's journalists—at least during hot national campaigns.

Nevertheless, the similarity of most mass media owners is cause for worry. Though coverage of national politics has improved, most media owners are still conservatives—and their conservatism is inevitably reflected in the media they own. Media owners are remarkably alike in viewpoint. When they influence news coverage through policy—whether business, personal, or political—that influence is likely to be close to unanimous.

It is hard to find two mass media owners today as different from each other as, say, Horace Greeley and Joseph Medill. It is just as hard to find two owners as intimately involved in the day-to-day production of news. The modern publisher or broadcaster intervenes only occasionally

—but when he does his policy is predictably and conventionally that of Big Business.

Owners are potentially the most powerful individuals in the mass media, but most use their power sparingly. The vast majority of the important day-to-day news decisions are made by the staff—by reporters and editors. Certain positions within media bureaucracies inevitably involve tremendous influence over news content. Many of these are relatively low-level positions, in terms of status and salary. Their occupants are often dangerously unaware of their own power.

GATEKEEPERS

Every piece of news passes through many hands between the original source and the final consumer. A corporation, say, mails a press release to a local newspaper. A *mail clerk* opens the envelope, reads the release, and decides that it should go to the financial department. An *assistant financial editor* reads it and judges that it is worth the attention of the *financial editor*. He assigns the piece to a *reporter,* who goes out in search of more information. The reporter writes his story and submits it to an *assistant city editor,* who decides that it needs more flair, and therefore turns it over to a *rewrite man.* The revised article is checked over by the *night editor.* He makes a few changes, then gives the article to a *copy editor,* who corrects the grammar, writes a headline, and sends the manuscript to the *typesetter.* A *photographer,* meanwhile, is out taking a picture to accompany the article, and the *layout editor* is busy dummying it into the newspaper. Eventually the story is okayed by the *city editor* and his boss the *managing editor.* And it is printed.

In this simplified example, thirteen people got a crack at a single corporate release. Most of them had a chance to change the content of the article in significant ways; at least six of them could have ruled it out of the paper entirely.

Communications researchers refer to these thirteen individuals as "gatekeepers." A gatekeeper is any person in the news-gathering process with authority to make decisions affecting the flow of information to the public. The image is precisely that of a turnstyle gatekeeper at a sporting event—he examines the qualifications of each person in line, and decides whether or not to let him in. The difference is that what gets let in or left out is not a person, but a piece of news.

Turnstyle gatekeepers have very little room for flexibility. They are under orders to let in anyone with a ticket, and no one without a ticket. Occasionally mass media gatekeepers are in the same position—the owner decides how a story is to be handled and an editor mechanically does the job. Most of the time, however, the owner remains neutral, so the editorial gatekeepers are left to make the decision. San Francisco journalist Lynn Ludlow puts it this way:

> On the surface the newspaper is organized along strict lines of authority and responsibility. The reporter is responsible to the city editor, who works under the policies of the managing editor, editor and publisher, etc. The insider knows, however, that . . . the man who actually does the work is actually setting his own strategy, tactics and policy a good deal of the time.[16]

We turn now to a few specific examples of mass-media gatekeepers.

THE TELEGRAPH EDITOR

Just about all state, national, and international news reaches the mass media via teletype, sent out by the Associated Press, United Press International, and other wire services. The job of the telegraph editor is to sort through this news and decide what to use.

It's an incredible job. A large metropolitan newspaper may subscribe to as many as 25 wires (including specialized ones like stocks, weather, and entertainment). Out of maybe 2,500 separate news items a day, the metro telegraph editor must pick out 200 or so for use in the paper. Working pretty much on his own, he continually asks himself questions like: Did we have something about this in the paper yesterday? Is our competition using anything on it? Are we likely to get a better story later in the day, in time for our deadline? Is the story too narrow or technical to interest our readers? Does it need checking or a local angle? Are more important stories likely to come in later? Even if the story is good, do I have room for it?

On the basis of his answers to these questions, the telegraph editor either edits the wire copy for publication or tosses it into a giant wastebasket that waits beside his desk. Throughout the day he is busy comparing, figuring, squeezing, and discarding—in short, gatekeeping.

In 1949 researcher David Manning White spent a week with the telegraph editor of a small Midwestern daily newspaper. The editor received a total of 11,910 column inches of copy from three wire services. He was able to use only 1,297 column inches, less than 11 percent. Exactly 1,333 stories were not used. Just under half of them, White reported, were discarded solely because of lack of space. Many of the rest were eliminated because the editor chose to print the same item from another wire service.[17]

Seventeen years later, in 1966, Paul Snider duplicated the White study, using the same telegraph editor. In the intervening time the paper had merged with its opposition and cut down to one wire service. (This is unusual; most newspapers get more wire copy than ever before.) As a result, the editor had only 1,971 column inches available during a five-day period. That was more than enough—he used only 631 inches, less than a third of the total.[18]

Telegraph editors have no universal standards or criteria to apply in deciding which wire stories to use. They invent their own—and each editor makes a different choice. Consider a 1959 study of wire copy in six small Michigan newspapers.[19] During a typical week, 764 wire stories appeared in at least one of the six papers. Only eight stories appeared in all six, and only four were on the front pages of all six. The total number of wire articles used ranged from 122 to 385; the number on the front page ranged from 45 to 105. One newspaper printed almost no international stories; another ran nearly as many foreign datelines as domestic ones. Every newspaper included at least a few articles that none of the other five bothered with.

Clearly, then, the telegraph editor is a gatekeeper of tremendous importance. Working under deadline pressure with little time to think before making his decisions, he determines almost entirely what his paper will publish about the world beyond its own city limits.

OTHER MEDIA GATEKEEPERS

The telegraph editor is only one of dozens of mass media gatekeepers. An entire book could be filled with gatekeeper studies of the various media. In the pages that follow we will discuss only a few of the more important or less obvious examples.

1. The Wire Service Editor. Telegraph editors have plenty of news to choose from—but there is lots more they never see. Only a fraction of the stories prepared by AP and UPI reporters are put on the national wire each day. Every article must pass through a succession of local and regional wire service editors, who decide whether it is important enough to teletype. Any one of these editors can kill the story.

In 1948 the Mississippi state legislature approved the creation of the Mississippi Bureau of Investigation, a special police force with wide discretionary powers. The AP and UPI Southern regional editors decided it was a minor story, so they kept it off the national wires. Press critic A. J. Liebling read about it in a New Orleans newspaper, and disagreed. Liebling's *New Yorker* articles on the M.B.I. started a national controversy. Only then did the wire services carry the story outside the South.[20]

2. The Reporter. No matter how many gatekeepers get their hands on a news item before it reaches the public, the one who influences that item most is the reporter. He decides whom to interview and what questions to ask. He decides where and how to cover an event. He decides which facts to include in his manuscript and which to leave out. Editors can kill the story or cut it to ribbons, but only occasionally do they know enough to add or correct anything. The way a reporter sees an event is almost certain to be the way that event is described by his newspaper, magazine, or broadcast station.

But no two reporters see the same event in the same way. Most newsmen try hard for objectivity, but they know before they start that they are doomed to failure. It is a fundamental law of psychology that people perceive the same stimulus in different ways, depending on their own attitudes, interests, and biases. If you support a political candidate, your estimate of the size of his audience will be larger than the estimates of opponents. If you disapprove of a war, you will see war crimes in actions that less critical observers view as unfortunate accidents. If you distrust college students, you will miss the evidence of legitimate grievances behind campus rebellions. Conscientious reporters do what they can to control these influences—but inevitably their opinions and feelings show through in what they write.

3. The Headline Writer.   The people who write headlines for newspaper articles tend to be hurried, harried, and often careless. Yet many readers never get further than the headline.

Even those readers who plow through an entire article are greatly ininfluenced by its headline. In 1953, Percy Tannenbaum planted a story about an imaginary murder trial in the *Daily Iowan,* a student newspaper. Tannenbaum used three different headlines. "Admits Ownership of Frat Murder Weapon" was intended to imply that the defendant was guilty. "Many Had Access to Frat Murder Weapon" seemed to imply innocence. And "Approach Final Stage in Frat Murder Trial" was neutral. Each reader saw only one headline, followed by the identical article in every case.

Tannenbaum then asked a sample of students whether they thought the defendant was guilty or innocent. This was their response:

	Guilty	*Innocent*	*No Opinion*	*Total*
Guilty headline	44	20	65	129
Innocent headline	29	38	65	132
Neutral headline	35	25	77	137

Though everyone read the same article, the "innocent headline" group tended to feel that the defendant was innocent. The "guilty headline" group thought he was guilty, and the "neutral headline" group fell approximately in the middle. Tannenbaum concluded that the headline "has a most definite effect on the interpretation of a story." He added: tended to feel that the defendant was innocent. The "guilty headline" and who is aware of the reading habits of the public, is certainly in a position to exert a significant influence upon the opinions of his audience."[21]

4. The Assignment Editor. Every mass medium has someone whose job it is to tell the reporters what stories to cover. Whatever his title, the man who makes the assignments is an important gatekeeper. Nothing gets covered unless he asks someone to cover it.

William Whitworth offers this description of assignment editor Robert Northshield's role in preparing for the evening NBC network newscast:

> Assignments have been made the day before, by Northshield or by the show's producer, Lester Crystal. Correspondents are at work in other cities and other countries, and are in touch with Northshield and Crystal off and on all day. . . .
>
> By noon, Northshield has seen some film, discussed story ideas with his producer and with the Washington staff, spoken to a correspondent or two, and read as much wire copy as possible. These chores will occupy him throughout the day. . . . Northshield will begin trying to make a rundown—a list of the stories that will be used on the program, with an estimate of the time to be allotted to each—between three-thirty and four. Perhaps six or eight of these stories will be filmed or taped reports. . . . The twenty or so other stories will be briefer. . . . Shortly before five, Crystal holds a story conference with the writers and gives them their assignments. Each man's is likely to be brief—anywhere from thirty seconds to three minutes of copy.[22]

Assignment editors in network television are seasoned professionals. In radio and local TV, however, they are likely to be comparative newcomers. They receive much lower pay than on-the-air reporters, yet they—not the reporters—determine which stories are to be covered.

5. The Film Editor. The television film editor (or the radio tape editor) takes twenty minutes of an interview or press conference and cuts it down to a minute or less. His job is to pick the most important, pithy, memorable, and interesting statements of the news source—without distorting his meaning. This is an extremely difficult and vital task. Often it is performed by a trainee fresh out of college.

6. Other Media. When the editor of a small newspaper is unsure how to report a national story, he may well check to see what the big city papers did with it. When a telegraph editor is swamped with copy, he looks to see what's on the wire service list of the day's most important stories. When a radio disc jockey sits down to prepare his hourly five-

LEADING LEADS

Next to the headline, the lead of a news story—the first paragraph or two—
is by far the most important part. Few readers get any further. The following
excerpts all refer to the march on the Pentagon in October, 1967. Regardless of the articles that followed, these passages would create very different
impressions of that event.

1. Chicago *Tribune,* October 22, 1967, page 1:

HURL BACK PENTAGON MOB

An estimated 4,000 to 5,000 anti-war demonstrators settled down in front
of the Pentagon this evening, apparently planning to spend the night.

They were all that were left of an estimated 30,000 to 35,000 protestors
who earlier in the day stormed the Pentagon and were hurled back by armed
soldiers and club swinging United States marshals. They came close to
breaking the doors they consider a symbol of militarism.

2. Washington *Post,* October 22, 1967, page 1:

55,000 RALLY AGAINST WAR;
GIs REPEL PENTAGON CHARGE

More than 55,000 persons demonstrated here against the war in Vietnam
yesterday in what started out as a peaceful, youthful rally but erupted into
violence at the Pentagon late in the day.

At one point, a surging band of about 20 demonstrators rushed into the
Pentagon, only to be thrown out by armed troops.

Dozens of youthful demonstrators were arrested during two brief but
angry melees at the Pentagon's Mall Entrance. Several thousand demonstrators
surged across boundaries that the Government had prescribed.

3. *Time* magazine, October 27, 1967, page 23:

THE BANNERS OF DISSENT

[Starts with a physical and historical sketch of the Pentagon.] Against
that physically and functionally immovable object last week surged a self-
proclaimed irresistible force of 35,000 ranting, chanting protestors who are
immutably opposed to the U.S. commitment in Vietnam. By the time the demonstration had ended, more than 425 irresistibles had been arrested, 13 more had
been injured, and the Pentagon had remained immobile. Within the tide of
dissenters swarmed all the elements of American dissent in 1967: hard-eyed
revolutionaries and skylarking hippies; ersatz motorcycle gangs and all-too-
real college professors; housewives, ministers, and authors; Black Nationalists
in African garb—but no real African nationalists; nonviolent pacifists and non-
pacific advocates of violence—some of them anti-anti-warriors and American
Nazis spoiling for a fight.

4. London *Times*, October 23, 1967, p. 4.

BESIEGE THE PENTAGON

The anti-war demonstration continued outside the Pentagon and elsewhere today after a night of disorder and some violence. About 200 demonstrators marched on the White House this morning, but a strong police guard kept them at a distance.

The vast Defense Department building, which stands on 583 acres of lawn and car parks, was penetrated briefly yesterday by a few dozen youngsters. United States marshals, with clubs swinging, quickly turned their attack into a retreat.

---

minute news report, he borrows local stories from the front page of the nearest newspaper. In these and other ways, the larger and more established news media serve as gatekeepers of a sort for the smaller and less established ones.

There are many other gatekeepers in the mass media—from the deskman who writes photo captions to the TV cameraman who decides where to point his lens, from the librarian who supplies background for stories to the rewrite specialist who adds sparkle to dreary copy. All of them have two things in common. First, they exercise a tremendous influence over the flow of news to the public. And second, they are largely unaware of their power. From time to time a publisher consciously sets policy. Working newsmen unconsciously set policy minute by minute.

UNANIMITY AGAIN

The dangerous thing about mass media owners is that they are all so much alike. Can the same charge be leveled against media gatekeepers? At least one observer, Vice-President Spiro Agnew, thinks it can:

> A small group of men, numbering perhaps no more than a dozen "anchormen," commentators and executive producers, settle upon the 20 minutes or so of film and commentary that is to reach the public. . . .
>
> We do know that, to a man, these commentators and producers live and work in the geographical and intellectual confines of Washington, D.C. or New York City—the latter of which James Reston terms the "most unrepresentative community in the entire United States." . . . We can deduce that these men thus read the same newspapers, and draw their political and social views from the same sources. . . .
>
> The upshot of all this controversy is that a narrow and distorted picture of America often emerges from the televised news. . . .[23]

Though Agnew's comments here concentrated on television newsmen, he has made it clear elsewhere that he feels the same way about most newspaper reporters. Media owners, we have charged, tend to be conservatives. Working journalists, Agnew replies, tend to be liberals. Both statements are overgeneralizations, but both are more true than false.

The difference is that working journalists are presumably trained to overcome their biases and present as balanced and objective a picture of the news as possible. Most mass media owners have no such training. When a publisher walks into a newsroom, he often does so for the express purpose of coloring the news to suit his taste. The gatekeepers who belong in that newsroom, on the other hand, are striving—however unsuccessfully—not to color the news at all.

Fifty years ago political scientist Curtice N. Hitchcock wrote a review of Upton Sinclair's newspaper diatribe, *The Brass Check*. In his review, Hitchcock made the following statement:

> Granted an adequate standard of professional journalism—a body of highly trained men competent to weigh news in terms of social significance and to present it adequately—the problem of control becomes one of turning the control over to them.[24]

The journalism profession has a long way to go yet before it satisfies Hitchcock's premise. But at least it is moving in that direction.

In the final analysis, the difference between owners and gatekeepers is this: An owner sets policy (occasionally) in order to achieve his own business, personal, and political goals. A gatekeeper influences the news (constantly) despite his honest efforts to remain objective.

NOTES

1 David R. Bowers, "A Report on Activity by Publishers in Directing Newsroom Decisions," *Journalism Quarterly*, Spring, 1967, pp. 44–49.

2 Rodney W. Stark, "Policy and the Pros: An Organizational Analysis of a Metropolitan Newspaper," *Berkeley Journal of Sociology*, Spring, 1962, pp. 14–15, 26.

3 Charles E. Swanson, "Midcity Daily: News Staff and Control," *Journalism Quarterly*, March, 1949, p. 25.

4 "Confessions of a Managing Editor," *Collier's*, October 28, 1911, p. 19.

5 Ben H. Bagdikian, "News as a Byproduct," *Columbia Journalism Review*, Spring, 1967, p. 9.

6 Edward W. Barrett, "Books" (Review of *Annenberg*, Gaeton Fonzi), *Columbia Journalism Review*, Spring, 1970, p. 56.

7 Ben H. Bagdikian, "Case History: Wilmington's 'Independent' Newspapers," *Columbia Journalism Review*, Summer, 1964, pp. 15–17.

8 Jules Witcover, "The Indiana Primary and the Indianapolis Newspapers—A Report in Detail," *Columbia Journalism Review*, Summer, 1968, pp. 12–16.

9 John Kobler, *Luce, His Time, Life, and Fortune* (Garden City, New York: Doubleday & Co., Inc., 1968), pp. 6–7.

[10] *Ibid.*, pp. 151, 177.

[11] Lewis Donohew, "Newspaper Gatekeepers and Forces in the News Channel," *Public Opinion Quarterly*, Spring, 1967, pp. 62–66.

[12] Warren Breed, "Social Control in the News Room," reprinted in *Mass Communications,* ed. Wilbur Schramm (Urbana, Ill.: University of Illinois Press, 1960), p. 182.

[13] Jean S. Kerrick, et al., "Balance and the Writer's Attitude in News Stories and Editorials," *Journalism Quarterly*, Spring, 1964, pp. 207–15.

[14] Malcolm W. Klein, and Nathan Maccoby, "Newspaper Objectivity in the 1952 Campaign," *Journalism Quarterly*, Summer, 1954, p. 285.

[15] Guido H. Stempel III, "The Prestige Press in Two Presidential Elections," *Journalism Quarterly*, Winter, 1965, p. 21.

[16] Personal communication from Lynn Ludlow of the San Francisco *Examiner* to David M. Rubin, August, 1969.

[17] David Manning White, "The 'Gate Keeper': A Case Study in the Selection of News," *Journalism Quarterly*, Fall, 1950, p. 387.

[18] Paul B. Snider, " 'Mr. Gates' Revisited: A 1966 Version of the 1949 Case Study," *Journalism Quarterly*, Autumn, 1967, p. 423.

[19] Guido H. Stempel III, "Uniformity of Wire Content of Six Michigan Dailies," *Journalism Quarterly*, Winter, 1959, p. 48.

[20] A. J. Liebling, *The Press* (New York: Ballantine Books, Inc., 1961), pp. 126–43.

[21] Percy H. Tannenbaum, "The Effect of Headlines on the Interpretation of News Stories," *Journalism Quarterly*, Spring, 1953, pp. 189–97.

[22] William Whitworth, "An Accident of Casting," *New Yorker*, Aug. 3, 1968, pp. 48–50.

[23] Address of Vice-President Spiro T. Agnew before the Midwest Regional Republican Committee, Des Moines, Iowa, November 13, 1969.

[24] Curtice N. Hitchcock, "The Brass Check, A Study of American Journalism: By Upton Sinclair," *The Journal of Political Economy*, April, 1921, pp. 343–44.

SUGGESTED READINGS

BAGDIKIAN, BEN H., "Case History: Wilmington's 'Independent' Newspapers," *Columbia Journalism Review*, Summer, 1964.

BOWERS, DAVID R., "A Report on Activity by Publishers in Directing Newsroom Decisions," *Journalism Quarterly*, Spring, 1967.

BREED, WARREN, "Social Control in the News Room," reprinted in Wilbur Schramm, ed., *Mass Communications* (Urbana, Ill.: University of Illinois Press, 1960).

FONZI, GAETON, *Annenberg* (New York: Weybright and Talley, Inc., 1970).

KOBLER, JOHN, *Luce, His Time, Life and Fortune* (New York: Doubleday & Co., Inc., 1968).

STARK, RODNEY W., "Policy and the Pros: An Organizational Analysis of a Metropolitan Newspaper," *Berkeley Journal of Sociology*, Spring, 1962.

WHITE, DAVID MANNING, "The 'Gate Keeper': A Case Study in the Selection of News," *Journalism Quarterly*, Fall, 1950.

WITCOVER, JULES, "The Indiana Primary and the Indianapolis Newspapers—A Report in Detail," *Columbia Journalism Review*, Summer, 1968.

4 Monopoly Control

The concept of Freedom of the Press is based on the conviction that truth somehow emerges from the conflict of many voices. But freedom can become a dangerous luxury when the number of voices falls to just two or three. The growth of giant media monopolies—networks, chains, conglomerates, and the like—has drastically reduced the diversity of media voices. This concentration of power in the hands of a few media "barons" represents a major threat to our First Amendment freedoms.

For six years WAVA was the only all-news radio station in the Washington D.C. area. Then, in 1968, WTOP switched to the same format. WAVA immediately complained to the Federal Trade Commission, charging that a dangerous media monopoly was in the making. WTOP, it pointed out, is owned by the Washington *Post*, the largest newspaper in the Capital and one of the most distinguished in the nation. Other *Post* properties include one of Washington's three network television stations, one of its largest FM radio stations, and *Newsweek*, an influential national news magazine. Working together, WAVA's management argued, the various *Post* outlets could establish a near-monopoly over the flow of news in the Washington area.

The *Post* responded that WTOP and other *Post*-owned media were free to cover the news as they wished, without corporate control. The

FTC found this a persuasive answer. It dismissed the complaint, noting that its investigation "failed to produce any evidence of misuse of alleged monopolistic power possessed by the Washington Post Company."[1]

The FTC decision makes sense. The *Post* really does allow its subsidiaries great editorial freedom. And with 44 broadcast stations and three daily newspapers, Washington offers much more media diversity than the average American city.

Nevertheless, there is an inherent danger to democracy any time a single owner controls more than one mass media outlet. Freedom of the Press is predicated on the belief that if people have access to a wide range of opinions and information, they will make intelligent decisions. Supreme Court Justice Oliver Wendell Holmes put it this way: "The best test of truth is the power of the thought to get itself accepted in the competition of the market."[2] It follows that the government should not be permitted to regulate the media. Let each publisher "do his own thing," the theory goes, and the people will be able to figure out who's right and who's wrong.

The theory works only so long as Holmes's "market" remains competitive. The fewer the number of independent media outlets in a given location, the weaker the case for freedom becomes. Consider an extreme example. If there were only one newspaper publisher in the entire United States, it would obviously be very dangerous to leave that publisher free to "do his own thing." How could the people choose right from wrong if they had only one source of information? Every media combination brings us that much closer to this "one source" situation.

A media owner may allow his outlets to disagree with each other for a while, but later he may change his mind—or sell his holdings to a new owner with stronger convictions. Competing media may supply the necessary diversity at first, but they too may eventually be purchased by a monopolist—or be forced to fold in the face of concentrated economic pressure. To be sure, some media combinations are more dangerous than others, and the Washington *Post* combine must be counted among the safest. Yet it is not entirely safe. No media combination is entirely safe.

Media combinations come in many forms, but there are four major varieties:

1. *Chains and networks*—two or more outlets in the same medium (television, newspapers, or whatever) but in different cities are owned or controlled by the same person or group.
2. *Cross-media ownership*—two or more outlets in the same city but in different media are owned by the same person or group.
3. *Joint operating agreements*—Two separately owned outlets in the same medium (usually newspapers) and the same city arrange to combine certain operations, such as printing and advertising.

4. *Conglomerates*—A company not primarily in the communications business also owns mass media outlets.

We will discuss each briefly in turn.

CHAINS AND NETWORKS

In June, 1967, there were 1,767 daily newspapers in the United States. Of these, 871 were owned by chains—that is, 871 newspapers were owned by individuals or companies that also owned other newspapers.

In 21 states chains now own more than half the dailies. In California chain ownership totals more than 70 percent; in Ohio and Texas it's 62 percent; in Florida it's an astounding 83 percent. Most of the nation's largest newspapers today are chain-owned, including the New York *Daily News,* the Los Angeles *Times,* the Chicago *Tribune,* the Detroit *Free Press,* and the Philadelphia *Inquirer.*

And the statistics are getting worse. In 1930 chains controlled only 43 percent of total newspaper circulation. In 1960 they controlled 46 percent, a modest increase. By 1967 the figure had skyrocketed to 62 percent—and it is still going up. Bryce Rucker estimates that if current trends continue, chains will own all the dailies in the country by 1990.[3]

Among the largest chains are the following: Thomson (35 papers); Gannett (26); Newhouse (22); Copley (17); Scripps-Howard (16); Ridder (15); Cowles (10); and Chicago *Tribune* (7). These eight chains alone control 131 newspapers, with a total circulation of well over 13,000,000.

Magazine chains are frequently tied to newspapers. The Hearst organization, for example, owns 12 newspapers, plus *Good Housekeeping, Cosmopolitan, Harper's Bazaar, Popular Mechanics,* and sixteen other magazines. Other magazine chains include Time-Life, Cowles, Triangle, and Bartell; each of these owns several magazines at least, plus newspaper or broadcasting interests. Of the giant mass circulation magazines, only *Playboy* and the *Reader's Digest* are completely free of chain ownership.

Radio chains are almost as old as radio. In 1939 there were already 39 AM radio chains; they owned 109 stations, 14 percent of the total. In 1967 the number of radio chains had grown to 317; they owned 1,297 stations, 31 percent of the total. These figures are still growing. Television chains represent an even greater portion of the total. In 1967 there were 147 TV chains controlling 459 stations, almost three-quarters of the total number of channels on the air.[4]

The Federal Communications Commission limits broadcast chains to seven television stations (of which only five can be VHF), seven AM radio stations, and seven FM radio stations. As of 1970 there were seven broadcast chains that had just about reached these limits: Metromedia, Westinghouse, RKO General, Storer, and the three networks. These seven companies own a total of 125 broadcast outlets, nearly all of them in the nation's largest cities. Five of the six VHF television stations in New York City are owned by one or another of these seven companies.

The monopolistic power of the three networks is not restricted to the 21 stations each is allowed to own. The vast majority of all non-network-owned radio and television stations are affiliated with a network, and carry massive amounts of that network's programming. NBC has 213 TV affiliates and 221 radio ones. CBS has 192 and 246, respectively. For ABC the figures are 159 and 900. There are only 4,100 AM radio stations and 617 commercial TV stations in the country. A little arithmetic reveals that 33 percent of all AM radio, and 91 percent of all commercial television, is network-affiliated.

CROSS-MEDIA OWNERSHIP

At the close of the 1960s, a single owner controlled at least one television station and one newspaper in 34 of the nation's 50 largest cities. Overall, 94 television stations were owned by newspapers in the same city.[5]

Fifty-seven communities are served by only one commercial radio station and one newspaper, both owned by the same company. On the list are Coeur d'Alene, Idaho; LaSalle, Illinois; Vincennes, Indiana; Asbury Park, New Jersey; Urbana, Ohio; Shawnee, Oklahoma; and Gettysburg, Pennsylvania. Eleven cities have just one commercial TV station and one newspaper, both owned by the same company. These include Fort Smith, Arkansas; Albany, Georgia; Zanesville, Ohio; Bluefield, West Virginia; and Cheyenne, Wyoming.[6]

In the larger cities, cross-media ownership is often combined with chains and networks to produce nearly total control over local broadcasting. In Chicago, for example, the three largest TV stations are owned by the networks; the fourth is the property of the Chicago *Tribune*. In Detroit one station is owned by ABC, a second by the Detroit *News*, and the third by Storer Stations, a chain. The top three stations in St. Louis are owned by CBS, the St. Louis *Post-Dispatch*, and the St. Louis *Globe-Democrat*.

The list of the top 50 markets includes only two cities in which every television station is independently owned—Miami, Florida; and Manchester, New Hampshire. Over four-fifths of all VHF television stations today are owned either by broadcast chains or by newspapers. In eleven states every VHF station is so owned.[7]

Concentration is strongest in the nation's small towns. In 1967, 83 percent of all communities with a population of more than 200,000 had at least one newspaper and broadcast station that were not owned by the same company. This was true of only 71 percent of the communities of 10,000 to 200,000—and of only 25 percent of the communities with fewer than 10,000 residents.[8]

Cross-media ownership is not limited to the newspaper-broadcast combination. Within broadcasting, the vast majority of FM radio stations are owned by AM stations. Most of the larger AM stations, in turn, are owned by TV stations—as are roughly half the existing cable television systems in the country. Many newspapers own their own feature syndicates; a number of them publish local or national magazines as well. Several magazine companies, meanwhile, own broadcast chains, or newspapers, or both. Nearly half of the major book publishing houses either own or are owned by broadcasting, newspaper, or magazine interests. A few movie companies are into broadcasting in a big way, while all three broadcast networks own their own movie companies. It is hard to imagine any field with more interconnections than the communications industry.

JOINT OPERATING AGREEMENTS

Albuquerque, New Mexico, has only two newspapers, the morning *Journal* and the afternoon *Tribune*. In 1933 the two papers negotiated, in secret, the first newspaper joint operating agreement. They arranged to do all their printing in one plant, and to employ a single business office, circulation department, and advertising department. Commercial expenses were split down the middle. At the end of each year the profits were to be divided according to a set ratio, regardless of either paper's circulation or advertising revenue.

By 1970, 46 newspapers in 23 cities had established joint operating agreements. In the following list, the combinations that involve chain-owned newspapers as well are marked with an asterisk:

> Albuquerque *Journal* and *Tribune*
> * Birmingham *Post-Herald* and *News*
> Bristol *Herald-Courier* and *Virginia-Tennessean*
> Charleston *Gazette* and *Daily Mail*
> * Columbus *Citizen-Journal* and *Dispatch*
> El Paso *Times* and *Herald-Post*
> Evansville *Courier* and *Press*
> * Fort Wayne *Journal-Gazette* and *News-Sentinel*
> Honolulu *Advertiser* and *Star-Bulletin*
> * Knoxville *Journal* and *News-Sentinel*
> Lincoln *Star* and *Journal*
> Lynchburg *News* and *Advance*

* Madison *State Journal* and *Capital Times*
* Miami *Herald* and *News*
  Nashville *Tennessean* and *Banner*
  Oil City-Franklin *Derrick* and *News-Herald*
* Pittsburgh *Post-Gazette* and *Press*
* St. Louis *Globe-Democrat* and *Post-Dispatch*
* Salt Lake City *Tribune* and *Deseret-News*
* San Francisco *Chronicle* and *Examiner*
* Shreveport *Times* and *Journal*
  Tucson *Arizona Star* and *Citizen*
  Tulsa *World* and *Tribune*[9]

Some of the advantages of the joint operating agreement are obvious: It reduces the cost of advertising sales, printing, and distribution. As long as the agreement is confined to these points it is harmless, even helpful. But many newspapers have used joint operating agreements as an excuse for manipulating advertising rates in such a way that no third newspaper can possibly develop. And a few papers have extended their cooperation to include news and editorials as well as advertising and circulation, posing a clear threat to media diversity.

CONGLOMERATES

A conglomerate is a company that operates in a number of different and unrelated markets. RCA General owns the NBC television network, more than a dozen individual radio and TV stations, the Random House publishing firm, RCA records, and RCA television sets. That makes it a media monster of tremendous size, but not a conglomerate—its holdings are all in the communications industry. CBS, on the other hand, not only owns a network, a bunch of stations, a record company, a publishing house, and the like. It also has a toy manufacturing firm (Creative Playthings) and a baseball team (the Yankees). It therefore qualifies as a conglomerate.

Most media conglomerates work in the other direction—they start out manufacturing something, then work their way into the media. There are many examples.

* Litton Industries owns Monroe adding machines, Henke syringes, Stouffer frozen food—and the American Books textbook company.
* Norton Simon Industries owns Hunt foods, Canada Dry beverages —and *McCall's* magazine.
* Gulf and Western owns machine tool companies, cigar manufacturers, zinc plants—and Paramount Pictures.
* Kinney National Service owns parking lots, funeral chapels—and comic books.

NEWSSTAND POWER

Most media monopolists are publishers or broadcasters. Henry Garfinkle is an exception.

Garfinkle is chairman of Ancorp National Services Inc. Ancorp, in turn, is owner of the Union News Company, the largest newsstand retailer of newspapers and magazines in the United States. Newsstand sales are an important revenue source for nearly every established metropolitan newspaper in the country, and for most of the major magazines. And of course a new publication requiring large circulation—whether newspaper or magazine—absolutely depends on newsstand exposure.

All of which gives Henry Garfinkle a great deal of power. In 1969 Garfinkle was feuding with the owners of *Newsweek, McCall's,* and *U.S. News and World Report.* Ancorp, it seems, also runs a wholesale distributing business—but these three publishers were working with a rival wholesaler. To help them see the light, Garfinkle kept the three magazines off the stands along the Long Island Railroad in Queens.[10]

- Kaiser Industries owns gravel, aluminum, cement, and steel manufacturers, an aerospace research firm, a jeep company—and a group of UHF television stations.

The danger of media conglomerates is, of course, that they may use their communications outlets to advance the interests of their other operations.

AN OVERVIEW

The trend toward media combination might not be so serious if there were an ever-increasing number of media outlets. Unfortunately, this is not the case.

In 1790 there were only eight daily newspapers in the entire United States. By 1850 the number of papers had risen to 387. By 1900 it was up to 2,190, and in 1910 it hit a high of 2,433. Then the figure began to slip—to 2,042 in 1920, to 1,878 in 1940. Throughout the 1960s the figure was stable at roughly 1,750 daily newspapers in the country—considerably fewer than in the 1890s.

There are many reasons why the number of newspapers declined in the first half of the Twentieth Century—increased operating costs, recurrent labor problems, competition from broadcasting, etc. But the most important reason was simply that newspapering became a business. When a publisher decides that he'd rather earn money than advocate a viewpoint, he naturally eliminates most of the ideological advocacy from his paper, and cares very little about the advocacy that's left. There is then no reason not to merge with another paper. One publisher is bought out and retires with his profit; the other publisher gains a monopoly and increases his profit.

The broadcast media, meanwhile, are limited in number by the technology of broadcasting. The spectrum has room for only so many stations. There are still more than 1,000 unclaimed TV frequencies available, but few are likely to prove profitable—so there are no takers.

So far we haven't said anything at all about the abuse of media monopolies. The very existence of these monopolies—of chains and networks, cross-media ownership, joint operating agreements, and conglomerates—represents a serious threat to the democratic process, even without abuses.

Every media monopolist possesses the dangerous power to advance his own interests at the expense of others—including the public. Many monopolists have used this power; others may do so in the future. It is not practical, however, to outlaw all forms of media combination. One must choose among evils, and for this purpose pro-monopoly arguments are instructive. So far, the federal government has taken some action against all the forms of media monopoly, but decisive action against none of them. Apparently it has not decided yet which forms are the most dangerous.

ABUSES OF CONCENTRATION

Any form of media combination reduces, at least in theory, the total number of independent voices that can be heard. It therefore runs contrary to the fundamental premise of the First Amendment, that if the people hear all sides they can make the right decision. As the Federal Communications Commission phrased it: "Centralization of control over the media of mass communications is, like monopolization of economic power, *per se* undesirable."[11]

But the dangers of media monopoly are far more than just theory. Two specific abuses have frequently been documented: news management and unfair economic competition. We will offer a few examples of each.

1. News Management.   Between 1926 and 1937, conservative George Richards acquired an impressive chain of AM radio stations, including major outlets in Detroit, Cleveland, and Hollywood. He left standing orders for all his news staffs to give no favorable coverage to President Roosevelt, but rather to depict the President as a lover of "the Jews and

Communists." When Mrs. Roosevelt was in an auto accident in 1946, Richards ordered his stations to make it seem that she had been drinking. Local newsmen who refused to follow the Richards line were fired.[12]

A less ideological example of news management came to light in 1969, when the FCC began its investigation of KRON-TV, a local station owned and operated by the San Francisco *Chronicle*. Station employees testified that when the *Chronicle* and the afternoon *Examiner* formed a joint operating agreement in 1965, KRON failed to report the story. Returning the favor, the *Chronicle* grossly underplayed the events leading to the FCC hearings on KRON.

And *Chronicle* columnist Charles McCabe testified that a piece he had written deploring violence on television was "killed" by higher-ups at the paper.[13]

Karl Nestvold has studied the relationships between 128 newspapers and the radio stations they owned. He found that 25 of the stations were located right within the newspaper building. Over 40 of them used newspaper personnel on the air. And roughly half the stations had access to prepublication carbons of newspaper articles.[14] Regular readers of the newspapers in Nestvold's study had little to gain from listening to the radio stations those newspapers owned.

In 1967 the International Telephone and Telegraph Company attempted to purchase the ABC network. Despite the fact that IT&T was already a giant international conglomerate, the FCC approved the sale. Three commissioners dissented. "We simply cannot find," they wrote, "that the public interest of the American citizenry is served by turning over a major network to an international enterprise whose fortunes are tied to its political relations with the foreign officials whose actions it will be called upon to interpret to the world."

Their fears were borne out by IT&T's conduct while the sale was under scrutiny by the FCC and the Justice Department. IT&T officials phoned AP and UPI reporters and asked them to make their stories more sympathetic to the company position. A New York *Times* correspondent who had criticized the merger received a call from an IT&T senior vice president. The man asked if she was following the price of ABC and IT&T stock, and didn't she feel "a responsibility to the shareholders who might lose money as a result" of what she wrote.[15] If IT&T was pressuring newsmen now, one might ask, what would it do after it owned its own reporters to pressure? Fortunately, the Justice Department balked at the merger, and IT&T eventually withdrew the offer.

2. Unfair Economic Competition. The *Examiner-Chronicle*-KRON combination can be used to illustrate unfair competition as well as news management. Before 1965 the two newspapers were involved in a bitter circulation war for the morning San Francisco market. *Chronicle* owners used the profits from KRON to win the battle, forcing the *Examiner* to move to the afternoon and sign a joint operation agreement.

Once the agreement was reached, the *Chronicle* doubled its advertising rate, while the weaker *Examiner* raised its rate by about fifty percent. The joint rate for placing the same ad in both papers was set only slightly higher than the *Chronicle*'s rate alone. The *Chronicle* had a monopoly, so advertisers were forced to pay its doubled rate. It then made sense for them to pay just a little more and get into the *Examiner* as well. The result: Suburban afternoon papers that were hoping to compete with the *Examiner* suffered a loss in advertising linage. And, more important, metropolitan competition was rendered impossible.

Not every media combination has made use of its power to slant the news. Not every media combination has taken advantage of its economic muscle to squelch the opposition. But every media combination is capable of these things—and some have done them.

COMPETITION

The most common criticism of media combinations is that they reduce competition. This raises a vital question: Does media competition really produce better media?

The assumption of the critics is that competitive media tend to produce more aggressive journalists than noncompetitive ones. To test this hypothesis, Gerard Borstel examined news and editorials in four kinds of newspapers—independent papers with local competition, chain papers with local competition, independent papers without competition, and chain papers without competition. He found absolutely no differences of any sort. The chain and monopoly papers were every bit as good as the independent and competitive ones.[16] It can be argued, then, that competitive papers are simply "rivals in conformity," offering the public no real diversity of viewpoint.

There may even be some advantages to a monopoly. Paul Block Jr., publisher of both the Toledo *Blade* and the Toledo *Times*, states his case persuasively:

> For one thing, a newspaper which isn't competing against a rival can present news in better balance. There is no need to sensationalize. . . .
>
> Competing newspapers live in fear of each other. They may be stampeded into excesses by their fear of losing circulation to a competitor less burdened with conscience. . . .
>
> The unopposed newspaper can give its reader . . . relief from the pressures of time. Deadlines no longer loom like avenging angels just this side of the next edition. . . . There is more freedom from financial

pressure on the business side. A single ownership newspaper can better afford to take an unpopular stand. It can better absorb the loss of money in support of a principle. . . .[17]

In a similar vein, the National Association of Broadcasters sponsored a study which tried to prove that cross-media ownership produces better, not worse, media. Author George Litwin interviewed owners, journalists, and citizens in six cities, three with strong cross-media ownership and three with independent media. He concluded that owners of two or more media are more likely than independent owners to adopt a hands-off policy, leaving the management of the station and the newspaper to professional journalists. In addition, Litwin said, giant media barons can afford a larger staff and more facilities, resulting in better news coverage.[18]

The advantages of newspaper chains have also been developed at some length. There are eight of them. (1) Newsprint, ink, and other supplies can be purchased more cheaply in bulk. (2) One representative can sell national ads for the entire chain. (3) Standardized accounting methods turn up errors in individual papers that can be quickly corrected. (4) Editors and reporters can exchange ideas and criticize one another. (5) Valuable feature material can be obtained for the chain more easily and cheaply. (6) High salaries and employee stock benefits can be maintained more easily, even in hard times. (7) Costs can be cut by centralizing some business functions. (8) Staff members from different papers can be used to work on an important story for the entire chain. Many of the eight factors apply also to cross-media ownership, joint operating agreements, and conglomerates.

There are rebuttals to all these arguments. Researcher Bryant Kearl, for example, has shown that monopoly media do not in fact use their added economic resources to improve performance. Specifically, he found that monopoly newspapers purchase no more wire services than competitive ones[19]—though wires are among the cheapest and easiest ways to improve a paper. Economics Professor Harvey Levin surveyed 60 joint newspaper-broadcast operations in 1954, and concluded that "no significant management economies seem to result from affiliation because the jobs of directing newspapers and radio or TV stations are markedly different." The main benefit of cross-media ownership, Levin found, is not increased profits, but rather increased economic security through diversification.[20]

Defenders of media monopoly always seem to miss the central point. Obviously media combinations offer some advantages; otherwise there wouldn't be so many of them. No doubt a conscientious media baron can turn these advantages to the benefit of the public. No doubt a few media barons have done so. The fact remains: Every case of media combination is one less independent voice in the community. If our independent media are not making sufficient use of their freedom, that is a serious

ABSENTEE OWNERSHIP

One of the charges often leveled against chains and conglomerates is that they lead to media run "by remote control" with "absentee landlords" at the helm. There is much justice in the claim. After the Newhouse chain purchased two newspapers in Mobile, Alabama, in 1966, every major daily in the state was in the hands of an absentee owner. The weekly Montgomery *Independent* felt compelled to editorialize:

> Ninety per cent of the people in Alabama read daily newspapers whose owners they will never know or see. . . . It is profoundly sad and dangerous that the newspapers of Alabama are passing into the hands of cartels. . . . [T]he only hope of restoring locally responsible ownership is by the application of the anti-monopoly laws.[21]

But the problem of absentee ownership is much less serious today than one might expect. The "new breed" of chain owners—Knight, Thomson, Newhouse—are far more interested in profit margins than in local news coverage. They encourage member newspapers to make their own news and editorial decisions, and are unconcerned when the papers wind up opposing each other.

Roy Thomson, for example, owns an international chain of 128 newspapers and 80 magazines. "I buy newspapers to make money to buy more newspapers to make more money," Thomson declares. "As for editorial content, that's the stuff you separate the ads with." Thomson leaves his editors alone; when he ran for the Canadian Parliament in 1953, some of his own papers did not support him.[22]

problem, worthy of serious attention. But at least they *are* independent; when they do raise their voices, they don't all say the same thing. Diversity is the strength of democracy. And no media monopoly can supply diversity.

GOVERNMENT REGULATION

From what has been said about the dangers of media monopolies, it should come as no surprise that the federal government has made efforts to contain and restrict them. What is surprising is the weakness of those efforts, at least until the end of the 1960s. Let us examine the extent of government restraint on each of the four forms of media combination.

1. Chains and Networks. Commercial radio was barely out of its infancy when the Federal Communications Commission began to worry about broadcast networks. The big problem was NBC, which owned two of the three existing networks and the vast majority of the strong metropolitan stations. In 1941 the FCC finally acted, ordering that "no license shall be issued to a standard broadcast station affiliated with a network organization which maintains more than one network."[23] This forced NBC to get rid of its so-called Blue Network. Lifesaver king Edward J. Noble bought the holdings; they became the nucleus of what is now ABC.

The FCC took two other actions in the early 1940s, known jointly as the Duopoly Rule. First, it ordered that no licensee could operate two stations of the same kind (AM, FM, or TV) in the same community. Second, it put a limit on the number of stations throughout the country that one licensee could own. Today that limit stands at seven AM, seven FM, and seven TV (of which no more than five may be VHF).

In the thirty years that followed, the FCC has done little or nothing about the growth of broadcast chains. Aside from a proposed rule requiring local stations to originate their own shows at least one prime-time hour a day, the Commission has also largely ignored the massive influence of the networks. Chains and networks continue to dominate the broadcasting scene.

The FCC, of course, can regulate only broadcasting; the government agency that watches over print monopolies is the Department of Justice, with the help of the Federal Trade Commission. From time to time Justice has opposed a particular newspaper sale or merger, but on the whole it doesn't object to newspaper combinations unless they are within a single city. In 1970, for example, the Justice Department approved the sale of *Newsday*, a large Long Island tabloid, to the Times Mirror Company of Los Angeles. That company already owned the Los Angeles *Times*, the Dallas *Times-Herald*, and assorted other publishing and broadcast properties—but the Justice Department didn't seem to mind. Mused one *Newsday* editor: "The *Times* has the best national reporting in the country for my money. But it's a long way from Long Island."[24]

2. Cross-media Ownership. The FCC has no rule governing the extent to which newspaper publishers are permitted to operate broadcast stations. Instead, it decides cross-media applications on a case-by-case basis.

In 1938 the Commission denied a newspaper applicant its license for the first time, awarding it to an independent instead. The Supreme Court intervened, holding that newspaper ownership was insufficient grounds for denying a license application or renewal. Eighteen years passed, and then in 1956 the FCC tried again. It picked an untried applicant with no media holdings over one with an extensive newspaper and broadcast chain. This time the courts upheld the Commission, ruling that diversity may be one factor—though not the sole factor—in deciding who gets a license.[25] But the Commission seldom took advantage

ONE-CITY CHAINS

The Justice Department doesn't worry much about broad-based newspaper chains, but when the chains are local Justice begins to get interested.   In 1968, for example, the department forced the Los Angeles *Times* to sell the San Bernardino *Sun and Telegram*.   The two cities are only twenty-odd miles apart, and getting closer every year.   Apparently Justice didn't want the *Times* to wind up owning both papers in the Southern California megalopolis.

Later that year, the department required the afternoon Cincinnati *Post & Times-Star* (a Scripps chain paper) to divest itself of the morning Cincinnati *Enquirer*, in order to "restore competition between downtown papers."[26]   And in early 1970 it forced the Chattanooga *Times* to close its sister paper, the *Evening Post,* because the latter was started with the sole intention of driving the competitive *News-Free Press* out of business.   The *Evening Post* was deliberately published at a loss, Justice claimed, just to make it impossible for the *News-Free Press* to compete.[27]

of its newly won power, and newspaper-broadcast combinations continued to flourish.

Then, in 1968, the Department of Justice entered the scene.   It filed with the FCC a formal objection to the purchase of station KFDM-TV in Beaumont, Texas, by the owner of the only two Beaumont newspapers. Justice argued that the merger would substantially lessen the competition for advertising.   Before the FCC could make up its mind, the application for transfer of the license was withdrawn.

Justice next presented to the FCC a legal rationale for moving against cross-media combinations on antitrust grounds.   Combined ownerships, it submitted, "may facilitate undesirable competitive practices by which the 'combined' owner seeks to exploit his advantages over the single station owner."[28]   Justice urged the FCC to take action against cross-media combinations.

To the surprise of almost everyone, the Commission agreed.   In 1969 it refused to renew the license of Boston station WHDH-TV, owned by the Boston *Herald-Traveler*.   Instead, it awarded the license to a committee of local educators and businessmen.

That was only the beginning.   In March, 1970, the FCC ruled that no new licenses would be granted to the owners of existing stations (radio or TV) in the same market.   It also announced a "declaration of proposed rulemaking"—a statement of what it hoped to do in the near future.   The terms were severe:

• Within five years all newspaper owners would be required to get rid of all their broadcast holdings in the same city.

- After five years no owner of a television station would be permitted to operate a radio station in the same city.
- Any broadcaster who purchased a newspaper in the same market would be required to give up his broadcast license.

Industry response to this bombshell was immediate. NBC, for example, announced that the FCC "is seeking a rule requiring divestiture (if not forfeiture) in the absence of any showing either of monopoly power or of any restraint of trade."[29]

So far the FCC proposed rulemaking is only proposed; it is not yet a rule, and may never become a rule. Yet the FCC has clearly declared itself in agreement with the Justice Department that cross-media ownership is a serious problem.

3. *Joint Operating Agreements.* In 1965 the Justice Department filed suit against the Tucson *Arizona Star* and *Citizen,* charging that the two newspapers had entered into a joint operating agreement that violated antitrust laws. The papers were accused of price-fixing, profit-pooling, and creating a total monopoly over the daily newspaper business in Tucson. The U.S. District Court in Arizona agreed, and declared the agreement unlawful. The U.S. Supreme Court upheld the decision. The newspaper joint operating agreement (except for limited arrangements involving papers in genuine danger of folding) was dead.

It was born again in 1967, when Arizona Senator Carl Hayden introduced the Failing Newspaper Act, which explicitly legalized agreements like Tucson's. The act died in committee, but was reintroduced as the Newspaper Preservation Act. In 1970 it passed both houses of Congress and was signed into law.

The act was vigorously lobbied through Congress by the powerful newspaper industry. Proponents argued that only the joint operating agreement could keep weak metropolitan papers from folding, leaving their cities with just a single newspaper. The act, they said, was therefore an attempt to preserve competition and forestall monopoly.

Opponents saw it differently. They pointed out that in most American cities it is the *third* newspaper, not the *second,* that is in imminent danger of folding. They marshalled statistics to establish that any city with more than 200,000 population can support two independent newspapers. They concluded, as John J. Flynn put it:

> It is dangerous to think the bill is designed to preserve the struggling and crusading editor of yesteryear whose only devotion is to the noncommercial aspects of journalism. It is ridiculous to think that the bill is anything other than an open invitation to further concentrate an already overconcentrated industry, thereby destroying the few remaining independent editorial voices.[30]

Even if a newspaper is in danger of folding, many argued, the goals of democracy are better served by letting it fold than by propping it up with a joint operating agreement. A newspaper that cannot survive as one of two in a big city must be doing something wrong. Perhaps if it were allowed to fold another paper might take its place—and do a better job. At a minimum, weekly and suburban papers in the area would benefit from the increased availability of advertising.

Nevertheless, the Newspaper Preservation Act is now law, and joint operating agreements are legal once again.

4. Conglomerates. The FCC is dead set against what it calls "trafficking in licenses." That is, it will refuse to grant or renew a broadcast license if it believes the applicant is interested only in selling the license at a profit. This is the only action any arm of the government has ever taken specifically against media conglomerates. As long as a conglomerate steers clear of trafficking and doesn't violate the rules about chains and cross-media ownership, it is quite safe.

CHOOSING AMONG EVILS

We have discussed four forms of media combination—chains and networks, cross-media ownership, joint operating agreements, and conglomerates. It is not feasible to outlaw them all. This is the age of Big Business, in communications as in all other industries. Critics of media monopoly must therefore decide which forms to fight, and which to leave alone as the lesser among evils.

The government, too, must make this decision. So far none of the four forms has been outlawed. Still, it is possible to examine the actions of Congress, the FCC, and the Justice Department, and to deduce from them how the government views the problem. The "official government" ranking, from most dangerous to least dangerous, would probably look like this:

1. Cross-media ownership
2. Chains and networks
3. Joint operating agreements
4. Conglomerates

Since the FCC's proposed rulemaking, cross-media ownership is under fire or likely to be. By comparison the other three are not targets.

The authors would rate conglomerates as the most serious threat to democracy, because an industrial corporation has the greatest incentive to slant the news. We consider cross-media ownership second in importance, because it limits the number of independent voices within a community. Joint operating agreements come third, for the same reason. And chains, so long as they remain loose and decentralized, we view as a comparatively minor problem.

That is our opinion. Others may choose a different order. But on the central point nearly all observers agree: Diversity of viewpoint is vital to Freedom of the Press; and media monopoly—*every* form of media monopoly—is antithetical to diversity.

NOTES

[1] Richard L. Worsnop, "Competing Media," *Editorial Research Reports,* July 18, 1969, pp. 538–39.

[2] *Abrams v. United States,* 250 U.S. 616, 630 (1919).

[3] Bryce Rucker, *The First Freedom* (Carbondale, Ill.: Southern Illinois University Press, 1968), pp. 21–23.

[4] *Ibid.,* pp. 189, 194.

[5] Federal Communications Commission, "Further Notice of Proposed Rulemaking," 70–311 46096, March 25, 1970, paras. 30–31.

[6] Federal Communications Commission, "Newspaper-Broadcast Joint Interests as of November 1, 1969," Table 1.

[7] Rucker, *The First Freedom,* p. 196.

[8] Guido H. Stempel III, "A New Analysis of Monopoly and Competition," *Columbia Journalism Review,* Spring, 1967, pp. 11–12.

[9] Walter B. Kerr, "S.1312 and All That," *Saturday Review,* May 10, 1969, pp. 77–78.

[10] Ronald Kessler, "Control of Newsstands Gives Henry Garfinkle Power Over Publishers," *Wall Street Journal,* July 3, 1969, p. 1.

[11] Federal Communications Commission, "First Report and Order," 70–310 46095, para. 17.

[12] Erik Barnouw, *The Golden Web* (New York: Oxford University Press, Inc., 1968) pp. 221–24.

[13] "McCabe Testifies at TV Hearings," San Francisco *Chronicle,* April 15, 1970, p. 6.

[14] Karl J. Nestvold, "Local News Cooperation Between Co-owned Newspapers and Radio Stations," *Journal of Broadcasting,* Spring, 1965, pp. 145–52.

[15] Quoted in Nicholas Johnson, "The Media Barons and the Public Interest," *The Atlantic,* June, 1968, pp. 44–46.

[16] Gerard H. Borstel, "Ownership, Competition and Comment in 20 Small Dailies," *Journalism Quarterly,* Spring, 1956, pp. 220–21.

[17] Paul Block, Jr., "Facing Up to the 'Monopoly' Charge," *Nieman Reports,* July, 1955, p. 4.

[18] George H. Litwin and William H. Wroth, *The Effects of Common Ownership On Media Content and Influence,* prepared for the National Association of Broadcasters, July, 1969, pp. 5–13.

[19] Bryant Kearl, "Effects of Newspaper Competition on Press Service Resources," *Journalism Quarterly,* Winter, 1958, p. 64.

[20] Harvey J. Levin, "Economics in Cross Channel Affiliation of Media," *Journalism Quarterly,* Spring, 1954, pp. 167–74.

[21] Ronald L. Bottini, "Group Ownership of Newspapers," Freedom of Information Center Report No. 190, Columbia, Missouri, pp. 4–5.

[22] "The Collectors," *Time,* November 26, 1965, p. 53.

[23] Barnouw, *The Golden Web,* pp. 170–71.

[24] "Thank You, Mr. Smith," *Newsweek,* April 27, 1970, p. 94.

[25] Christopher Sterling, "Newspaper Ownership of Broadcast Stations, 1920–1968," *Journalism Quarterly,* Summer, 1969, pp. 231–33.

[26] Walter B. Kerr, "The Problem of Combinations," *Saturday Review,* October 12, 1968, p. 82.

[27] "Antitrust Consent Decree Closes Chattanooga Post," *Editor & Publisher,* February 28, 1970, p. 9.

[28] Department of Justice Memorandum of August 1, 1968, p. 6.

[29] Federal Communications Commission, Further Notice of Proposed Rulemaking, 70–311 46096, March 25, 1970, para. 19.

[30] John J. Flynn, "Antitrust and the Newspapers, A Comment on S.1312," *Vanderbilt Law Review,* 1968–69, p. 114.

SUGGESTED READINGS

BARNOUW, ERIK, *The Golden Web.* New York: Oxford University Press, Inc., 1968.

JOHNSON, NICHOLAS, "The Media Barons and the Public Interest," *The Atlantic,* June, 1968.

MINTZ, MORTON, and JERRY S. COHEN, *America, Inc.* New York: The Dial Press, 1971.

RUCKER, BRYCE, *The First Freedom.* Carbondale, Ill.: Southern Illinois University Press, 1968.

5 Advertiser Control

Most of the money in the mass media comes from advertising. If money means power, then advertisers must have enormous power to control the media. And they do. Surprisingly, they exercise that power only on occasion, and usually for business rather than political reasons. Advertiser control does have an effect on overall media performance, especially in broadcasting, but the effect is usually more subtle than most critics imagine.

Newspapermen are not easy to embarrass, but this time the Denver *Post* offices were filled with red faces. Someone had spirited an inter-office memorandum from the newspaper's files and published it. Addressed to the managing editor, the memo read as follows:

> Regarding "editorial" commitment on advertising schedules for Villa Italia Shopping Center. . . .
>
> I'm open to review on figures, based on Hatcher's [retail advertising manager] stated commitment of 25 per cent free space ratio to advertising, but believe this is reasonably accurate. . . .
>
> We have since Feb. 2 . . . published in various sections of the *Post* 826 column inches of copy and pictures directly related to Villa Italia, through March 7.
>
> Coverage beyond Monday (three days of grand openings . . . which we can't ignore and must cover with pix and stories) won't come close to

the total commitment, but probably would put it over the half-way mark. If we did a picture page each day of the opening . . . we would be providing another 546 column inches and thus be beginning to get close to the commitment figure. . . .[1]

Why is this memo so damning? All it reveals, after all, is that the *Post* had promised the shopping center one inch of free "news stories" for every four inches of paid advertising—and that the paper was having trouble finding the necessary news angles. Such a commercial arrangement is straight-forward, legal, and very common. It is also typical of the way advertisers influence the content of the mass media. The Villa Italia Shopping Center did not bribe the *Post* to support a particular political candidate, or even to fight for a zoning change it might have wanted. It simply purchased a little free space along with its ads. That seems harmless enough.

Nonetheless, the loss to Denver *Post* readers is clear. For one thing, they were falsely led to believe that the newspaper's editors considered Villa Italia an important news story. Moreover, in just over a month 826 column inches of genuinely important stories (roughly 30,000 words, the equivalent of a short novel) were eased out of the paper to make room for this disguised advertising.

WHO PAYS THE PIPER

Almost all American mass media are commercial. Some, like the book and motion picture industries, earn their revenue directly from the consumer. Most earn it—or at least the bulk of it—from advertising.

Newspapers: Sixty percent of the space in the average newspaper is devoted to ads, which account for three-quarters of the paper's income.

Magazines: A little over half of all magazine income is derived from ads, which fill just about half the available space.

Broadcasting: One quarter of the nation's air time is reserved for commercial messages, which pay the entire cost of the other three quarters.

In 1968 advertisers spent $5.24 billion on newspapers; $3.14 billion on television; $2.07 billion on magazines and business papers; and $1.15 billion on radio. Each year the figures are larger. It is obvious that none of these media could exist in the form we know them without advertising.

Imagine that you are the Vice-President for Advertising of Procter & Gamble, which in 1970 spent over $120,000,000 on television advertising alone, much of it for daytime serials. Imagine also that the script for one of your serials calls for an episode in which the heroine goes swimming in detergent-polluted water and suffers a psychotic breakdown because of the slime. You would almost certainly feel tempted to ask the producer to skip that part, and you might well feel cheated if he refused. As far as we know P&G does not monitor TV shows before broadcast. But then, as far as we know no soap opera has ever featured the dangers of detergent pollution. With $120,000,000 of Procter & Gamble's money at stake, no soap opera is likely to do so.

The advertiser pays the piper. If he wants to, he can more or less call the tune.

IDEOLOGY VERSUS BUSINESS

In the late 1950s, General Motors signed with CBS to sponsor a series of television documentaries. When it was learned that the first program would be entitled "The Vice-Presidency: Great American Lottery," the company guessed that the show might attack V.P. Richard Nixon. Nixon was a great favorite of many GM executives, so GM withdrew from the entire series.[2]

This anecdote has been told and retold many times over, and for good reason: It is rare. Advertisers almost never exercise their power, as GM apparently did, purely for ideological reasons. Their goal, after all, is to sell a product, and they pick their outlets on commercial grounds, not political ones. No matter how conservative a company may be, if it wants to sell to young people it will be pleased to have an ad in the middle of "Laugh-In." Wherever the market is, that is where the advertiser hopes to be. In a 1962 speech, conservative business editor Donald I. Rogers described (and criticized) this devotion to circulation:

> When businessmen place their advertising in Washington, where do they place it?
> They place 600,000 more lines per month with the liberal, welfare-state loving *Post* than in the *Star*, and the poor old conservative *News* runs a poor—a very poor—third. . . .
> The picture is no different here in New York. We find that the greatest amount of advertising placed by businessmen goes into the liberal *Times*. . . .
> The influential conservative New York papers, the *Herald Tribune* and the *World Telegram & Sun*, get very sparse pickings indeed from the American business community which they support so effectively in their editorial policies.[3]

Rogers considered the ideological neutrality of advertisers short-sighted. Perhaps it is, but it is also very fortunate for the democratic

ADVERTISER BOYCOTT

William F. Schanen Jr. is publisher of three weekly newspapers in suburban Ozaukee County, Wisconsin. At least he was when this sentence was written. By the time it is published, Schanen may well have lost all three papers.

In addition to his newspapers, Schanen does job-lot printing for a number of smaller publications. These include conservative political, religious, and business newsletters—and *Kaleidoscope*, an underground newspaper serving Milwaukee's "hippie" community. *Kaleidoscope* is not very popular in Ozaukee County, nor does Schanen himself like it—but he believes that "no printer should deny his facility to any . . . legal use."

Benjamin Grob, a local machine-tool manufacturer, disagrees. In June, 1969, Grob sent a letter to 500 influential businessmen, charging that Schanen "prints obscene literature for profit." Grob continued: "I will not buy space in his newspapers, and I will not buy from anyone who advertises in his newspapers. Ladies and gentlemen, I am looking for company."

Almost immediately, Schanen's gross advertising returns plummeted from $4,000 a week to $700—a loss of $165,000 a year. Support for Schanen has come from many sources—the American Civil Liberties Union, the Milwaukee *Journal*, the University of Wisconsin journalism school, and hundreds of sympathizers around the country. The National Newspaper Association established a special fund to buy full-page ads in Schanen's newspapers. Despite this help, the papers are still published at a loss, and Schanen is on the verge of folding.[4]

The boycott is the most potent form of advertiser control—as well as the rarest. Ozaukee businessmen had no complaints about the selling power of Schanen's three newspapers. They didn't even object to the content of the papers. But they shared an ideological disapproval of a fourth paper, *Kaleidoscope*, which Schanen printed to earn some extra money on the side. On the strength of that disapproval, they may well force a reputable "establishment" publisher to fold.

---

process. Because of this neutrality, a publisher or broadcaster who attacks the business establishment will be kept in business *by* the business establishment so long as he can attract an audience. In the early 1940s, Marshall Field owned two Chicago businesses: a giant department store and a liberal newspaper, the *Sun*. While the *Sun* battled the conservative *Tribune* for the morning market, the department store continued to advertise in the *Tribune*—for business reasons. A decade later the Milwaukee *Journal* led the nation in advertising linage, despite its opposition to Red-baiting Joseph McCarthy and its support for Democrat Adlai Stevenson. Advertisers agreed that the *Journal* was "anti-business," but

Hearst's conservative Milwaukee *Sentinel* was a loser in the circulation race—and so the ads stayed with the *Journal.*[5]

Every underground newspaper today, from the Berkeley *Barb* to the (N.Y.) *East Village Other,* depends for its survival on advertisements from the business establishment, especially record and film companies. The ideological tension between the underground paper and the large corporation is obvious. Even open hatred, apparently, does not often prevent businessmen from putting their ads where they will help sales the most.

PATTERNS OF ADVERTISER CONTROL

The fact that most advertisers are ideologically neutral does not mean that they ignore the content of the programs they sponsor or the publications they appear in. Some companies, of course, are satisfied to pay for their ads and let it go at that. But many like to have at least a little say over what comes before and after.

There are four major types of advertiser control over the content of the mass media:

1. The ads themselves.
2. Connecting the product to nonadvertising content.
3. Making the company and product look good, never bad.
4. Avoiding controversy at all costs.

We will discuss each of these in turn.

1. The Ads Themselves. It may be obvious, but it is worth emphasizing that roughly half the content of the mass media is written directly by advertisers—the ads. The average American adult is exposed to well over a hundred separate advertising messages each day. Many find their way into the language as symbols of our culture—"The Pepsi Generation," "The Dodge Rebellion," "Progress Is Our Most Important Product." Besides selling goods, these ads undoubtedly have a cumulative effect on American society. Philosopher Erich Fromm has defined Western Man as *Homo consumens*—Man the Consumer. If the description fits, the institution to blame is advertising.

Legally, a publisher or broadcaster is free to reject most kinds of ads if he wishes, but as a practical matter only the most egregiously dishonest or offensive specimens are ever turned away. It is a strange paradox that advertisers have more power over the content of the media than the media have over the ads.

2. Connecting the Product to Non-advertising Content. The clearest example of the blurred line between advertising and non-advertising is the common newspaper custom of trading free "news stories" for paid ads, as in the Denver *Post* case already discussed. A parallel practice in the magazine world is the disguising of advertisements as editorial copy. The November, 1967, issue of the *Reader's Digest,* for instance, contained a special section advocating the use of brand-name drugs instead of the cheaper generic versions. The whole section was laid out to look like standard *Digest* fare. Only a small box at the end informed readers that it was paid for by the Pharmaceutical Manufacturers Association. Are readers confused by such ads? Evidently advertisers think so, for they pay dearly for the privilege of running them.

Nearly every newspaper has a department or two whose main purpose is to keep advertisers happy by giving them something "appropriate" to appear next to. Frequent offenders include the real estate section, entertainment page, church page, and travel and dining pages. There is nothing evil about a newspaper deciding to run a weekly ski page. But if the only function of the page is to give skiing advertisers a place to locate—and if the page disappears when the ads fall off—then the editor's news judgment has been replaced by the business manager's. In his book *The Fading American Newspaper,* Carl Lindstrom calls these sorts of articles "revenue-related reading matter."[6] Many newspaper executives use another term: BOMs, or Business Office Musts. The reader, of course, pays the price—a steady diet of pap and puffery.

In broadcasting, the best way to connect paid and unpaid content is to hire the performer to do his own ads. It was Dinah Shore herself who sang, at the end of every show, "See the U.S.A. in your Chevrolet." Between monologues and interviews, Johnny Carson tells millions of viewers what to buy.

Almost from the beginning, network television newscasters refused to do commercials, believing that it was unfair and misleading to slide from a review of the day's action in Vietnam to a review of the reasons for taking Excedrin. Many local TV newsmen are not so conscientious, and nearly all radio announcers are willing to alternate between news and commercials. Even on network TV news, some combination is permitted. NBC's coverage of the 1964 political conventions, for example, was sponsored by Gulf Oil. At the company's request, the luminous orange Gulf disc was installed behind every commentator's desk. Blurring the line between news and advertising is intended to strengthen the credibility of the ads. It may also lessen the credibility of the news.

3. Making the Company and Product Look Good, Never Bad. Advertisers go to a great deal of trouble to look good in their ads; wherever possible, they would like to look good between ads as well. It is often possible. CBS newsman Alexander Kendrick recalls the case of a cigarette sponsor that "dictated that on none of its entertainment programs, whether drama or studio panel game, could any actor or other participant smoke a pipe or cigar, or chew tobacco, or even chew gum that might be mistaken for tobacco. Only cigarettes could be smoked, and only king-sized, but no program could show untidy ashtrays, filled with cigarette butts. . . ."[7]

Though cigarettes are no longer advertised on television, other companies have similar policies. If Bufferin sponsors a television drama, the hero is unlikely to take a plain aspirin for his headache. If Jello sponsors a family comedy, the desserts served on the show will rarely be layer cakes. If TWA sponsors a spy story, the CIA man will not fly the friendly skies of United—though the Communist agent might. Needless to say, neither plane will crash.

When a plane does crash, newspapers and news broadcasts must report it, and they even mention the name of the airline (though there was a time when they didn't). But if an airline ad is scheduled next to the news show, it is quietly moved to another spot. And even the newspapers are unlikely to report which airlines have the worst crash records.

The following additional newspaper practices are designed to preserve the "good image"—and therefore the goodwill—of advertisers and potential advertisers:

- When someone dies or commits suicide in a downtown hotel, the name of the hotel is rarely mentioned.
- When a big advertiser gets married, the story is almost certain to receive big play on the society page; when he gets divorced the story is often ignored—no matter how juicy.
- The names of shoplifters and embezzlers are printed, but whenever possible the names of the stores and businesses they stole from are not.
- Government suits against advertisers, especially those that involve consumer protection, are sometimes killed or quietly buried.

When an entertainment show is "rigged" to make an advertiser look good or to keep him from looking bad, the problem is a petty one. When news is similarly affected, the danger to democracy is great.

4. Avoiding Controversy at All Costs. A major advertiser of breakfast foods once sent the following memo to the scriptwriters of the television series it sponsored:

> In general, the moral code of the characters in our dramas will be more or less synonymous with the moral code of the bulk of the American middle class, as it is commonly understood. There will be no material that will give offense, either directly or by inference, to any organized minority group, lodge or other organizations, institutions, residents of any state or section of the country, or a commercial organization of any sort.

. . . We will treat mention of the Civil War carefully, mindful of the sensitiveness of the South on this subject. . . . There will be no material for or against sharply drawn national or regional controversial issues. . . . There will be no material on any of our programs which could in any way further the concept of business as cold, ruthless and lacking in all sentiment or spiritual motivation.[8]

The goal of this broad coat of whitewash is to give advertisers an antiseptic environment in which to peddle their goods—an environment that nobody could possibly find offensive. This is especially important on television, which caters to an audience of millions.

In a celebrated incident in 1969, CBS was quick to edit out of the Merv Griffin talk show an appeal by actress Elke Sommer for postcards and letters to be sent to Mrs. Martin Luther King calling for world peace. Comedienne Carol Burnett made a similar appeal on the Christmas Day show and it, too, was censored. Peace, apparently, is a controversial issue. In his book *Television and The News*, critic Harry Skornia of the University of Illinois, Chicago Circle, lists these noteworthy subjects which he believes the broadcast media have ignored over the years in deference to advertisers: poverty in America; public utilities bilking the public; the harmful effects of liquor, tobacco, and coffee; air and water pollution; and the problems of labor in labor-management disputes.[9]

The aversion of advertisers to controversy is largely responsible for the homogenized quality of most television entertainment. More important, it is a factor in the consistent avoidance by the news media of many problems of national importance.

THREATS, BRIBES, AND UNDERSTANDINGS

When the average citizen thinks of advertiser influence, two images are likely to come to mind: the sumptuous party at which newsmen are wined and dined into the "right" attitude, and the irate businessman who storms into an editor's office and threatens to withdraw all advertising unless. . . . Both images—the bribe and the threat—have some truth to them. There isn't an editor, reporter, or broadcaster of experience who hasn't experienced both at one time or another. But such tactics are too gauche, and so they tend to fail as often as not. In the mid-1950s, the *Wall Street Journal* managed to get the details on the new General Motors cars before the information was officially released. GM quickly cancelled $11,000 worth of advertising in retribution. The *Journal* was not intimidated, and published the story anyhow.[10]

More recently, St. Louis Cardinal owner Gussie Busch fired his radio commentator Harry Caray. The word went out that any station that hired Caray would not only get no ads from Busch's Budweiser beer, but also no business from the two largest advertising agencies in town. Months later Caray was back on the air in St. Louis—sponsored by Schlitz.

More subtle techniques are more effective, and always have been. During the oil pipeline wars of the 1890s, the Ohio press was highly critical of John D. Rockefeller's Standard Oil Company. The boss assigned his trusted "fixer," Dan O'Day, to sweeten the sour press. O'Day did not threaten anybody, nor did he offer any outright bribes. Instead, he planned a heavy advertising campaign for Mica Axle Grease, a very minor Standard product. Huge ads were purchased on a regular basis in every Ohio newspaper. Editors got the point: Don't bite the hand that feeds. After a year of receiving monthly checks from the axle grease subsidiary, most had quit knocking John D. and the parent corporation. Mica, by the way, became a top seller.[11]

Even this indirect sort of bribe is not often necessary. Over the years, editors have come to know what advertisers expect, and they supply it without questioning. Nobody has to tell the copy editor of a newspaper to cut the name of the car out of that traffic accident article. He understands without being told that including the name might embarrass the manufacturer. He understands that embarrassing the manufacturer would be in "bad taste" for the newspaper. He understands that that just isn't the sort of thing one business (publishing) does to another business (automotive). He doesn't have to be threatened or bribed; such tactics would only offend and bewilder him.

Can you call this advertiser control? Only in the sense that in the back of every editor's mind is the need to keep advertisers happy. The local auto dealer, after all, does not even know that the newspaper copy editor is "censoring" the name of the car. Should the name slip in, he would probably take no action whatever; at worst he might mention the matter to his friend the managing editor at the country club or the next Chamber of Commerce meeting. Certainly he would be most unlikely to threaten to withdraw his ads. He needs the newspaper at least as much as the newspaper needs him. The important point is that this conflict of wills seldom takes place. The copy editor knows his job, and so the name of the car rarely gets into the traffic accident report.

BROADCASTING: A SPECIAL CASE

When radio was invented at the turn of the century, few thought it would ever be a profit-making medium, and fewer still expected it to earn its profit from advertising. Events reversed expectations:

1919:   Dr. Frank Conrad begins the first regular entertainment broadcast, offering Pittsburgh crystal set owners a few hours of music each week.

1920:   Westinghouse obtains the first commercial radio license, KDKA, also in Pittsburgh.
1921:   Thirty commercial stations are in operation throughout the country.
1922:   WEAF in New York sells the first radio advertisement.
1923:   The Eveready Battery Company produces its own radio program, The Eveready Hour, on WEAF.
1924:   A "network" hook-up is arranged to broadcast The Eveready Hour on several stations at the same time.

By 1927, only eight years after the Conrad broadcast, The Eveready Hour was a part of a nation-wide NBC radio network. It offered a varied diet of concert music, dance music, and drama. Programs were prepared jointly by the station, the company, and its advertising agency. They were submitted to the sponsor three weeks before air time, and if declared unsatisfactory they were revised or abandoned.

There were objections voiced to the delivery of the radio medium into the hands of the advertisers—but they were quickly outshouted by soaring profit curves. Throughout the 1930s and 1940s, advertisers produced almost every radio program broadcast. The job of the station was merely to sell the time and man the transmitter; the sponsor and its ad agency handled everything else. When commercial television was introduced in the late forties, this pattern of advertiser control and advertiser production was accepted from the very start.

By the late 1950s, the cost of even a single prime-time network television show had grown too big for all but the largest advertisers to afford. When the "quiz show scandals" at the end of the decade brought public pressure on the networks to accept responsibility for programming, broadcasters were only too happy to comply. It was good business as well as good politics. ABC set the trend in encouraging sponsors to scatter their ads among several different programs; NBC and CBS soon followed suit. By 1962 it was rare for a sponsor to produce its own show. Some continued to sponsor particular network-produced programs, while most settled for the ABC "scatter plan" system. This is still the pattern in broadcasting today.

Though the networks took over programming control from advertisers in the early sixties, they did nothing to alter the fundamental nature of the programs. Advertisers no longer write their own shows, but they still decide where to put their ads. A show without advertiser appeal is unlikely to be produced, unlikelier to be broadcast, and unlikeliest to be renewed for a second season.

To most Americans this sounds like a truism, an inevitable result of the free-market system. It isn't. Even within the context of commercial broadcasting, advertisers need not be all-powerful. In England, for example, sponsors are not permitted to choose where in the day's program

THE QUIZ SHOW SCANDALS

On June 7, 1955, emcee Hal March posed before the world's first "isolation booth" and announced to a massive CBS network audience: "This is The $64,000 Question." The era of big-money TV quizzes had begun. NBC countered with "Twenty-One," and within a year six similar programs were on the air.

"The $64,000 Question" was the invention of Revlon, Inc., a cosmetics firm, with some assistance from Revlon's ad agency, a few independent producers, and CBS. It was a package product: Revlon and its agency supervised the content of the show as well as the commercials, and paid CBS $80,000 for each half hour of network time. CBS had some say in how the show was run, but not much. The other quiz programs were similarly organized.

Syndicated columnist Steve Scheuer was the first to suggest that the shows were frauds, fixed to allow certain participants to win. Soon a former contestant on NBC's "Twenty-One" told a Congressional subcommittee that he had been forced to lose to Charles Van Doren.

1959 was a year of television soul-searching. Van Doren admitted that he had been fed the questions and answers for his $129,000 streak on "Twenty-One." The packagers of "The $64,000 Challenge," meanwhile, revealed that Revlon executives had personally decided which contestants to bump and which to keep. Both networks claimed to know nothing, fixing the blame on the sponsors, ad agencies, and producers. In November, 1959, CBS President Frank Stanton told a House subcommittee:

> I want to say here and now that I was completely unaware . . . of any irregularity in the quiz shows on our network. When gossip about quiz shows in general came to my attention, I was assured by our television network people that these shows were completely above criticism of this kind. . . . This has been a bitter pill for us to swallow. . . . We propose to be more certain . . . that it is we and we alone who decide not only what is to appear on the CBS Television Network but how it is to appear.[12]

Stanton kept his promise, as did the other two networks. Broadcasters resumed control of programming content, and the scandals since have been few and far between.

---

schedule their advertising spots will be placed. They simply purchase so many minutes of television time, and the station decides which minutes to put where. British advertisers are free to utilize television or not as they like. But they cannot pick their program, and therefore cannot influence programming to any great extent.

American television is designed to attract advertising, and advertising is designed to influence the largest possible audience. It follows that the great majority of TV programming must be aimed at the "mass market," at the lowest common denominator of public viewing tastes. The potential audience for a classical opera may be, say, one million viewers. The potential audience for a soap opera in the same time slot may be ten million. Naturally television will choose the soap opera, not the classical opera, to broadcast. The classical opera will not even be allotted one-tenth as much broadcast time as the soap opera (though it has one-tenth the potential audience)—for what advertiser would be willing to sponsor such a minority-interest program?

Even when advertisers can be found for small-audience shows, television stations are reluctant to broadcast them. A single "highbrow" program can force millions of viewers to switch to another channel; once switched, they may stay there for hours or even days. The ratings on adjacent shows are therefore lowered. Other advertisers begin to complain, and station profits begin to drop.

Exactly this happened to the Firestone Hour in the early 1960s. Sponsored by the Firestone Tire & Rubber Company, the classical music program had a consistently low rating. Firestone did not mind; it wanted an "elite" audience for its ads. But adjacent mass-market programs were suffering. After moving the show around a few times in an effort to reduce the adjacency problem, the network finally gave up and refused to continue the show. Companies like Bell Telephone and Xerox, which like to sponsor documentaries and cultural programs, have had similar difficulties finding a time slot.

More recently, United Press International moved the following news item: "Armstrong Cork Co., whose Circle Theater was one of television's best known dramatic shows, said . . . it has dropped video advertising because the networks offer only childish programming."[13] Apparently Armstrong was unable to find a network willing to produce another Circle Theater.

Advertising revenue is at the heart of the debate over the quality of television programming. In the 1959–60 season NBC and CBS tried an experiment, offering several "high quality" music and drama shows. ABC, financially weakest of the three networks, refused to go along. Instead, it chose that season to introduce its gory detective series "The Untouchables," plus ten westerns a week. Ratings were excellent and ABC closed the gap on its older rivals. The next season, NBC and CBS followed the ABC lead, with detective and western series galore. The experiment was over.

Comments critic Robert Eck: "In the audience delivery business, you do not have the luxury of setting either your standards or those of your audience. Instead, they are set for you by the relative success of your competitors."[14] This is another way of saying what NBC President

Robert Kintner answered in response to the question "Who is responsible for what appears on network cameras?": "The ultimate responsibility is ours," Kintner replied, "but the ultimate power has to be the sponsor's, because without him you couldn't afford to run a network."[15]

NOTES

[1] "News for Advertisers: A Denver Case," *Columbia Journalism Review,* Summer, 1966, p. 10.

[2] William L. Rivers and Wilbur Schramm, *Responsibility in Mass Communication,* rev. ed. (New York: Harper & Row, 1969), p. 107.

[3] Donald I. Rogers, "Businessmen: Don't Subsidize Your Enemies," *Human Events,* August 11, 1962, pp. 599–600.

[4] Bernice Buresh, "Boycott Turns on Wisconsin Publisher," *Chicago Journalism, Review,* September, 1969, pp. 7–11.

[5] Vern E. Edwards, Jr., *Journalism in a Free Society* (Dubuque, Ia.: William C. Brown Company, 1970), p. 176.

[6] Carl E. Lindstrom, *The Fading American Newspaper* (Gloucester, Mass.: Peter Smith, 1964).

[7] Alexander Kendrick, *Prime Time* (Boston: Little, Brown & Co., 1969), p. 449.

[8] Dallas Smyth, "Five Myths of Consumership," *The Nation,* January 20, 1969, p. 83.

[9] Harry Skornia, *Television and the News* (Palo Alto, Calif.: Pacific Books, 1968), pp. 87–90.

[10] Rivers and Schramm, *Responsibility,* pp. 108–9.

[11] Will Irwin, "Our Kind of People," *Collier's,* June 17, 1911, pp. 17–18.

[12] Fred W. Friendly, *Due to Circumstances Beyond Our Control . . .* (New York: Random House, Inc., 1967), pp. 101–2.

[13] United Press International, April 8, 1970.

[14] Robert Eck, "The Real Masters of Television," *Harper's,* March, 1967, p. 49.

[15] "The Tarnished Image," *Time,* November 16, 1959, pp. 72–80.

SUGGESTED READINGS

Eck, Robert, "The Real Masters of Television," *Harper's,* March, 1967.

Skornia, Harry, *Television and the News.* Palo Alto, Calif.: Pacific Books, 1968.

6   Source Control

Only a small percentage of the news covered by the mass media comes from on-the-scene reporting. The vast majority must be obtained from news sources—often through interviews, even more often through mimeographed press releases and the like. Sources are seldom unbiased. In one way or another they usually try to control the form and content of the news they offer. Such news management on the part of both governmental and private sources has a tremendous effect on the nature of the news reaching the public.

Throughout his eight years in the White House, President Dwight Eisenhower depended heavily on his press secretary, James Hagerty. One of Hagerty's main jobs was covering up for his boss's longish vacations. *Time* magazine described the process:

> Hagerty struggled valiantly and, to a point, successfully in stressing work over play. . . . He took with him on trips briefcases full of executive orders, appointments, etc., and parceled them out daily to make news under the Augusta or Gettysburg dateline. He encouraged feature stories on the Army Signal Corps' elaborate setup to keep Ike in close touch with Washington. . . . He did anything and everything, in short, to keep the subjects of golf and fishing far down in the daily stories about the President.[1]

If Hagerty had been working for General Motors, say, instead of Eisenhower, his job would presumably have been a little different. In place of diligence, he would have stressed the economic health of the company and the beauty of its new models. In place of vacations, he would have obscured price hikes and auto safety complaints.

But wherever he works, the purpose and technique of a press secretary or public-relations man are the same. The purpose: to protect and advance the good image of his employer. The technique: news management.

In one form or another, news management is probably as old as news. But conscious, full-time, *professional* news management is a relatively recent invention. The first corporate press agent was hired in the 1880s. The first presidential press secretary was hired twenty years later (by Theodore Roosevelt). Today there are more than 100,000 public-relations men working for private companies, plus tens of thousands more in government. The federal government now spends more than $400,000,000 a year on public relations and public information. The executive branch alone spends more on publicity and news than the entire combined budgets of the legislative and judicial branches. All together, the cost of federal government P.R. is more than double the total news-gathering expenses of AP and UPI, the three television networks, and the ten largest American newspapers.[2] News sources, in short, pay more to manage the news than the media pay to collect it.

PRESS RELEASES

By far the most important vehicle for news management is the press release. Preparing such releases and distributing them to the media is the main job of nearly every public-relations man.

Releases are ground out by the bushel. In a single ten-day period, one small country newspaper in Vermont received 149 handouts from 68 different sources, totaling to 950 pages or nearly a quarter of a million words—more than the length of this book. The list included 80 releases from businesses; 16 from philanthropic organizations; 14 from government; 6 from lobbies and pressure groups; 29 from educational institutions; and 4 from political parties.[3] That's for a *small* newspaper. The average metropolitan daily receives well above a hundred releases a day; the average big-city broadcast station gets at least sixty.

Most releases—say around three-fifths—are thrown away. The bulk of the rest are either used as is or rewritten and condensed in the office, usually the latter. Only a few releases (all the staff has time for) are actually investigated by reporters.

Though most releases are never used, those that are account for an incredible share of the average news hole. In many newspapers more than half the articles printed started as press releases. Some departments are almost entirely dependent on handouts—finance, travel, etc. Even the political reporter has time to cover only the most important stories himself; for much of the day-to-day news of local government he counts on the City Hall mimeograph machine. The backbone of every news beat is the press release.

However important releases may be in reporting local news, they are far more vital on the state, national, and international levels. A Washington correspondent covering the White House spends little of his time chatting with the President, or even the President's aides. Most of his effort is devoted to reading and rewriting White House releases. And a reporter covering the "minor" executive departments has even less time for in-person digging and interviewing. Instead, he spends a few hours each morning picking up the day's handouts from the various agencies and offices within his assigned department. The rest of the day he sorts through the stack—throwing out most, rewriting many, following up on maybe one or two.

As for Congress, releases dominate news coverage there too, as this item from the Washington *Post* shows:

> A freshman Senator outslicked his veteran colleagues to pick off the easiest publicity plum available last week. He was Clifford P. Case (R-N.J.), whose reaction comment to the President's decision [to veto the Natural Gas Bill] was the first to hit the Senate press gallery. His prize was a prominent play in the afternoon newspapers.
>
> Behind his speed was the quick thinking and faster legs of Sam Zagoria, Case's administrative assistant. . . .
>
> Zagoria had run off several copies of the Senator's "isn't it grand" statement early Wednesday morning. He then parked himself by the Associated Press teletype in the Senate lobby. When the flash came through, he hightailed it back to the press gallery, one floor above, where eager reporters were waiting to write reaction accounts. Zagoria beat a runner for Sen. William A. Purtell (R-Conn.) by one minute flat.[4]

Governments (as well as private organizations) use press releases to announce new policies and procedures, to publicize plans and accomplishments, to reveal facts and research findings, etc. They may also use releases to influence the course of events. The Defense Department, for example, might issue a release on the "tight nuclear race" between the U.S. and the Soviet Union just as the State Department is planning strategy for arms limitation talks. It seems fair to surmise that at least one purpose of the release is to force the negotiators to adopt a tougher stand.

The danger of press releases is obvious—they put the initial decision as to what is and is not newsworthy in the hands of the source instead

LEAKS AND TRIAL BALLOONS

When a top public official wants to try out a new policy without committing himself to it, he may release the proposal to the press in secret. In late 1956, for example, the Eisenhower administration began formulating a new policy toward the Middle East. Secretary of State John Foster Dulles invited a select group of Washington correspondents to his home and *leaked* to these reporters the nature of the change. The story was published, on Dulles's instructions, with the source identified only as a high, unnamed State Department official. This was the *trial balloon*. Dulles now waited to see how the public, other government officials, and foreign governments reacted to the proposal. The response was favorable, so Dulles formally announced the new "Eisenhower Doctrine" for the Middle East. If the feedback had been discouraging, Dulles was free to change the plan or to disavow it entirely.

The leak and the trial balloon are accepted tactics of diplomacy, but they are subject to abuses. A politician can punish critical reporters by leaking exclusive stories to those who are not so critical. Alternatively, he can force a reporter to write a one-sided article by trading exclusive information for the reporter's promise not to interview anyone else on the subject. Both practices are common in Washington today.

At best, leaks and trial balloons are invidious. They enable a government official to say anonymously what he does not dare to say on the record. Beyond doubt they are a useful tool of diplomacy, and beyond doubt they are here to stay. But they may mislead the public. Conscientious reporters participate in them reluctantly and cautiously.

---

of the reporter or editor. Even when the media follow up a release on their own, the questions they ask and those they forget to ask are likely to be determined by what's in the release. And most releases are *not* followed up. The blatant propaganda may be edited out, but the substance is printed—and it is substance that the source, not the reporter, has selected. It is substance designed to help build the image and advance the aims of its source. It is, in short, public relations. But it passes for news.

OTHER TECHNIQUES

Press releases are the most useful weapon in the arsenal of news management, but they are by no means the only one. There are four additional techniques of some importance:

1. Canned news and editorials
2. Pseudoevents
3. Junkets and favors
4. Direct access

We will discuss each in turn.

1. Canned News and Editorials.   In the early 1960s, Rafael Trujillo, dictator of the Dominican Republic, hired a New York press agent named Harry Klemfuss to help build pro-Trujillo sentiment in this country. Klemfuss, in turn, hired the U.S. Press Association, Inc., a company specializing in canned news and editorials.   For a fee of only $125, the company mailed the following "news item" to 1,300 dailies and weeklies throughout the country: "Today the Dominican Republic . . . is a bulwark of strength against Communism and has been widely cited as one of the cleanest, healthiest, happiest countries on the globe.   Guiding spirit of this fabulous transformation is Generalissimo Trujillo who worked tirelessly . . . ."[5]   It is not known how many papers actually carried the story, but Klemfuss and Trujillo considered their money well spent.

Canned articles and editorials are like releases, except that they are carefully designed to be used without editing—hence the term "canned." Many come in the form of mats or plates to be inserted right into the paper; all are in standard newspaper style.   Most metropolitan dailies refuse to use canned material.   But smaller papers may be desperate for content, and the temptation of a well-written, well-researched, *free* article or editorial is often too great to resist.

For corporations and political pressure groups, canned material offers an opportunity to publish anonymous propaganda.   Among the clients of the U.S. Press Association are the American Cotton Manufacturers Institute, the American Legion, the Bourbon Institute, and the Right to Work Committee.   The American Medical Association and the National Association of Manufacturers regularly employ similar services.   Typically, a canned article or editorial will be picked up by roughly 200 newspapers. Ben Bagdikian calculates that the cost of placing advertisements in all 200 papers would run at least ten times as much—and the canned stuff is more effective than ads.[6]

The most successful canned articles are fillers and light features, which many editors slip into their papers without even noticing.   The North American Precis Syndicate, for example, has done very well with stories like "Candy Through the Ages" (sponsored by the candy industry), "How to Keep Your Dog in Condition" (plugging the use of veterinarians), and "How to Be a Two-Faced Woman" (promoting eye glasses).[7]

2. Pseudoevents.   The cognac industry of France wanted to introduce the product to the American market with a splash, so in the late

1950s it hired a P.R. man named Bill Kaduson. On President Eisenhower's 67th birthday in 1957, Kaduson offered the President several bottles of 67-year-old cognac as a gift. He insured the bottles for $10,000, then took them to the city room of the Washington *Daily News* for photos. The cognac was poured into a special keg and conveyed to the White House by two uniformed guards, where secret service agents accepted the gift on behalf of Eisenhower. The stunt received newspaper headlines throughout the country.

Kaduson also arranged for French Premier Pierre Mendes-France to be photographed drinking cognac when he visited the United States in 1954. He got a French chef onto the Jack Paar television show to create on camera the world's biggest crepe suzette, sprinkled with a gallon of cognac. Between 1951 and 1957 cognac sales in the U.S. increased from 150,000 to 400,000 cases a year. Bill Kaduson claimed much of the credit.[8]

The interesting thing about Kaduson's antics is that they took place solely to gain the attention of the mass media. In Daniel Boorstin's terms, they were not real events at all, but rather "pseudoevents," performed in order to be reported.[9] The media are easily manipulated through pseudoevents. By their very nature they feel compelled to cover conventions, demonstrations, dedications, press conferences, stunts, and the like. Anyone who desires news coverage is therefore wise to arrange a convention, a demonstration, a dedication, a press conference, or—like Kaduson and his cognac—a stunt.

The Congressional committee hearing is a perfect example of a government-sponsored pseudoevent. Some hearings, of course, aim at obtaining information on proposed legislation. But many have a different goal—to provide publicity for the committee, its members, and its legislative goals. Perhaps the most famous Congressional hearing in recent history was held by the Senate Crime Investigating Committee under Estes Kefauver in 1951. The Kefauver hearings were the first ever to be televised, and they catapulted Kefauver to national fame. The chief

---

THE DANGERS OF HAIR

The power of a good public relations expert is incalculable. Throughout the 1920s, P.R. man Edward L. Bernays promoted the idea that loose or long hair is a health and safety hazard in restaurants, manufacturing plants, and such. As a result, many states passed laws requiring waitresses and female factory workers to wear hair nets at all times. Bernays was working for the Venida hair net people.

"I HAVE HERE IN MY HAND. . . ."

Perhaps the greatest news manager of them all was Senator Joseph Mc-Carthy, the Red-baiting Wisconsin Republican.   He began as soon as he reached Washington in 1948, treating newsmen to Wisconsin cheese and making himself available night and day for comment on any subject.

McCarthy was a master of the pseudoevent.   Often he would call a morning press conference solely to announce an afternoon press conference, thus earning headlines in both editions.   His lists of Communists in government service were released only minutes before newspaper deadlines.   This insured that he could not be questioned closely, and also made it impossible for the accused to reply in the same edition as they were charged.   McCarthy made his most damaging allegations from the Senate floor, where he was protected by law from libel suits.   He seldom permitted reporters to examine the "documentary evidence" that he habitually carried in his briefcase and frequently waved in his hand.

By 1952, most of the Washington press corps already knew that Mc-Carthy's claims were often fraudulent and always self-serving.   Yet they continued to accord him headlines, day after day.   They were caught in the mechanics of the pseudoevent: When a famous Senator accuses someone of Communism it's news—even if the charge is without foundation.

Then came the televised Army-McCarthy hearings of 1954.   This time the news management was in the Army's hands, and McCarthy could do nothing to halt the pitiless publicity that brought his career in demagoguery to a quick end.

---

witness was Frank Costello, an over-the-hill ex-con, with no real power and little inside information.   Kefauver knew that Costello's testimony would have great public impact on TV, despite its limited value as a source of new knowledge.   And he was right.[10]

Television is uniquely susceptible to manipulation by means of pseudoevents.   The chief advantage of TV over the other media is its ability to reproduce talking pictures.   Quite naturally, TV news directors strive constantly to make use of this ability, to come up with effective films or videotapes.   But most television news departments are severely understaffed.   They can seldom afford to let a reporter-cameraman team spend a day or two digging into a story the hard way.   It is much, much easier to send the team to cover a ready-made story—a press conference, say, or a demonstration.

A news source who arranges for easy-to-shoot effective footage will always get better coverage from television than a source who fails to do so.

3. Junkets and Favors.   From the November 20, 1954, issue of *Editor & Publisher* comes the following article:

> Schenley Distributors, Inc., [threw a party] for the first American importation of Canadian OFS, Original Fine Canadian. It seems that the first shipment was due in New York aboard the SS President Monroe. So a special car on a New Haven Railroad train was arranged to take the press representatives from New York to Boston . . . [followed by] an overnight trip on the Monroe to New York. The letter of invitation said: "I know you will thoroughly enjoy it, for we are prepared with sumptuous cuisine and delightful entertainment." An *E&P* staffer noted: "And with a boat load of whiskey, it sounds like a perfect lost weekend."[11]

The goal of a press junket like this is, of course, to put reporters in a good mood, thus insuring favorable news coverage. Apparently it works, or junkets wouldn't be the tradition they are. Most large corporations and many small ones organize junkets from time to time. So do some philanthropic groups, and others interested in keeping reporters happy. Even the federal government has been known to take newsmen on tours of foreign military installations and the like.

News sources generally do their best to make life pleasant for journalists. Customary favors run the gamut from free movie tickets for reviewers to cash "contests" for articles, from banquet invitations to outright bribes. Some of these practices are obnoxious and some are not, but all have the same purpose—to influence the news in the source's favor.

4. Direct Access.   Where possible, news sources generally prefer to have their say directly to the public, without "interference" from reporters and editors. Paid advertising is the most obvious example of direct access, but it has disadvantages—it costs money, it gets low readership, and it is distrusted. Advertising may be the best that private companies can manage, but the government can do better.

Before the development of radio, a public official had only two means of reaching the public. He could speak personally with small groups, either in his office or publicly. Or he could direct his efforts to the reporter as middleman and work through the mass-circulation newspapers.

Radio opened up a third method. It permitted the politician to address a mass public directly, with no reporter to interpret his words. President Franklin Roosevelt was the first to make use of this medium; his "Fireside Chats" told millions of listeners how he planned to halt the Depression of the 1930s. Roosevelt had everything he needed to make effective use of radio—a warm voice, an easy manner, and the right to demand free air time whenever he wanted it. In theory, perhaps, a broadcaster can turn the President down, but no broadcaster ever has.

Television, like radio, offers direct access to the public. It is also a far more powerful, ubiquitous, and believable medium. This raises a problem, aptly expressed by New York *Times* editor James Reston: "Thoughtful observers have wondered, ever since the inception of nationwide television, what would happen if a determined President, who had both the will and the ability to use the networks effectively, really set out to exploit television for his political advantage."[12]

Reston believes that the first American President to make this effort was Richard Nixon. Nixon requested air time far more frequently than any of his predecessors. In January of 1970 he became the first Chief Executive ever to take to the air simply to explain his reasons for vetoing a bill (an appropriation for the Department of Health, Education, and Welfare). Three months later he was on television twice within a ten-day period, discussing the war in Southeast Asia.

There are two dangers here. First, the President's opponents cannot so readily obtain free air time for rebuttal. Only after sharp controversy did the networks offer some time to critics of the war, and critics of the H.E.W. veto were not able to talk back. Perhaps more important, people automatically tend to support the President in times of crisis—and a direct television address gives the impression of crisis. Pollster George Gallup found increased public approval of the President after every major TV speech. "The public traditionally rallies around the President immediately following a major foreign policy decision," writes Gallup.[13] The

---

GOVERNMENT AS PUBLISHER

The Government Printing Office was authorized by Congress in 1860. Today it sells 67 million publications a year. The G.P.O. currently has about 25,000 titles in stock, ranging from a booklet on how to cook fish to the *Congressional Record* and the *Public Papers of the Presidents*. Each of these publications is a chance for the government to speak directly to the reader, without the mass media in the middle.

The government underwrites book publication in more controversial ways as well. Often a federal agency will put a security classification on essential information on some subject. It then approaches a writer and offers to reveal the information for his use in return for permission to edit the finished book. Such books have been published commercially without mention of the fact that they were censored. The United States Information Agency and the Central Intelligence Agency pay authors and commercial publishers subsidies for political books favorable to the official government position. The books are distributed overseas through USIA libraries. They are sold domestically, however, with no indication of their origin.[14]

effect is heightened when that decision is announced live and in color on national television.

We have described four techniques used by news sources to help them control what is said about them in the mass media—canned news and editorials, pseudoevents, junkets and favors, and direct access. Add to these the omnipresent press release, and a picture of the extent of news management in the United States today begins to emerge. Much of the content of newspapers and broadcasting is the way it is because someone wanted it that way. And the "someone" in question is likely to be, not a reporter, but a public-relations man.

Most cases of news management involve public-relations men who want the story told, and told their way. But sometimes the goal of a news source is not publicity, but secrecy. When the government censors a reporter's article, that too is news management. It is news management also when a reporter is forbidden to attend a meeting, examine a record, or interview an official. And it is news management when the media are threatened, bribed, or even politely asked to keep an item to themselves. These practices are associated mainly with government—but private companies and associations have their secrets too.

KEEPING SECRETS

By and large, everyone is free to keep whatever secrets he wants to keep —everyone but the government. There are exceptions to this freedom; corporations, for example, are required to make public their financial statements and the names of their principal stockholders. But if a corporation wants to say absolutely nothing to the press about its activities, it is within its rights.

Governments, on the other hand, are obligated to talk—at least in theory. The very heart of the democractic process is that public officials are accountable to the public. But accountability is meaningless unless the public is told what the officials are doing. "The people's right to know" is therefore a cardinal principle of democracy. In practice this means the media's right to know—because only the media are capable of keeping tabs on the government and reporting back to the public.

Some day the United States may decide that large corporations, like governments, should be held accountable to the people. We seem to be moving in that direction. But for the moment at least, only the government must have a good reason for hiding anything from the public. Private groups may hide—or try to hide—whatever they wish.

GARDEN CLUB NEWS MANAGEMENT

News management can turn up in the unlikeliest places. One afternoon in 1964, reporter Alex Dobish of the Milwaukee *Journal* showed up at the Wauwatosa Woman's Club to cover its monthly meeting. The featured speaker was a local attorney, and his topic was "managed news."

No, said club chairlady Mrs. Cyril Feldhausen, Mr. Dobish could not cover the lecture. "What he says is for us," she vowed, adding that she would "give the papers what is to be said." Before booting Dobish she reminded him that "we are not getting the news from the news media."[15]

What counts as a "good reason" for government secrecy? The most frequent answer—and the most frequently abused—is national security. Nearly everyone agrees that wartime information on troop movements, battle plans, and the like should be kept secret. During World War Two an American newspaper revealed that U.S. forces had broken the Japanese Navy Code. (The government of Japan somehow missed the article, and thus failed to change the code.) Certainly the Defense Department should have prevented publication of that fact.

But most cases are not so clear. Troop movements are related to national security all right, but what about troop morale? Which is more important, that the Viet Cong should be misled about the mood of American forces, or that the American people should be fully informed? And how does national security apply to cold wars, or to internal "wars" against dissident groups? These are not easy questions to answer.

John B. Oakes of the New York *Times* has pointed out that "the natural bureaucratic tendency to hide mistakes or stupidity behind the sheltering cover of 'national security' is almost irresistible."[16] So is the temptation to use national security as an excuse for political expediency. In 1957, Assistant Secretary of Defense Murray Snyder refused to release photographs of the Titan missile—though the missile itself had been sitting on an open launching pad in Boulder, Colorado, for months. Snyder waited until just before the 1958 elections, then handed the press a picture of President Eisenhower viewing the Titan.[17] Was national security behind the delay, or vote-getting?

In 1971, a former Defense Department consultant delivered to the New York *Times* a complete copy of a 47-volume top secret report on Vietnam policy-making throughout the 1960s. Despite the report's security rating and the fact that its release was unauthorized, the *Times* selected huge segments of it for publication. *Times* editors argued that the report revealed nothing that was dangerous to American national security, but much that was significant in understanding the tragic U.S.

involvement in Southeast Asia. In particular, the report made clear how consistently the American government had lied to the American people about the war.

As soon as the first installment was published in the *Times,* the federal government applied for a temporary injunction to forbid any further installments. When the Washington *Post* began reprinting the report, it too was served with an injunction. This exercise of prior restraint of the press—a technique characteristic of authoritarian dictatorships—was unprecedented in modern American history. The government argued that the circumstances were unprecedented as well; never before had a major American newspaper determined to reveal vital defense secrets to the entire world. The conflict between freedom of the press and national security seemed unresolvable.

If the report had actually contained vital defense secrets, as the government claimed, the resulting court decision would have been a legal landmark. But a federal district court, a federal circuit court, and finally the U.S. Supreme Court all studied the documents in question, and all were unable to find any important secrets. True, the report would embarrass certain government officials, and even the government itself—but embarrassment is not the same as national security. The Supreme Court dissolved both injunctions, and the "Pentagon Papers" (as they came to be called) was widely reprinted. Even the U.S. Government Printing Office came out with an almost complete edition.

EXECUTIVE PRIVILEGE

In 1792 a committee of the House of Representatives asked President George Washington to hand over all documents relating to the Indian massacre of Maj. Gen. Arthur St. Clair and his troops. Washington refused. He told the Congress that the executive branch of government had a right to withhold any information that might injure the public if disclosed. This is called the doctrine of Executive Privilege. It has been used by many Presidents since Washington to thwart not only Congressional investigations, but inquisitive newsmen as well.

In 1946 the concept of Executive Privilege was formalized into the Administrative Procedure Act. The act provided that all official documents of the federal government were open to the public, with three exceptions:

1. "Any function of the United States requiring secrecy in the public interest."
2. "Any matter relating solely to the internal management of an agency."
3. "Information held confidential for good cause found."[18]

In other words, everything was open to the public except whatever the executive branch wanted to keep secret.

During the Eisenhower administration, the veil of government secrecy was extended even further. In a series of Executive Orders, Eisenhower established the security classifications of confidential, secret, and top secret, thus forbidding disclosure of defense-related information. He also commanded all executive employees to keep quiet about their internal discussions, debates, and disagreements. So far as Congress and the public were to know, Eisenhower decreed, the executive branch was unanimous on every issue.

Such matters became far removed from national security. In 1959, for example, a reporter for the Colorado Springs *Gazette-Telegraph* was unable to obtain from the Forest Service a list of ranchers with permits to graze in the Pike National Forest. Explained a Forest Service official: "We have to protect the permittees. We consider their dealings with the Forest Service and their use of Forest Service land strictly a private affair between them and the Forest Service."[19]

Executive Privilege, remember, helps the President keep information from Congress as well as from the mass media. In 1955, therefore, the House Subcommittee on Government Information was set up to look into

LOCAL GOVERNMENT SECRECY

City, county, and state authorities are at least as tempted as the federal government to withhold information from the media. But they don't have the excuse of national security. As a result, considerable progress has been made in guaranteeing the people's right to know on the local level.

As of 1969, 42 states have open-record laws, and 38 have laws requiring public agencies to hold open meetings. These regulations are binding on every level of government within the state, right down to the neighborhood Board of Education. They allow some exceptions—for income tax files and personnel hearings, for example—but by and large they insure that any reporter can get at the local news if he works at it. News coverage of local government is often shoddy, but only occasionally can official secrecy be blamed.

The philosophy behind the right to know is well-expressed in the preamble to the Ralph M. Brown Act, California's open-meeting law:

> The people of the State do not yield their sovereignty to the agencies which serve them. The people, in delegating authority, do not give their public servants the right to decide what is good for the people to know and what is not good for them to know. The people insist on remaining informed so that they may retain control over the instruments they have created.[20]

CORPORATE "NATIONAL SECURITY"

In the early 1960s the federal government began safety tests on various airplanes, carefully crashing the planes and studying the debris. The tests were open to the public, and were frequently filmed by network television crews. Several airlines complained that the crash telecasts were hurting their image, so the government obligingly declared the tests to be secret.[21]

National security? Or good public relations?

---

the problem. Under Democrat John E. Moss of California, the committee accumulated 31 volumes of testimony. In several cases it forced executive departments to reveal information they had been keeping hidden. In many more cases, it simply documented the need for a stronger federal law protecting the people's right to know.

The Moss Subcommittee was instrumental in drafting the 1966 Federal Public Records Law (also known as the Freedom of Information Act). The bill was designed to put a stop to unnecessary government secrecy—but by the time President Lyndon Johnson signed it into law, nine exemptions had been added. The law thus leaves plenty of loopholes for government officials who want to evade public accountability for their actions.

Still, the Freedom of Information Act is a definite step forward. It puts the burden of proof on the government to justify each secret, and it empowers any citizen (or reporter) to sue in federal court for release of a public record. Among the documents that have been "sprung" under the law in recent years are: Labor Department lists of corporations violating federal safety standards; Interstate Commerce Commission travel vouch-

---

VARIATION ON A THEME

The National Aeronautics and Space Administration is as secret-prone as most other federal agencies. Yet it frequently boasts that the American space program—unlike Soviet Russia's—is completely open and aboveboard.

How does NASA resolve the conflict? Easy. It simply floods reporters with mountains of technical facts and figures—too much to understand and much too much to publish or broadcast. NASA aides ("public-relations scientists") are available night and day to help reporters figure out what it all means. The job of interpreting the handouts has kept the press too busy to look into more controversial aspects of the NASA program—subcontracting deals, excessive costs, safety problems, etc. Which, of course, is probably what NASA had in mind all along.

---

ers; Renegotiation Board records on excessive corporate profits from defense contracts; and Federal Aviation Agency handbooks.

In each of these cases, however, someone had to go to court to *force* the government to release the information. The government did not do so willingly. Frequently there is no one sufficiently interested in a particular secret to bother to sue for it. Certainly the typical reporter with a deadline to meet is not free to kill a few weeks or months in a federal courthouse.

Speaking of the Freedom of Information Act, consumer advocate Ralph Nader recently charged that "Government officials at all levels . . . have violated systematically and routinely both the purpose and the specific provisions of the law."[22] As long as many of our public servants do not seriously believe in the people's right to know, government secrecy will remain a critical problem.

COOPERATION AND INTIMIDATION

When the British government is anxious to prevent a certain piece of information from appearing in the British media, it uses what is called the D notice system. A D notice is a formal letter circulated confidentially to the media, warning them that some fact is of secret importance to the government and should not be published. The notice is only advisory, but the implication exists that any item covered in a D notice may also be protected under the British Official Secrets Act. Very few D notices are ever ignored, even when they seem to the media less concerned with national security than with national scandal.

The United States has nothing like the D notice system. But a confidential chat between a reporter and a government official often serves the same purpose, as does a phone call from the President to the publisher. This is called voluntary self-censorship. In wartime it is necessary, and far safer than government-enforced censorship. In peacetime, however, it is a dangerous form of government news management.

President Franklin Roosevelt had a standing request that no pictures be taken of him while in pain from the polio that crippled him for decades. Once, surrounded by dozens of photographers, the President fell full-length on the floor—and not a single picture was snapped. This was very polite of the photographers—but are newsmen supposed to be so polite? In May of 1970, a Nixon adviser asked the New York *Times* to skip certain details of the resumption of bombing in North Vietnam, because those details were "embarrassing" to the President.[23] The *Times* printed them anyhow—a blow to politeness, perhaps, but a victory for the people's right to know.

Traditionally, the American media have tended to cooperate with the

American government on the matter of keeping secrets, especially when national security was involved. But in recent years—largely because of the government's "credibility gap" in foreign affairs—such cooperation has waned. The New York *Times* dutifully downplayed the planned Bay of Pigs invasion in 1961, and kept the secret of the Cuban missile crisis in 1962. But by 1971 the *Times* was willingly reprinting top secret government documents stolen by a former Defense Department consultant.

When cooperation fails as a tool of government news management, intimidation may be tried in its stead. On November 3, 1969, President Richard Nixon appeared on national television to explain, in person, his Vietnam policy. Immediately after the speech, network commentators and their guests began to discuss the President's remarks—analyzing, interpreting, often criticizing.

Ten days later, addressing the Midwest Regional Republican Committee in Des Moines, Vice-President Spiro Agnew delivered a stinging attack on network television news. He focused particularly on the "instant analysis" that had followed the Nixon speech, arguing that TV commentators comprised a "tiny and closed fraternity of privileged men." Agnew continued:

> I am not asking for government censorship or any kind of censorship. I am asking whether a form of censorship already exists when the news that forty million Americans receive each night is determined by a handful of men responsible only to their corporate employers and filtered through a handful of commentators who admit to their own set of biases.[24]

On November 20, the Vice-President delivered his second attack on the media, this time before the Montgomery, Alabama, Chamber of Commerce. Now he concentrated on "fat and irresponsible" newspapers, especially the New York *Times* and the Washington *Post*, both critics of Nixon's war policy. A third onslaught the following May made it crystal clear that Agnew was fighting against "the liberal news media in this country"—media that were helping to make life difficult for the Nixon administration.

There is much truth in what the Vice-President had to say. That is not the point. The question is, to what extent was President Nixon, through Agnew, trying to cow the media into being less critical of White House policies? And to what extent did he succeed?

Positive proof is hard to find. But shortly after Agnew's first speech, the Federal Communications Commission asked all three networks to submit transcripts of their commentary on the Nixon Vietnam telecast—clearly implying at least the possibility of government interference. White House Director of Communications Herbert Klein made the threat even more explicit. "If you look at the problems you have today," Klein said, "and you fail to continue to examine them, you do invite the government to come in. I would not like to see that happen."[25] As for the effectiveness of the attack, many observers have noted that television commentary on the President's later war messages tended to be bland and noncommittal.

Veteran ABC broadcaster Edward P. Morgan summed it all up. He called the first Agnew speech "one of the most significant and one of the most sinister . . . I have ever heard made by a public figure." Morgan added: "It is significant because it is a perfect gauge of what this administration is doing. They've been trying to manage the news ever since the campaign."[26]

When a high government official publicly attacks the mass media, there is more at stake than merely whether or not his criticisms are justified. Even the most valid arguments, coming from him, constitute a form of news management—an attempt to intimidate the media.

Intimidation is by no means confined to the White House. It seems most frequent, in fact, in the military. During the postwar occupation of Japan, General Douglas MacArthur branded several newsmen Communists, and demanded the removal of others because they were unfair or overly critical. Some correspondents were threatened or interrogated,

A STAGED ATROCITY?

Late in 1969, the CBS evening news program broadcast a film of a South Vietnamese soldier stabbing to death a North Vietnamese prisoner. The Pentagon asked CBS to turn over the unused portion of the film for study, and CBS refused. At that point Presidential Assistant Clark Mollenhoff went to work. Mollenhoff decided that CBS had staged the entire episode. He passed along his conclusion to syndicated columnists Jack Anderson and Richard Wilson, who then published versions of the Mollenhoff theory.

On May 21, 1970, CBS responded to the attack. In a seven-minute segment incorporating the original film, the network convincingly demonstrated that it was genuine. CBS newsmen even tracked down the South Vietnamese sergeant who had done the stabbing, and put his cheerful confession on the air. The White House was forced to back down.

Walter Cronkite concluded this unprecedented nationwide rebuttal with the following words:

> We broadcast the original story in the belief it told something about the nature of the war in Vietnam. What has happened since then tells something about the government and its relation with news media which carry stories the government finds disagreeable.

and one had his home raided by Army investigators. The harrassment continued until only friendly reporters were left.

In 1962, Assistant Secretary of Defense Arthur Sylvester directed all Pentagon employees to file a report on "the substance of each interview and telephone conversation with a media representative . . . before the close of business that day."[27] Sylvester also had Public Information Officers sitting in on many of the interviews—effectively terrorizing both the source and the reporter. Hanson Baldwin of the New York *Times* recalls that his fellow military writers were investigated by the FBI, shadowed in the halls of the Pentagon, and subjected to frequent telephone wire taps—all on stories without any overtones of national security.[28]

In 1970, CBS produced and broadcast a documentary entitled "The Selling of the Pentagon." One of the most admirable (and controversial) programs of the year, the documentary dealt with the public relations activities of the Defense Department.

The government's response to this exposé of Pentagon news management was more news management. The Defense Department immediately issued a statement claiming that the documentary was biased, that interviews with Pentagon spokesmen were edited out of context to make them appear more damning than they actually were. Some of the specific complaints were probably justified, but they effectively obscured the main point—that the documentary itself was essentially accurate. When the Defense Department demanded rebuttal time, CBS agreed—and rebutted the rebuttal in the same program. It also rebroadcast the original documentary for those who had missed it the first time.

In the wake of these events, a Congressional committee headed by Rep. Harley O. Staggers (D.-W.Va.) decided to investigate the documentary. The Staggers Committee asked CBS to supply all film used in preparing the program, including film that was not broadcast. Despite a subpoena, CBS refused, risking a Contempt of Congress citation. It is conceivable, of course, that the Staggers Committee actually contemplated some sort of government regulation of broadcast documentaries (though any such regulation would almost certainly be unconstitutional). But most observers agreed that the purpose of the investigation was more probably to intimidate the media, to make broadcasters think twice before planning another documentary critical of the federal government.

Private corporations are also fond of intimidation as a form of news management. Back in the 1950s, syndicated columnist Ray Tucker wrote a scathing account of airline lobbying for the rights to a new route. The day before the column was scheduled to appear, Pan American Airways sent the following telegram to every newspaper that subscribed to the syndicate: "Pan American understands that you may be planning to publish a column by Ray Tucker containing numerous scurrilous references to Pan American. We feel it our duty to tell you that we believe a number of these statements to be libelous. You may also wish to take into consideration the columnist's obvious bias against the airline that has earned for the United States first place in world air transport." Many papers decided not to carry the column.[29] The threat to withdraw advertising if a certain story is published (see Chapter 5) is another common variety of corporate intimidation.

In the final analysis, the best answer to secrecy is a professional attitude on the part of the mass media. The reporter must be willing to dig, to ask embarrassing questions, to play off one source against another, to follow up unpromising leads. The editor must be willing to back up his reporter, to give him the time and freedom he needs in tracking down elusive secrets. And the owner must be willing to publish or broadcast what the reporter and editor have found, without bowing to polite requests or overt threats.

It can be done. In the 1960s, while columnist Joseph Alsop was complaining about "total news control" by Defense Secretary Robert McNamara, his brother Stewart Alsop was publishing a detailed story on American defense planning, based on unauthorized interviews with forty senior Pentagon officials.

THE MADDOX CRUSADE

In May of 1970 Governor Lester Maddox of Georgia announced the opening round of a personal campaign against the two major Atlanta newspapers, the *Journal* and the *Constitution*. Maddox claimed that both papers had published articles slanted against him. He was probably right; certainly both were anti-Maddox papers.

The Governor's response was a ban against selling either newspaper on state capitol property. Maddox removed the papers' vending machines from every state building in Atlanta. He personally picketed the offices of both papers, and appealed to all Georgia residents to stop their subscriptions for a month as a warning. If these tactics weren't enough to force reform, Maddox claimed he would "call on the business community to drop its advertising in the papers and, perhaps, give consideration to issuing an executive order taking all liquor advertisements out of their papers."[30]

Some of these steps are unconstitutional; some are amusing. Together they could do the Atlanta *Journal* and *Constitution* serious harm. Neither paper seems likely to change its news coverage in the near future—but a more subtle and less public approach might have worked—and no one need ever have known.

NOTES

[1] "Authentic Voice," *Time*, January 27, 1958, pp. 16–20, quoted in Douglass Cater, *The Fourth Branch of Government* (N.Y.: Vintage Books, Inc., 1959), p. 163.

[2] William L. Rivers, *The Adversaries* (Boston: Beacon Press, 1970), pp. 49–50.

[3] Evan Hill, "Handouts to the Country Editor," *Nieman Reports*, July, 1954, pp. 8–9.

[4] Quoted in Cater, *The Fourth Branch of Government*, pp. 52–53.

[5] Ben H. Bagdikian, "Journalist Meets Propagandist," *Columbia Journalism Review*, Fall, 1963, p. 30.

[6] Ben H. Bagdikian, "Behold the Grass-roots Press, Alas!" *Harper's*, December, 1964, pp. 102–5.

[7] Ralph Blizzard, "How to Edit Without Hardly Being an Editor," *Grassroots Editor*, March–April, 1969, pp. 5–6.

[8] Irwin Ross, *The Image Merchants* (Garden City, New York: Doubleday & Co., Inc., 1959), pp. 23–24, 129.

[9] Daniel J. Boorstin, *The Image* (New York: Atheneum, 1962).

[10] Ivan Doig, "Kefauver Versus Crime: Television Boosts a Senator," *Journalism Quarterly*, Autumn, 1962, p. 490.

[11] Quoted in Wilbur Schramm, *Responsibility in Mass Communication* (N.Y.: Harper & Brothers, 1957), p. 145.

[12] James Reston column appearing in the "Sunday Punch" section of the San Francisco *Sunday Examiner and Chronicle*, February 1, 1970, p. 3.

[13] George Gallup, "Nixon's Rating After Cambodia," San Francisco *Chronicle*, May 11, 1970, p. 5.

[14] Rivers, *The Adversaries*, pp. 157–64.

[15] Curtis D. MacDougall, *Reporters Report Reporters* (Ames, Ia.: Iowa State University Press, 1968), pp. 95–96.

[16] John B. Oakes, "The Paper Curtain of Washington," *Nieman Reports*, October, 1958, p. 3.

[17] Samuel J. Archibald, "Secrecy from Peanuts to Pentagon," Freedom of Information Center Publication No. 20, Columbia, Missouri, pp. 1–2.

[18] "Press-Endorsed Info Act Restrictive, Frustrating," *Editor & Publisher*, November 12, 1966, p. 11.

[19] Archibald, "Secrecy from Peanuts to Pentagon," p. 1.

[20] Ralph M. Brown Act, California Government Code, Sec. 54950.

[21] Marvin Alisky, "Safety Test Casts Discouraged," *RTNDA Bulletin*, June, 1964, p. 2.

[22] "Government's Urge to Hide Facts," San Francisco *Sunday Examiner and Chronicle, This World*, April 12, 1970, p. 21.

[23] Jack Anderson, "A Reminder of McCarthy Era," San Francisco *Chronicle*, May 8, 1970, p. 41.

[24] Address of Vice-President Spiro T. Agnew before the Midwest Regional Republican Committee, Des Moines, Iowa, November 13, 1969.

[25] "Beat the Press, Round Two," *Newsweek*, December 1, 1969, p. 25.

[26] "Agnew's Complaint: The Trouble with TV," *Newsweek*, November 24, 1969, p. 89.

[27] Clark R. Mollenhoff, "News 'Weaponry' and McNamara's Military Muzzle," *The Quill*, December, 1962, p. 8.

[28] Hanson W. Baldwin, "Managed News, Our Peacetime Censorship," *Atlantic Monthly*, April, 1963, p. 54.

[29] Schramm, *Responsibility in Mass Communication,* p. 154.
[30] Associated Press, May 30, 1970.

SUGGESTED READINGS

BAGDIKIAN, BEN H., "Behold the Grass-roots Press, Alas!" *Harper's,* December, 1964.

BALDWIN, HANSON W., "Managed News, Our Peacetime Censorship," *Atlantic Monthly,* April, 1963.

ROSS, IRWIN, *The Image Merchants.*   Garden City, N.Y.: Doubleday & Co., Inc., 1959.

7 Government Control

The mass media are so important to society that they are often referred to as "the fourth branch of government." Quite naturally, the other three branches are very interested in what this "fourth branch" is doing. In some countries the government rules the media. In others, including the United States, government control of the media is more relaxed. Nowhere does the government leave the media entirely free to do whatever they wish.

The First Amendment to the United States Constitution reads in part: "Congress shall make no law . . . abridging the freedom of speech or of the press." This is the earliest and most important statement of the relationship between the U.S. government and the mass media. Because it is part of the Constitution, all other laws and government policies must be consistent with it—otherwise they are unconstitutional and therefore illegal.

Freedom of the Press is not limited to newspapers and magazines. In a series of judicial decisions, the courts have made it clear that the First Amendment applies also (though somewhat differently) to broadcasting, film, and the other mass media. Nor is it only Congress that must respect press freedom. The other arms of the federal government are equally bound by the First Amendment. By means of the Fourteenth Amendment, it is binding on state and local governments as well.

It is fair, then, to rephrase the First Amendment as follows: "No arm of any government shall do anything . . . abridging the freedom of speech or of the press." That is where we start.

Throughout our history, there have been judges on the Supreme Court who believed that the First Amendment meant exactly what it said: "no law." The most recent representative of this viewpoint was the late Justice Hugo Black, who steadfastly held that anything any government does to regulate the mass media is unconstitutional. Justice Black was in the minority. His colleagues believe that libel laws are needed to protect individuals from unfair attacks, that the FCC is needed to hold broadcasters to the public interest, that antitrust legislation is needed to prevent newspapers from gaining a monopoly. They believe, in other words, that Freedom of the Press is not absolute, that it has exceptions.

This chapter—one of the longest in the book—is devoted to the exceptions, to the ways our government permits itself to control our mass media. We will start by examining some alternative theories on the proper relationship between government and the media.

THE AUTHORITARIAN THEORY

The printing press was born in the wholly authoritarian environment of Fifteenth Century Europe. The Church and local political leaders exercised their waning power with little thought for the will of the people. Infant nation-states flexed their new-found muscles. Absolute monarchies demanded absolute obedience. It was no time for a small man with a small hand press to insist on his freedom.

The first books to be published, Latin Bibles, posed no particular threat to the Establishment. But before long books and pamphlets began to be printed in the vernacular, and a growing middle class soon learned to read them. Here was an obvious danger to the aristocracy—who could tell what seditious or heretical ideas those books and pamphlets might contain? Every government in Europe recognized the urgent need to regulate the press.

A philosophy of regulation quickly developed. By definition, the ruling classes were right in everything they did and said. Any published statement that supported or benefited the government was therefore "truth." Any statement that questioned or damaged the government obviously had to be "falsehood." Consistently truthful publishers—those who regularly supported the government—were rewarded with permission to print religious tracts, commercial newsletters, and other nonpolitical material. Untruthful publishers—dissenters—were denied permission to print anything; many wound up in prison as well. As one scholar has put it, the function of the mass media in the Sixteenth Century was to "support and advance the policies of government as determined by the political machinery then in operation."[1] This is the authoritarian theory of the press.

Johann Gutenberg and his successors were not government employees. The printing press was invented well before State Socialism, and for the first 400 years of post-Gutenberg history the presses were privately owned. From the very beginning, private ownership was the major problem of the authoritarian theory: How can the government control the media when it doesn't own them?

The earliest answer was licensing. Each printer was required to obtain a "royal patent" or license to print. Usually the license included vast privileges, often a local monopoly. It was understood that if a printer deviated from the government-defined truth, his license would be revoked. Licensing by itself didn't work very well. Unlicensed printers appeared by the hundreds, and even some licensed ones occasionally published anti-government materials, possibly by accident. For a while precensorship was tried—a government censor for each press, reading every word it printed. But the volume of copy soon made precensorship impossible except for emergencies.

By the end of the Seventeenth Century, the primary tool of authoritarian governments was postcensorship. A printer could publish whatever he liked. Eventually the government got around to reading it—and if the government didn't like what it read, that was the end of that printer. Stiff fines, long jail sentences, and occasionally even death were the penalties for a seditious publication. The mere threat of these punishments was enough to keep most printers in line.

The authoritarian theory is not some dead notion dredged up from Seventeenth Century history. It is the dominant relationship between government and the media in most of Asia, Africa, and South America today. To find the authoritarian theory in action, look for a country where the government forbids the media to say certain things, and uses techniques like censorship and licensing to enforce its prohibitions. You won't have far to look.

THE SOVIET THEORY

The problem of controlling private owners of the media is solved in the Soviet Union and mainland China through state ownership. Newspapers, magazines, and broadcast stations are all owned and operated by the government itself. It is no mere metaphor in Russia to speak of the media as "the fourth branch of government"; it is a simple statement of fact. The chiefs of *Pravda* and *Izvestia*, for example, are high officials in the Communist Party—rather as if the Vice-President ran the New York *Times.*

Under state ownership there is no question of whether the mass media will support or oppose government policy. They are *part* of government policy. The fundamental purpose of the press, states the 1925 Russian Constitution, is "to strengthen the Communist social order." Consider these instructions offered to a broadcasting trainee in the Soviet Union: "The Soviet radio must carry to the widest masses the teachings of Marx-Lenin-Stalin, must raise the cultural-political level of the workers, must daily inform the workers of the success of socialist construction, must spread the word about the class struggle taking place throughout the world."[2]

Professor Fred S. Siebert offers this description of the Soviet theory:

> The function of the press is not to aid in the search for truth since the truth has already been determined by the Communist ideology. No tampering with the fundamental Marxist system is tolerated. . . . The stakes are too high and the masses too fickle to trust the future of state policies to such bourgeois concepts as "search for truth," "rational man," and "minority rights."[3]

Paradoxically enough, the Soviet media are free to criticize the government—not the basic dogmas of Communism, of course, but the actions of specific government agencies and officials. Because the media are part of the government, such criticism is considered to be *self*-criticism, and is therefore acceptable. A few years ago *Pravda* ran an article on factory production shortages, headlined: "Bring Parasites To Account!" Undoubtedly, the article was part of a carefully orchestrated government campaign. Nonetheless, such a story could never have appeared in a country with privately owned media governed by the authoritarian theory.

These, then, are the three essential differences between the authoritarian and Soviet theories of the press: (1) The media are privately owned in the authoritarian theory, state-owned in the Soviet theory; (2) Authoritarian control of the media is negative, while Soviet control is affirmative; (3) The authoritarian theory permits no criticism of the government, while the Soviet theory forbids only the questioning of ideology. You could sum it up this way. In the authoritarian theory, the government decides what the media should not do, and punishes it. In the Soviet theory, the government decides what the media should do, and does it.

THE LIBERTARIAN THEORY

Apples fall from trees because of gravity, not the whim of some dictator or the dogma of some church. One does not need a dictator or a church to understand the law of gravity; one needs only one's own mind. This was the great insight of the scientific Enlightenment of the Seventeenth and Eighteenth Centuries: Man is a rational being, and as such he can discover natural laws on his own.

If it's true of natural laws, reasoned the philosophers of the Enlightenment, it should be true of man's laws as well. Men like Voltaire and J. S. Mill based entire philosophies on this notion:

> If men were free to inquire about all things, . . . to form opinions on the basis of knowledge and evidence, and to utter their opinions freely, the competition of knowledge and opinion in the market of rational discourse would ultimately banish ignorance and superstition and enable men to shape their conduct and their institutions in conformity with the fundamental and invariable laws of nature and the will of God.[4]

How does this philosophy apply to the mass media? Man is a rational being. Offered a choice between truth and falsehood, he will unerringly choose truth—at least in the long run. It follows that the best thing a government can do with the media is to leave them alone, let them publish whatever they want to publish. This is the libertarian theory of the press.

The libertarian theory developed out of the Enlightenment, out of science, but it is doubtful that it would have done so without the parallel development of democracy. Even if a dictator accepted the philosophical premise of libertarianism—that the people can tell truth from falsehood—there would be no reason for him to relax his hold on the mass media. Why should a dictator want the people to know the truth in the first place? He does the governing, not they. It is important for *him* to know the truth, perhaps—and for his people to know whatever he feels like telling them, no more, no less.

In a democracy, on the other hand, the people do the governing. If they are to make the right decisions, they must know the truth. James Madison put it this way: "Nothing could be more irrational than to give the people power, and to withhold from them information without which power is abused. A people who mean to be their own governors must arm themselves with power which knowledge gives. A popular government without popular information or the means of acquiring it is but a prologue to a farce or a tragedy, or perhaps both."[5] Thomas Jefferson was more blunt: "If a nation expects to be both ignorant and free it expects what never was and never will be."[6]

It is no coincidence, then, that the growth of libertarian theory in Eighteenth Century England was accompanied by the rising power of Parliament over the King. Nor is it accidental that libertarianism achieved its most nearly ideal form in the democracy of Nineteenth Century America. Other countries with a libertarian press include Canada, Australia, New Zealand, Sweden, Norway, Denmark, and Israel—all democracies.

The greatest assets of the libertarian theory, one scholar has said, "are its flexibility, its adaptability to change, and above all its confidence in its ability to advance the interests and welfare of human beings by continuing to place its trust in individual self-direction."[7]   There is no doubt about the last point.   Libertarianism is almost incredibly optimistic about the rationality of man.   The other two points—flexibility and adaptability —are more debatable.   It can be persuasively argued, in fact, that the libertarian theory has failed to keep up with social change, that it is now obsolete and should be discarded.

What are the implicit assumptions of the libertarian theory?   The most important one, of course, is that the people are capable of telling truth from falsehood, given a choice between the two.   Some of the other assumptions include:

1. That there are enough voices in the mass media to insure that the truth will be well represented.
2. That the owners of the mass media are different enough to include all possible candidates for truth.
3. That the mass media are not under the control of some nongovernmental interest group, such as news sources or advertisers.
4. That it is not difficult for those who wish to do so to start their own newspaper, broadcast station, or other mass media outlet.

All of these premises were more or less satisfied by conditions in the Eighteenth and Nineteenth Centuries.   As we have seen in the last several chapters, all of them are considerably less well-satisfied today.   The modern mass media are a vital part of Big Business.   The number of media voices decreases every year, as the similarity of the remaining voices increases.   Media owners are extremely responsive to the wishes of pressure groups.   And starting a new mass medium is difficult and costly.

Even the first premise of libertarian theory—that the people can tell truth from falsehood—may be less valid today than it was three hundred years ago.   Life and government are far more complex now than they were then.   Decisions are harder to make, harder even to understand.   It is no longer so obvious that common sense is enough to solve the problems of the world.

THE SOCIAL RESPONSIBILITY THEORY

The social responsibility theory was first articulated in 1947, by the Hutchins Commission Report on a Free and Responsible Press.   This important piece of press criticism from scholars in many fields accepted the basic assumption of libertarian theory.   It agreed, in other words, that the way to run a democracy is to expose the people to all kinds of information and all kinds of opinions, and then let them decide for themselves. But the Hutchins Commission questioned whether the libertarian theory was working, whether the people were getting enough information and opinions to give them a fair chance of making the right decision. It therefore proposed five "requirements," designed to guarantee that the media include "all important viewpoints, not merely those with which the publisher or operator agrees."[8]   According to the Hutchins Commission, the mass media should:

1. Provide a truthful, comprehensive, and intelligent account of the day's events in a context which gives them meaning.
2. Provide a forum for the exchange of comment and criticism.
3. Provide a representative picture of the constituent groups in society.
4. Be responsible for the presentation and clarification of the goals and values of society.
5. Provide full access to the day's intelligence.[9]

The difference between the libertarian and social responsibility theories is subtle, but most important.   The libertarian theory holds that if each publisher "does his own thing," all will work out for the best.   The social responsibility theory disagrees.   It *urges* the media to do what the libertarian theory *assumes* they will do—provide a free marketplace of ideas.   "A new era of public responsibility for the press has arrived," stated the Hutchins Commission.   "The variety of sources of news and opinion is limited.   The insistence of the citizen's need has increased. . . . We suggest the press look upon itself as performing a public service of a professional kind."[10]

The essence of the social responsibility theory is that the media have an obligation to behave in certain ways.   If they meet that obligation voluntarily, fine; otherwise the government may be forced to make them meet it.   Theodore Peterson interprets the theory this way:

> Freedom carries concomitant obligations; and the press, which enjoys a privileged position under our government, is obliged to be responsible to society for carrying out certain essential functions of mass communication in contemporary society.   To the extent that the press recognizes its responsibilities and makes them the basis of operational policies, the libertarian system will satisfy the needs of society.   To the extent that the press does not assume its responsibilities, some other agency must see that the essential functions of mass communication are carried out.[11]

THEORY AND PRACTICE

The four theories of the press are less concerned with what the media should and should not do than with *who decides* what the media should and should not do.   Consider the following chart:

	Who decides what the media should do?	Who decides what the media should not do?	Who enforces these decisions?
Authoritarian theory	The media	The state	The state
Soviet theory	The state	The state	The state
Libertarian theory	The media	The media	The media
Social responsibility theory	The experts	The experts	Ideally the media; if necessary the state

In libertarian theory there is no control over the media. In Soviet theory the state controls everything, while in authoritarian theory the state has only negative controls. In social responsibility theory the "experts" suggest answers; the media carry them out either voluntarily or through state control.

Which theory offers the most freedom? The most obvious answer is the libertarian theory, under which the media are free to do whatever they choose. But that is freedom for the publisher and the broadcaster, not for the private citizen. Soviet philosophers argue that a government-run press is likely to be freer than a press that is controlled by businessmen, whose special interests seldom mirror those of the general public. Authoritarian theorists assert that the freedom to oppose the government is not freedom, but anarchy. And advocates of social responsibility claim that the people are truly free only when the media are required to inform them properly.

Different theories of the press follow inevitably from different theories of government. Dictators invariably choose the authoritarian model; communism leads naturally to the Soviet model; simple democracies follow the libertarian model; more complex, bureaucratic democracies require the social responsibility model. It is hard to imagine a communist state with a libertarian press, or a democracy with an authoritarian press, or any other mismatched combination of media and government.

Yet it is just as hard to find a pure example of any of the four theories. In practice, everything turns out to be a combination—with one element dominant, perhaps, but with the other three represented as well. The First Amendment to the U.S. Constitution perfectly embodies the libertarian theory; yet the Constitution itself was debated and passed in secret, and newsmen were told only what the Founding Fathers thought they ought to know. This authoritarian strain has persisted throughout the history of our country. Sedition is *the* mass media crime under authoritarian regimes. It is still a crime in the United States today.

There has never been a pure example of the libertarian theory in action. The United States probably comes closest. But the authoritarian elements in American press-government relations are many: sedition and blasphemy laws; government news management; post office mailing permits; licensing of broadcast stations; etc. And the social responsibility elements are even more prevalent: libel, obscenity, and privacy restrictions; antitrust laws; the fairness and equal time doctrines; etc. If there are no elements of Soviet theory in this country, it is only because all the mass media are privately owned. In Canada, England, Australia, and many other democracies, broadcast stations are state-owned, lending a Soviet tinge to their mass media systems.

Despite the First Amendment and the heritage of libertarian theory, the United States government exercises many direct controls over mass media content. Among the most important are: copyright, sedition, obscenity, libel, privacy, free press/fair trial, and advertising regulation. Some of these controls (like copyright) are designed to protect the individual citizen. Others (like sedition) aim at protecting the government itself. Still others (like obscenity) are intended to protect the society as a whole. All limit the freedom of the mass media.

COPYRIGHT

The authors of this book have in front of them at all times a copyright manual prepared by the publisher. It tells us what we may and may not use from the work of others, when we must give credit, and when we must write for permission. Without its help we would undoubtedly violate the law many times.

We begin our discussion of press law with copyright, not because it is the most important example of government control of the media (it isn't), but because it is the most ubiquitous. Every country has some kind of copyright law. In the United States, it is embodied in the Constitution itself—the same Constitution that contains the First Amendment: "The Congress shall have power . . . to promote the Progress of Science and useful Arts by securing for limited Times to Authors and Inventors the exclusive Right to their respective Writings and Discoveries."

Copyright law is an obvious necessity. Without it, no writer or publisher could earn a living, and hence few would bother to try. Yet strictly

BACK TO PRIOR RESTRAINT

Prior restraint of the press (also called precensorship) is almost a defining characteristic of the authoritarian theory. Nothing could be more basic to the libertarian notion of freedom of the press than the right to publish absolutely anything without prior interference by the government. Once an item has been published, the publisher may be subject to suit or prosecution—but according to libertarian theory his right to publish it first is ironclad.

Nonetheless, in 1971 the U.S. government successfully obtained a temporary injunction forbidding the New York *Times* to publish further installments of the "Pentagon Papers" (see pp. 153–54). The government justified this unprecedented move by arguing that continued publication of the top secret documents could irreparably damage U.S. national security. The Supreme Court disagreed. It could find no vital secrets in the Pentagon Papers, and therefore permitted the *Times* to continue publishing them. Quite possibly the *Times* can be prosecuted for releasing secret documents after it has done so, but it cannot be stopped in advance.

But even the Supreme Court admitted that if the Pentagon Papers actually had contained information dangerous to American national security, then the government might have been entitled to prevent their publication. Under American law, the authoritarian tactic of prior restraint is so severely curtailed that it has never once been successfully invoked. But it is not impossible.

---

speaking, copyright law is a violation of the libertarian theory. It is a government-enforced limitation on what the mass media are permitted to publish.

Copyright is a civil, not a criminal, affair. The government doesn't arrest you for it; the owner of the copyright sues you. The amount of money he can collect is limited to the amount you profited by stealing his material, plus a little extra for his time and effort. For newspapers, then, copyright is seldom a serious matter. Very little money is made or lost when one newspaper steals an article from another; unless it becomes a habit, no one is likely to sue. When a national magazine or a college textbook infringes on a copyright, however, the settlement is likely to be several thousand dollars, enough to justify a lawsuit. And when a best-selling novel or a successful movie is involved in copyright litigation, the winner may stand to gain $100,000 or more.

According to American copyright law, a published work is protected for 28 years, and may be renewed for an additional 28 years. The copyright covers the style and organization of the work, but not its ideas or facts. Brief quotations (less than 250 words from a book, less than two lines from a poem) are usually not considered to be copyright violations, even without the author's permission.

A work is automatically copyrighted if it is published with a formal copyright notice on its title page; the copyright may then be registered with the federal government any time in the next 28 years. Unpublished works are copyrighted forever—as long as they carry the notice.

The most recent revision of the American copyright law was in 1909. That was before the invention of television, computers, talking movies, and photocopy machines. It was also before the invention of cable television systems. A few years ago, a movie company sued a cable TV operator in West Virginia, charging that it had carried copyrighted films without obtaining (and paying for) permission. The case eventually reached the Supreme Court, which reluctantly ruled that the 1909 copyright law does not apply to cable television.

Which only proves that we need a new copyright law.

SEDITION

Sedition is by far the oldest crime of the mass media. It consists of saying or writing something that displeases the government, usually because it criticizes the government. In early English common law, the name of the crime was "seditious libel." Besides sedition, it included blasphemy, obscenity, and ordinary libel. Today these three are separate offenses, and so is sedition.

Even when sedition was a kind of libel, it was a very special kind. In ordinary libel, truth is a defense; in seditious libel it wasn't. On the contrary—since true criticisms of the government are more dangerous than false ones, the English courts felt they ought to be more libelous too. This authoritarian tradition was carried to the American colonies, where it was seldom questioned until the trial of Peter Zenger. Accused of writing and publishing anti-government articles, Zenger defended himself by arguing that the articles were true. The judge ruled that truth was no defense against seditious libel, but the rebellious jury turned in a verdict of not guilty anyhow. By 1798, when the Sedition Act was passed, truth was accepted as a legitimate defense against charges of sedition.

The Sedition Act made it a crime to publish "any false, scandalous and malicious writing" that might bring into disrepute the U.S. government, Congress, or the President. Seven editors were convicted under the act; all were Republicans and opponents of the Federalist Adams administration. When Jefferson took office in 1801, he pardoned all seven men and allowed the Sedition Act to lapse.

Exactly a hundred years later, after the assassination of President William McKinley in 1901, sedition reappeared as a crime in the United States. This time the definition was a lot narrower. It was no longer illegal merely to criticize the government. But it was (and still is) illegal to advocate the violent overthrow of the government—the government of the United States, the government of New York, the government of Wisconsin, and the governments of literally thousands of states, counties, cities, and towns.

Sedition statutes are all designed to protect the government from subversive attacks: from anarchists and socialists at the turn of the century, from Germans during World War I, from Germans and Japanese during World War II, from communists during the 1950s and 1960s.

There is an obvious conflict between any sedition law and the First Amendment. Over the years, the courts have tried to resolve this conflict through compromise, proposing various standards to limit the crime of sedition without eliminating it entirely. In *Schenck v. United States* (1919), for example, Supreme Court Justice Oliver Wendell Holmes offered the "clear and present danger" standard:

> The question in every case is whether the words used are used in such circumstances and are of such a nature as to create a clear and present danger. . . . When a nation is at war many things that might be said in time of peace are such a hindrance to its effort that their utterance will not be endured.[12]

The "clear and present danger" test lasted for nearly 40 years, as court after court tried to interpret its meaning. Then, in 1957, the Supreme Court chose another criterion. It is not sedition, the court said, to advocate the violent overthrow of the government as an abstract principle. That is protected by the First Amendment. Sedition is confined to advocacy of the violent overthrow of the government as an incitement to immediate action.[13]

In recent years there have been very few prosecutions for sedition. The "incitement" standard is too tough, and the government has easier ways of getting rid of revolutionaries—notably the conspiracy laws. But sedition is still a crime; the law is still on the books. Come another crisis, another war, or another Senator Joseph McCarthy, it will no doubt be used again.

As a practical matter, mainstream publishers and broadcasters never have to worry much about sedition. They don't customarily advocate the violent overthrow of the government anyhow. Nevertheless, the very existence of a crime called sedition illustrates the authoritarian strain in American press law. Sedition was born in Sixteenth Century Europe, where any criticism of the government was a threat to the established order. In a healthy, free society, criticism is no crime.

Blasphemy is to religion what sedition is to government.   There are still blasphemy laws on the books of some 15 states today, but they are almost never used.   They are holdovers from an earlier era, when Americans viewed Christianity as the one true religion.   Most of them, possibly all, are unconstitutional by current Supreme Court standards.

OBSCENITY

The purpose of copyright law is to protect the individual.   The purpose of sedition law is to protect the government.   The purpose of obscenity law is to protect the society as a whole—from what, no one is quite sure.

What is obscene?   Until 1933, American courts answered this question by quoting the so-called "Hicklin rule," first enunciated by a British judge in 1868.   The Hicklin test of obscenity is "whether the tendency of the matter charged as obscene is to deprave and corrupt those whose minds are open to such immoral influences and into whose hands a publication of this sort might fall."[14]   Translated into English, this means that if a neurotic child might be affected by some photograph, say, and there's a chance the child might see the photo somewhere, then the photo is obscene.

American judges added to the Hicklin rule the doctrine of "partial obscenity," which holds that if some passages in a book are obscene (by Hicklin standards), then the whole book is obscene.

Then, in 1933, U.S. customs officials refused to allow the importation of James Joyce's book *Ulysses* on grounds of obscenity.   The importer took the case to court.   The judge threw out both Hicklin and partial obscenity.   He insisted on judging the book as a whole, and decided that it did not "lead to sexually impure and lustful thoughts . . . in a person with average sex instincts."[15]   In 1957 the Supreme Court finally got around to endorsing this new standard.   The case was *United States v. Roth,* and the court declared that the big question was "whether to the average person, applying contemporary community standards, the dominant theme of the material taken as a whole appeals to prurient interest."[16]   This is the "Roth test."   It's a long way from the Hicklin rule.

Recent interpretations of the Roth test have made obscenity almost a dead issue in the Supreme Court.   To be judged obscene, a book or film must be completely pornographic, with no "redeeming social value" whatever.   Just about anything with a plot or a few moralistic sentences can pass muster.   And *Ulysses*, which started it all less than forty years ago, now seems incredibly tame.

Establishment newspapers and radio and television stations seldom have cause to worry about obscenity laws. By custom they blue-pencil or blip out anything that might conceivably be offensive to anyone; their standards of self-censorship are far more severe than even the Hicklin rule. Underground newspapers, racy magazines, and many books and movies operate from a different premise. They try to come as close as possible to the legal limits of obscenity, without crossing the border into arrests and lawsuits. If every case went immediately to the Supreme Court, this would present no special problems. Unfortunately, it takes money, time, and luck to fight a case that far. In theory, of course, lower courts and local police departments are supposed to follow the Supreme Court's lead. In practice, they are very likely to revert to the Hicklin rule, or even more stringent standards.

Obscenity is not, therefore, the pointless issue it may seem to be. There are novelists, editors, and filmmakers who claim with total sincerity that they cannot say what they want to say without risking prosecution for obscenity. The argument is especially sound when applied to the underground newspapers, which use obscenity to help carry a distinct political message. When an underground editor finds his paper banned and his staff jailed on grounds of obscenity, there is often good reason to agree that his political stance has been intentionally stifled.

Under pure libertarian theory there would, of course, be no such thing as an obscenity law. Social responsibility theory would permit obscenity legislation only if the mass media were unwilling to restrain themselves within the bounds of good taste. Most of the media *do* restrain themselves in this way. Of those that do not, many are apparently trying to convey a viewpoint that cannot be conveyed "tastefully." When the government censors these media, is it following a social responsibility model or an authoritarian one? To put the question another way: If "dirty" words have come to stand for an ideology, then what is the difference between sexual repression and political repression?

LIBEL

Libel law is an incredibly complicated affair, but for beginning journalists it is by far the most important kind of law to learn. And there is no better illustration of how an essentially libertarian government tries to protect the rights of the individual without abridging the rights of the mass media. We must start with some definitions.

Defamation is any statement about an individual which exposes him to hatred, contempt, or ridicule; or which causes him to be avoided; or which tends to injure him in his occupation. Libel is essentially written defamation. The distinction between libel and slander (spoken defamation) was written into the law long before radio and TV came along to confuse the issue. As a rule, scripted broadcasts and films are treated as libel, while live radio and TV ad libs fall under the heading of slander. Since the laws and penalties are pretty much the same, we will ignore the distinction and call them all libel.

There are two kinds of libel—civil and criminal. In civil libel the person who's libeled sues the person who libeled him, and if he wins he collects money. In criminal libel the government prosecutes the libeler, and if it wins it fines him or puts him in jail; the person libeled is no more than a witness.

For every case of criminal libel today there are hundreds of cases of civil libel. Criminal libel, in fact, is little more than a holdover from the days of "seditious libel" (see pp. 174–75). But it is still used from time to time, when someone libels a dead person, or a group, or a local government official.

There are two kinds of civil libel too. Some statements are libelous by definition; judges call them libel *per se*. Accusing a person of a crime, for instance, is automatically libel. So is charging him with immorality, or a contagious disease, or professional incompetence. Other statements are libelous only sometimes, depending on the conditions; they are called libel *per quod*. Suppose, for example, you wrote a gossip column for your school newspaper, and in it accused a fellow student of getting drunk last weekend. Now getting drunk is not the worst thing a college student can do, so the judge might decide that your statement did not constitute libel *per se*. It would then be up to the jury to say whether or not it was libel *per quod*. If your classmate happened to be president of the local temperance union, the jury would probably say that it was; if he was a regular tippler, on the other hand, the jury might well rule that there was no libel at all.

There are three important defenses against libel: (1) Truth, (2) Privilege, and (3) Fair comment.

1. Truth. A libelous statement that's true is still technically a libel, but it's a legal libel. In all but a few states (where lack of malice is also required), proof that the statement is true is enough to win a libel case, regardless of any other factor. Literal truth on every point is not required, only on the important ones. If the newspaper says that Jones was arrested for shoplifting in Detroit, when he was really arrested for shoplifting in Chicago, the newspaper is still substantially accurate—and Jones loses his case.

2. Privilege. Certain official documents and proceedings are said to be "privileged." This means that the mass media may quote from them without fear of a lawsuit, even if they contain libelous statements. The

LIBEL BY MISTAKE

Ninety percent of all libel cases are the result of an accident.   John Smith of 119 Jones Street is arrested for shoplifting.   A careless typesetter prints it as John Jones of 119 Smith Street, and that's how it goes into the newspaper. Next morning Jones and his lawyer arrive at the publisher's office to discuss their libel suit.

Jones has an open-and-shut case.   The fact that it was an error is no defense, and accusing a man of shoplifting is libel *per se*.   Most such cases are settled out of court, and every metropolitan newspaper and book publisher has at least a part-time attorney to handle them.

Although error is not a defense in libel actions, it is an advantage.   This is because there are two kinds of judgments awarded in libel suits—actual damages and punitive damages.   Actual damages are assessed according to how much harm (financial, emotional, and otherwise) the person libeled actually suffered as a result of the libel.   They seldom amount to much. Punitive damages—which is where the big money comes in—are granted only if the libeler is shown to be malicious or grossly incompetent.   Many states have a law that if a newspaper promptly retracts a libelous statement, that in itself is proof that no malice was intended.   John Jones will get his retraction, and can collect only actual damages.

---

precise definition of privilege varies from state to state, and it is important to learn the local variation.   A police arrest record, a trial, and a Senate speech are all privileged, but an unofficial interview with the police chief, the judge, or the Senator is not.   Quoting an interview accurately is no defense if the interview happens to include a libel.   The person interviewed can be sued—but so can the reporter who copied it down and the publisher who let it be printed.   Usually the publisher is the one with the most money, so he's the one most likely to be sued.

In 1970 the Supreme Court vastly expanded the definition of privilege, ruling that any statement on a public issue made at a public meeting (such as a city council session) is privileged, and may be quoted with impunity.   As later interpretations clarify the meaning of this case, privilege may become even more important than it is today.

What is the purpose of the defense of privilege?   The authors of the Constitution recognized that a legislator would be unable to debate many issues effectively if he had to steer clear of possible libels.   So they wrote a clause providing that "for any Speech or Debate in either House, they [Senators and Representatives] shall not be questioned in any other place."   This was quickly expanded to include a variety of other federal, state, and local government officials.   How could a judge conduct a trial, or a policeman file an arrest report, if what they said could be held against them in a libel suit?

But the single most important function of the mass media in a democracy is to report on the actions and statements of government officials. Unless governmental privilege were extended to the media, the police report, the trial, and the Senate speech all would be secret. It soon became apparent that the media must be privileged to report everything that government officials are privileged to say. No doubt some individuals are damaged (libeled) in the process, but without the defense of privilege the mass media would be paralyzed.

3. Fair Comment. Statements of opinion that are not malicious and are of legitimate interest to the public are protected against libel charges by the defense of fair comment. A theater review is the most common example. A reviewer who writes that a particular actor gave a rotten, incompetent performance last night cannot be sued for libel. But if he says the actor was drunk on stage (a statement of fact, not opinion), then he can be sued. Ditto if he never bothered to attend the play (malice). And he most certainly can be sued if he adds the actor is also a rotten, incompetent golfer (not of legitimate public interest). But as long as the reviewer sticks to his honest opinion of the performance, he is safe from a libel action.

So much for theater reviewers. But what about political reporters? The survival of democracy, after all, depends at least in part on the ability of the mass media to tell the public all there is to know about political candidates and public officials. Wouldn't it be a good idea to extend the defense of fair comment to political reporters, leaving them free to give their honest opinions without fear of a libel suit? Perhaps we should go even further. A reporter who is afraid to say something untrue will hesitate to say a lot of things that *are* true, for fear he might not be able to prove them. If we really want the mass media to offer a free-wheeling discussion of politics and government, perhaps we should exempt these topics from libel actions altogether.

So far no state has gone quite this far. But the Supreme Court took a giant step in this direction in 1964, with the landmark case of *New York Times Company v. Sullivan.*

The case centered on a protest advertisement placed in the *Times* by a civil rights group in Montgomery, Alabama. The ad accused the Montgomery police of a "wave of terror" against black activists. L. B. Sullivan, Commissioner of Public Affairs for the city (responsible for the police department), sued the *Times* for libel. He had a strong case. Newspapers are, of course, liable for anything they print, including the ads. This particular ad undoubtedly contained factual errors of a libelous nature; even though Sullivan wasn't named, the ad reflected badly on his department and therefore (to anyone who knew the governmental set-up in Montgomery) on him. An Alabama jury awarded Sullivan $500,000, and the Alabama Supreme Court upheld the verdict.

The U.S. Supreme Court reversed it. In order to insure free debate on issues of public importance, the court said, critics of public officials must be given more leeway than those who write about private individuals:

> The constitutional guarantees require, we think, a federal rule that prohibits a public official from recovering damages for a defamatory false-hood relating to his official conduct unless he proves that the statement was made with "actual malice"—that is, with knowledge that it was false or with reckless disregard of whether it was false or not.[17]

In other words, a public official cannot sue for libel at all except under circumstances where a private citizen could collect punitive as well as actual damages.

Three years later, the Supreme Court extended the *"Times* rule" still further. Two cases were involved. In one, retired General Edwin A. Walker sued the Associated Press for a dispatch claiming he had led an attack against federal marshals in an attempt to halt the integration of the University of Mississippi. In the other, University of Georgia athletic director Wallace Butts sued the *Saturday Evening Post* for an article charging that he had fixed a Georgia-Alabama football game.

Both articles were clearly libelous. Neither man was a public official. The cases seemed open-and-shut, and so the lower courts thought. The Supreme Court disagreed. Reviewing both decisions at once, the court ruled that a public figure can win a libel suit only "on a showing of highly unreasonable conduct constituting an extreme departure from the standards of investigation and reporting ordinarily adhered to by responsible publishers."[18] On the basis of this standard, the court reversed the *Walker* verdict (the AP was under deadline pressure and made an honest error), but upheld the *Butts* decision (the *Post* was blatantly irresponsible).

The "Butts-Walker rule" for public *figures* is a little more narrow than the *Times* rule for public *officials,* but both are plenty broad enough to give the mass media a lot of freedom. Nearly everyone mentioned in the media, after all, is either a public official or a public figure—otherwise he wouldn't be news.

The purpose of libel law is not to make the job of the press harder, but rather to protect the rights of individuals. Yet the fear of libel suits *does* interfere with the freedom of the media to report and comment on the news. Over the last decade the courts have devoted themselves to lessening this interference—by expanding the notion of privilege, and by invoking special rules for public figures and public officials. Libel law is still inconsistent with the libertarian theory, but it is no longer the practical barrier to Freedom of the Press that it once was.

PRIVACY

The right of privacy is a comparative newcomer to the law. It was first suggested by two young Boston lawyers, Samuel Warren and Louis D. Brandeis, in an 1890 article in the *Harvard Law Review*. The authors argued that precedent for privacy law already existed in legal areas like defamation and trespass. They urged the courts to expand the notion to include the right to be left alone by the mass media.

The courts refused, so various state legislatures did the job instead. In 1903 New York passed the first specific privacy law, making it illegal to use the name or picture of any person for advertising purposes without his permission. Today, 35 states recognize the right of privacy in one form or another. So does the Supreme Court—though it has severely limited that right as applied to subjects "of legitimate news interest."[19]

The law of privacy is different in every state and changing all the time. But in general the following rules hold: (1) A person's name or picture may not be used in an advertisement or for purposes of trade without his consent. (2) A person's name or picture may not be used in a fictional story without his consent. (3) A person's name or picture may be used in a true story without his consent, so long as the story is of some conceivable legitimate interest to the reader. Anything said about public officials, and almost anything about public figures, is considered to satisfy this requirement. (4) A person's name or picture may not be used in a fictionalization of a true story without his consent, if significant parts of the story are known, or should be known, to be false. More fictionalization is permitted for public officials than for public figures, and more for public figures than for private citizens.

So far privacy law hasn't had much effect on the day-to-day work of the mass media. But give it time. Perhaps the single most frequent complaint about the media is that they unnecessarily invade the privacy of their news sources (see pp. 85–86). As the social responsibility theory becomes more and more dominant, this complaint may eventually find itself written into law.

FREE PRESS/FAIR TRIAL

The First Amendment to the Constitution guarantees Freedom of the Press. The Sixth Amendment to the Constitution guarantees the right of every defendant to an impartial jury. When the mass media set out to report a sensational trial, the two amendments come into inevitable conflict. Consider the most extreme case in modern history: the assassination of President John F. Kennedy. After the incredible publicity surrounding the assassination, how could you possibly find an impartial jury to decide the guilt or innocence of Lee Harvey Oswald (accused of shooting Kennedy) or Jack Ruby (accused of shooting Oswald)?

Until recently, the courts have tried to resolve the free press/fair trial dilemma within the judicial system itself. Sensational trials were moved to distant cities, juries were locked up and denied access to newspapers, and so forth. When even these techniques failed to insure a fair trial, the defendant was simply released. In 1966, for example, the Supreme Court reviewed the case of Dr. Sam Sheppard, convicted of murder in Cleveland twelve years before. The court ruled that newspaper publicity before and during the trial (headlines such as "Sheppard Must Swing!" were common) had denied Sheppard his right to an impartial jury. Because the judge failed to insulate the jury from this furor, the Supreme Court reversed the conviction.

For our purposes, the important thing about the Sheppard case is that no action whatever was taken against the news media. Everyone agreed that the Cleveland newspapers had been irresponsible, but no one claimed that they had done anything illegal.

Today the Cleveland papers would probably be found in contempt of court, with a stiff fine attached. Judges have been consistently unable to solve the free press/fair trial problem on their own. So in the last four or five years, they have tried to solve it by restricting the mass media. From the day Martin Luther King was assassinated to the day James Earl Ray was convicted of the crime, the media were under strict judicial supervision. They were forbidden to publish anything that might possibly prejudice Ray's jury; those who violated the rules were held in contempt of court. The same procedure was followed in the trial of Sirhan Sirhan for the assassination of Robert Kennedy, and again in the Mylai massacre courts-martial. Literally hundreds of local judges have continued the new trend, even in simple cases of divorce or assault. It is no longer unusual for a newsman to find himself in legal hot water for writing something a judge didn't want him to write.

Some judicial restrictions on the press are traditional. Most judges have always refused to allow photographers and TV cameramen into their courtrooms. The American Bar Association endorses this common-sense rule, and in 1965 the Supreme Court held that the televising of the Billie Sol Estes trial was unconstitutional. But barring the courtroom door to a photographer is one thing; following a reporter to his desk and checking what he writes is something else again.

In 1970, commenting on the on-going murder trial of hippie Charles Manson, President Richard Nixon offhandedly stated that the defendant was "either directly or indirectly guilty." He soon corrected himself, but the papers headlined his error anyhow. Manson himself displayed the headline to his jury, raising the possibility of a mistrial or a reversal on appeal. Question: Should the mass media have published Nixon's statement? Another question: Should the mass media be forbidden by the government to publish such statements?

The answer to the first question may be No, but the answer to the second question may also be No. Responsible newsmen do their honest best to protect the rights of criminal defendants. The notion that the government should *enforce* this responsibility is an extremely dangerous one, potentially suggestive of the secret, torture-ridden "Star Chamber Courts" of medieval England. Yet many state legislatures today are considering bills to control what the press may say about crimes and trials. By the time this book is published, some of those bills will almost certainly have become laws.

Sometimes the public's right to know is more important even than the defendant's right to a fair trial. If the alleged murderers of Vietnamese civilians at Mylai cannot find an impartial jury, then let them go free. Even that is better than hiding the facts of the massacre from the public.

ADVERTISING

Like everything else in the mass media, advertising is at least theoretically covered by the First Amendment. Nevertheless, the federal government and every state government have laws forbidding deceptive or irresponsible advertising practices. The purpose of these laws is obviously to protect the reader, listener, and viewer. Sensible though they are, they are not consistent with strict libertarian theory.

Regulation of national advertising is mostly in the hands of the Federal Trade Commission, with a little help from the Post Office Department and other government agencies. The FTC has five weapons against misleading ads: (1) Letters of compliance, in which the advertiser informally promises to shape up; (2) Stipulations, containing a formal agreement to drop a specific ad; (3) Consent orders, handed down in the middle of a hearing before a verdict is reached; (4) Cease and desist orders, issued after a formal finding of guilty; and (5) Publicity.

None of these weapons works very well, mostly because the FTC takes so long to use them. Advertising messages are by their very nature ephemeral. By the time the FTC gets around to opposing a particular campaign, the campaign has just about run its course. The advertiser already has a new one in the works, perhaps every bit as deceptive as the original. The FTC starts all over again—and never catches up.

Government regulation of broadcast advertising is somewhat more stringent and more effective. Cigarette ads, for example, are no longer permitted on the air at all. This seems a direct violation of the First Amendment, but the courts have ruled it legal.

Are the mass media free to accept or reject advertising as they wish? As the cigarette example proves, the broadcast media may be forbidden to accept advertisements for certain products. Except for the requirements of the fairness doctrine and the equal time rule, however, they may reject any ad they wish.

The print media, meanwhile, have traditionally been free to accept and reject whatever ads they please. The Post Office, however, prohibits lottery promotions and certain other kinds of advertisements from being sent through the mails—which effectively bars them from most newspapers and magazines. And some experts (a small minority so far) have argued that all the media should be required to accept any ad dealing with an issue of public importance, and to reject any ad that has been found to be fraudulent.

To the extent that the government ever requires the mass media to print or broadcast a specific advertisement, it does so in flagrant violation of the libertarian theory. Of the four theories of the press, several permit the government to tell the media what they must not do. Only one— Soviet theory—permits the government to tell the media what they must do. Yet the alternative to this sort of government control is to let each publisher reject any advertisement with which he disagrees. Certain viewpoints might thus be completely frozen out of the mass media, despite their willingness to pay their own way. Such is the dilemma of an essentially libertarian society, trying to preserve the freedom of the media without endangering the freedom of everyone else.

––––––––––

Not every example of government control over the mass media consists of direct regulation of content. Licensing and antitrust laws, for instance, control who may become a media owner. Government secrecy and news management control what sorts of information become available to the media. Postal mailing permits control how the media may be distributed. These forms of government control have a significant, though indirect, effect on the content of the mass media.

ACCESS

Until 1969, the United States government had for years flatly prohibited newsmen from visiting Cuba, mainland China, Albania, and a number of other places. Today these rules are somewhat relaxed, but it is still difficult for a reporter to get permission to travel to certàin communist countries. Whatever the purpose of this policy, it is an important infringment on the freedom of the mass media. The right to publish the news is of very little value without the right to investigate it first.

From the very beginning, the U.S. government recognized both the need for media access to the news and the convenience to government of restricting that access. Though the Constitution was debated in secret, the newly established House of Representatives immediately opened its doors to reporters, and the Senate followed suit in 1795. Yet even today much of the important work of Congress takes place in the executive sessions of Congressional committees, which are closed to newsmen.

On the whole, the formal enactments of government tend more to protect than to restrict the right of access. On the federal level, there is the "Freedom of Information Act," which requires government officials to release everything that is in the public interest for the public to know. At least 42 states have their own open-record laws, and 38 have statutes specifically permitting journalists to attend meetings of various government bodies. Municipal governments usually provide press passes for local reporters, allowing them to cross police and fire lines in order to collect the news.

Yet there are many laws which have the opposite effect. Government regulation of foreign travel is one example. Executive sessions of Congressional committees are another. Restricted access to juvenile court and certain other trials is a third. Even the Freedom of Information Act includes a collection of nine exceptions—everything from national security to personnel, from interagency memos to geological data. State versions have their own lists of exceptions.

Moreover, the practical policies of most government officials are far more restrictive than the laws on the books. For a journalist the problem is access to news. But for a city councilman or an undersecretary of agriculture, the problem is access to news *about him*—news that may damage his reputation or impair his flexibility. We have already discussed the news management activities of government (see Chapter 6). It is hardly surprising that public officials do their best to manipulate the news, to emphasize what is favorable and to hide what is unfavorable. In the process, the reporter's "right of access" often gets forgotten.

Sometimes government officials lie—the ultimate form of news management. Shortly after the Cuban missile crisis in 1962, Assistant Secretary of Defense Arthur Sylvester addressed the Deadline Club of Sigma Delta Chi. Many of the reporters had complained about government secrecy and news management during the crisis. Said Sylvester: "It's in the government's right, if necessary, to lie to save itself for when it's going up toward a nuclear war. It seems . . . this seems to me basic—basic." Later Sylvester clarified the statement: "The government did not have the right to lie to the American people, but it did have the right in time of extreme crisis to attempt to mislead the enemy, which might in turn mislead the American people."[20] If government officials feel free to lie to the media, then the right of access to those officials is of questionable value.

The government has a case, of course. Public officials often hide news from the media in order to protect their own skins, but perhaps as often they hide news in order to advance the policies of the government. Their purpose is laudable and legitimate. So is the purpose of the media: to inform the people. Perhaps it is best to conceive of the government-media interaction as an "adversary relationship." When a newsman gets a controversial story, the efficiency and flexibility of government may be impaired. When the government succeeds in keeping the story secret, the ability of the public to make sound decisions may be impaired. Both media and government are motivated by valid goals—but the goals are mutually exclusive. Inevitably they come into conflict.

In this adversary relationship, the strength of the government lies in the fact that it makes and controls most of the news. The main weapon of the media is the right of access. To keep the battle even, then, the right of access must remain strong.

CONFIDENTIALITY

In 1966, an editor of the University of Oregon *Emerald* wrote an article on campus drug use. Shortly thereafter, the editor was subpoenaed by a local grand jury and ordered to reveal the names of the students (the users) she had interviewed. When she refused, she was convicted of contempt of court.

The right of the mass media to keep their sources of information confidential is essential. New York *Times* columnist Max Frankel explains why:

> In private dealings with persons who figure in the news, reporters obtain not only on-the-record comments but also confidential judgments and facts that they then use to appraise the accuracy and meaning of other men's words and deeds. Without the access and without such confidential relationships, much important information would have to be gathered by remote means and much could never be subjected to cross-examination. Politicians who weigh their words, officials who fear their superiors, citizens who fear persecution or prosecution would refuse to talk with reporters or admit them to their circles if they felt that confidences would be betrayed at the behest of the Government.[21]

There are many relationships in this country that are considered "privileged"—which means that the government is not permitted to pry into them in search of information. Among these are lawyer-client, doctor-patient, priest-parishioner, and husband-wife; in some states the list also includes social worker-client, accountant-client, and psychologist-patient.

In some foreign countries and in fifteen states, the reporter-source relationship is also privileged. New York's statute, for example, protects "journalists and newscasters from charges of contempt in any proceeding brought under state law for refusing or failing to disclose information or sources of information obtained in gathering news for publication."[22] In the federal system and the remaining 35 states, however, a reporter has no more right than the average citizen to withhold information demanded by a court, a grand jury, or a legislative committee.

In early 1970, for example, the Justice Department asked a number of mass media to hand over their unused film, notes, correspondence, memos, and other materials on the Black Panther Party and the Weatherman faction of the Students for a Democratic Society. The government was in the process of preparing cases against members of both groups. It believed that *Time*, *Newsweek*, CBS, NBC, the New York *Times*, and various other media representatives had information in their files that would be useful to the prosecution. When the media hesitated to comply with the request, the Justice Department went into court and obtained subpoenas for what it wanted.

None of the media gave in willingly—but most gave in. The New York *Times* put up the toughest fight. It editorialized: "Demands by police officials, grand juries or other authorities for blanket access to press files will inevitably dry up essential avenues of information." An even more serious danger, the *Times* noted, is that "the entire process will create the impression that the press operates as an investigative agency for government rather than as an independent force dedicated to the unfettered flow of information to the public."[23]

With the support of his newspaper, *Times* reporter Earl Caldwell took his subpoena to court. (Supporting briefs were submitted by CBS, the Associated Press, *Newsweek*, the American Civil Liberties Union, and the Reporter's Committee on Freedom of the Press.) Caldwell argued that the First Amendment guarantees reporters the right of confidentiality: "Nothing less than a full and unqualified privilege to newsmen, empowering them to decline to testify as to any information professionally obtained, will truly preserve and protect the newsgathering activities of the media."

Federal District Judge Alfonso J. Zirpoli wasn't willing to go that far. But he did limit the subpoena powers of the government over journalists:

> When the exercise of grand jury power . . . may impinge upon or repress First Amendment rights of freedom of speech, press and association, which centuries of experience have found to be indispensable to the survival of a free society, such power shall not be exercised in a manner

likely to do so until there has been a clear showing of compelling and overriding national interest that cannot be served by alternative means.[24]

Later Zirpoli ruled that this protection applies to reporters for all kinds of publications, including the Black Panther Party newsletter.

Eventually the U.S. Supreme Court will be asked to deal with this problem, to determine the extent and limits of journalistic privilege implied by the First Amendment. In the meantime, it is up to the media to resist attempts by government to "borrow" confidential information and identify confidential sources. Many of the most vital news stories of our time—from pot use on campus to the plans of the Black Panther Party—can be reported only if sources feel they can trust the media. Anything that destroys that trust is a tremendous danger to Freedom of the Press.

ANTITRUST

The Sherman Act of 1890 provides that "every contract, combination in the form of a trust or otherwise, or conspiracy, in restraint of trade or commerce among the several states, or with foreign nations, is hereby declared illegal." The Clayton Act of 1914 further outlaws all practices that "tend to lessen competition or to create a monopoly in any line of commerce." These two laws are the basis for all antitrust action in federal courts today.

As we have seen (see Chapter 4), the mass media are by no means immune to the Twentieth Century trend toward monopoly. It is not surprising, then, that the Sherman and Clayton Acts have sometimes been invoked again the media—the First Amendment notwithstanding.

The first such case occurred in 1945, when the Supreme Court decided *Associated Press v. United States*. The Jusice Department brought suit against the Associated Press, charging that it was a "conspiracy in restraint of trade." At issue were two AP bylaws: One provided that AP members could not sell news to nonmembers, and the other gave each member virtual veto power over the applications of competitors for the service. Together, these two regulations permitted a one-newspaper monopoly of wire news within each city. The Supreme Court agreed that this constituted an illegal news monopoly, and outlawed the two bylaws.

The following are typical of antitrust actions against the mass media since 1945:

- *Lorain Journal Company v. U.S.* A local newspaper refused to accept advertising from any company that advertised on a competing radio station. The court outlawed the practice.
- *Times-Picayune v. U.S.* Two New Orleans newspapers required

advertisers to buy ads in both papers or neither. The court permitted the practice so long as it had no deleterious effects on competing media.

- *U.S. v. Kansas City Star.* A morning-evening-Sunday newspaper combination killed its daily competitor by requiring advertisers to buy space in all three at once. The court stopped the practice, and made the company sell its radio and TV outlets.
- *U.S. v. Times Mirror Corporation.* The court refused to allow the Los Angeles *Times* to buy the nearby San Bernardino *Sun,* since the two competed for the same advertising and some of the same readers.
- *U.S. v. Citizen Publishing Company.* The court outlawed a Tucson newspaper joint operating agreement because it involved profit pooling, price fixing, and other monopolistic practices. (Congress later passed a law legalizing such arrangements once again.)

As these five cases indicate, antitrust prosecutions against the mass media have tended to concentrate on advertising. This is because advertising is more obviously related to "trade" and "commerce" than news is. To base an antitrust suit on *news* monopoly would weaken the government's case and make First Amendment objections more persuasive. Yet, as we have seen, it is news monopoly that is the real problem for today's mass media. By confining itself to regulation of advertising—and not too much of that—the government has essentially ignored the most serious threat to freedom of information in modern times: media monopoly.

This is a real dilemma for libertarian theorists. Even the current wishy-washy regulation of media monopoly runs contrary to the First Amendment, though the courts have ruled it legal. Who is the Justice Department, after all, to tell the Los Angeles *Times* it cannot buy the San Bernardino *Sun?* In libertarian theory such an action is evil incarnate. Yet only the government is powerful enough today to reverse the trend toward monopoly in the mass media. Is the threat of government interference still the greatest danger to Freedom of the Press, as it was when the First Amendment was written? Or is monopoly now a greater danger? Which is the lesser of the two evils?

PERMITS AND LICENSES

Licensing of communications media is a traditional device used by authoritarian governments to insure control over the news. The licensed publisher is permitted to print whatever he likes; if he prints something the government *doesn't* like, he loses his license. Unlicensed publishers, of course, are forbidden to print anything at all.

Government licensing of the media has always been held to be unconstitutional.   In 1938, for example, the Supreme Court ruled that a local ordinance requiring all distributers of literature to get permission from the City Manager was contrary to the First Amendment.   A few years later, the court outlawed a local ten-dollar license fee for booksellers.   Today, cities may regulate the street sales of publications only if their regulations have nothing to do with the content of those publications.   If the Boy Scouts are allowed to distribute their leaflets on Main Street, then the Berkeley *Barb* is free to distribute as well.

There is one big exception to this principle: broadcasting.   Because of the limited number of available broadcast frequencies, the government of nearly every country in the world—including the United States—has taken on the job of licensing broadcasters.   We will return to this exception in a few pages.

A less-known exception is the postal mailing permit.   The United States government decided many years ago to encourage the distribution of knowledge by establishing the second-class postage category.   Second-class mail is reserved for printed matter "published for dissemination of information of a public character, or devoted to literature, the sciences, arts, or some special industry."[25]   Second-class mail travels as fast as first-class, but costs much less; the government takes a financial loss on every second-class item mailed.

In order to qualify for second-class postal privileges, a publication must apply to the Post Office Department for a permit.   By deciding which publications "deserve" the permit, the post office can set itself up as a licensing authority very much like the English kings of the Sixteenth Century.

In 1946, for example, the Post Office Department withdrew the second-class permit from *Esquire* magazine because of its "smoking car humor."   Loss of the permit would have cost *Esquire* $500,000 a year in extra postage, so the magazine appealed the decision to the Supreme Court.   The court ruled that the Postmaster General had overstepped his authority, that he could not on his own declare a publication to be obscene.

Nevertheless, the Post Office Department still has the power to ban from the mails any book or magazine that has been ruled obscene by the courts.   It may also issue "adminstrative stop orders" to keep such items out of the mails pending court action.   And it may revoke the second-class mailing permit for any number of reasons—too much advertising, misleading content, sedition, etc.

No matter what it's called, this is licensing.   The government, through the post office, offers publishers a special subsidy to help them distribute their publications.   Then the government, again through the post office, takes away the subsidy from publishers of whom it disapproves.

A much more dangerous form of licensing was recently suggested by

Dr. W. Walter Menninger, a psychiatrist and a member of the National Commission on the Causes and Prevention of Violence. Dr. Menninger recommended that individual newsmen be licensed by the government, in order to increase public confidence and to weed out "individuals who are totally inept."[26] Fortunately, there is no indication that anyone in government took the suggestion seriously.

Closely related to licensing is restrictive taxation—also a traditional tool of authoritarian regimes. The so-called "Stamp Act" was passed by the English Parliament to impose a heavy tax on colonial printers in America; it was one of the major issues of the American Revolution. Punitive taxation is uncommon in U.S. law, but it is not unknown. In the 1930s, Governor Huey Long of Louisiana put a two-percent tax on the gross receipts of every large newspaper in the state (all were critical of the Long administration). One paper appealed the tax to the courts, and eventually the Supreme Court declared it unconstitutional.

We have discussed four kinds of government control over the mass media in this section: (1) Restricted access to the news; (2) Invasion of confidential sources and information; (3) Antitrust legislation; and (4) Permits and licenses. None of the four has any *direct* effect on the content of the media. But all four have vast *indirect* effects. The first two concern what the media are able to find out; the last two involve who is able to own the media and make use of media privileges. A government with such powerful indirect tools of control has little need for direct ones.

———

The authority of the government over radio and television is far greater than government control of the print media. In theory, at least, any broadcast license may be revoked by the government if the station fails to fulfill its obligation to the public. In practice, however, government regulation tends to concentrate on the pettier aspects of broadcasting. Though the fear of government intervention often motivates the behavior of broadcasters, the government has done little to justify that fear.

WHY BROADCASTING?

Government regulation of radio began in 1910, when Congress ratified a treaty providing that ships at sea and shore stations must answer each other's emergency radio messages. Two years later came the Radio Act, another common-sense law. It required private broadcasters to steer clear of the wave lengths used for government transmissions. The Secretary of Commerce was given the job of administering the law. Each applicant was awarded his own radio "license," which authorized him to broadcast whatever he wanted, wherever he wanted, whenever he wanted, on whatever frequency he wanted—as long as he avoided the government-used wave lengths.

By 1927, there were 733 private radio stations in the country. Most were concentrated in the big cities. They spent much of their time jumping from point to point on the radio dial, trying to avoid interference—but the stronger stations still managed to smother the weaker ones. In some areas there were more stations than frequencies, making interference inevitable. The situation was intolerable. Radio manufacturers, the National Association of Broadcasters, and the listening public all called on the federal government to do something about it. The air waves belong to the public, they argued. Since the air waves were a mess, it was the government's job to clean the mess up.

Thus was born the Radio Act of 1927. A five-man Federal Radio Commission was given the power to license broadcasters for three-year periods, allotting each one a specific frequency in a specific location. If there were more license applicants than available frequencies (as there were bound to be), the Commission was to favor those applicants most likely to serve "the public interest, convenience, or necessity." The same standard was to be used in judging whether a licensee deserved to keep his license at the end of the three years. And in case new problems came up, the Commission was empowered to "make such regulations not inconsistent with law as it may deem necessary to prevent interference between stations and to carry out the provisions of this Act."

Seven years later, Congress passed the Communications Act of 1934. Besides radio, the Commission was given authority over telephone, telegraph, and television as well. It was expanded to seven members and renamed the Federal Communications Commission. The other provisions were essentially the same as those of the Radio Act. They are still the same today.

The government began broadcast regulation by popular request, in order to allocate frequencies. But there were more would-be station owners than available wave lengths. At that point the government *could* have assigned licenses by picking numbers out of a hat, or by raffling them off to the highest bidder. But it decided instead to judge program content, to award the license to the most "deserving" applicant, not the luckiest or the richest.

If this sounds like censorship to you, it did to some broadcasters too. The 1927 Radio Act provides:

> Nothing in this Act shall be understood or construed to give the licensing authority the power of censorship . . . and no regulation or condition shall be promulgated or fixed by the licensing authority which shall interfere with the right of free speech by means of radio communication.

The Communications Act of 1934 included a nearly identical provision.

Its meaning was tested in 1931, when the Federal Radio Commission refused to renew the license of station KFKB, because the owner used a daily medical program to plug his own patent medicines. The station took the case to court—and lost. The court ruled:

> In considering the question whether the public interest, convenience, or necessity will be served by a renewal of appellant's license, the commission has merely exercised its undoubted right to take note of appellant's past conduct, which is not censorship.[27]

It is fruitless to debate the point. Licensing has traditionally been a tool of authoritarian governments, which used it as a form of censorship. The power to license a broadcast station is—beyond doubt—the power to control what it broadcasts. Yet licensing of radio and television is inevitable, simply because there are not enough channels to go around. Every libertarian government has faced this dilemma. The only ones that didn't wind up licensing their broadcast stations wound up owning them instead—an even more authoritarian solution.

The First Amendment does apply to broadcasting—but not in the same way it applies to newspapers and magazines. As the Federal Court of Appeals put it in 1966: "A newspaper can be operated at the whim or caprice of its owner; a broadcasting station cannot. After nearly five decades of operation, the broadcasting industry does not seem to have grasped the simple fact that a broadcast license is a public trust subject to termination for breach of duty."[28]

LICENSING

The fundamental power of the Federal Communications Commission is its power to grant and renew broadcast licenses. The standard to be used in this operation is, of course, the "public interest, convenience, or necessity." Over the years, the FCC has expanded this notion to include many different criteria. Pike and Fischer, the chief law digest for communications law, classifies them this way:

1. Fair, efficient, and equitable distribution of facilities.
2. Interference.
3. Financial qualifications.
4. Misrepresentation of facts to the Commission.
5. Difficulties with other government agencies; involvement in civil or criminal litigation.
6. Violation of Communications Act or FCC rules.
7. Delegation of control over programs.

8. Technical service.
9. Facilities subject to assignment.
10. Local ownership.
11. Integration of ownership and management.
12. Participation in civic activities.
13. Diversification of background of persons controlling.
14. Broadcast experience.
15. New station versus expansion of existing service.
16. Sense of public service responsibility.
17. Conflicting interests.
18. Programming.
19. Operating plans.
20. Legal qualifications.
21. Diversification of control of communications media—newspaper affiliation.
22. Diversification—multiple ownership of broadcast facilities.
23. Effect on economic interest of existing station.
24. "Need."
25. Miscellaneous factors.[29]

In deciding between competing applicants for an open frequency, the FCC actually uses these 25 criteria. But this happens only on occasion. Most of the desirable frequencies are already taken—which is why the government got into broadcast regulation in the first place. In practice, then, the FCC spends most of its time considering license *renewal* applications. And that's another story entirely.

Between 1934 and 1962, the FCC failed to renew a grand total of *NINE* broadcast licenses. There were a few before 1934, and a couple after 1962—pulling the all-time total up to roughly fifteen. That's fifteen no votes out of approximately 50,000 licenses considered during the last forty years. It would seem that the average broadcaster hasn't much to worry about.

The FCC is severely limited in the penalties it is allowed to impose on errant broadcast stations. It can assess a small fine, which for a profitable station is a wrist-slap of no particular importance. It can renew the license for a probationary period of one year, which merely prolongs the agony. Or it can take the license away altogether. The FCC is rather like a judge with only two sentences in his repertoire: five minutes in jail or the gas chamber. He knows the first sentence is too light to be effective, but the other one is far too severe—so he's stuck with the first. Loss of the license is the gas chamber for a radio or TV station. Understandably, the FCC imposes that penalty only on the most egregiously irresponsible broadcasters. A station that falsifies its records or tries to bribe the Commission stands a good chance of losing its license. A station that merely does a poor job is reasonably safe.

The prevailing attitude on the FCC is well illustrated by the WLBT-

TV case. In 1964, Dr. Everett Parker of the United Church of Christ led a drive to deny the Jackson (Mississippi) station its license renewal, on the grounds that it had made no effort to serve the black population. At first the Commission simply dismissed the complaint, claiming that a citizens group had no standing in a license hearing. Dr. Parker went to court and had the ruling overturned. Then the Commission decided that there wasn't enough proof of discrimination by the station to justify taking away the license. Dr. Parker went to court again, and won the right to still a third hearing. Said Judge Warren Burger:

> The intervenors [Dr. Parker and his colleagues], who were performing a public service under the mandate of this court, were entitled to a more hospitable reception in the performance of that function. As we view the record, the examiner [for the FCC] tended to impede the exploration of the very issues which we would reasonably expect the commission itself would have initiated; an ally was regarded as an opponent.[30]

In an unprecedented (and so far unrepeated) move, the court *itself* revoked the license of WLBT. It instructed the FCC to consider the matter from scratch, reviewing all applications for the license—including the original licensee's—as if it had never seen them before. Reluctantly, the Commission obeyed, and in 1971 it finally awarded the license to the black citizens group.

But the attitude of the Commission itself remained unchanged, as a January, 1970, policy statement indicates. The statement proclaimed that license holders would retain their licenses so long as their programming remained "substantially attuned to meeting the needs and interests" of their audience. In other words, the FCC explained, applicants for license renewal would first be judged on their own merits. Only if they appeared unworthy would competing applications be considered. Never would the competing applicant be measured against the renewal applicant on an even basis.[31]

The FCC uses its power to take away broadcast licenses only on very rare occasions. But lurking in the back of every broadcaster's mind is the fear that *his* license might be the one to go. This fear, however unjustified, makes radio and television somewhat more responsive to the public interest than they might otherwise be.

DIVERSITY

In the last few years of the 1960s, the FCC appeared to be very concerned about the problem of diversity versus monopoly. In quick succession, it took a number of actions which seemed about to change fundamentally the structure of the broadcast industry. The furor has since died down, and most observers expect it to stay dead—but there is at least a chance that it may not.

It all started in March of 1968, when the Commission issued a notice of proposed rule-making, providing that no licensee could acquire a second broadcast station in the same market area (but it could keep the ones it already owned). This was not a rule, just a "proposed rule." The FCC has often followed that procedure. Sometimes the purpose of the proposal is nothing more than publicity; sometimes it is to see how the public will react; and *sometimes* it is to notify the broadcast industry of what's coming. Many more proposed rules have been abandoned than adopted. Nevertheless, broadcasters were scared.

They were a lot more scared in January of 1969, when a bare 3–2 majority of the Commission refused to renew the license of Boston station WHDH-TV. WHDH was known for lackadaisical programming (it had never once included an editorial), but that was not the reason for the decision. The station was owned by the Boston Herald-Traveler Corporation, publisher of a Boston daily newspaper and also owner of local AM and FM radio stations. The FCC decided that this was too much news control in the hands of one company. It awarded the license to a local citizens group instead.

The fear reached its height in 1970, when the FCC adopted the "one-to-a-customer" proposed rule of 1968. Also in 1970, the Commission came up with another proposed rule-making. This one was much more stringent, because it would require licensees to get rid of their newspaper holdings and other broadcast stations (the details of the proposal are listed on pages 125–26). In effect, the 1970 proposed rule would limit each licensee to one broadcast station per market area, period.

No doubt about it: The one-to-a-customer rule is burdensome, the revocation of the Boston license is unprecedented, and the 1970 proposed rule is incredibly radical. But don't count on the FCC to follow through. Since 1968, the Commission has quietly renewed the licenses of literally scores of stations owned by chains, conglomerates, or local newspapers. WHDH is only one station. And the proposed rule is still only proposed. Moreover, two liberal FCC commissioners retired at the close of the Sixties. President Nixon replaced them both with conservatives, including the new FCC Chairman Dean Burch (who was national chairman of the Republican Party under Barry Goldwater). A third liberal, Nicholas Johnson, is due to leave the Commission in the early 1970s. The balance of power is shifting. The 1968 FCC was seriously worried about the dangers of media monopoly. The 1971 FCC was marking time.

Aside from the one-to-a-customer rule, government regulation of broadcast monopoly today is precisely what it was thirty years ago: the "duopoly rule." This provides that no single company may own more than

REGULATING THE NETWORKS

There is one additional rule worth mentioning, passed by the FCC in May of 1970. It forbids television stations in the fifty largest market areas to present more than three hours of network programming between 7 p.m. and 11 p.m. Special network documentaries are exempt. The purpose of the regulation is to get *something* besides the network shows onto prime-time TV. It will have that effect; most stations are now looking elsewhere to fill the extra hour. Unfortunately, the new rule has also killed network plans to consider expanding the early evening news program from thirty minutes to an hour.

TV networks are in some ways the greatest threat to broadcast diversity. Most local stations are network-affiliated, and just about all the powerful ones are. At any given evening hour, the vast majority of the nation's viewers are forced to choose among the same three network programs. Yet the FCC is powerless to regulate the networks directly, since they are not in themselves broadcast stations, and require no license. The new prime-time restriction is the first attempt of the Commission to get at the networks by way of their local outlets. It isn't much, but it's a start.

seven television stations (five VHF), seven AM radio stations, and seven FM radio stations. Even a rabid libertarian would put up with that much.

PROGRAMMING REGULATIONS

The FCC is empowered to look at programming when it considers a license renewal, but it seldom bothers. The real strength of the Commission's control over programming is embodied in three specific regulations: the equal time law, the obscenity provision, and the fairness doctrine.

1. Equal Time. The equal time law, Section 315 of the Communications Act, requires any station that provides time for a political candidate to provide the same amount of time, on the same terms, for every other candidate for that office. The station needn't provide time for anyone, of course. But if one would-be Senator gets a free half hour, every other "legitimate" candidate for that seat is entitled to an equivalent free half hour. If one would-be city councilman buys a prime-time minute, every other city council candidate is entitled to his own prime-time minute at the same price. Regularly scheduled newscasts and interviews, on-the-spot stories, and documentaries are exempt. No station may censor or edit the equal-time remarks of a political candidate.

The purpose of the equal time law is, of course, to make sure that broadcasters do not use their power to influence political campaigns by freezing out one candidate and plugging his opponent. But the law raises almost as many problems as it solves. Suppose there are 27 declared candidates for mayor of some city. A local broadcaster may wish to schedule half-hour interviews with the two or three top contenders. He knows that if he does so, the other two dozen (Vegetarian, Prohibitionist, Communist) candidates will all be entitled to a free half-hour apiece. So he drops the interview idea entirely. The Nixon-Kennedy debates of 1960 were a public service of major importance; they took place only because Congress passed a special amendment temporarily suspending the equal time law. There were no Presidential debates in '64 and '68 because Congress didn't want any, and therefore let the equal time law stand.

2. Obscenity. Federal law specifically forbids "obscene, indecent, or profane language" in broadcasting. Control of broadcast obscenity is far more stringent than the comparable rules for the print media, presumably because broadcasting reaches into every living room. Many stations have been fined—and several almost lost their licenses—simply for letting a single "dirty word" slip out over the air waves. Poems and plays that were manifestly legal in print and on stage have suddenly become very illegal when repeated over radio or television.

Early in 1970, the FCC levied a fine against a Philadelphia educational radio station for allowing a rock musician to use obscene words during an interview. The Commission invited the station to appeal the fine to the courts as a test case. It is hard to guess what the judges will decide. The trend in obscenity law is toward greater and greater liberalization—but broadcasting is a special case. In the meantime, most radio and TV stations are extremely leery of four-letter words.

3. Fairness Doctrine. The equal time and obscenity regulations are laws passed by Congress; the FCC merely administers and interprets them. The fairness doctrine, on the other hand, is entirely the invention of the Commission.

From the very beginning of radio, the government has held that broadcasters must not present only one side of controversial issues. As early as 1929, the FRC revoked a station's license for bias, insisting that "the public interest requires ample play for the free and fair competition of opposing views."[32] Over the years, on a case-by-case basis, this notion has evolved into the fairness doctrine.

Between 1929 and 1941, several stations lost their licenses for "unfair" treatment of controversial issues. And in 1941, radio station WAAB nearly lost its license simply for running editorials on various issues. The FCC finally decided to give the station another chance, but it firmly declared that "the broadcaster cannot be an advocate."[33]   The effect of these decisions was to scare the hell out of most radio and TV owners. They not only dropped their editorials; they dropped just about all their controversial programming.   As long as they didn't talk about anything important, broadcasters reasoned, they couldn't possibly be unfair about anything important.

This was not what the FCC had intended.   In the late 1940s the Commission reconsidered the whole fairness problem, and in 1949 it announced its conclusions.   Although it has changed over the years, the fairness doctrine today retains the following major provisions:

1. Licensees must devote a reasonable amount of broadcast time to controversial public issues.
2. In doing so, they must encourage the presentation of all sides of those issues.
3. Licensees are encouraged to editorialize so long as the end result is balanced programming on public controversies.
4. Whenever a licensee broadcasts a specific attack against a person or group, the victim must be offered comparable free time in which to reply.   Newscasts, news interviews, and on-the-spot coverage are exempt.
5. Licensees have an "affirmative obligation" to seek out representatives of opposing viewpoints.
6. Those who reply to earlier broadcasts under the fairness doctrine have no obligation to pay for the time; the licensee must provide it without charge.

The fairness doctrine is *not* an attempt to insure that individuals and groups will have access to the broadcast media.   Aside from the personal attack provision (#4), no one has a right to appear on radio or television. Broadcasters may pick whomever they want to represent "the opposing view."   The purpose of the fairness doctrine is to protect the listener or viewer, to insure that he has a chance to hear both sides.   It pictures the broadcast audience as a collection of passive sponges, with no viewpoint of their own to present, but in imminent danger of accepting someone else's viewpoint uncritically.

The fairness doctrine also applies, by the way, to broadcast advertising.   In 1967, the FCC declared that cigarette smoking was in fact a controversial issue.   Stations that carried cigarette commercials were therefore obliged to give "a significant amount of time" to antismoking messages.   Since then Congress has outlawed cigarette commercials entirely.   But fairness in advertising is by no means a dead issue.   An effort is now underway to get antipollution messages accepted as the fairness doctrine answer to gasoline ads.

Does the fairness doctrine violate the First Amendment?   Many broadcasters, perhaps most, think so—but the Supreme Court disagrees. In 1969 the court stated:

> The Congress and the Commission do not violate the First Amendment when they require a radio or television station to give reply time to answer personal attacks and political editorials.[34]

Be that as it may, the fairness doctrine (like the equal time and obscenity regulations) is certainly a violation of libertarian theory. It is undoubt-

---

RULES AND MORE RULES

The 1970 *Broadcasting Yearbook* includes a 17-page list of specific FCC regulations pertaining to the broadcast media. We have already covered the important ones. But it is the "unimportant" ones—hundreds and hundreds of them—that keep the FCC always on the mind of every broadcaster. The following is a sample of ten, selected more or less at random.[35]

1. Two television stations operating on the same channel number may not be located less than 155 miles apart.
2. No station may move its main studio across any state or municipal boundary without first receiving a special permit from the FCC.
3. Every station must remain on the air at least two-thirds the number of hours per day that it is permitted to be on the air, except Sundays.
4. FM radio stations in cities of over 100,000 people must not devote more than half of their programming to programs duplicated from an AM station owned by the same company in the same market area.
5. One or more persons holding a valid first-class radio-telephone operator license must be on duty at all times at the transmitting facility of every station.
6. No licensee may sign an exclusive contract with any network, which forbids the station to buy and use programs distributed by other networks.
7. Every station must file a detailed financial report and a complete programming log with the FCC every year.
8. Every licensee must announce its call letters and location at least once every hour that it is on the air.
9. Every station must announce the name of the sponsor of every program which is paid for, in whole or in part, by some source outside the station.
10. No licensee may broadcast advertisements for or information concerning any lottery, gift enterprise, or similar scheme.

Remember, these are only ten rules. We could list hundreds—and a broadcaster must know and obey them all.

edly the most powerful weapon in the government arsenal for controlling broadcast content.

There are two dangers implicit in the fairness doctrine. The first is that broadcasters, reluctant to assume the burdens of fairness, will avoid some controversies altogether. There is considerable evidence that this has happened; broadcast editorials, for example, are still mostly of the apple-pie-and-motherhood variety. The second danger is more acute. In the average broadcast day, literally hundreds of opinions on various issues are either stated or implied. It is the government that gets to decide which issues are controversial and which are not. In the past, fairness complaints brought by aetheists and communists have been dismissed by the FCC, on the grounds that aetheism and communism are so obviously evil that no fairness is required. What would the FCC have to say about a Christian Scientist who wanted to reply to a blood-donor ad? Or a pot smoker who opposed a keep-off-the-grass announcement? Or a Black Panther who thought a recent "Dragnet" episode was unfair to his point of view? Is it safe to leave such decisions in the hands of the federal government?

In the long run, which is more important: the right of the audience to balanced broadcasting, or the right of the broadcaster to free broadcasting?

THE FUTURE

The FCC began its career by allocating frequencies in order to eliminate interference. As befits this beginning, the Commission is always very preoccupied with technology. The vast majority of FCC regulations are technical—they concern the height of the transmitter, the precise wavelength of the signal, the number of "dots" per square inch on the TV screen, etc.

Regulation of today's technology is of interest only to technicians, but regulation of *tomorrow's* technology is (or should be) of interest to everyone. More than ten years ago, the FCC decided to encourage the development of UHF television, a technological gimmick that nearly sextupled the number of available TV channels. It passed several rules to achieve this goal, culminating in a 1962 law that required every new television set made after 1964 to include a UHF receiver and antenna. During the same period, the Commission adopted a wait-and-see approach to subscription television ("pay TV"). The result: Pay TV made little progress, while UHF is now a booming industry. Had the FCC made the opposite decision, the shows available on your television screen tonight might be quite different.

After a slow start, the FCC is just now coming to grips with the problems and potential of community antenna television (CATV) and satellite transmission. Within the next year or two it must make decisions on these topics that will largely determine the nature of American broadcasting in the 1980s.

No other single entity exercises so much control over the mass media in the United States as the federal government. No other mass medium is so stringently controlled by government as broadcasting. Many of these controls, perhaps most, are inconsistent with the American tradition of libertarian theory, with the spirit of the First Amendment.

Yet anyone who spends much time with the media, including the broadcast media, eventually comes to a puzzling conclusion: The government does not seem to be having much effect.

There is a paradox here. Look at any specific government control over the media, and you are likely to conclude that it is too much and too strong. Then look at the totality of government control, and you are likely to conclude that it is too little and too weak. Perhaps it is neither too much nor too little, but simply misdirected. Somehow the government has managed to inhibit seriously the freedom of the mass media without improving seriously their performance. Perhaps what we need is not *more* government control or *less* government control, but *different* government control.

NOTES

[1] Frederick S. Siebert, "The Historical Pattern of Press Freedom," *Nieman Reports,* July, 1953, p. 43.

[2] Fred S. Siebert, Theodore Peterson and Wilbur Schramm, *Four Theories of the Press* (Urbana, Ill.: University of Illinois Press, 1963), p. 135.

[3] Siebert, "The Historical Pattern of Press Freedom," *Nieman Reports,* July, 1953, p. 44.

[4] Carl Becker, *Freedom and Responsibility in the American Way of Life* (New York: Vintage Books, 1945), p. 34.

[5] Alvin E. Austin, "Codes, Documents, Declarations Affecting the Press," Department of Journalism, University of North Dakota, August, 1964, p. 55.

[6] Letter from Thomas Jefferson to Colonel Charles Yancey, January 6, 1816, quoted in Austin, "Codes, Documents, Declarations," p. 56.

[7] Siebert et al., *Four Theories of the Press,* p. 71.

[8] *Ibid.,* p. 90.

[9] *Ibid.,* pp. 87–92.

[10] *A Free and Responsible Press* (Chicago: University of Chicago Press, 1947), p. 92.

[11] Siebert et al., *Four Theories of the Press,* p. 74.

[12] *Schenck v. U.S.,* 249 U.S. 47, 39 S.Ct. 247 (1919).

[13] *Yates v. U.S.,* 354 U.S. 298, 77 S.Ct. 1064 (1957).

[14] *Regina v. Hicklin,* L.R. 3 Q.B. 360, 370 (1868).

[15] *U.S. v. One Book Called "Ulysses,"* 5 F.Supp. 182, 184 (S.D.N.Y. 1933).

[16] *U.S. v. Roth*, 354 U.S. 476, 77 S.Ct. 1304, 1311 (1957).

[17] *New York Times Co. v. Sullivan*, 376 U.S. 254, 279–80, 84 S.Ct. 710 (1964).

[18] *Associated Press v. Walker*, and *Curtis Publishing Co. v. Butts*, 388 U.S. 130, 87 S.Ct. 1975 (1967).

[19] *Time Inc. v. Hill*, 385 U.S. 374, 87 S.Ct. 534 (1967).

[20] Quoted in Martin Gershen, "The 'Right to Lie'," *Columbia Journalism Review*, Winter, 1966/67, pp. 14–15.

[21] Quoted in "Passing Comment," *Columbia Journalism Review*, Spring, 1970, p. 3.

[22] Associated Press, May 13, 1970.

[23] United Press International, Feb. 4, 1970.

[24] "How Much Privilege?" *Newsweek*, April 13, 1970, p. 77.

[25] *Hannegan v. Esquire*, 327 U.S. 146, 148–49, 66 S.Ct. 456, 457–58 (1946).

[26] Associated Press, Feb. 5, 1970.

[27] *KFKB Broadcasting Ass'n v. FRC*, 47 F.2d 670, 60 App.D.C. 79 (1931).

[28] *Office of Communication of United Church of Christ v. FCC*, 359 F.2d 994, 1003 (1966).

[29] William L. Rivers and Wilbur Schramm, *Responsibility in Mass Communication* (New York: Harper & Row, 1969) pp. 63–64.

[30] Marvin Barrett, ed., *Survey of Broadcast Journalism 1968–1969* (New York: Grosset & Dunlap, Inc., 1969), p. 32.

[31] "Test Case," *Newsweek*, Sept. 28, 1970, and Barrett, *Survey of Broadcast Journalism 1969–1970*, p. 70.

[32] *Great Lakes Broadcasting Co.*, 3 F.R.C. 32 (1929).

[33] *Mayflower Broadcasting Corp.*, 8 F.C.C. 333 (1941).

[34] *Red Lion Broadcasting Co. v. FCC* (1969) in Barrett, *Survey of Broadcast Journalism 1968–1969*, p. 39.

[35] *1970 Broadcasting Yearbook*, pp. C49–C66.

SUGGESTED READINGS

FRANKLIN, MARC A., *The Dynamics of American Law*. Mineola, N.Y.: The Foundation Press, Inc., 1968.

GILLMOR, DONALD M. and JEROME A. BARRON, *Mass Communication Law*. St. Paul, Minn.: West Publishing Co., 1969.

JOHNSON, NICHOLAS, *How to Talk Back to Your Television Set*. New York: Bantam Books, Inc., 1970.

NELSON, HAROLD L. and DWIGHT L. TEETER, *Law of Mass Communications*. Mineola, N.Y.: The Foundation Press, Inc., 1969.

SIEBERT, FRED S., THEODORE PETERSON, and WILBUR SCHRAMM, *Four Theories of the Press*. Urbana, Ill.: University of Illinois Press, 1956.

8 Public Control

A democracy works only if every important democratic institution is somehow responsive and responsible to the public. The mass media are a vital democratic institution. Since media executives are not elected, other means must be found to guarantee that public opinion will play a role in the determination of media content. Existing channels for public control of the media are weak, and new channels have been slow in developing.

When the Army Corps of Engineers first announced its plan to widen a creek running through a small park in a poor section of town, no one thought much about it. But soon it became clear that the operation would almost totally destroy the park. Mrs. Green, a local resident, organized a small citizens group which petitioned the Corps to abandon the project. The request was denied. Mrs. Green next asked the support of the weekly newspaper in her area, and the metropolitan paper about fifteen miles away. "Bring us a petition with a thousand names and we'll run something," both editors said. "We can't get a thousand names unless the issue is presented in the press," Mrs. Green replied. "Sorry," said the editors, "we can't do much on an organization with only a few dozen women." Finally Mrs. Green asked, "Do we have to stage a sit-in and block the bulldozers in order to get any attention?" No one answered.

Mr. Henderson was a roller derby nut. He attended every game in the area and hoped to follow his favorite competitors in the papers. But in weeks of combing the sports pages and tuning in as many radio and TV sports shows as he could, Mr. Henderson heard not a mention of roller derby. "Why don't you run writeups of the roller derby events?" he demanded of the local sports editor. "It's a phony sport, like wrestling," the editor told him wearily. "We don't cover anything like that." Mr. Henderson received the same answer from the TV and radio sportscasters he consulted. "Why don't you get interested in ice hockey?" one sympathetic radio man suggested. "We cover that all the time."

Every day hundreds of Mrs. Greens and Mr. Hendersons across the country discover to their surprise that they are unable to influence the content of the mass media. Control over the flow of information is exercised by publishers and reporters, station owners and editors, advertisers and government officials. What about the public?

All successful communication is two-way. In the jargon of communication theorists, the mechanisms that permit two-way communication are called "feedback loops." When we talk about public control of the mass media, then, we are really talking about the ability of the media to accept and deal with feedback.

Suppose you are listening to a speech in a large auditorium. There are two kinds of feedback you may wish to give the speaker. First, you may want to influence what he says or the way he says it—asking him to speak louder or explain a point further, perhaps requesting that he move to a different topic. Second, you may want to respond to what he says—disputing his evidence or his conclusions, telling him what you think. A good speaker will usually find some way to accommodate both kinds of feedback.

The mass media must also accommodate both kinds of feedback. Mr. Henderson is interested in the first kind; he *wants the media to tell him* about something (roller derby) that they do not customarily deal with. Mrs. Green, on the other hand, is concerned with the second kind of feedback; she *wants to tell the media* about something (danger to the park), and through the media she wants to reach the government and other citizens. We will discuss Mr. Henderson's problem first, then Mrs. Green's.

CONSUMER CONTROL OF THE MEDIA

Mr. Henderson is a mass media consumer. There is nothing that he particularly wants to say to the media. He just wants the media to say something to him—something about the roller derby.

There are five mechanisms available for helping the media consumer control media content:

1. Consumer boycotts.
2. Ratings.
3. Letters to the editor.
4. The fairness doctrine.
5. Press councils.

As we shall see, all five are unsatisfactory.

1. Consumer Boycotts. The simplest way to register protest against a print medium is to stop buying it. If the circulation drop is enough to be noticeable, advertisers will leave the publication—both because it is reaching fewer people and because it is obviously offending some of them. The publisher will soon see the error of his ways and reform.

A single lost subscriber, of course, won't even be noticed. It takes a well-organized mass boycott to stand a chance—and even then the tactic rarely works. In Richmond, California, for example, the people are served by one local newspaper, the *Independent*. The paper is notorious for ignoring the needs of the substantial black population in Richmond. In 1968 a subscription cancellation drive was organized. Although it was backed by leaders of the black and white liberal communities, the drive failed miserably. Out of a total circulation of nearly 40,000, the *Independent* lost perhaps a hundred subscribers. Many who agreed with the goals of the boycott were unwilling to cut off their only source of local news by canceling their subscriptions to the daily.

Though rarely successful, local newspaper boycotts stand a far better chance than national magazine boycotts—simply because it is nearly impossible to organize a nationwide cancellation drive.

The only mass medium regularly influenced by consumer boycotts is the film industry. For many years the Legion of Decency, for example, rated all new movies on their acceptability for Catholic audiences. The Legion was able to dictate hundreds of alterations in various films, threatening a box office boycott if the changes were not made. Recently, however, even the Legion's power has been waning, as American society becomes more permissive and more pictures are aimed at the youth market.

At best, the consumer boycott is a negative weapon. It can help an organized group fight objectionable media practices, but it cannot help them substitute something better. And for the individual media consumer it is next to useless.

2. Ratings. The broadcast equivalent of a consumer boycott is switching channels or turning off the set—actions which presumably show up in the ratings. The broadcast industry pictures its rating system as a democratic one in which each sampled home (representing tens of thousands throughout the country) has one vote in determining the nation's radio and television content.   Arthur C. Nielsen, president of the rating company that bears his name, put it this way to the Oklahoma City Advertising Club in 1966:

> After all, what is a rating?   In the final analysis, it is simply a counting of the votes, . . . a system of determining the types of programs that people prefer to watch or hear.   Those who attack this concept of counting the votes—or the decisions made in response to the voting results— are saying, in effect: "Never mind what the people want.   Give them something else."[1]

But ratings are not the perfect feedback device that Nielsen describes. In most cases, the public can only voice an advisory yes or no vote on the programs presented to it.   It cannot suggest new forms of programming via the ratings, nor can it communicate to the programmers *how much* and *why* it likes or dislikes a show.   Most ratings simply measure what channel the television is tuned to.   They do not determine whether anybody is actually watching, much less whether those who watch are enjoying the program.   Finally, the ratings serve a broadcast industry that demands mass audiences of 20 or 30 million for network programs.   A mere five or six million people would constitute far too small a minority to influence broadcast content.   A single individual (like Mr. Henderson) will get very little help from the ratings.

3. *Letters to the Editor.* The letter to the editor is primarily a method for gaining access to the mass media, and it will therefore be dis-

---

RIGGED RATINGS

Network programmers have little trouble manipulating ratings in order to justify eliminating a show.   In the late 1950s, for example, "Playhouse 90" was perhaps the most highly acclaimed dramatic series on CBS.   Yet the sponsors of adjacent shows complained that the program was too high-brow, and they put pressure on CBS to get it off the air.   In 1959 the network started moving "Playhouse 90" around in its program schedule like a pea in a shell game.   First it was biweekly; then it alternated with a program called "The Big Party"; then it appeared infrequently as a Special.   Ratings began to slide, and by 1961 "Playhouse 90" was dead.   Asked why such a highly-praised program was dropped, then CBS-TV President James Aubrey replied that "the public lost interest in it completely."

Writes critic Harry Skornia: "It is well known that, using tactics such as this, there is no difficulty in getting poor ratings for a show one wants to drop. Network officials then can quote the ratings they have achieved as the reason for dropping the program involved."[2]

---

cussed in the next section of this chapter. It is worth mentioning here as well because the letter can be used (though it seldom is) as a way of making consumer demands on the media. Most letters discuss public issues, but roughly one in ten addresses itself instead to media coverage of those issues. If editors read their own letters columns—which many do not— such a tactic can occasionally be successful.

4. The Fairness Doctrine. Strictly speaking, the Federal Communications Commission's fairness doctrine is not a form of public control of the mass media. Rather, it is an example of government control exercised on behalf of the public. The fairness doctrine requires two things of all broadcasters: (1) They must include some discussion of controversial issues in their programming; and (2) when discussing controversies, they must make a reasonable effort to provide a balance of conflicting viewpoints. A viewer or listener who feels that the fairness doctrine has been violated may complain to the station involved, or directly to the FCC. Though it almost never happens, a station *can* lose its license because of flagrant or continued violations.

In theory, the purpose of the fairness doctrine is to protect the media consumer from unbalanced commentary on controversial issues. In practice, the doctrine has been used by activists as a wedge to gain access to the media for their own views. We will therefore return to it in the next section of this chapter.

5. Press Councils. The first press council was founded in Sweden in 1916. An appointed, voluntary body of professional journalists and distinguished laymen, it was organized to field complaints from the public about media performance. The council had no statutory power, but the moral force of its decisions was considerable. Today, similar press councils exist in many countries, including Denmark, Germany, India, Australia, Chile, and Great Britain.

The British press council has been a model for many American attempts. It was born in 1953 as a result of criticism of newspaper sensationalism, and complaints by Labour Party officials that the press was biased against them. The council has no general code or standards. It decides each case as it comes—an average of two complaints per week.

In each case, the injured party is asked to try to work things out with the local editor first. If that fails, the council will act as a mediator between the two. Only as a last resort does the council issue a public rebuke to the newspaper involved. When that happens the council action is given wide publicity; it is almost always carried even by the offending paper. Cases fall into five categories: regulation of content; privacy and news sources; professional ethics; access to news sources; and sex in the news.

A typical council action came when a British newspaper printed the story of a married woman whose ex-lover had committed suicide. The woman had begged the paper to leave her connection to the victim out of the article. When the story was run anyhow, she also committed suicide. The council charged the newspaper with needless invasion of privacy.[3]

While the British press council monitors the media on a national level, experiments in the United States have all involved local councils—mainly because this country has no national press to speak of. A private press council was started in Littleton, Colorado, in 1967. A year later the Mellett Fund for a Free and Responsible Press sponsored press councils in four American communities—Bend, Oregon; Redwood City, California; and Cairo and Sparta, Illinois. Similar groups have sprung up in a variety of U.S. cities and towns.

Typically, the local press council is made up of a cross-section of residents, who meet regularly with publishers to air their gripes. The sessions have usually been kept secret, and have produced few if any significant changes in press performance. So far, in fact, the councils have paid more attention to teaching citizens the problems of newspapermen

---

RECEIVER-CONTROLLED COMMUNICATION

All the mass media today are controlled, not by the receiver, but by the sender—the publisher or broadcaster. One new medium, the computer, promises receiver-control in the not too distant future. Edwin Parker, a professor of communication at Stanford University, envisions what it will be like:

> Imagine yourself sitting down at the breakfast table with a display screen in front of you. You touch a key and the latest headlines appear on the screen. Not the headlines that were written last night—or even those of six or seven hours ago. But headlines that may have been rewritten and updated five minutes or just 50 microseconds before you see them on the screen. You type another key or poke a light pen at the appropriate headline and the whole story appears on the screen. . . .
>
> Are you interested in something that hasn't made the major headlines? Like a bill on education being considered in Congress. . . . Perhaps there's something you missed yesterday or the day before that's not front-page news today; the computer has stored it for you. You can have the latest information whether it's on today's or yesterday's story. . . .
>
> There's a person in the news you'd like to know more about. Ask your computer for a biographical sketch. You don't understand the economics of the gold market. Request a tutorial program on the subject. You want the comics? Press the right button. Catch up on the strips you missed while you were on vacation. . . .[4]

Dr. Parker's dream is technologically feasible today. Whether it will actually come about is another question.

---

than to forcing the papers to solve those problems more effectively. And of course broadcasting, magazines, films, and the vast majority of local newspapers are so far not touched by the press council movement.

Consumer boycotts, ratings, letters to the editor, the fairness doctrine, and press councils are all inadequate to the task of enabling the mass media consumer to control what he sees and hears. For the moment, at least, Mr. Henderson will have great difficulty getting the media to tell him about the roller derby.

ACCESS TO THE MEDIA

So far we have considered only the obligation of the media to tell the public what the public wants to be told. We turn now to an equally important obligation—to permit the public to respond to what it is told. The mass media do not serve merely as a means of molding public opinion; they are also a vital channel for *expressing* that opinion. This is Mrs. Green's problem. She wants the local media to cover her save-the-park campaign, not so that *she* can read about it, but so that *others* (local residents; the Army Corps of Engineers) can do so.

The problem of access to the media has been ignored for many years, but it is not being ignored today. Dozens of special-interest groups— ghetto blacks and middle-class whites, young people and senior citizens, radicals and rightists—have come to recognize that access to the media plays a vital role in the fulfillment of their goals. As Hazel Henderson has put it:

> The realization is now dawning on groups espousing . . . new ideas, that in a mass, technologically complex society, freedom of speech is only a technicality if it cannot be hooked up to the amplification system that only the mass media can provide. When our founding fathers talked of freedom of speech, they did not mean freedom to talk to oneself. They meant freedom to talk to the whole community. A mimeograph machine can't get the message across anymore.[5]

The complex problems of access to the media will come up again and again in this book, especially in chapters 15 through 19, where we discuss media coverage of various social issues. We will see then that special-interest groups have devised a number of strategies, such as the protest demonstration, to insure big play in the mass media. Smaller and less organized groups—like Mrs. Green's—have a more difficult task. What can they do to gain access to the media?

There are four major access mechanisms available:

1. Letters to the editor.
2. Talk shows.

3. Paid advertisements.
4. The fairness doctrine.

As we shall see, none of the four is really adequate for the job.

1. Letters to the Editor. The most common method of expressing one's feelings in public is the letter to the editor. It is also the oldest; the New York *Times* published its first letter in 1851, four days after the newspaper was founded. In 1931 a special page was set aside for the letters. Today the *Times* receives over 40,000 letters a year, of which two thousand are printed. Letters are edited for grammar and style, but not for content.

Most newspapers today run around 20 column inches of letters a day, usually on the page opposite the editorial page. With a few exceptions, editors are scrupulously fair to use letters that are critical of the newspaper and its editorial stand.

Numerous researchers have found that letter-writers are able to "blow off steam"[6] and "get something off their chest"[7] by writing the editor their thoughts. Letter-writers tend to be educationally well above average, definitely not cranks or crackpots. They are usually well-read and highly individualistic; they are also predominantly male, white, and members of business and professional groups.

Letters to the editor are among the best-read parts of the newspaper. Letter-writing is therefore an excellent device for those who write persuasively to communicate with those who read critically. For individuals who are less literate, or who want to reach audiences other than the elite, the letter to the editor is of limited value.

2. Talk Shows. Though radio and television stations do not broadcast letters to the station manager, in recent years many have instituted phone-in "talk shows" instead. These programs give the public an opportunity to converse with moderators and their expert guests on almost any topic of interest. Callers are limited to once every three or four days,

---

TOP LETTER-WRITERS

The current champion letter-writer in the New York *Times* is Martin Wolfson, an economics teacher at Brooklyn Tech High School in New York. Wolfson writes five or six letters a week to the *Times,* and has had over 2,000 printed in various publications since 1927.

The all-time champion is Charles Hooper, who lived off a private income in Coeur d'Alene, Idaho, from 1913 to 1941 and wrote letters to newspapers all day, every day. Hooper's goal, which he nearly reached, was to get at least one letter in every newspaper in the United States.[8]

---

and the calls are screened to weed out drunks, young children, and other undesirables. The "talk show" format has proved to be immensely popular, as well as an unusually cheap way for broadcasters to fill time. The value of the talk show in providing public access to the media is obvious. Its limitations are equally apparent—no caller stays on for more than a minute or two, and most callers never get through at all.

3. Paid Advertisments. During the battle over Prohibition, both the Brewers Association and the Prohibitionists attempted to lobby public officials by taking out newspaper ads supporting their positions. It wasn't until the mid-1960s, however, that the tactic gained much popularity with private citizens and citizens groups. Then ads began to appear in metropolitan dailies condemning everything from the bombing of North Vietnam to the massacre of baby seals in Canada. Between 1955 and 1965 an average of two protest advertisements per month were placed in the New York *Times* (ads for political candidates are not counted). By the first years of the Kennedy administration the average was 4.2 protest ads per month, and the first years of the Johnson administration saw the average rise to 5.7 per month. Nonprotest ads that take a stand on some issue have also increased dramatically in number over the last decade.

The popularity of the protest advertisement does not seem to be based on any conviction that it works. In a study of one antiwar ad placed by a hundred professors at a New England college, J. David Colfax found that only twenty percent of all readers recalled having seen the ad. More than ninety percent disagreed with it, and not a single reader said he was heeding the ad's call to write his Congressman and protest the war. On the other hand, more than half the sponsors of the ad admitted that they expected it to have no effect—though seventy percent said they would sponsor another such ad anyhow.[9] If the Colfax study is typical, then access to the media through paid advertisements is apparently not a very practical solution.

4. The Fairness Doctrine. When a broadcaster presents a controversial viewpoint on the air and does not balance it with opposing viewpoints, he is in violation of the FCC fairness doctrine. A representative of some opposing view is entitled to demand that the station give him (or someone like him) time to reply. If necessary, he can go to the FCC to enforce his demand.

This is precisely what New York lawyer John Banzhaf did in 1968. Banzhaf was the founder of A.S.H. (Action on Smoking and Health), which contended that cigarette smoking was a controversial issue of public importance, and therefore subject to the fairness doctrine. A.S.H. singled out WCBS-TV in New York for a test case. Banzhaf asked the FCC to order WCBS to broadcast information on the hazards of smoking, to balance its steady diet of cigarette commercials. The FCC agreed, and the entire broadcast industry was forced to give millions of dollars worth of free time to such groups as the American Cancer Society. This decision was a prelude to the removal of all tobacco ads from the broadcast media in 1971.

Banzhaf chose to challenge an advertisement rather than the regular editorial content of the broadcast media. The fairness doctrine applies to both, as long as the issue presented is a genuinely controversial one. Future challenges may elevate the fairness doctrine to an important method for gaining access to broadcast time.

Nevertheless, the fairness doctrine is not essentially an access tool. It was designed to protect the broadcast audience from unbalanced comment, not to permit members of that audience to get on the air themselves. If a station ignores some issue altogether, it has no need to balance comment. If the station does discuss an issue, it can claim that the topic is not controversial. If the topic is ruled controversial, the station

---

THE RIGHT OF ACCESS

In 1967 the *Harvard Law Review* published an article by Jerome A. Barron, entitled "Access to the Press—A New First Amendment Right." The article argued that the entire mass communications industry "uses the free speech and free press guarantees to avoid opinions instead of acting as a sounding board for their expression."[10] Barron urged a new interpretation of the First Amendment, which would recognize the obligation of all the media to afford access to minority viewpoints. A publisher might, for example, be required to print all letters replying to earlier articles in the newspaper.

There are already some judicial and legislative precedents for the Barron theory. The state of Florida now requires all publications to print replies from political candidates who have been attacked; Nevada extends the same right to the average citizen as well. And a recent court decision held that members of the Students for a Democratic Society must be permitted to advertise their antiwar views in New York's public bus and subway stations. Barron would like to go still further, opening up all the media to all viewpoints.

Opposition to the Barron theory stems from a potent fear of any increased government control of the press. Someone would have to determine, on a day-to-day basis, which spokesmen for which views are offered time and space. That someone would probably be the government—a cure that many feel would be even worse than the disease. Dennis E. Brown and John C. Merrill of the University of Missouri's Freedom of Information Center assert that Barron's theory will take root "only when our society has proceeded much further along the road toward Orwell's 1984, wherein a paternalistic and omnipotent Power Structure makes our individual decisions for us."[11]

---

can claim that its other programming has already provided balance. And if that doesn't work the station can pick whomever it wants to represent the other side—or one of many "other sides." John Banzhaf himself never got onto WCBS.

The fairness doctrine will not do Mrs. Green any good in her campaign to save the park from Army bulldozers. Paid advertisements, talk shows, and letters to the editor will help her somewhat more. But even those who oppose Jerome Barron's theory of the "right of access" (see box) would agree that Mrs. Green has rough sledding ahead. Her chances of building a movement through the mass media are almost as small as Mr. Henderson's chances of getting the media to cover the roller derby.

Individuals and groups that fail in their efforts to influence existing mass media are often tempted to start their own. Though this was once a feasible goal, today it is nearly impossible to found a mass-market newspaper, magazine, or broadcast station without vast capital reserves. Nevertheless, attempts at media competition have occasionally succeeded, at least to the extent of forcing changes in the established media. And the "underground" media today, though not truly competitive with the Establishment press, are in a healthier condition than ever before.

PRINT COMPETITION

When Daniel C. Birdsell founded the Hartford (Conn.) *Telegram* in 1883, he became the fifth newspaper publisher in that city. From the very start he was able to compete successfully with the other four. The first issue of the *Telegram* sold 2,000 copies, as opposed to 10,000 copies a day for the established *Courant* and *Times*. Within months Birdsell's *Telegram* was also considered an "established" newspaper, and a sixth publisher was no doubt preparing to enter the fray.[12]

Modern-day Birdsells are few and far between. Today the outlook for a freshman publisher in Hartford—or any other American city—is exceedingly glum. The following are some of the more important barriers to starting a new newspaper.

1. *Start-up costs.* Birdsell began the *Telegram* for under $10,000; his press cost him $900. By contrast, when the Hartford *Times* bought a new press in 1959, the price was more than $1,000,000. Equipment prices have continued to soar. So has the cost of labor, ink, paper, distribution, and just about everything else. In 1968 the New York *Times* surveyed the afternoon market in that city with an eye to competing with the *Post*. Estimates were that the *Times* would lose $60,000,000 in ten years before

the new p.m. paper turned the corner.[13]   Even the *Times* decided it couldn't afford that large an investment.

2. *Mass market demands.*   The Nineteenth Century newspaper was an individual.   It had its own editorial policy, its own style, its own quirks and favorite topics—and its own special readership.   In comparison today's newspapers are all pretty much alike.   It is that much more difficult, then, for a new paper to woo readers from the old ones.   And unless a newspaper attracts large numbers of readers, it has nothing to offer advertisers.

3. *Wire service problems.*   A new paper cannot survive without a wire service for national and international news.   Yet neither the Associated Press nor United Press International is overly cooperative with new publishers.   During the Detroit newspaper strike of 1964, Mike Dworkin founded the Detroit *Daily Press* as an interim paper.   He recalls his negotiations with UPI: "We were told we had to sign a five-year contract, at close to $2,500 per week, and pay the last year in advance—an amount in excess of $128,000.   These were impossible and unrealistic conditions. We told them we did not want the entire package of services.   They said all or nothing.   We offered to pay them $3,000 per week, payable two weeks in advance, in cash, and again this wasn't for everything.   We offered to assume all installation costs. . . . Their answer was 'No.' "[14]

4. *Syndicated problems.*   A new publication may also have trouble subscribing to syndicated comics, columnists, and news features.   Syndicates often offer their clients exclusive contracts for an entire geographical area.   The Los Angeles *Times*, for example, controls the West Coast from San Diego to Santa Barbara and east to the Colorado River.   The Philadelphia *Evening Bulletin* holds territorial rights over Delaware, southern New Jersey, and all of eastern Pennsylvania.   Some newspapers buy the rights to syndicated materials they rarely print, just to insure that no competing paper will get them.

5. *Circulation audits.*   The Audit Bureau of Circulation refuses to vouch for a newspaper's circulation unless at least half of it is paid.   A new paper that wants to give away introductory copies is thus denied the ABC audit—and without ABC figures few advertisers are willing to purchase space.

6. *Other problems.*   A host of seemingly petty problems confront the beginning publisher.   Newsboys who carry the established paper are forbidden to sell the new rival.   It may take up to 14 months for the paper to be listed in the local telephone book, perhaps even longer to get an entry in the standard advertising rate books.   Established papers buy up the printing equipment of failing newspapers so that cheap, used presses are kept off the market.   And if he surmounts all other barriers, the fledgling publisher may be faced with a protracted circulation and advertising war designed to force him out of business.

THE WASHINGTON EXAMINER

In 1968, O. Roy Chalk decided to start a second morning newspaper in Washington, D.C., to compete with the Washington *Post*. Chalk was prepared to lose from $20,000,000 to $50,000,000 on his Washington *Examiner* before hitting the break-even point. But even that estimate was overoptimistic, and the *Examiner* folded within months of its first issue.

Chalk's biggest problem was his inability to get syndicated and wire service material. The only features he could find that weren't tied up in exclusive contracts were the mailed services of the Toronto *Star* and the San Francisco *Chronicle*. The only available wire service was Agence France Presse, which is printed almost entirely in French.

The Associated Press, meanwhile, refused to serve the *Examiner* until after a six-month survey to prove that at least half its circulation was paid. United Press International at first demanded proof of 85 percent paid circulation. It then offered a five-year contract at roughly $2,000 a week, with the *entire fifth year* paid in advance without interest. If the *Examiner* folded before its fifth year, UPI would keep the money. (The cost of the service to UPI, it was estimated, would run about $200 a week.[15]) As UPI general sales manager Wayne Sargent explained in a letter to Chalk: "We believe in free enterprise and will do everything we can to make your operation successful. But we cannot fall into the trap of fostering competition at the expense of existing clients."[16]

Faced with nearly insurmountable odds, the best a competing newspaper can hope to do is to force an improvement in the established paper. In 1957 the Lima (Ohio) *News* was sold to Freedom Newspapers, Inc., a very conservative newspaper chain. The staff of the paper decided to quit and start their own in competition. Over the next seven years the new Lima *Citizen* cost the *News* $4,000,000 in a hard-fought circulation and advertising battle. Although the *Citizen* was finally forced to fold, the *News* had to become a much better newspaper in order to keep its readers.[17]

However overwhelming the problems of a fledgling local newspaper, they are nothing compared to those of a new national magazine or book publisher. The sums of money required to finance even the most rudimentary nationwide distribution system are counted in seven digits. The Atheneum book publishing company is considered something of a miracle because it started in 1959 with only a million dollars—a mere shoestring. Even big money is no guarantee of success. The magazine *Careers Today* was capitalized at $10,000,000 when it was founded in 1968. It folded after two issues.

Folding is, in fact, the most likely outcome of any attempt to compete with established print media, whether newspapers, magazines, or book publishers. As a means of "control" over print media content, starting one's own medium may sound like an admirable idea—but it seldom succeeds.

BROADCAST COMPETITION

Though the economics of print journalism makes competition exceedingly difficult, it is at least theoretically possible. In broadcasting this is not always the case. The electronic spectrum has room for only so many radio and so many television stations. Once they are all gone, no amount of money can make space for one more.

Not quite all the stations are gone. The Federal Communications Commission, which is responsible for dividing the spectrum and handing out broadcast licenses, still has over a thousand television and radio frequencies that are up for grabs.[18] Nearly every one of them, unfortunately, has some kind of catch to it. Either the station is reserved for noncommercial use, or it's an unprofitable UHF, or it's located out in the country where there's no audience to hear it, or it's already got five competing applications—or, most likely, some potent combination of these and other disadvantages. Certainly there are few commercial AM radio or VHF television licenses in good-sized cities going begging for lack of interest. For those interested in operating such a station, transfer of an existing license is the only way.

The entire question is really an academic one. Running a full-scale broadcast station, especially a TV station, is an incredibly expensive undertaking. It requires massive support from national and local advertising (or, in the case of noncommercial stations, from government and private philanthropies). In practice, only a big business can afford to go into broadcasting. Having to buy an existing station instead of getting one free from the FCC only adds to the start-up cost—which customarily runs in the millions anyhow. Every once in a while someone starts a small FM radio station somewhere with just ten or twenty thousand dollars, and runs it the way *he* thinks a station ought to be run. But by and large competing with the established broadcast media is simply out of the question.

There is another way. Every three years a broadcaster is required to apply to the FCC for renewal of his broadcast license. In the past renewal procedures have been simple and straightforward, with no embarrassing questions asked. Most renewals still are. But in recent years a number of citizens groups have made use of license renewal time to question the performance of established broadcasters. This is one sort of "competition" that does not require tens of millions of dollars.

The change began in 1964, when two black leaders in Jackson, Mississippi, challenged the license of Jackson station WLBT. Aided by Dr. Everett Parker, head of the Office of Communications of the United Church of Christ, they charged that WLBT had systematically promoted segregationist views in its editorials and news coverage.

The FCC dismissed the challenge, asserting that the public had no "standing" before the Commission—no right, that is, to help decide whether a broadcaster has earned the privilege of keeping his license. The Jackson citizens appealed this decision to the federal courts, and in 1966 the FCC was ordered to hold a hearing and let the men testify. It did so, then renewed WLBT's license anyhow, claiming that the Negroes had not proved racial discrimination. So Dr. Parker and the citizens of Jackson went back to the courts.

On June 23, 1969, appeals court judge Warren Burger (now Chief Justice on the Supreme Court) announced his decision. The FCC was rebuked for shifting the burden of proof from the licensee to the challenger, and was ordered to consider new applications for the WLBT license. In 1971, the license was awarded to a local citizens group.

Even though it took seven years, the WLBT case established once and for all that local residents are entitled to fight broadcast license renewals without applying for the license themselves. Regional "watchdog" groups now exist to monitor the air waves and aid challengers to poorly-operated stations. Such groups include the National Citizens

---

A CONTRACT WITH THE PUBLIC

In 1969 station KTAL-TV of Texarkana, Texas, received its license renewal only after it signed a 13-point contract with local citizens groups, promising to improve its performance.

Twelve local black groups had challenged the license, charging that the station failed to meet the needs of the black community. They agreed to withdraw the challenge on condition that the station sign the contract. Among other points, KTAL-TV is now legally obligated to hire a minimum of two full-time black reporters; to preempt network programs only after consultation with minority groups; to solicit public service announcements from those groups; and to meet with them once each month to discuss programming plans.[19]

This is the only known case to date in which a license challenge led to a binding contract between the challenger and the station.

Committee for Broadcasting (New York), the National Association for Better Broadcasting (Los Angeles), and the American Council for Better Broadcasts (Madison, Wisconsin). On a national level, the Office of Communications of the United Church of Christ and the Television, Radio and Film Commission of the Methodist Church have both been active. Local groups from Media, Pennsylvania to Los Angeles, California have successfully demanded public hearings on the license renewals of specific stations.

The license renewal challenge is the most potent weapon now available for influencing the broadcast media. But it is by no means a cure-all. For one thing, license challenges cost money—not as much as running your own station, but at least a few thousand dollars or so. They also require more time and effort than any individual and most groups can spare. And even today most challenges fail. Former FCC Commissioner Kenneth A. Cox warns that "possession is nine points of the law. FCC will not put a license holder out of business if he has even a halfway decent record."[20]

TECHNOLOGY AND THE UNDERGROUNDS

The best hope for increased public participation in the media is the development of new communication technologies. Cable television (see chapter 12) may one day permit scores of TV stations in areas where there are now only two or three, solving the spectrum space problem and putting a channel or two within the grasp of every major special-interest group. Cheaper and more flexible movie equipment allows independent film-makers to produce high-quality products, which may eventually find outlets in cable and UHF television as well as neighborhood movie theaters. Time-shared computer terminals (see box on page 210) may offer individual subscribers an opportunity to input what they want to say and output what they want to hear. If and when these innovations begin to fulfill their promise, the problem of public control of the media may be greatly alleviated.

The most significant technological contribution of the moment is photolithograph printing, also known as offset or cold-type printing. The offset process has reduced the cost of small-scale publishing to a level that is within the reach of nearly everyone. Using equipment like a Varityper, a Justowriter, or even an ordinary electric typewriter, a would-be publisher can turn out neat and attractive copy in his basement and his spare time. Job-lot printers can produce 5,000 copies of an eight-page offset newsletter for as little as $80. Many of them print literally hundreds of such publications every month.

Offset printing has spurred the growth of weekly newspapers in many communities too small to support a letter-press paper. It has also fostered thousands of "shoppers," mini-papers that are distributed free to area residents, paid for by local advertisers. But the most exciting effect of offset technology is neither of these. It is the special-interest newsletter, the ideological bulletin, and the underground newspaper.

Suppose you are deeply involved in the ecological problems of your local community, devoting most of your leisure time to the fight for cleaner air and water. Naturally you will do your best to get the mass media to discuss your activities. But your best may not be good enough. So in addition to lobbying the local newspapers and broadcast stations, you may also put out a monthly publication of your own—which you will mail to other ecology activists and potential converts.

Economically, of course, you are in no way competing with the mass media. You do not want, and cannot get, their mass readership and mass-market advertisements. But in a more important sense you *are* competing. You are providing your community with specialized information that the mass media do not provide. Offset printing makes it possible for you to do so on a very low budget.

In 1955 the *Village Voice* carved a small niche for itself in the New York City newspaper market with a potpourri of film and theater reviews, hip features, and acid political commentary. Ten years later the *Voice* had a circulation of 56,000 and a respectable profit for the first time. It had become the newspaper of the "Establishment Left"—and in 1966 the anti-Establishment Left was forced to start another publication, aptly named the *East Village Other.* Said Jack Newfield of the *Voice:* "EVO

THE PEOPLE'S NEWSPAPER

The purest example of public control of the mass media was voted into being by the citizens of Los Angeles in 1911. A special referendum established the Los Angeles *Municipal News,* with a budget of $36,000 a year in tax money and a mandate to cover city government without bias. The *News* endorsed no candidates and took no editorial stands. It gave all the established political parties free space to use as they liked. It reported the proceedings of every municipal agency, and kept an eye on every city project and proposed project. Its credo was accuracy.

Its downfall was disinterest. Advertising started at 60 percent of the space, but within three months fell to 28 percent. Circulation—even with most copies free—never got above 60,000. At the urging of L.A.'s commercial newspapers, a measure was put on the 1912 ballot to abandon the experiment; it was worded so that a "no" vote was needed to save the paper. By a margin of 8,000 votes, the Los Angeles *Municipal News* was abolished.[21]

---

is for the totally alienated. We're the paper for the partially alienated."[22]

In *The Open Conspiracy*, a book on underground newspapers, author Ethel G. Romm defines the underground as a paper with "a peculiar sense of what was news, a mad eye for design, an instinct for the shocking."[23] Others would say that the underground newspaper combines social revolution, sexual titillation, and psychedelic exultation into a single tabloid package. By either standard the *Village Voice* no longer qualifies. But there are plenty of others to take its place—from the *Rat* in New York to the *Free Press* in Los Angeles. In 1965 Romm could find only four genuine underground newspapers; in 1969 she counted 111 of them. By 1970 they were uncountable. Illinois had 27 established undergrounds and 70 more published irregularly. A month's supply of Boston undergrounds weighed over five pounds.

The Bell and Howell Corporation operates a microfilm service for university libraries. Mostly it concentrates on the large metropolitan dailies, but by 1970 its special "underground" list included more than 150 titles. Nearly every big city, army base, and college campus has at least one underground paper—and so do more than 500 high schools throughout the country.

Two major news services now supply underground clients with appropriate national and international copy. The Underground Press Syndicate permits member papers to reprint each other's articles without writ-

---

STARTING AN UNDERGROUND

Writing in the New York *Guardian*, Margie Stamberg describes what it is like to start an underground newspaper:

> The little papers began to come out the summer the kids ran away. It was 1967, when the acid-rock bands sang for free in Provo Park and the drug experience awakened people to color and sound. Then, to reject what it meant to be young and white in America would make it go away for a little while.
>
> You felt a need to talk about it, share it, make it grow. . . . You discovered all it takes is a carbon-ribbon typewriter, a jar of rubber cement, and $200 hustled from friends. The first issue comes out, you stand on the street corner and hawk it, gathering money for the next issue, rapping to people, finding out what's happening.
>
> The papers become the lifelines of the community. Calls pour in. "Where can I get some draft counseling?" "My friend just got busted—where can he get a free lawyer?" "I'm 14 and just got in from Iowa." "Help. . . ."
>
> As the politics of alienation mature through struggle into revolutionary consciousness, the underground press is slowly changing from a reflection of an isolated phenomenon into a self-conscious agent of revolution. Editors have begun to learn the skill of propaganda. . . .[24]

ing for permission. Liberation News Service, the larger of the two, mails out twice-weekly packets of news, features, photos, and drawings—all for a monthly fee of $15.

Despite incessant legal harrassment (most often on charges of obscenity or peddling without a license), the underground press has been immensely influential. Occasionally an underground paper manages to earn a profit. Occasionally one succeeds in winning a convert or two from the middle class. But neither of these is the main goal of the undergrounds. Their aim is to help build a cohesive nationwide community of the young, the hip, and the radical. There is little doubt that in this they are succeeding.

George A. Cavalletto of Liberation News Service has put it as simply as it can be put. "As hundreds of new communities develop across the country," he says, "they start their own newspapers. The information they want they can't get through the regular press."[25]

The radical young have no monopoly on offset technology. Every serious ideology and special interest has its own publication or publications—from the John Birch Society to the Black Panthers, from the Sierra Club to the lumber lobby. If you are unable to convince the mass media to cover what you think they ought to cover, then you must cover it yourself—and offset helps you do it. An admiring critic of the monthly muckraking San Francisco *Bay Guardian* sums it all up: "That's what the First Amendment is all about."[26]

NOTES

[1] Arthur C. Nielsen, Jr., "If Not the People . . . Who?" Address to the Oklahoma City Advertising Club, July 20, 1966, p. 5.

[2] Harry J. Skornia, *Television and Society* (N.Y.: McGraw-Hill Book Co., 1965), p. 57.

[3] Helen Nelson, "Watchdog of the British Press," *Saturday Review*, August 8, 1964, p. 42.

[4] Quoted in William L. Rivers and Wilbur Schramm, *Responsibility in Mass Communication* (N.Y.: Harper & Row, 1969) pp. 9–10.

[5] Hazel Henderson, "Access to the Media: A Problem in Democracy," *Columbia Journalism Review*, Spring, 1969, p. 6.

[6] Sidney A. Forsythe, "An Exploratory Study of Letters to the Editor and Their Contributors," *Public Opinion Quarterly*, 1950, p. 144.

[7] William D. Tarrant, "Who Writes Letters to the Editor?" *Journalism Quarterly*, Fall, 1957, p. 502.

[8] Irving Rosenthal, "Who Writes the 'Letters to the Editor'?" *Saturday Review*, September 13, 1969, pp. 114–16.

[9] J. David Colfax, "How Effective is the Protest Advertisement?" *Journalism Quarterly*, Winter, 1966, pp. 697–702.

[10] Jerome A. Barron, "Access to the Press—A New First Amendment Right," *Harvard Law Review*, 1967, pp. 1646–47.

[11] Dennis E. Brown and John C. Merrill, "Regulatory Pluralism in the Press," Freedom of Information Center Report No. 005, Columbia, Missouri, p. 4.

[12] Carl E. Lindstrom, *The Fading American Newspaper* (Gloucester, Mass.: Peter Smith, 1964), pp. 82–83.

[13] O. Roy Chalk, "The High Cost of a Fresh Voice," *Grassroots Editor,* May/June, 1968, p. 16.

[14] Keith Roberts, "Antitrust Problems in the Newspaper Industry," *Harvard Law Review,* 1968, p. 334.

[15] *Ibid.,* p. 334.

[16] Chalk, "The High Cost of a Fresh Voice," pp. 17–18.

[17] John M. Harrison, "How a Town Broke a Newspaper Monopoly," *Columbia Journalism Review,* Winter, 1963, pp. 25–32.

[18] *Broadcasting Yearbook,* 1970, *passim.*

[19] Marvin Barrett, ed., *Survey of Broadcast Journalism, 1968–69* (N.Y.: Grosset & Dunlap, Inc., 1969), pp. 44, 122–24.

[20] *Access to the Air,* A Report on a Conference Held in New York City, September 28–29, 1968, conducted by The Graduate School of Journalism, Columbia University, p. 25.

[21] Robert W. Davenport, "Weird Note for the Vox Populi: The Los Angeles *Municipal News,*" *California Historical Society Quarterly,* March, 1965, pp. 3–14.

[22] "Voice of the Partially Alienated," *Time,* November 11, 1966, p. 92.

[23] Ethel Grodzins Romm, *The Open Conspiracy* (Harrisburg, Pa.: Stackpole Books, 1970), p. 17.

[24] Romm, *The Open Conspiracy,* p. 16.

[25] Richard Askin, "The Underground Press: Where It's At" (unpublished paper, University of Texas, 1970), p. 1.

[26] Personal communication from Wallace Turner to David M. Rubin, April, 1970.

SUGGESTED READINGS

Bagdikian, Ben H., "Right of Access: A Modest Proposal," *Columbia Journalism Review,* Spring, 1969.

Barron, Jerome A., "Access to the Press—A New First Amendment Right," *Harvard Law Review,* 1967.

Chalk, O. Roy, "The High Cost of a Fresh Voice," *Grassroots Editor,* May/ June, 1968.

Henderson, Hazel, "Access to the Media: A Problem in Democracy," *Columbia Journalism Review,* Spring, 1969.

Roberts, Keith, "Antitrust Problems in the Newspaper Industry," *Harvard Law Review,* 1968.

Romm, Ethel Grodzins, *The Open Conspiracy* (Harrisburg, Pa.: Stackpole Books, 1970).

PART THREE

MEDIA

So far in this book we have discussed the functions of the mass media, their history, and their control by various groups and institutions. By and large, our discussion has treated the media as a whole, not stressing the differences from one medium to another. But those differences are extremely important. It is impossible to understand the mass media without, at some point, considering them one by one.

We have now reached that point. Our discussion will begin with newspapers, traditionally the most prototypic of the media. Next will come magazines, because they share so many newspaper characteristics. The following chapter—the longest—is devoted to broadcasting, which has replaced the print media as the public's main source of news and entertainment. After broadcasting, we will turn our attention to three less important media: wire services, movies, and books. The final chapter in this section will consider a "mass medium" that is, in the long run, perhaps the most influential of all—advertising.

We will discuss a grand total of eight different media: newspapers, magazines, television, radio, wire services, movies, books, and advertising. It is important to recognize that these eight are by no means the only mass media in existence. Consider the following list:

Comic books
Matchbooks
Posters

Buttons
Phonograph records
Record jackets
Tape recordings
Plays
Light shows
Happenings
Nightclubs
Lectures
Operas
Concerts
Billboards
Graffiti
Paintings
Sculptures
Museums
Boxtops
Postcards

All of these—and many more—are in some sense mass media.

Some of them are extremely important mass media. You don't have to be under thirty to know that rock music, for example, has replaced everything else as *the* medium of expression and communication for many young people.

Before starting in on newspapers, we want to make some general points about the differences among the media. The first chapter in this section is therefore addressed to the following questions: How do the different media work? What are they good at and not good at? What do they accomplish? How do people use the different media and what do they think of them? In the last half of the chapter we will draw heavily on the thinking of Marshall McLuhan.

9 The Medium and the Message

Different mass media cover different events, and cover them differently. Some are fast, others slow. Some are shallow, others deep; some narrow, others broad. Some media are primarily for information, others for entertainment. Some appeal to the intellect, others to the emotions. Some are superlative vehicles for advertising and persuasion; others are not. The differences among the media have been studied for many years, but Marshall McLuhan was the first to argue persuasively that those differences were responsible for Western Civilization.

The mass media differ from each other in many ways. The most important ways tend to be the most obvious as well. You will find very little to suprise you in the next few pages, but much that is worth keeping in mind as you examine the media one by one. Remember also that only a few of these differences are essential characteristics of the media themselves; most could be otherwise if the people who ran the media wanted them otherwise.

1. Speed. The first medium to find out about an event is almost always the nearest newspaper. The wire services get the story from the paper, and everyone else gets it from the wires. Speed in reaching the public is another matter. Radio is usually first, followed by television. Newspapers come next, then magazines, and finally books. Advertising and movies are not concerned with the reporting of events, and wire services do not reach the public directly.

2. Depth. Depth is inversely proportional to speed. The slowest media, books and movies, are (at least potentially) the deepest. Magazines are next in line. Of the faster media, newspapers are the most likely to treat a subject in depth. Television and the wire services seldom do, and radio almost never does. Advertising could, but doesn't.

3. Breadth. The broadest range of subjects and interests is covered by books and magazines. By comparison, the rest of the media are appallingly narrow. Film and radio are the narrowest, except for advertising of course.

4. Ubiquity. Virtually every American has access to both a radio receiver and a television set—and spends at least a few hours a day with each. Newspapers reach more than 90 percent of the homes in the country, but seldom get more than ten minutes attention from any reader. Two-thirds of all American families subscribe to at least one magazine; roughly half of the adult population sees at least one movie a month. By contrast, less than one-tenth of the adult population reads a book a month. Every American, of course, is exposed to advertising on a daily— if not hourly—basis.

5. Permanence. Books are the most permanent of the mass media. Magazines are next, followed by newspapers. Only film companies save films; only ad agencies save ads; only editors save wire service teletypes. Almost nobody saves radio and television shows.

6. Locality. Newspapers are the only purely local medium. Radio is mostly local; advertising, wire services, and television are both local and national. Magazines, books, and movies are almost entirely national.

7. Openness. Of all the mass media, only books and magazines are truly open to new ideas and new owners; you can publish your own book or magazine tomorrow and reach your intended audience. Independent producers have made film a halfway open field. Offset printing has done the same for newspapers. Television, radio, and wire services are closed shops.

8. Sensory Involvement. Books appeal only to the eye, usually in black and white and without pictures. In sensory terms, they are the dullest of the mass media. Newspapers have pictures, and magazines have pictures and color—but they are still designed only for the eye. Radio, on the other hand, reaches only the ear. Television and film (and much advertising) appeal to both the eye and the ear, with moving pictures and often in color.

9. Credibility. The print media have traditionally been considered more believable than broadcasting or film. This is probably still valid in most cases, but recent surveys have found that most people believe television more readily than newspapers or magazines.

FUNCTIONS

As we have stressed throughout this book, the mass media have essentially four functions: to make money, to inform, to entertain, and to influence. How do the different media compare according to these four criteria?

1. To Make Money. It is difficult to rank the media in terms of profit; there are too many exceptions to the rules. Nevertheless, one can safely say that television is by all counts the most profitable. The advertising industry comes second, followed by newspapers, magazines, and radio—probably in that order. Book publishing earns a small but steady profit; movies alternately earn huge sums and lose huge sums. And the wire services are losing money.

2. To Inform. The United States, unlike many other countries, has no purely informational mass media. Books probably come closest, since the majority of all book titles published are textbooks. Most magazines also contain more information than anything else. Newspapers (which get most of their information from the wire services) are split about evenly, news versus advertising. Though television and radio do less than they should to inform the public, they are the main source of news for most people. Films and advertising are least intended to inform—but even they teach us something about our world and ourselves.

3. To Entertain. Although the purest entertainment medium is undoubtedly film, television is a close second—and is watched a great deal more. Entertainment is also the principal purpose of most radio stations, and of many magazines and books. Just about every newspaper sugarcoats its information with a heavy dose of entertainment. Even advertising tries hard to entertain, and often succeeds.

4. To Influence. Only one medium exists solely to influence people: advertising. It is remarkably successful. By contrast, newspapers usually confine their efforts at outright influence to the editorial pages. Many books (but not most) are written with influence in mind; some magazines and a few films have the same purpose. Television and radio make little if any conscious attempt to influence our society; their influence is of course enormous, but it is unplanned. The wire services are the most objective and least influence-conscious of the mass media.

THE AUDIENCE

Most Americans, it must be said, are happy with their mass media. They have complaints, of course—too much depressing news, too many commercials, and so forth. But on the whole they are quite satisfied. When survey researchers go out into the field and ask people what they would like from the media that they are not already getting, almost invariably the response is "Nothing." It is possible, of course—perhaps even likely—that there are public needs which are not adequately served by the mass media. But if so, the public is largely unaware of them.

Audiences use the mass media for their own purposes—which need not be the media's purposes. The goal of advertising, we have said, is to persuade people to buy. Yet many people watch TV ads solely for their entertainment value, with no intention of buying anything. Many others read the ads in newspapers for information—to find out what's available, what's on sale, what people are wearing these days. Still others use the ads primarily for reassurance; they try to convince themselves that the car or dishwasher they own was really the right one to buy.

Similarly, broadcast entertainment does not simply entertain. It informs and influences as well. A classic study of radio soap operas, for example, found that many listeners used the shows for guidance in their everyday activities. One faithful follower commented: "If you listen to these programs and something turns up in your own life, you would know what to do about it."[1]

Additional examples are easy to come up with. A movie like "Easy Rider" helps sell motorcycles. Black models in television commercials help reduce racism. Many people read newspaper feature stories purely for entertainment; they read the columnists for prestige and cocktail party conversation; they read the front page in order to avoid staring at their fellow bus or subway passengers. People listen to the radio out of boredom, or as background, or to keep from talking or thinking. People buy magazines to show them off on the coffee table; they read them because they bought them. People go to movies to get away from their kids, or to get away from their parents.

Before judging any mass medium, it is a good idea to ask three questions. First, what is the medium, as a medium, capable of doing? Second, what do the people and groups who control that medium permit it to do? And third, what does the audience do with it?

THE MEDIUM AND THE MESSAGE

For decades social scientists have been extremely interested in the study of attitude change. Supported by advertising agencies, political groups, and others with vested interests, they have sought the answer to one basic question: How can we persuade people to change their opinions? Many lesser questions had to be attacked first. One of the most important of those was this one: Does the same persuasive message have different effects if carried by different media?

Back in the 1930s, scholars like W. H. Wilke, Franklin R. Knower, Hadley Cantril, and Gordon Allport addressed themselves to this question. In a typical experiment, they would expose matched groups of college students to an identical argument about war, religion, or some other controversial topic. One group would get the lecture in person; another would hear it on radio; a third would read it in print. Then everyone was tested to see how much his attitude had changed. In experiment after experiment, the results were consistent. The face-to-face lecture was more persuasive than radio, and radio was more persuasive than print.[2]

The same order of effectiveness turned up in the real world. Paul Lazarsfeld and his colleagues studied the 1940 Presidential election campaign in Erie County, Ohio. They found that voters were most influenced by neighbor-to-neighbor conversations. Radio was the second most influential medium in the campaign, and print was third.[3] Later experiments showed that television and film were both better persuaders than radio, but still less effective than personal contact.

That problem solved, social scientists turned to more complicated ones. For more than a decade nobody wrote much about the differential effects of different media. Then, in 1964, a Canadian scholar named Marshall McLuhan published his book, *Understanding Media*. McLuhan's thinking relies heavily on the ideas of another Canadian scholar, Harold Innis—but it was McLuhan who first popularized those ideas.

Trained in engineering and English literature, McLuhan was (and is) an intellectual eclectic. He ignores the findings of social science even when they support his ideas. He does not bother to prove his statements with evidence, but rather illustrates them with examples—drawn from such varied sources as James Joyce and professional football. The reaction of traditional scholars to these tactics is summed up by critic Dwight Macdonald:

> One defect of *Understanding Media* is that the parts are greater than the whole. A single page is impressive, two are "stimulating," five raise serious doubts, ten confirm them, and long before the hardy reader has staggered to page 359 the accumulation of contradictions, nonsequiturs, facts that are distorted and facts that are not facts, exaggerations, and chronic rhetorical vagueness has numbed him to the insights. . . .[4]

These accusations do not seem to bother McLuhan, who claims that his unrigorous style is ideally suited to the world of television. Nor do they bother his disciples, who number in the thousands.

THE MEDIUM IS THE MESSAGE

McLuhan's central assertion is that "the medium is the message." The customary distinction between the two, he argues, is mythical. What a medium communicates, quite apart from its content, is the nature of the medium itself. "Our conventional response to all media, namely that it is how they are used that counts, is the numb stance of the technological idiot. For the 'content' of a medium is like the juicy piece of meat carried by the burglar to distract the watchdog of the mind."[5] McLuhan entitled one of his later books *The Medium Is The Massage*, purposely turning the title into a pun in order to emphasize that the real "message" of a medium is the way it pokes, jabs, and kneads its audience—not what it says.

Media for McLuhan are extensions of one or more of the five senses. Face-to-face speech (the oldest of the media) extends all five senses. Print extends only the eye, radio the ear. Television is an extension of both the eye and the ear. (Elsewhere, McLuhan insists that TV is primarily a tactile medium, but he never makes clear the meaning or significance of the remark.) The impact of a medium is determined by which senses it extends and the way it extends them.

Media, says McLuhan, are either "hot" or "cool." This is a crucial distinction for McLuhan, and he describes it lucidly:

> There is a basic principle that distinguishes a hot medium like radio from a cool one like the telephone, or a hot medium like the movie from a cool one like TV. A hot medium is one that extends one single sense in

---

BRAINWAVES AND McLUHAN

Dr. Herbert Krugman, a physiological psychologist in New York, recently reported some findings that seem to support a McLuhanesque view of the importance of the medium, though they contradict McLuhan's notion of how media differ. Says Krugman: "The basic electrical response of the brain is clearly to the media and not to content differences."

In one typical experiment, Krugman attached an electrode to the skull of a college student. He recorded her brain waves as she first read a cosmetics ad, then watched a few television commercials. For the printed ad, the electroencephalograph registered five seconds of slow Delta waves and 28 seconds of fast Beta waves. When the commercials came on, the Delta waves jumped up to 21 seconds, while the Beta waves dropped to 15 seconds. Krugman believes the girl "was trying to learn something from the print ad, but was passive about television."[6]

"high definition." High definition is the state of being well filled with data. A photograph is, visually, "high definition." A cartoon is "low definition," simply because very little visual information is provided. Telephone is a cool medium, or one of low definition, because the ear is given a meager amount of information. And speech is a cool medium of low definition, because so little is given and so much has to be filled in by the listener. On the other hand, hot media do not leave so much to be filled in or completed by the audience. Hot media are, therefore, low in participation, and cool media are high in participation or completion by the audience. Naturally, therefore, a hot medium like radio has very different effects on the user from a cool medium like the telephone.[7]

A hot medium is hot, in other words, because it provides a lot of information and requires little audience participation. A cool medium is cool because it provides little information and requires a lot of audience participation. Print, film, radio, and nylon stockings are hot. Telephone, modern art, and open-mesh stockings are cool. Television is cool, too—a fuzzy collection of tiny dots that the viewer must connect and fill in.

McLuhan wants to know only two things about any medium: which senses it extends, and whether it does so in high definition (hot) or low definition (cool).

RETRIBALIZATION

History for McLuhan is divided into three stages. The first may be called the "tribal" stage. It is characterized by local, oral communication within each tribe or community. Person-to-person speech is, in McLuhan's view, a cool medium, involving all five senses. It thus requires the maximum amount of participation.

The second stage begins with the invention of the printing press. Print, of course, is the hottest of McLuhan's media, and extends only one sense: the eye. Instead of participation and involvement, it requires dispassionate attention to the words on the page. James W. Carey notes that "the desire to break things down into elementary units . . . the tendency to see reality in discrete units, to find causal relations and linear serial order . . . to find orderly structure in nature" can be traced to the influence of print.

Carey goes even further: "To live in an oral culture, one acquires knowledge only in contact with other people, in terms of communal activities. Printing, however, allows individuals to withdraw, to contemplate and meditate outside of communal activities. Print thus encourages privatization, the lonely scholar, and the development of private, individual points of view."[8]

In addition, McLuhan says, print created the price system—"for until commodities are uniform and repeatable the price of an article is subject to haggle and adjustment."[9]   Print is also responsible for the growth of nationalism, because it permitted "visual apprehension of the mother tongue and, through maps, visual apprehension of the nation."[10]   All these effects, taken together, McLuhan calls the detribalization of man.

McLuhan's third stage begins with the invention of television.   TV, he tells us, is a cool medium; it requires its audience to participate.   TV is also an extension of at least three senses—the visual, the aural, and the tactile.   Through television, involvement has once again become a fundamental part of the communication process.   Instead of the "tribal village" of the first stage, we are faced now with a "global village," mediated by television.   We are in the process of being "retribalized" by television.

Most adults can't take it.   "We are no more prepared to encounter radio and TV in our literate milieu than the native of Ghana is able to cope with the literacy that takes him out of his collective tribal world and beaches him in individual isolation.   We are as numb in our new electric world as the native involved in our literate and mechanical culture."[11]

But in McLuhan's view, anyone born after 1950 doesn't need retribalizing.   He grew up with television, and hence he has always been a member of the tribe.   Print man, writes Tom Wolfe, "always has the feeling that no matter what anybody says, he can go check it out. . . . He can *look* it up. . . . The aural man is not so much of an individualist; he is more a part of the collective consciousness; he *believes*."[12]   James Carey summarizes McLuhan's views this way:

> The generational gap we now observe by contrasting the withdrawn, private, specializing student of the fifties with the active, involved, generalist student of the sixties McLuhan rests at the door of television. . . . The desire of students for involvement and participation, for talking rather than reading, for seminars rather than lectures, for action rather than reflection, in short for participation and involvement rather than withdrawal and observation he ascribes to the reorchestration of the senses provoked by television.[13]

The impact of television is so enormous that McLuhan does not hesitate to assert that it "has begun to dissolve the fabric of American life." He has recommended, apparently quite seriously, that TV be banned in the United States before it destroys the country by driving us "inward in depth into a totally nonvisual universe of involvement."[14]

TRUTH AND FANTASY

Is McLuhan right?   Certainly he is right about some things.   The mass media do have far-reaching effects on society, effects too broad to be measured in the experiments of social scientists.   And at least some of those effects, it seems, stem from the nature of the media themselves, irrespective of content. McLuhan has looked at the history of civilization from a new perspective. Much of what he sees no one else has seen.

Much of what he sees probably isn't there. Listen to critic Tom Nairn: "Take the example of the so-called 'global village.' To anyone who can extricate himself from the McLuhanite trance for a few seconds, it is reasonably clear that the existing global village was created by European imperialism, not by television; that it is not a 'village,' but a cruel class society tearing humanity in two; that the techniques which made it, and sustain it, are overwhelmingly pre-electronic—private property and the gun; and that the *actual* use made of media like television in our society, far from pushing us toward a healing of the gap, reinforces our acceptance of it. . . ."[15]

Or listen to critic Richard Kostelanetz, talking about the notion that the medium is the message: "The fifth rerun of *I Love Lucy* is a considerably different TV experience from a presentation of George F. Kennan addressing the Committee on Foreign Relations on the War in Vietnam; and I doubt if many people watching Kennan stayed with that channel when Lucy appeared in his stead. Even on the medium which has perhaps the narrowest range of quality, content does count."[16]

McLuhan and his disciples share a complete disdain for evidence. One of the distinctions between print and broadcasting, according to McLuhan, is that print follows a linear one-thing-at-a-time sort of logic, while broadcasting is global, everything-at-once. As a result, McLuhanites claim, Western Civilization is now undergoing a change from a linear lifestyle to a global one. This is, in the language of social science, a testable hypothesis. But McLuhan and his followers do not bother to test it, or even to find out whether it has already been tested. Instead, they simply point out that baseball, a linear game, is now less popular than football, a global game. Q.E.D. If you want more proof than that, you are obviously a linear personality, unfit for the television age.

Evidence for McLuhan's propositions turn up in unexpected places. Professor John Wilson of the African Institute of London University, for example, tried to use a movie to teach African natives how to read. He found, to his surprise, that the natives did not "see" the film the same way he did. In each scene of the movie, they picked out a familiar object like a chicken and fastened on that, switching to a different object only when the scene switched. They made no effort to connect the scenes or follow the story line.[17] Several studies of children watching television have produced intriguingly similar results. The children did not focus on the whole screen as their parents did; instead, they scanned the screen for details to fasten on.[18] Perhaps television is retribalizing us after all.

To summarize Marshall McLuhan in a single paragraph (and only a linear mind would try): He is impossible to understand, difficult to accept, and dangerous to ignore. He is one part nonsense, one part insight, and several parts unproved supposition. All the social science Ph.D.s in the country could spend their lifetimes testing McLuhan's guesses—and maybe they should.

NOTES

[1] Herta Herzog, "Motivations and Gratifications of Daily Serial Listeners," in *The Process and Effects of Mass Communication,* ed. Wilbur Schramm (Urbana, Ill.: University of Illinois Press, 1954), p. 51.

[2] Joseph T. Klapper, *The Effects of Mass Communication* (New York: The Free Press, 1960), p. 106.

[3] *Ibid.,* p. 107.

[4] Gerald Emanuel Stearn, ed., *McLuhan: Hot and Cool* (New York: Signet Paperback, 1967), p. 205.

[5] Marshall McLuhan, *Understanding Media* (New York: Signet Paperback, 1964), p. 32.

[6] "TV vs. Print," *Newsweek,* November 2, 1970, pp. 122–23.

[7] McLuhan, *Understanding Media,* p. 36.

[8] Raymond Rosenthal, ed., *McLuhan Pro and Con* (Baltimore: Penguin Books Inc., 1968), pp. 285–86.

[9] Marshall McLuhan, *The Gutenberg Galaxy* (Toronto: University of Toronto Press, 1962), p. 164.

[10] Rosenthal, *McLuhan Pro and Con,* p. 286.

[11] McLuhan, *Understanding Media,* p. 31.

[12] Stearn, *McLuhan: Hot and Cool,* p. 37.

[13] Rosenthal, *McLuhan Pro and Con,* p. 288.

[14] Stearn, *McLuhan: Hot and Cool,* pp. 270–71, 291.

[15] Rosenthal, *McLuhan Pro and Con,* p. 150.

[16] *Ibid.,* p. 220.

[17] McLuhan, *The Gutenberg Galaxy,* pp. 36–37.

[18] Stearn, *McLuhan: Hot and Cool,* p. 37.

SUGGESTED READINGS

McLuhan, Marshall, *The Gutenberg Galaxy.* Toronto: University of Toronto Press, 1962.

———, *Understanding Media.* New York: Signet Paperback, 1964.

Rosenthal, Raymond, ed., *McLuhan Pro and Con.* Baltimore: Penguin Books Inc., 1968.

Stearn, Gerald Emanuel, ed., *McLuhan: Hot and Cool.* New York: Signet Paperback, 1967.

10 Newspapers

The newspaper is the oldest and traditionally the most important source of current information. Even today, the average daily paper contains far more news than is available on television or elsewhere. But most of that news is not read, and the newspaper appears to be growing less influential every year. This is a source of profound dissatisfaction for many publishers and reporters, and a possible threat to American society.

A newspaper is an unbound, printed publication, issued at regular intervals, which presents information in words, often supplemented with pictures.

Don't memorize that definition. It is accurate, but not very useful. Perhaps more useful is this rough breakdown of the content of a typical daily newspaper:

60%	Advertising
15%	Wire service news (state, national, and international)
10%	Syndicated features and columns
10%	Sports, society, and other specialized departments
5%	Local hard news

The breakdown tells you some important things about newspapers: that more than half of their content isn't news at all, but advertising; that almost half of the remainder is really features and specialized departments; that the bulk of what's left is written by wire service reporters dozens, hundreds, or thousands of miles away; that only a tiny fraction of each paper is local hard news.

That is what a newspaper is. What should it be? Most observers agree that the main function of the daily newspaper is to tell readers what's happening in the world, the country, the state, and the city. It should strive to report significant political and social developments, to include news of special relevance to particular groups of readers, to scrutinize the actions of local government, and to act as a forum for various community viewpoints.

Students of journalism and political science are agreed that this is the role of the daily newspaper. Readers, reporters, and publishers, however, have somewhat different notions of the purpose of the paper. And it is their views (not ours) that control what actually happens.

THE NEWSPAPER READER

The best way to tell what readers think of their newspapers is to see what they read. What percentage of the audience reads each kind of news? The following list shows one typical set of findings.[1]

Picture pages	74.3%
Comic pages	42.6
Page One	34.3
Solid news-feature pages	24.0
Editorial pages	23.1
Amusement	21.3
Split news-advertising pages	18.2
Solid advertising pages	15.7
Society and women's pages	15.5
Sports pages	13.9
Financial pages	5.4

The readership pattern is clear. Most people turn to the least taxing, most entertaining sections first, glance at the front page, and then stop. Nearly twice as many read the comics as the editorials. Almost as many read solid ad pages as inside news pages. It is figures like these that feed the cynicism of newspapermen, that prompted one city editor of the 1920s to say: "You and I aren't hired to make the world a better place to live in, or to fight and die for noble causes, or even to tell the truth about this particular main street. We're hired to feed human animals the kind of mental garbage they want. We don't have to eat it. I don't read our paper for instruction or even for fun. I just read it for errors and to see if we're handing out regularly what the boobs like for breakfast."[2]

The statement is exaggerated. Newspaper readers aren't boobs. They are, in fact, considerably higher in education and income than nonread-ers. And a study conducted in 1965 by the Louisville *Courier-Journal* found that more than 90 percent of "influential decision-makers" in the Louisville area were regular readers of the paper.[3] The newspaper audi-ence is, relatively, an elite audience.

Elite or not, most newspaper readers are not very interested in news. When a strike deprives them of their daily paper, what do they miss most? They miss the ads, the "news" of supermarket sales, apartments for rent, and new movies in town. And they miss the service announce-ments; weddings go uncongratulated, funerals unmourned, and the weather unprepared for. Above all, they miss the habit of reading the paper, and turn desperately to the backs of cereal boxes in search of an adequate sub-stitute. But newspaper *news* they can do without—there's always tele-vision.

Television is, in fact, the preferred source of news for most Americans today. In 1959, Roper Research Associates asked a sample of Americans where they got their news. Newspapers were mentioned by 57 percent of the respondents; television by 51 percent; radio by 34 percent; and magazines by eight percent (multiple answers were accepted). In 1968, Roper repeated the survey. This time, 59 percent mentioned television; newspapers were down to 49 percent, radio to 25 percent, and magazines to seven percent.

The decline in newspaper credibility at the expense of television is even more dramatic. When Roper asked his sample which medium is most believable, this is what he found.[4]

	1959	*1968*
Television	29%	44%
Newspapers	32	21
Magazines	10	11
Radio	12	8
No answer	17	16

Students of journalism believe that the newspaper is the best avail-able daily source of news. But newspaper readers prefer to get their news from television. They rely on the paper for entertainment and ser-vice, for comics, crosswords, and classifieds.

THE NEWSPAPER REPORTER

For reporters, newspapering is first and foremost a job—and not a very well-paid job at that. The average metropolitan daily newspaper pays a starting reporter roughly $150 a week—less if the paper has no contract with the American Newspaper Guild. After five years on the job, the reporter will rise to $250 a week or so. He will never get much higher unless he specializes, becomes an editor, or wins a Pulitzer Prize.

To be sure, prestige papers like the New York *Times* and the Washington *Post* pay 5-year veterans as much as $350 a week. And most large papers have at least a few top reporters who are paid far more than their colleagues. Small-town and weekly newspapers, on the other hand, often pay less than $100 a week. Perhaps more important, reporters' salaries do not keep pace with wage hikes in other industries, nor do they reflect increases in newspaper profits. In comparison with the average newspaper reporter, advertising salesmen earn one-third again as much, printers and stereotypers earn half again as much, radio journalists earn nearly twice as much, and television newsmen earn well over twice as much.

Besides the bad pay, newspapermen must learn to live with low status, terrible hours, and total insecurity (every time a newspaper folds, a roomful of reporters starts looking for work.) They must also put up with the whims of publishers, the anger of news sources and would-be sources, and the tedium of covering press conference after press conference after press conference.

Why do they stay? Many don't. One typical study traced the careers of 35 outstanding journalism students. Only 19 of them (just over half) went into newspaper work after graduating. Ten years later, only eight of them were still holding down newspaper jobs. The rest had left for public relations, advertising, broadcasting, insurance, or whatever.[5] It can be persuasively argued that the best college students don't major in journalism, the best journalism majors don't go into the media, the best media people don't work for newspapers, and the best newspapermen quit.

What's left after this winnowing process is the typical newspaperman. He is in his late forties and earns around $12,000 a year. He's been in the newspaper business for half his life, and though he doesn't find it especially exciting any more, he doesn't intend to leave either. He has a college diploma, a wife, and a mortgage. He believes in the mystique of journalism, and will occasionally remark that he has "ink in his veins." But he is a little resentful of the younger reporters who expect to take the world by storm, and is secretly pleased whenever one of them quits and takes a job in public relations.

The experienced reporter is something of a cynic. He has seen the worst in life and been unable to report it, or has reported it and been unable to change it. Theodore Dreiser described him this way:

> One can always talk to a newspaper man, I think, with the full confidence that one is talking to a man who is at least free of moralistic mush.

Nearly everything in connection with those trashy romances of justice, truth, mercy, patriotism, public profession of all sorts, is already and forever gone if they have been in the business for any length of time.[6]

The cynicism of the newspaperman is largely the result of frustration —the frustration of a man of action forced to play the role of an observer. What city hall reporter has not fancied himself a LaGuardia? What education writer a Dewey? What sports columnist a Mays? Many journalists pick newspaper work, it seems to us, in order to change the world. They soon discover that they *can't* change the world, that the most they can do is to report the world-changing decisions of others. And so the activist reporter becomes a passive writer of articles. After work he adjourns to the neighborhood bar to tell his colleagues what the mayor *should* have done.

Perhaps this is an exaggerated view of newspaper work. No doubt there are reporters around who exult with editor Walter Humphrey that "every human activity is on my beat and I am interested in everything that happens in the world, for everything is my concern."[7] No doubt there are other reporters who simply do their job, and do it well, with a minimum of frustration or cynicism. But the typical reporter, we maintain, is a disillusioned idealist. He wants to change the world, but his readers and his publisher, he often feels, want mostly pap.

THE NEWSPAPER PUBLISHER

For publishers the newspaper is a business, and like all businessmen the publisher wants his paper to earn a profit. By and large, he gets what he wants.

Newspaper financial statements are hard to come by. Publishers are constantly pleading that the wolf is halfway in the newsroom door, and treat any inquiry into profits as a direct assault on Freedom of the Press. The Tucson *Daily Citizen* and *Arizona Star* told Congress that only their joint operating agreement kept them barely in the black (see p. 126). Yet Tucson Mayor James N. Corbett testified that the two papers together earned an annual profit of two million dollars.[8] If that's what a "failing newspaper" looks like, then solvent newspapers must be doing very well indeed.

The New York *Times* is among the few newspapers that freely report their profits. In the first quarter of 1969, the *Times* earned a net of $3,332,000 on gross revenues of $57,367,000. The paper's total profit in 1968 was $14,204,671—up nearly three million dollars from the 1967 figure.

There are several newspapers in the country with higher advertising revenues than the *Times,* and nearly every newspaper has lower editorial expenses. The following list shows the 1969 advertising leaders and their total ad linage. It is safe to assume that all these papers are earning very healthy profits.

Los Angeles *Times*	5,168,022
Miami *Herald*	4,930,815
Fort Lauderdale *News*	4,025,072
Chicago *Tribune*	3,919,620
Houston *Chronicle*	3,681,655
Washington *Post*	3,628,460
New York *Times*	3,454,739
San Jose *Mercury*	3,316,382
San Jose *News*	3,294,486
Phoenix *Republic*	3,175,386

The profitability of today's newspaper is reflected in the difficulty and cost of buying one. Only two or three metropolitan papers change hands each year; most of the available action is in the 5,000 to 50,000 circulation range. A few decades ago, you could have bought the Athens, Georgia, daily paper (circ. 7,000) for a mere $50,000. The asking price in the mid-1960s was $1.7 million. And the 400,000-circulation Cleveland *Plain Dealer* was sold to the Newhouse chain in 1968 for a cool $51 million.

Occasionally, of course, a newspaper loses money. The Cowles chain dropped nearly $2.2 million on the Suffolk *Sun* before giving up in 1969. But on the whole, a newspaper is a good, safe, solid investment.

Newspaper profits are steady, but they are by no means exorbitant. The New York *Times* first quarter 1969 figures work out to a profit of only six percent on gross income—nothing to write home about. In recent years operating costs have climbed steadily, especially labor and newsprint. Many publishers are afraid to pass the increase along to advertisers, for fear they might switch to radio and television. They are just as reluctant to raise the newsstand and subscription price; readers might quit buying. (The New York *Times* and the New York *Post* both conquered the fear and jumped to 15¢ in 1970; many others followed suit in 1971.) So they have absorbed much of the cost increase themselves, in the form of reduced profits. Very few publishers are going broke, but not too many are getting rich either. Television has been called "a license to print money." By contrast, a newspaper is only a permit to coin pocket change.

Publishers could probably increase newspaper profits if they put their minds to it. The oldest of the mass media, newspapering is also the most old-fashioned. Many publishers are not especially eager to streamline their operations. In an age dedicated to speed, cleanliness, and efficiency, there is a certain thumb-your-nose pleasure in slow, dirty, inefficient newspaper work. It seems many publishers (like most editors and re- porters) are traditionalists; they like doing things the old way.

People own newspapers for old-fashioned reasons. They enjoy the powerful role they play in local politics. They appreciate being courted by Senators and Presidents. They delight in lecturing the Lions and Rotarians on world affairs. They love the chance to write their own weekly column. And there is a very personal feeling of historical pride in performing a task protected by the Constitution itself—the only occu- pation so protected. As long as they are earning adequate profits, pub- lishers are content to leave well enough alone.

This traditional attitude of newspaper owners may be changing. Only twenty years ago, the typical publisher owned his paper, period. Today, he may own four papers, or forty—plus a couple of TV stations, a cable system, and maybe some real estate on the side. And he is no longer on his own; he may be the salaried president of a corporation listed on the New York Stock Exchange. The head of a chain or con- glomerate has neither the time nor the inclination for local ego-tripping. He boosts his ego with financial statements, not editorials or lectures. His god is profit.

If this man has his way, the newspaper business will become far more efficient and far less romantic. It's a trade-off that many will applaud. Most working reporters will be unsurprised, but bitterly disappointed. And the readers won't even notice the difference.

THE NEWSPAPER

The content of a newspaper is the product of the conflicting goals of the reader (to be entertained), the reporter (to change the world), and the publisher (to make money and make his mark). In this conflict the re- porter usually loses. For one thing, the reader and the publisher have all the power; for another, their goals are highly compatible. The reporter is odd man out.

Consider, for example, the syndicated feature. Syndicated material— comic strips, advice columns, and the like—makes up as much as one- third the editorial content of many daily newspapers. Why? Because it's cheap; a cost-conscious publisher can use the syndicates to fill 35 percent of his news hole for only ten percent of his editorial budget. And because it's entertaining, which is what the public wants. To be sure, the feature syndicates also bring us Jack Anderson, Joe Alsop, and many other important political columnists. But most of what they move is cheap junk. Reporters scorn it, but publishers and readers approve it.

The decline of the newspaper editorial is another perfect example of the publisher-reader coalition at work. Until the Penny Press era the unsigned editorials were the most important part of most newspapers. But today's reader finds the editorial page too heavy for his taste. That's okay with the profit-oriented publisher. He uses his edit page to praise the weather and pontificate on the latest news from Afghanistan—or he fills it with canned editorials supplied free-of-charge by special interest groups. Even the power-hungry publisher sees little point in editorials, since nobody reads them. Said William Rockhill Nelson of the Kansas City *Star:* "Give me the front page and I don't care who has the editorial page."[9] There are still a few newspapers left in the country that regularly publish strong local editorials. But you can count them on your fingers and toes.

A third example is the growing ascendency of advertising over news copy. In 1941, the average newspaper was 52 percent news, 48 percent advertising. Today, a respectable ratio is 60 percent advertising and 40 percent news. (In all fairness, the size of the typical newspaper has also increased, leaving a bigger news hole by absolute measures than ever before.) Reporters and editors fight for every column-inch of news they can get. But publishers prefer to print ads. And readers often prefer to read ads.

Regardless of whether they're in the business for profit or for power, publishers are always pleased to own the only newspaper in town. Without competition, costs are lower and ad revenues higher—and the publisher can sound off without fear of contradiction. As long as the survivor picks up the dead paper's comics and columns, readers seldom object to the loss of a newspaper.

THE ENDOWED NEWSPAPER

Press critic A. J. Liebling was fond of comparing the job of running a newspaper with that of running a university. He reasoned that newspapers, like universities, should be endowed, thus freeing the publisher from the effort to please readers and advertisers.

"The hardest trick, of course, would be getting the chief donor of the endowment (perhaps a repentant tabloid publisher) to a) croak, or b) sign a legally binding agreement never to stick his face in the editorial rooms." The best kind of endowment for a newspaper, Liebling continued, "would be one made up of several large and many small or medium-sized gifts."

"Personally," he added, "I would rather leave my money for a newspaper than for a cathedral, a gymnasium, or even a home for street-walkers with fallen arches, but I have seldom been able to assemble more than $4.17 at one time."[10]

The result: merger after merger, ending in monopoly after monopoly. In 1910, there were 689 American cities with competing daily newspapers. By 1930, the figure was down to 288; by 1960, it was down to 61. Today, Chicago is the only city in the country with two competing newspapers in the morning, and two more in the afternoon (two companies own all four papers). The vast majority of Americans live in towns with no effective newspaper competition.

When newspaper competition dies, part of the challenge of newspapering dies too. Most reporters swear that newspaper quality declines as a result. Management claims the opposite. Without competitive pressure, publishers argue, a paper is free to stress accuracy and balance instead of speed and sensationalism.

The debate is hard to resolve. One researcher studied the *Tri-City Herald* in Washington during periods of monopoly and of competition. He found that sensational copy filled 30 percent of the paper's news hole during its competitive era, but only 22 percent when it was a monopoly. On the other hand, the *Herald* devoted more space to local news when faced with competition (51 percent of the news hole) than it did with no competition (41 percent).[11] Monopoly, in other words, improved the paper in some ways, but hurt it in others.

Another study found that competitive newspapers tended to have a larger news hole than monopoly papers. They also allowed more space for letters to the editor and wrote more editorials on local subjects. The differences, however, were very small.[12]

A third study focused on competing dailies in Pottstown, Pennsylvania. Author Stanley Bigman compared the two papers on many characteristics, and concluded that they were identical. Because the two publishers were so similar in social class and political ideology, Bigman asserted, the town would lose nothing if it lost one of the papers.[13]

The central lesson of Bigman's study is that it's the publisher, not the reporter, who controls newspaper quality. No doubt a conscientious reporter does a better job if he has another paper to compete with. But competition or no competition, the publisher has it in his power to produce any sort of paper he wants. The Louisville *Courier-Journal* and the Atlanta *Constitution* are monopoly newspapers, yet they are excellent newspapers. The Detroit *News* and the Cleveland *Press* have competition, but they do a poor job anyhow. Perhaps the competitive publisher has to make a greater effort to keep his readers happy—but pleasing the readers doesn't necessarily make for a better newspaper.

One man can change the face of a newspaper. In 1960, the Los Angeles *Times* was "best represented by a middle-aged lady in a mink shrug on her way to a Republican tea."[14] It had three men in its Washington bureau, a total news staff of 220, and an annual editorial budget

of $3 million. Then Otis Chandler took over as publisher. Today, the
Times has 18 men in Washington, a news staff of more than 500, and an
operating budget of $12 million a year. And it is one of the most aggres-
sive, respected (and profitable) newspapers in America. Under Colonel
William Rockhill Nelson, on the other hand, the Kansas City *Star* was once
ranked among the top papers in the country. Today it is just another
big-city daily.

Publishers control their newspapers. And, as Bigman points out, most
publishers are very much alike—conservative, well-to-do businessmen, confirmed members of the Establishment. Their newspapers reflect their
values, and the values of their friends. Editor H. Lang Rogers of the
Joplin (Missouri) *Globe* comments that the average publisher tries "to
mold his newspaper around the comments, desires, and complaints of
his country club buddies."[15] The result is a newspaper responsive only
to the upper classes, not to the entire community.

"Country club journalism" is nothing new. William Allen White had
this to say about it back in 1939:

> If he is a smart go-getting up-and-coming publisher in a town of
> 100,000 to 1,000,000 people, the publisher associates on terms of equality
> with the bankers, the merchant princes, the manufacturers, and the in-
> vesting brokers. His friends unconsciously color his opinion. If he lives
> with them on any kind of social terms in the City club or the Country
> club or the Yacht club or the Racquet club, he must more or less merge
> his views into the common views of the other capitalists. . . .
>
> So it often happens, alas too often, that a newspaper publisher, re-
> flecting this unconscious class arrogance of the consciously rich, thinks he
> is printing news when he is doctoring it innocently enough. He thinks
> he is purveying the truth when much that he offers seems poison to hun-
> dreds of thousands of his readers who don't move in his social and eco-
> nomic stratosphere. . . .[16]

Country club journalism is strongest in newspapers whose publishers
are more interested in power than profit. Money-hungry publishers
confine their ideology to the editorial page, where it won't alienate so
many readers. Some readers are alienated anyhow, and stop reading.
But most newspaper readers are interested in entertainment, not politics.
They may never notice the bias in their daily paper.

The fact remains that large groups of citizens find little of value to
them in today's newspaper. These include blacks and other minority
groups, high school and college students, and to a lesser extent blue-collar
workers. In the past, the existence of an audience unserved by established newspapers has always spurred the growth of a new kind of newspaper—the Penny Press in the 1830s, yellow journalism in the 1890s, the
tabloid in the 1920s, etc. Today this audience has nurtured the urban
weekly and the underground paper.

In the last section we detailed five characteristics of newspapers that are approved by publishers and readers, but bitterly resented by most reporters:

1. The growth of syndicated features.
2. The decline of the editorial.
3. The supremacy of advertising over news.
4. The trend toward newspaper monopoly.
5. Country club journalism.

Reporters are powerless to change any of these characteristics.

Although reporters lose most of their battles with publishers and readers, they are bound to win a few. Two such victories have had a significant effect on the quality of today's newspaper—specialized reporting and personal writing.

Specialized reporting is not a recent invention. The New York *Sun* had its own police reporter back in the 1830s. But except for a few areas (sports, society, business), specialization didn't begin to take hold until the last twenty years or so. A study of 52 major metropolitan dailies revealed that in 1945 only ten of them had specialized education writers. By 1955 there were 23 such writers; by 1960 the number was up to 40. In 1966, only three of the 52 papers still had no education reporter on their staffs.[17]

In 1970 the Milwaukee *Journal* (a better-than-average metropolitan daily) listed the following specialized departments and beats: art, auto, aviation, boating, books, business/financial, civil rights, education, farm, fashion, food, garden, home furnishings, labor, medicine, men's, motion pictures/theatrical, music, outdoor, radio/television, real estate, religion, science, society, sports, state, theater, travel, and women's. In addition, a number of the paper's "general assignment" reporters consistently covered certain areas—city hall, police, etc.

There is little doubt that specialized reporters do a better job than those on general assignment. The specialist gets to know both his subject and his sources. He has the background necessary to interpret the story for his readers.

But specialization is of little value unless reporters are free to include their expertise in their articles. The traditional who/what/where/when/why kind of journalism allows almost no leeway for this sort of interpretation. A complicated political or economic story written in the traditional style is almost completely incomprehensible. It is not enough for the reporter to understand the issues; he must be permitted to explain them to the reader in a way that the reader can follow, understand, and enjoy.

The growth of "personal journalism" may well turn out to be the most important newspaper development of the 1970s. It is not a new development. The colonial press was intensely personal; so was the Penny Press in the 1830s and the yellow press in the 1890s. It can be argued, in fact, that newspaper "objectivity" is nothing but a passing fad—a fad that peaked in the 1960s and is already on the wane. Perhaps by 1980 reporters will write as personally and subjectively as publishers and editors wrote in the early history of American journalism.

In any case, the current renaissance of personal journalism is still in its infancy. No Establishment paper comes even close to the "New Journalism" of Norman Mailer, Tom Wolfe, and your local underground rag. The first person is still forbidden in most news stories, and so are the opinions of the writer. But interpretive news articles are getting more and more common every day—and more and more outspoken. Consider the following UPI story, chosen more or less at random:

> WASHINGTON (UPI)—The Senate has voted to permit children to pray, to protect women from war and to save America from sin. Can election day be far away?
>
> The god-mother-and-morality triple-header came Tuesday, three weeks to the day before the Nov. 3 congressional elections. Separate roll-call votes within the space of four hours put the Senate on record in favor of:
> —Amending the Constitution to permit prayer in the public schools.
> —Exempting women from the draft.
> —And repudiating the Presidential Commission on Obscenity and Pornography, which favored legalized smut for consenting adults.
> None of the votes, however, was expected to change anything.
> The prayer and draft measures were amendments to a proposed constitutional amendment that would grant equality to women—a measure which is destined for the post-election scrap-heap. And the condemnation of smut was in a simple resolution that has no apparent binding legal effect. . . .[18]

Publishers object to specialized reporting because it costs more; most readers couldn't care less. Both publishers *and* readers object to personal journalism, because it opens the door to biased reporting. Newspaper reporters tend to be more liberal than their readers, and far more liberal than their publishers. H. Lang Rogers of the Joplin (Missouri) *Globe* puts the objection this way: "We find fewer of the young journalists with the basic honesty and integrity to seek to write entirely objectively and to bend over backwards to keep their own beliefs from slanting their writings."[19]

The problem of biased reporters is a serious one, as Vice President Spiro T. Agnew pointed out in 1969 (see pp. 109–10, 158). But a little bias is not, we think, too high a price to pay for intelligent, informed, interpretive reporting. The typical publisher, after all, wants only to make money and give speeches. The typical reader wants only to be entertained. The reporter—especially the under-thirty reporter—wants to change the world. Perhaps we should give him a chance.

The process of creating a newspaper is a good reflection of the paper's character. That process is, of course, different for different papers, and the process differs even for different stories in the same paper. But always it is hurried, harried, and demanding. Many of the developing trends in newspaper work are changes in the way the paper is produced. They will inevitably result in a different kind of paper.

THE EVERYDAY PROCESS

The typical reporter on a typical newspaper may spend his morning covering a fire in a downtown jewelry store—good for fifteen inches on an inside page. That afternoon he may sit in on a zoning board hearing, trying to summarize a complex dispute in three or four paragraphs to be buried among the classified ads. Late in the afternoon he may put in some overtime preparing a feature on the opening of a suburban carnival. All three stories will be skimmed quickly by an assistant city editor, and then inserted into the paper.

Occasionally the reporter is assigned a more important story—perhaps a local strike. As each deadline approaches, he dictates his article by phone to a rewrite man in the newsroom. The rewrite man revises it as he writes. A copy boy rips each page out of the typewriter and brings it to the city editor himself. This personage checks it over, adds a few paragraphs of background, and hands it to a copy editor. The copy editor corrects the style and grammar, then writes a headline. He shoots the page through a pneumatic tube to the composing room, where a lino-typist is assigned the job of setting it in type. By the time the reporter has finished dictating his story, the first ten paragraphs are ready to go. Since the city editor has decided to put the story on the front page, his boss the managing editor will read it before he gives the order to start the presses.

If newspapers lavished this much care on every story, they would be a lot better than they are. Unfortunately, nobody can spare the time. Most newspaper pages are part news and part advertising. Each day the advertising department "dummies" its ads into the paper. It tells each editor—city, state, telegraph, sports, business, women's, etc.—exactly how much space he has left for news. The editor makes his assignments, then devotes most of his time to the three or four top stories of the day. The routine articles are left to subordinates—or to chance. More often than not, they appear in the newspaper almost exactly as they came off the teletype machine or the reporter's typewriter.

THE REST OF THE STAFF

The vast majority of a newspaper staff is made up of neither reporters nor editors. Consider the following:

The advertising salesmen, who sell the ads that fill 60 percent of the paper.

The circulation department, made up of hundreds of executives, secretaries, truck drivers, and delivery boys.

The dispatch department, which turns scrawled-out display advertising into printer-ready copy.

The linotypists, scores of them, who set all of the news and many of the ads in type (other ads are set by hand).

The make-up staff, which arranges the type into pages and somehow makes it fit.

The photographers and photoengravers, who illustrate the news and then prepare the illustrations for printing.

The rim staff, or copy readers, who write every headline, check every article for grammar and spelling, and then check it again for printer's errors.

The stereotypers, who convert the flat beds of type into curved plates for high-speed printing.

The pressroom staff, which operates the presses that turn out the finished newspapers.

The telephone operators; the receptionists; the classified ad department; the repairmen; the janitors; the librarians; the cafeteria workers; the suppliers of ink and paper; the elevator operators; and many, many more.

Few if any of the above groups consider themselves "newspapermen." But without their help, the real newspapermen—the reporters and editors—would be powerless.

THE FUTURE

In the process of describing today's newspaper, we have already depicted some of the trends of the future—increasing specialization, for example, and newspaper monopoly, and the move toward personal and interpretive journalism. There are at least five other trends of importance:

1. Suburban newspapers.
2. New technology.
3. Magazine-style layout.

4. New information sources.

5. Underground and weekly papers.

We will consider these one at a time.

1. Suburban Newspapers. In the mid-1960s, Field Enterprises discovered that the suburban circulation of its Chicago *Daily News* was decreasing. Suburbanites, it found, were getting their national and state news from the morning Chicago *Sun-Times,* also a Field paper. What they wanted in the afternoon was local news—and that the *Daily News* wasn't equipped to provide.

The company considered reorganizing the *Daily News* into zoned editions, with a different page or two of local news for each suburb. But that solution looked too expensive. It also thought about buying out the existing weekly and semi-weekly suburban papers. But that might have provoked an antitrust suit. Finally, Field decided to start its own daily newspapers in Arlington, Prospect, Des Plaines, and a number of other Chicago suburbs.[20] Though the competition proved tougher than expected, the trend was clear.

Nearly every major metropolitan area has witnessed a similar renaissance in the suburban press. In Los Angeles County alone, there are now 21 suburban dailies, with circulations ranging from 5,000 to more than 180,000. Their combined circulation increased 163 percent from 1945 to 1962. Since then it has nearly doubled again.

Two factors make suburban newspapers profitable. First, the suburbs themselves are growing at an unprecedented rate, while many inner city areas actually decline in population. Second, suburbanites have plenty of money to spend, and they spend it in nearby shopping centers. The small suburban daily is the perfect advertising medium for the stores in these shopping centers.

Some suburban papers hardly deserve to be called newspapers. Consider, for example, the Van Nuys (Calif.) *News and Green Sheet,* delivered free to 250,000 homes every Tuesday, Thursday, Friday, and Sunday. The paper generally runs 300 pages or more a week, up to 166 pages in a single issue—about four times as large as the average daily newspaper. Its content: page after page of ads from neighborhood stores and shopping centers, with just a sprinkling of local news and photographs.[21] Publications like the *News and Green Sheet* are called, appropriately enough, "shoppers." Whether mailed or hand-delivered, they almost always earn good money for their publishers.

2. New Technology. Slowly but surely, newspaper owners—especially chain owners—are overcoming their distaste for change and modernizing their plants. The most important newspaper innovation is undoubtedly the computer. Already a number of publishers have worked out the necessary agreements with the backshop unions and installed computerized typesetting machines. Many more will do so in the next few years.

The larger newspapers may also use the computer to build libraries of information for reporters. In April, 1969, the New York *Times* announced the start of the Times Information Bank. According to *Times* vice president Ivan Veit, this computerized information retrieval system will permit "instantaneous accessibility of a gigantic store of background information on virtually every subject of human research and inquiry."[22] At first the data bank will be for the exclusive use of *Times* staffers; later it will be available for use by scholars and perhaps (at a price) by other newspapers.

The ultimate impact of computer technology might be the placing of a computer terminal in every home. Such a "home console" could make all the conventional mass media obsolete overnight. An individual could sit down at his terminal and request whatever he felt like—the latest news from South Africa, a rerun of last year's World Series, or the past three weeks of Dick Tracy. Should this actually happen, the newspaper industry will have to reorganize itself for the task of gathering news for the computer.

3. Magazine-Style Layout. For the foreseeable future, newspapers will continue to publish on paper, not on computers. But they may not continue to look the way they look today—which is more or less the way they have looked for the last hundred years.

Today's newspaper is made up largely of features and interpretive news stories. Its content more closely resembles a magazine than a newspaper of fifty years ago. Yet its layout is still modeled on the old "hard news" concept. Though there are eight or nine columns on a page, type is set only in single columns, giving the paper a "vertical" look. Banner headlines are used to grab the reader's attention even if there's no big story to justify the fuss. Dozens of articles are squeezed onto the front page, scattergun fashion. Photos are most often one-column "mug shots" or splashy space-wasters.

In the early 1960s, the New York *Herald Tribune* (possibly influenced by the weekly *National Observer*) pioneered the move toward magazine-style newspaper layout—horizontal, simple, and neat. Stories were laid out in blocks, no more than four or five to the page. Headlines were lighter and more varied, with bold type saved for the truly important stories. White space, centered heads, and unusual column widths were used to suit the look of an article to its subject matter. In the last ten years, many newspapers have adopted these techniques, especially for their Sunday editions. Almost certainly these are the newspaper design principles of the 1970s.

Photos, drawings, and color may be extensively used by the newspaper of the future to heighten the visual appeal of the page. The city editor will no longer be forced to throw the front page together as he goes along; instead, an art director will be hired to design it each day. The inside pages, meanwhile, may become compartmentalized like those of the weekly newsmagazines—Washington news on one page, police news on another, education news on a third. All in all, the newspaper of 1980 should be a great deal easier and more pleasant to read than that of 1970.

4. New Information Sources. Historically, newspapers have relied almost exclusively on four information sources: wire services, feature syndicates, press releases, and reporters. To a large extent this is still the case today—but it will not be tomorrow. Newspapers can be expected to make increasing use of the following sources:

1. Special-interest magazines.
2. Underground papers and news services.
3. Scientists, politicians, and other outside experts.
4. Books and libraries.
5. University research findings.
6. The newspaper's own morgue.

This expansion of horizons is essential if the newspaper is to meet the challenge of the new media. Newspapers must keep pace with the expanding consciousness of the American reader, or they risk becoming the medium of the elderly.

5. Underground and Weekly Papers. The weekly newspaper used to be a rural phenomenon. It was also a dying phenomenon; throughout the 1950s and 1960s, the number of country weeklies dropped steadily.

KEEPING UP WITH THE TUBE

The sports department of the Miami *Herald* has contrived a unique way to compete with live television broadcasts of sporting events. One staffer covers the game, while another watches it on TV. Afterwards, the two men work out the best approach for the story, trying to come up with an angle that the sportscasters missed. Sometimes this means a special post-game interview; sometimes it involves a lengthy explanation of the fine points of a rule or a play. In any event, Miami fans get something in the *Herald* that wasn't on TV.[23]

Slowly but surely, the newspaper industry is shaping a new role for itself, in the face of up-to-the-second radio and TV coverage. Some day it may be standard practice for a news editor to monitor the newscasts, in a conscious effort to offer readers something they cannot get elsewhere.

During the same period, however, the number of *urban* weeklies rose to unprecedented heights. In 1970, the city of Detroit supported 13 weekly papers; Brooklyn had 19. Neither figure includes the undergrounds or special-interest publications.

Even today, most of the nation's 8,000 weeklies are pretty bland. But the outspoken, muckraking metro weekly has become a feature of nearly every large city. Such papers are havens for dissatisfied readers and re-porters.

The Detroit *Inner City Voice*, for example, bills itself as "The Voice of Revolution" in the black ghetto. "It's funny," says assistant editor James Williams, "but when we started we wanted to have an objective paper with a hard militant editorial page. It didn't take us long to realize that that wouldn't work. People just don't read the editorial page in the paper. You have to put your editorials everywhere—in every article so they'll see it."[24] Williams and his colleagues are trying to tell the truth about the ghetto, which they believe the white press ignores or distorts. Their main problem—which they share with all anti-establishment papers —is finding enough advertising to survive.

The Pittsburgh *Point* and the San Francisco *Bay Guardian* are ex-amples of white urban weeklies. Both are latter-day muckrakers. They delight in exposing sacred cows—public utilities, grand juries, real-estate developers, draft boards, and the like. Any story the established dailies won't touch is their kind of story. "We're not just accepted" by readers, says *Point* editor Charles Robb. "We're seized upon as a beacon of light. The paper has become important to them."[25]

Even a small weekly newspaper possesses the "power of the press." The *Southern Courier*, for example, was founded in 1965 by two former editors of the Harvard *Crimson*. Its goal was to cover—and protect—the civil rights of Alabama's blacks. Bertha Godfrey, a black housewife, was involved in an automobile accident with a white woman. A white police-man decided it was Mrs. Godfrey's fault. "Just because I'm a Negro woman you want to treat me like this," she snapped at him. The officer promptly arrested her for interfering with his investigation. When the case came to trial, Judge Woodrow Barnes led the policeman and Mrs. Godfrey into his chambers. He told them he was dismissing the case in order to avoid nasty publicity. A reporter for the *Southern Courier*, it seems, was in the courtroom.[26]

The so-called underground press is a much broader phenomenon than the hippie-acid-sex-rock papers peddled on city street-corners and college campuses. It is much broader than the political Movement papers that cater to the New Left or the New Right. It embraces, perhaps for the first time in our history, a growing number of very straight, Establish-ment-type people. They are ignoring their daily papers and turning to the weeklies in search of fresh news and new insights.

The typical daily newspaper is mildly entertaining—though not as entertaining as television. It is reasonably informative—though not as informative as many magazines. And it is a superlative vehicle for local advertising. Will that be a sufficient rationale for a mass medium in 1980?

NOTES

1 Charles E. Swanson, "What They Read in 130 Daily Newspapers," *Journalism Quarterly,* Fall, 1955, p. 414.
2 "Sell the Papers!" *Harper Monthly,* June, 1925, p. 5.
3 Chilton R. Bush, *News Research for Better Newspapers* (New York: American Newspaper Publishers Association Foundation, 1967), II, p. 18.
4 Richard L. Worsnop, "Competing Media," *Editorial Research Reports,* July 18, 1969, p. 537.
5 W. J. Galbraith, Jr., "Sigma Delta Chi Outstanding Graduates of 1955—Where Are They Now?" (Region 2 Sigma Delta Chi Conference, March 17, 1966), as reported in Bush, *News Research for Better Newspapers* (New York: American Newspaper Publishers Association Foundation, 1968), III, pp. 80–82.
6 Theodore Dreiser, *A Book About Myself* (New York: Boni and Liveright, 1922), p. 396.
7 Quoted in Alvin E. Austin, "Codes, Documents, Declarations Affecting the Press," Department of Journalism, University of North Dakota, August, 1964, p. 17.
8 "Pig Paper Profits," *Grassroots Editor,* July–August, 1969, p. 3.
9 Will Irwin, "If You See It In the Paper, It's ——?" *Collier's,* August 18, 1923, p. 11.
10 A. J. Liebling, *The Press* (New York: Ballantine Books, 1961), p. 23.
11 Galen Rarick and Barrie Hartman, "The Effects of Competition on One Daily Newspaper's Content," *Journalism Quarterly,* Autumn, 1966, pp. 461–62.
12 Raymond B. Nixon and Robert L. Jones, "The Content of Non-Competitive vs. Competitive Newspapers," *Journalism Quarterly,* Summer, 1956, pp. 299–306.
13 Stanley K. Bigman, "Rivals in Conformity: A Study of Two Competing Dailies," *Journalism Quarterly,* June, 1948, pp. 130–31.
14 John Corry, "The Los Angeles *Times,*" *Harper's Magazine,* December, 1969, pp. 75–81.
15 "Newspapers Blamed for Loss of Image," *Editor & Publisher,* April 5, 1969, p. 12.
16 George L. Bird and Frederic E. Merwin, eds., *The Press and Society* (Englewood Cliffs, N.J.: Prentice-Hall, Inc., 1951), p. 74.
17 Charles T. Duncan, "The 'Education Beat' On 52 Major Newspapers," *Journalism Quarterly,* Summer, 1966, pp. 336–38.
18 United Press International, October 14, 1970.
19 "Newspapers Blamed for Loss of Image," p. 12.
20 Gene Gilmore, "News Conflict in the Suburbs," *Columbia Journalism Review,* Fall, 1968, p. 19.
21 Carroll W. Parcher, "Anatomy of the Suburban Newspaper Phenomenon," ASNE (American Society of Newspaper Editors) *Bulletin,* April 1, 1964, p. 4.
22 "New York Times Develops Public Information Bank," *Editor & Publisher,* April 5, 1969, p. 9.

23 John Hohenberg, "The New Foreign Correspondence," *Saturday Review,* January 11, 1969, pp. 115–16.

24 Roger M. Williams, "The Irrepressible Weeklies," *Columbia Journalism Review,* Summer, 1968, p. 31.

25 *Ibid.,* p. 33.

26 Stephen E. Cotton, "The Southern Courier," *The Harvard Crimson,* March 17, 1967, p. 19.

SUGGESTED READINGS

CORRY, JOHN, "The Los Angeles *Times,*" *Harper's Magazine,* December, 1969.

LIEBLING, A. J., *The Press.* New York: Ballantine Books, 1961.

TALESE, GAY, *The Kingdom and the Power.* New York: World Publishing Co., 1969.

WILLIAMS, ROGER M., "The Irrepressible Weeklies," *Columbia Journalism Review,* Summer, 1968.

11   Magazines

The typical magazine of the past was a potpourri of features and fiction, aimed at a general audience. Such magazines still exist, but today they are losing money. The successful magazine of the present and future is highly specialized. It is run by an editor who knows precisely who his readers and his advertisers are. In a sense magazines are no longer a mass medium—but they are once again a highly profitable one, and they perform a valuable service for their audiences.

Caskie Stinnett, former editor of *Holiday* magazine, tells this story which he says "sums up the magazine business today." Stinnett was on a travel junket to Portugal with a number of other writers, including *Holiday* contributor Marc Connelly. At a reception for the mayor of Lisbon each visitor was asked to stand and identify his magazine. Connelly announced that he represented *Popular Wading*, a journal for enthusiasts of shallow-water sports. It specialized, said Connelly, in medical articles, particularly the ravages of immersion foot.

Comments Stinnett: "It was hilarious, and we were all howling. But you know, I don't think anyone would laugh today. In fact, I'll almost bet that somewhere out there, you could find a special-audience magazine for waders."[1]

The term "magazine" comes from the French word *magasin,* meaning "storehouse." The earliest magazines were literally storehouses of sketches, poems, essays, and assorted other content. Their incredible diversity led journalism historian Frank Luther Mott to offer this definition of the magazine: "A bound pamphlet issued more or less regularly and containing a variety of reading matter."[2]

For more than two hundred years, the most general magazines were invariably the most popular, and the most profitable. The mass circulation leaders in the late 1800s were the *Saturday Evening Post, Collier's, Leslie's,* and *Harper's Weekly. Collier's* and the *Post* continued into the Twentieth Century, and were joined by *McCall's, Life, Look,* and the *Reader's Digest.* All these magazines earned substantial profits from subscriptions and newsstand sales. Except for the *Digest,* they earned even more from advertising.

In 1929, the nation's 365 leading magazines had an average circulation of 94,836. By 1950, the 567 top magazines were averaging 223,581 readers apiece.[3] Magazine circulation—and magazine revenue—was at an all-time high.

Then came television. TV did comparatively little damage to the public's appetite for general magazines. But it devastated their appeal to advertisers. The largest magazines could offer a readership of only a couple of million; a run-of-the-mill network series offered tens of millions of viewers. And television ads cost less too. In 1970, a minute of time on NBC's *Laugh-In* (with 17 million viewers) sold for $3.82 per thousand households. A full-page four-color ad in *Look* (with 7 million readers) ran $7.16 per thousand households. Nearly three times as many people watched NFL football as read *Life* magazine—yet both ads sold for the same amount, $64,200. Naturally, advertisers preferred *Laugh-In* to *Look,* NFL football to *Life.*

The mass magazines responded to the challenge of television by trying to build TV-size circulations. In the dozen years after 1950, both *McCall's* and *Look* doubled their readership. In 1960, the *Saturday Evening Post, Life, Look,* and the *Reader's Digest* proudly noted that a single ad in each of the four magazines would reach every other Amercian 2.3 times.[4]

The technique for building circulation was simple: offer cut-rate subscriptions at a price so low that no one could afford not to subscribe. Newsstand sales, naturally, declined. During World War Two, *Life* and *Look* sold 55 percent of their copies at the newsstand price. By the mid-1960s, the number of newsstand sales had dropped to less than ten percent. As the subscription price went down, production and distribution

costs rose steadily. Some time in the late 1950s the two passed each
other. It was now possible to subscribe to a magazine for less than the
cost of printing it. Advertisers, of course, were expected to make up the
difference.

They didn't. Take *Life* for example. The magazine sells for an average of 12 cents per copy. It costs 41 cents per copy to edit, print, and
distribute. For *Life* to break even, advertisers must cough up the remain-

DEATH OF THE POST

For 72 years the *Saturday Evening Post* was the flagship of the Curtis Publishing Company empire. It had a circulation of 6.8 million satisfied readers in
1968. Then it folded.

When Martin Ackerman became president of Curtis in 1968, the *Post* was
deep in debt. Advertisers, it seems, simply were not interested in the *Post's*
rural readership and middle-American appeal. Ackerman's battle plan was
simple and straight-forward: stop fighting for circulation, cut back to three
million readers, and turn the *Post* into "a high-class magazine for a class
audience." The subscribers to be retained were those living in designated
Nielsen A and B counties. These are television rating terms for the most
affluent counties in America—the ones advertisers are most eager to reach.

Of the *Post's* 6.8 million subscribers, 4.5 million lived in the Nielsen A and
B areas. Ackerman instructed his computer to drop not only the 2.3 million
C and D area people, but 1.5 million of the B area people as well—leaving
him with a circulation of three million big spenders. *Life* agreed to purchase
the extra B subscriptions. But no one was interested in the small-town C
and D folks. Form letters went out, telling subscribers that the *Post* no
longer wanted them. Among those so informed were Arkansas Governor
Winthrop Rockefeller, former *Post* editor Ben Hibbs, and small-town boy
Martin Ackerman.

In an effort to impress Madison Avenue, Ackerman spent a lot of money
advertising the "new" *Post*. He prepared four dummy issues of the magazine
to show off the planned "classy" approach. But advertisers were uncon-
vinced. They doubted the magazine could slough off its rural image so
easily. The *Post* earned millions of enemies in 1968, but very few new advertisers. It continued to lose upwards of $400,000 a month. Ackerman finally
admitted defeat, and the *Saturday Evening Post* folded.

At the very end, a prosperous rock-and-roll group offered to buy the *Post*
for $250,000 and turn it into a pop music magazine. The offer was refused,
but the lesson was clear. Pop music magazines have a future in this country.
General interest magazines don't.[5]

ing 29 cents per copy.   At the start of 1970, ad revenues amounted to only 27 cents per copy.   Every week *Life* was actually losing two cents on each copy sold.[6]

It has taken nearly 20 years for the magazine industry to learn that it cannot beat television at the numbers game.   In the process, such giants as *Collier's, Coronet, Women's Home Companion, Look,* and the *Saturday Evening Post* have died.   But magazines offer advertisers something that neither television nor any other medium can provide: a specialized national audience.

SPECIALIZED MAGAZINES

The special-interest magazine is nothing new.   When film stars first captured the public's imagination, *Photoplay* was founded to cater to that interest.   A new hobby in the 1930s gave rise to *Model Railroader;* a manpower shortage in the 1940s led to *Jobs;* a sudden craze of the 1950s gave birth to *Skin Diver.*   But the number of such magazines has increased dramatically in recent years.   For hunters and fishermen alone there are now 60 different magazines.   Boaters and yachtsmen claim 37 magazines.   Travel and camping is the subject of 44 magazines.   Name any special interest and you will likely find a magazine devoted to it— even wading.

The more general magazines have done their best to specialize.   The *Reader's Digest* covers dozens of topics in each issue—but its treatment and style are designed with the busy business executive in mind.   Similarly, *Playboy* is aimed at young, urban males with money to spend; *Cosmopolitan* is edited for big-city women in search of a husband; *Seventeen* appeals to teenage girls with fashion on their minds.   None of these magazines is as specialized as, say, *Business Week* or *True Frontier.*   But all are a good deal more specialized than *Life*—and a good deal more profitable.

Some are immensely profitable.   Consider, for example, *Sunset,* which offers recipes, gardening help, and the like to just under a million West Coast homeowners.   In 1969, *Sunset* averaged 218 pages per issue, with more regional advertising in its four editions than any other major magazine.   Profits ran 10 to 15 percent of gross revenues.   The *New Yorker* is a very different magazine—urbane, sophisticated, strictly Eastern.   With a circulation of less than half a million, it earned $2.2 million in 1969.   Comments one Madison Avenue executive: "Their salesmen do not see you, they grant you an audience; their advertising departments do not sell advertising, they accept it."[7]

The specialized magazine is a perfect vehicle for advertising.   It offers advertisers a chance at a hand-picked audience. Suppose, for example, that you were a manufacturer of low-calorie foods. If you could afford it, you'd probably advertise on television and in the newspapers. But despite the higher cost per thousand, you certainly wouldn't miss a chance to take out an ad in *Weight Watchers Magazine.* The average reader of that publication is far more likely to be interested in your product (and hence your ad) than the average newspaper reader or TV viewer.

Some magazines earn so much money from advertising that they don't even need to sell copies; they give them away instead. This is most common among trade journals. A magazine for plastics manufacturers, for example, is well advised to send a free copy to every plastics manufacturer in the country. That makes it a superlative advertising vehicle for companies that make the sorts of supplies and equipment plastics manufacturers use. Aside from trade publications, free-circulation magazines include the *American Legion Magazine, Scouting, Today's Education, Signature* (for Diner's Club members), *TWA Ambassador,* and *Nation's Business.*

Free-circulation magazines almost always have a "controlled" readership; only certain people are permitted to receive them. Sometimes the readership is made up of members of an organization. Sometimes it is a captive audience like airplane passengers. But usually the major common ground of a free magazine's readers is that they are a ready market for some specialized group of advertisers. Very often the editorial content of such a magazine is quite weak. It is read for its ads.

But specialized magazines not only appeal to advertisers. They attract readers as well—readers who are willing to pay high subscription prices for just the right magazine. Martin Gross, editor and publisher of

---

CAN LIFE *SPECIALIZE?*

The mass magazines have done their best to copy their specialized colleagues. *McCall's* and *Better Homes and Gardens,* for example, now publish special zip-coded editions for high income areas only. *Time* now has a college student edition, a doctor's edition, and an educator's edition. And the *Reader's Digest* offers advertisers one million households with incomes in excess of $15,000 a year. The *Digest* charges $11.25 per thousand for this edition, compared with only $3.33 per thousand for its general edition.

Such tactics have limited potential. In the short term, they earn the mass magazines a little extra income. But in the long term, they do nothing to make those magazines more specialized. General-interest magazines have millions of readers that advertisers simply aren't interested in reaching. Until that is no longer the case, such magazines will continue to lose money.

---

the *Intellectual Digest,* predicts that in the next few years "you'll see more and more magazines supported almost totally by circulation. This has to come with the trend toward specialized reading and a stronger reader commitment."[8]

Whichever way specialized magazines go, they have a good future in front of them. As one advertising executive points out:

> Don't look at it like a mass medium. Look at it like a medium that is catering to special interests. I think there is a whole new way to use print that we are not using today. And I think that's the challenge of the Seventies.[9]

Lewis Gillenson sums it all up in one sentence: "When a magazine skillfully exploits its own individuality, it offers a product impossible to copy."[10]

THE EDITOR

Once upon a time, a strong-willed would-be editor started a newspaper. Today, he is far more likely to start a magazine.

Why? For one thing, it's cheaper. Printing can be farmed out to another company, and the post office handles distribution. Hugh Hefner founded *Playboy* on $7,000 in the early 1950s. Many of the 94 magazines begun in 1968 had just as little cash.

Magazines are a growth industry. The number of magazines in the country has grown from just over 5,000 in the mid-1930s to just under 10,000 in the late 1960s. This figure does not include the 17,000-odd corporate publications now in existence; Pittsburgh Plate Glass, for example, produces 13 magazines of its own. Total magazine circulation is impossible to estimate, but it almost certainly surpasses total newspaper circulation—and the number of magazines is far in excess of the number of newspapers.

Most important, the magazine industry is extremely fluid. Of the 20 most profitable magazines in 1927, half were gone by 1950. Of the top 20 magazines in 1962, 15 were not yet founded in 1920.[11] It is possible to start a magazine today and be an instant success tomorrow. This can be said of none of the other mass media.

Magazines, notes Clay Felker (himself editor of the highly successful *New York* magazine), are "peculiarly and stubbornly personal products."[12] *Time, Life,* and *Fortune* are the vision of Henry R. Luce. *Playboy* is Hugh Hefner. Arnold Gingrich guided *Esquire* to popularity; Helen Gurley Brown made a winner of *Cosmopolitan;* Robert Peterson did the same with *Hot Rod*.   It is hard to think of a successful magazine that is not the reflection of one man.   Historian James Playsted Wood writes:

> A strong editor, even a strongly wrongheaded editor, has usually meant a strong and influential magazine; whereas intelligent editors of moderate means and no firm opinions have often produced colorless and comparatively ineffective magazines.[13]

Perhaps, as Roland E. Wolseley claims, this is no longer true of the mass-circulation magazines, whose voices now tend to be "institutional rather than individual."[14]   But the mass-circulation magazines are no longer successful in any case.   Most of the outstanding specialized magazines, at least, are the work of one man.

They almost have to be.   The typical magazine staff is much, much smaller than its readers imagine.   Take *Wastes Engineering*, for example, a successful monthly for the sanitation industry.   It has one editor, one associate editor, one managing editor, one editorial assistant, and one part-time editorial consultant.   It also has an 18-man editorial advisory board to read and comment on articles—but they work only a few hours a month.   Obviously the editor of *Wastes Engineering* has a chance to give personal attention to every word in his magazine.

Magazines are written by staff writers, free-lance writers, or some combination of the two.   Staff writers, of course, work on salary.   Free-lancers are paid by the article, at rates ranging from $20 an article all the way up to $3,000 an article.   While there are perhaps 25,000 writers in the country who consider themselves free-lancers, most work only part-time.   Fewer than 300 of them earn $10,000 a year or more from their writing.[15]   The same hard core of a few dozen free-lancers do 90 percent of the writing in all the top-paying publications.

Each article begins with an assignment.   Free-lancers usually think up their own topics, then "query" various magazines to see who's interested.   Staff writers, of course, are often told what to write.   Either way, one editor is always responsible for approving the topic, the research approach, and the finished manuscript.   On most magazines the top editor does this himself for every article.   Some of the larger and more decentralized magazines have department editors for the job.   *Better Homes and Gardens*, for example, has twelve of them: residential building, foods, furnishings and decorations, gardens and landscaping, kitchens and equipment, money management, family cars, home entertainment, family health, travel, sewing and crafts, and education.

Once a manuscript is approved, it goes to a copy editor for the finishing touches.   At the same time, a copy is sent to the art department, which begins work on drawings, photographs, and other illustrations.   The art director and the managing editor rough out an approximate layout, then tell the production editor to prepare the article for the printer.

The printer sends back galley proofs. A proofreader checks these for errors, while the production editor cuts-and-pastes them into a "dummy" of the magazine. The printer uses the dummies to prepare a set of page proofs, a one-color version of the magazine. After final adjustments are made on the page proofs, color proofs are prepared and checked. Finally, the magazine is okayed for printing.

All this takes time. When necessary (as for a weekly magazine), the entire process is squeezed into a single week of frenzied activity. The average monthly, though, takes about 90 days to process an article from accepted manuscript to printed copies. And still the activity can be frenzied.

THE NEWSMAGAZINES

The most influential magazines in the United States are probably the three newsweeklies: *Time, Newsweek,* and *U.S. News and World Report.* For 7.5 million readers, these three magazines are a vital source of news. They share three important characteristics: (1) Brevity—the week's news is compressed into as few pages as possible; (2) Subjectivity—fact, opinion, and colorful adjectives are blended together into a slick, highly readable puree; and (3) Group journalism—dozens of researchers, writers, and editors collaborate on each major article.

The oldest and most successful of the three newsweeklies is *Time,* founded by Henry R. Luce in 1922. In his biography of Luce, John Kobler describes the preparation of a single *Time* cover story. The following narrative is adapted from Kobler's account.[16]

On November 1, 1963, South Vietnam's General Duong Van Minh staged a successful coup d'etat against President Ngo Dinh Diem and his regime. It was a Friday morning. *Time* managing editor Otto Fuerbringer immediately decided to substitute the coup for the planned cover story on Calvin Gross, superintendent of the New York City public schools.

The previous Tuesday, the senior foreign news editor had begun the week by selecting a dozen stories for his section, based on suggestions from 260 correspondents in 30 bureaus. Writer Edward Hughes was assigned two of them—one on Italian politics, the other on an army coup in Dahomey. He was also assigned a research girl for each article. The researchers (there are 78 of them) quickly began culling *Time*'s massive files on 225,000 individuals and 100,000 subjects. In addition, Hughes asked them to interview certain local sources by phone. *Time*'s foreign bureau chiefs, meanwhile, were busy questioning sources at the scene, and cabling their findings to Hughes.

On Thursday Hughes was handed two new assignments, U.S. troop withdrawal from West Germany and sabotage in South Africa. The Italian story was just about done; the Dahomey piece was given to another writer. In three hours, Hughes whipped off the short sabotage article (it never ran) and went home, saving Germany for Friday.

But on Friday, with 36 hours till press time, Fuerbringer ordered Hughes to drop everything and do the cover story on the Vietnam coup. Working with him was Margaret Boeth. Mrs. Boeth spent the day in the *Time* Vietnam files. She put together a folder on recent Vietnamese political history, the biographies of the coup principals, and other relevant information—circling the most important items as she went along.

An unending series of cables began to pour into the *Time* offices in New York. A Saigon correspondent (who had witnessed the coup flat on his belly on a rooftop) sent in a 10,000-word dispatch. Reporters in Hong Kong interviewed Vietnamese who had fled the country in the wake of the coup. The Los Angeles bureau forwarded the comments of the touring Madame Nhu, while the Washington bureau described the reaction at the White House. A picture editor assembled a portfolio of appropriate photographs, from which Fuerbringer chose seven to illustrate the text. A staff cartographer prepared a map of Saigon showing the main events of the coup. At a cost of $7,000 the cover portrait of Calvin Gross was dumped, and by 10:30 that evening the Chicago printing plant (one of six around the country) had already engraved the new cover of General Minh.

As Hughes began to write, Fuerbringer and the foreign news editor bombarded him with suggestions—quotes to use, points to emphasize, phrases to work in. Hughes worked until midnight Friday; a rented *Time* Cadillac took him home.

Saturday morning he was back at his desk. New developments had to be worked in (Diem had been assassinated overnight). So did new suggestions from Fuerbringer and others. It was 8:30 Saturday night when Hughes ripped the last page of copy from his typewriter.

Now Margaret Boeth got back to work. She methodically checked Hughes' article against her files, putting a dot over each word to show that it had been verified. Some items she couldn't verify, and questions were phoned or cabled to correspondents on the scene. Mrs. Boeth argued with Hughes over the color of a Vietnamese cathedral, the source of a quote, the number of Buddhist monks who had burned themselves to death. The two debated whether or not the streets of Saigon were really "tree-lined" as Hughes had claimed. Once these battles were settled, the copy went to the foreign news editor, and then to Fuerbringer. Both requested insertions, deletions, and further checking before they would initial the article.

At 12:30 a.m. Sunday, the corrected story was given to a copyreader, who checked it for infractions of grammar, syntax, and "*Time* style."

Then back to the foreign news editor for a final look before going to the printer. Hughes followed the story to the printer, indicating where cuts could be made to fit the available space. At dawn on Monday, the Chicago plant confirmed that the article was ready to go. Hughes went home.

Tuesday morning the magazine was on the stands, and Hughes attended the weekly assignment conference. He was given two stories. . . .

IMPACT

There is no doubt that magazines have far less impact on American society than either broadcasting or newspapers. It wasn't always that way. Throughout the Eighteenth and Nineteenth Centuries, magazines were the nation's most important entertainment medium. Nearly all the great American authors published their novels in serial form first. And the muckraking magazines of the early Twentieth Century did much to revolutionize our system of government. The January, 1903 issue of *McClure's*, for example, contained three articles of lasting importance: Ida Tarbell on "The History of the Standard Oil Company," Lincoln Steffens on "The Shame of Minneapolis," and Ray Stannard Baker on "The Right to Work." These articles dealt with serious issues—monopoly, corruption, labor.

Today, the market for magazine fiction is reduced to three or four major publications and a host of tiny literary quarterlies. As for muckraking, that kind of writing can be found regularly only in opinion journals like the *New Republic* and the *National Review*. These magazines invariably lose money. They have small circulations and probably little influence.

Yet magazines are not unimportant. They offer three unique services:

First, magazines are the only mass medium that is both timely and permanent, quick and deep. Television and newspapers take only hours to report a story, but they can report it only briefly. And neither is customarily saved or savored. Books, of course, offer the maximum depth and permanence—but books take years to produce and seldom circulate more than a few thousand copies. Magazines are the ideal compromise. A writer (or an advertiser) can say more in a magazine than he could on TV or in a newspaper. He can say it sooner and to more people than he could in a book.

Second, magazines are national. So is television, of course—but television is sketchy, impermanent, and devoted almost entirely to light entertainment. The "American perspective" on everything from theater to politics to underarm deodorants is molded largely by magazines. When a serious writer wants to say something serious, and he wants to say it to the whole country, he says it in a magazine.

Third, magazines are specialized. If you want to know what's on television, you read *TV Guide*. If you want to know what explorers and anthropologists are doing, you read the *National Geographic*. If you want help repairing your car or building a stereo, you read *Popular Mechanics*. If you want to know where it's at in rock music, you read *Rolling Stone*. It is only in magazines that writers and advertisers can reach precisely those readers most interested in what they have to say.

The demise of magazines has been predicted many times—in the 1910s with the automobile, in the 1920s with radio, in the 1930s with movies, in the 1950s with television. Each time the prediction was nonprophetic. Magazines have changed greatly over the years, but they have survived, even flourished. They will continue to change, and survive, and flourish.

NOTES

[1] "The Hot Magazines Aim At Special Targets," *Business Week*, May 2, 1970, p. 64.

[2] Frank Luther Mott, quoted in Roland E. Wolseley, *The Magazine World* (Englewood Cliffs, N.J.: Prentice-Hall, Inc., 1951), p. 8.

[3] Theodore Peterson, *Magazines in the Twentieth Century* (Urbana, Ill.: University of Illinois Press, 1964), p. 59.

[4] *Ibid.*, pp. 60–61.

[5] Otto Friedrich, "I am Marty Ackerman. I am Thirty-Six Years Old and I am Very Rich. I Hope to Make the Curtis Publishing Company Rich Again," *Harper's Magazine*, December, 1969, pp. 95–118.

[6] "The Hot Magazines Aim At Special Targets," p. 68.

[7] Theodore Peterson, quoted in Lewis Anthony Dexter and David Manning White, eds., *People, Society, and Mass Communications* (New York: The Free Press, 1964), p. 259.

[8] "The Hot Magazines Aim At Special Targets," p. 72.

[9] *Ibid.*, p. 74.

[10] Lewis W. Gillenson, "The Struggle for Survival," *Columbia Journalism Review*, Spring, 1962, p. 38.

[11] John Tebbel, "Magazines—New, Changing, Growing," *Saturday Review*, February 8, 1969, p. 55.

[12] Clay S. Felker, "Life Cycles in the Age of Magazines," *Antioch Review*, Spring, 1969, p. 7.

[13] James Playsted Wood, *Magazines in the United States* (New York: The Ronald Press Co., 1956) p. 36. New, third edition published by Ronald Press, 1971.

[14] Roland E. Wolseley, *Understanding Magazines* (Ames, Iowa: Iowa State University Press, 1965), p. 203.

[15] Warren G. Bovee, *The Editor and Writer Relationship* (Milwaukee: Marquette University Press, 1965), p. 9.

[16] John Kobler, *Luce, His Time, Life, and Fortune* (Garden City, N.Y.: Doubleday & Co., Inc., 1968), pp. 189–201.

SUGGESTED READINGS

FELKER, CLAY S., "Life Cycles in the Age of Magazines," *Antioch Review,* Spring, 1969.

FRIEDRICH, OTTO, "I am Marty Ackerman. I am Thirty-Six Years Old and I am Very Rich. I Hope to Make the Curtis Publishing Company Rich Again," *Harper's Magazine,* December, 1969.

"The Hot Magazines Aim At Special Targets," *Business Week,* May 2, 1970.

KOBLER, JOHN, *Luce, His Time, Life, and Fortune.* Garden City, N.Y.: Doubleday & Co., Inc., 1968.

PETERSON, THEODORE, *Magazines in the Twentieth Century.* Urbana, Ill.: University of Illinois Press, 1964.

12 Broadcasting

Television is by far the most powerful and ubiquitous of the mass media. Yet it is used almost exclusively for entertainment. TV programming has been attacked by some as a degradation of American culture. Others assert that it is a dangerous corrupter of the nation's morals. More moderate critics claim that it is, at best, a waste of the viewer's time and the medium's potential.

Television is everywhere. There are, at present, roughly sixty million American homes with at least one TV set. That's nearly all the homes in the country. More families own televisions than bathtubs.

And they use them more. The average TV is on for approximately six hours a day—42 hours a week, 2,200 hours a year. The average American spends three and a half hours a day sitting in front of a television screen. Some of that time he is doing other things as well—eating, reading, or talking. But he devotes 15 hours a week *exclusively* to TV.[1] That comes to 28 percent of his leisure time. It is more time than he spends at any other activity except sleeping and earning a living. In a single day, 65 percent of the U.S. population is exposed to television; in a week, 87 percent of the population can be found watching the tube.[2]

Radio is almost as pervasive. There are half again as many radio sets in America as people. Nearly every American owns his own, and has it turned on an average of two and a half hours a day. Three quarters of the population listens to the radio at some time in a typical day; more than 90 percent tune in some time in an average week.[3]   Unlike television viewing, radio listening is usually a secondary activity.   The typical radio listener is busy driving or dancing.   The typical TV viewer is staring at the tube.

Any activity that takes up so much of the time of so many people is bound to exert a tremendous influence on society.   Harry J. Boyle of the Canadian Radio-Television Commission was not exaggerating when he stated that "the license to broadcast is almost the heaviest obligation society can allow individuals to bear."[4]

ENTERTAINMENT

How do broadcasters respond to this obligation?   As we have emphasized before, they respond with entertainment—hour after hour after hour of entertainment.   They respond with soap operas and situation comedies, with westerns and detective thrillers, with sporting events and music. The vast majority of all radio and television content is meant strictly to entertain.

Americans are so accustomed to the entertainment role of broadcasting that it is necessary to stress what should be an obvious fact: Television and radio are not *inherently* entertainment media.   In the developing countries of Asia, Africa, and South America, broadcasting is used almost exclusively for education and information.   Even in Western Europe, news and public affairs fill a substantial part of the broadcast day.   American broadcasting is entertainment-centered because American broadcasters want it that way.   They want it that way because they believe (rightly or wrongly) that that is what the public and the advertisers want.   But broadcast advertising isn't inevitable either; there are many countries without it.   And it is at least possible to give the public what someone decrees it should want instead of what it does want.

We are not arguing that American broadcasting should be turned into a government-controlled educational monopoly—though that has been argued.   Perhaps our system of broadcasting is the best possible system. But it is not, obviously, the only possible system.

To say that American broadcasting is mostly entertainment is not to depreciate its effect on American society.   No doubt our country would be different without televised moon landings and election results, assassinations and battles.   But it would also be different without TV coverage of the World Series and the Academy Awards.   Westerns and soap operas teach us some things.   They reflect and reinforce certain characteristic national traits—competition and aggression, materialism and racism, hu-

SPORTS ON THE TUBE

Once upon a time spectator sports were something you journeyed to the stadium to see. Today you stay home and watch them on TV. At least two football games are now televised every Sunday during the season. Basketball and hockey telecasts ease the transition into the baseball season, when viewers are offered a minimum of one game a week.

Television has revolutionized college and professional athletics in uncounted ways:

- Athletes on the field are forbidden to spit, scratch, or otherwise risk offending the home audience.
- Games are scheduled to meet the needs of television. The 1970 Stanford-Arkansas football game was played at 5 p.m. Arkansas time, so as not to conflict with the Miss America pageant.
- TV routinely calls its own time-outs (sometimes in the middle of a rally) in order to slip in a commercial.
- Elaborate playoff systems have been devised purely to provide more "big games" for the television audience.
- New rules have been devised to make the game more dramatic and more easily scheduled on TV. An example of the latter is the "thirteenth game rule" in professional tennis.
- Television has strapped cameras and microphones to players and coaches, so that even Grandma knows what it is like to be tackled by Sam Huff.

Television controls athletics because it pays the bills. In 1969, broadcasters put up $21,690,000 for the rights to major league baseball, and $49,430,000 for the rights to college and professional football. It is broadcast money that supports team expansion and astronomical player salaries. The sports world is hooked on television; it would collapse without it.

---

mor and openness, faith and ambition. It is as entertainers that the broadcast media have their greatest impact on American culture. And that in itself says something about the American character.

Most observers have been critical of broadcasting's emphasis on entertainment. In 1961, former FCC Commissioner Newton Minow told the National Association of Broadcasters: "When television is bad, nothing is worse. I invite you to sit down in front of your television set when your station goes on the air and stay there without [anything] to distract you—and keep your eyes glued to that set until the station signs off. I can assure you that you will observe a vast wasteland."[5] Robert M. Hutchins of the Center for the Study of Democratic Institutions made the point even more stringently:

> We have triumphantly invented, perfected, and distributed to the humblest cottage throughout the land one of the greatest technical marvels in history, television, and have used it for what? To bring Coney Island into every home. It is as though movable type had been devoted exclusively since Gutenberg's time to the publication of comic books.[6]

Read these two quotations carefully. Minow and Hutchins are criticizing more than just the *fact* of broadcast entertainment. They are criticizing the *quality* of that entertainment. There are some entertainment shows on television (symphony concerts and Shakespearean dramas, for example) that simply do not fit Minow's image of a vast wasteland or Hutchins' analogy to comic books. Minow and Hutchins argue that the vast majority of TV programming does fit.

Judging the quality of entertainment is a thorny problem. Broadcast executives assert that the proper standard is ratings. If people watch a show then they must like it, and if they like it then by definition it must be good entertainment. Critics of television are not satisfied with this standard. They judge programming according to their own criteria, esthetic or moralistic. The esthetic critics claim that broadcasting is degrading American culture. The moralists insist that it is corrupting American morals. Let us examine each argument in turn.

MASS CULTURE

Some time in the not too distant future, one of the networks may announce a new half-hour series called "Hawthorne Place," based loosely on Nathaniel Hawthorne's novel *The Scarlet Letter*. It will be billed as a sort of Calvinist Peyton Place, with the role of the fallen woman, Hester Prynne, played by Tina Louise. In keeping with the All-American spirit of the show, its theme song will be drawn from the works of Aaron Copland, arranged for jazz sextet.

Guardians of the sacred flame of Culture will no doubt greet "Hawthorne Place"—if they stoop to greet it at all— with cries of dismay. The mass media, they will say, are again raping and debasing our culture in pursuit of profit. In the face of such irreverence it is impossible to be a serious artist or critic in America. The series is just one more proof of the old saying that everything television touches turns to tripe. That's what they'll say.

What is culture? Edward A. Shils supplies this definition: "Superior or refined culture is distinguished by the seriousness of its subject matter, i.e., the centrality of the problems with which it deals, the acute penetration and coherence of its perceptions, the subtlety and wealth of its expressed feeling."[7] This is High Culture. Twentieth-century examples include the music of Stravinsky and Berg, the novels of Conrad and Hesse, the paintings of Picasso and Wyeth, and like works of esthetic and intellectual refinement. High Culture has traditionally been the province of the upper classes.

Before the industrial revolution, the only competitor with High Culture was Folk Art—the culture of the common man. Folk Art, says critic Dwight Macdonald, was "the people's own institution, their private little garden walled off from the great formal park of their masters' High Culture."[8] It was expressed in craftsmanship, dance, music, and poetry.

Then came the industrial revolution, the burgeoning middle class, and the mass media. With them came Mass Culture—also known as Masscult, Low Culture, Pop Culture, and *Kitsch* (the German word for mass culture). Unlike Folk Art, Mass Culture borrows from the basic content of High Culture. But unlike High Culture, it is designed to be popular, to "sell" to a mass audience. Alexis de Tocqueville described the difference as long ago as 1835:

> In aristocratic ages the object of the arts is . . . to manufacture as well as possible, not with the greatest speed or at the lowest cost. . . . In democracies there is always a multitude of persons whose wants are above their means and who are very willing to take up with imperfect satisfaction rather than abandon the object of their desires altogether. . . .
>
> In aristocracies a few great pictures are produced; in democratic countries a vast number of insignificant ones. In the former statues are raised of bronze; in the latter, they are modeled in plaster.[9]

America is by all counts the world's greatest producer of Mass Culture. And television is by all counts America's greatest producer.

Broadcasting is a mass medium in the literal sense of the word. In order to attract advertisers, networks must attract an audience of millions, not thousands or even hundreds of thousands. There is no conspiracy at work here. If broadcasters were convinced that the public appetite for ballet was enormous, they would gladly program hour after hour of ballet. But since there is almost no demand for televised ballet, there is almost no ballet on television. Of course it is hard to generate a massive demand for ballet when most people have never *seen* one. Television could probably teach the public to enjoy ballet in the same way it has taught the public to enjoy doctor shows and situation comedies. But broadcasters are not in the business of breaking vicious circles. As long as viewers are satisfied with Mass Culture, there is no reason to bother training them to appreciate High Culture.

Critics like Dwight Macdonald not only deplore the public's satisfaction with Masscult. They fear it. Macdonald puts the point this way:

"Bad stuff drives out the good, since it is more easily understood and enjoyed. . . . When to this ease of consumption is added *Kitsch's* ease of production because of its standardized nature, its prolific growth is easy to understand. It threatens High Culture by its sheer pervasiveness, its brutal, overwhelming *quantity*."[10]

Macdonald fears that television may destroy High Culture in America. Shils is more optimistic:

> There is much ridicule of *Kitsch,* and it *is* ridiculous. Yet it represents aesthetic sensibility and aesthetic aspiration, untutored, rude, and deformed. The very growth of *Kitsch,* and of the demand which has generated the industry for the production of *Kitsch,* is an indication of a crude aesthetic awakening in classes which previously accepted what was handed down to them or who had practically no aesthetic expression and reception.[11]

Only history can settle this dispute. Perhaps broadcasting will kill American High Culture. Perhaps it will create a new audience for that culture.

Whatever the eventual effects of broadcasting on High Culture, there is no doubt that the culture in today's broadcasting is anything but high. Despite their pompous élitism, Macdonald and Shils are right. So are Minow and Hutchins. Television is a vast wasteland, an endless succession of electronic comic books. Maybe that's all for the best, and maybe it isn't. But certainly it is what's happening.

BROADCAST CORRUPTION

Sex, violence, profanity . . . Our children are in danger! Such is the cry of many critics of the broadcast media.

While the fight against Mass Culture is confined to a few universities and literary magazines, the fight against broadcast corruption is out in the open—in Congress, in the FCC, in outraged letters to networks and stations. Broadcasters have more or less ignored their esthetic critics. But they have been forced to make major concessions to their moralistic ones.

The battle over sex in the mass media has traditionally centered on books, magazines, and movies, not broadcasting. The reason for this is not that sex is accepted in broadcasting, but rather that sex is nonexistent in broadcasting. From the very beginning of radio, obscene words were illegal; when television arrived, dirty pictures were also outlawed. Both are grounds for a stiff fine or even a license revocation.

These laws have seldom been tested in recent years, and few broadcasters are eager to test them. The typical station is so fearful of offending the public that it stays well on the right side of the law. Examples:

- Late night talk shows supply handkerchiefs to young ladies whose dresses might otherwise show a hint of bust.
- An educational radio station in Philadelphia was fined $100 by the FCC for letting rock musician Jerry Garcia use a four-letter word in an interview.
- When CBS broadcast the movie "Elmer Gantry," it cut out the scenes between Gantry and a prostitute, leaving gaping holes in the plot.
- The costumes for a female "genie" in a popular TV series were carefully designed to cover her navel.

The tradition of sexless broadcasting is not about to be reversed. In 1970, the President's Commission on Obscenity and Pornography concluded that adults should be completely free "to read, obtain or view explicit sexual materials." In 1970 also, FCC Chairman Dean Burch announced his intention of itemizing illegal broadcast obscenities. Burch's prudery is bound to have more influence on broadcasters than the research findings of the President's Commission. Television advertisers are permitted to imply all sorts of sexual advantages to their products. But forthright sex is forbidden on the TV screen.

The moralists have also won their battle against profanity. It, too, has been illegal since the inception of radio. In January of 1970, the Walter Cronkite news show aired the expression "goddamn" three times. First Joseph Yablonski Jr., the son of a murdered labor leader, declared that "the Federal government doesn't give us a goddamn bit of help anywhere along the line." Then a Chicago black, commenting on home mortgage problems, complained that his house was "a goddamn cracker box," and that "the goddamn foundation is cracking."

The government made no attempt to prosecute CBS for these minor infractions. But the public reaction was instantaneous. The Bible Belt was outraged, viewers everywhere objected, and station managers around the country called network headquarters in New York to protest. Cronkite later defended the Yablonski goddamn: "Our policy is to permit such language only when it seems essential to the development of the character or nature of the news." He apologized for the other two.[12]

The fight against broadcast violence has made considerably less headway than the fights against sex and profanity. Does media violence do any harm? The evidence is mixed.

One series of experiments exposed nursery school children to films of adults aggressively punching or kicking a pop-up "bo-bo doll." Afterwards the children were intentionally frustrated by taking away their toys. Then each child was put in a room containing several playthings, including the bo-bo doll. Those children who had seen the film were much more aggressive with the doll than those who had not.[13]

This experiment was interpreted to mean that children (at least frustrated children) can "learn" aggressive behavior from media violence. Perhaps all it really means is that children can learn that bo-bo dolls are fun to punch. Is hitting a toy that's made to be hit really a sign of aggression? Does laboratory behavior tell us anything about the real world? Would anybody actually object to bo-bo dolls on television?

Some researchers argue that exposure to media violence increases anxiety and arouses aggressiveness. In a typical study, college students were "hired" to administer electric shocks to other students in what looked like a learning experiment (the set-up was faked). After a while, some of the subjects were shown a film of a teenage knife fight, while others watched a nonaggressive control movie. At that point most of the first group switched to stronger and longer shocks. There was no change in the control group.[14]

A representative study on the other side involved an experimenter who purposely insulted his student volunteers. Then half of them were shown a prizefight film; the other half watched a neutral control film. When the subjects were asked to evaluate the nasty experimenter, the first group was actually *less* harsh in its judgments than the second. The researchers concluded that watching the brutal prizefight had had a cathartic effect—it drained the viewers of their anger at the experimenter.[15]

Conflicting findings have led some psychologists to a more complicated hypothesis. Perhaps exposure to violence itself arouses aggression, but exposure to the evil *results* of violence diminishes it. This suggestion goes a long way toward resolving the problem, but it has not yet been conclusively proved. If it is valid, then honest violence (like honest sex) may actually be a benefit to society. The danger may be in cleaned-up, sanitized violence. Perhaps it is healthy for Americans to see dead Vietnamese bodies on the evening news, but unhealthy for them to listen to impersonal or enthusiastic battle statistics. On another level, perhaps it is bad to watch the sheriff punch the villain on *Gunsmoke,* but good to contemplate the villain's bleeding face.

Paradoxically, the effect of complaints about television violence has been to sanitize that violence, not to eliminate it or make it honest. Brutal footage from Vietnam is seldom shown, but "Mighty Mouse" and "Road Runner" still get knocked around every morning in the cartoons. In an effort to stave off Congressional interference, the networks declared 1969 "the year of anti-violence." The superhero cartoons were eliminated, and so was most of the on-camera killing for adults. Says TV critic John Stanley: "It was the year that if you shot anybody on 'Bonanza' he

DIRTY WORDS?

Michigan State University has its own educational TV station, WMSB. In the fall of 1963, the station began negotiations with clergyman Malcolm Boyd to produce three of his plays on race relations. The plays are strong indictments of white conduct, laced with provocative language. They have been performed and praised throughout the United States.

WMSB backed out. According to station director Armand Hunter, the plays were "too strong," and contained words like "damn" and "nigger." Two of the three were eventually broadcast after the offensive words were removed. The strongest of the plays, *Boy*, was never shown. Hunter said his decision was based solely on vocabulary—not on the content or viewpoint of the plays.

The campus was outraged. "Suppression of an educational play on race relations by an educational television station hardly seems conducive to educational enlightenment on this campus or in the State of Michigan," the *Michigan State News* editorialized. "You just can't sweep naughty names under the rug. They are symptoms of a sickness in our society. Educational broadcasting media should take the lead in exposing that sickness."

Boyd found evidence of the station's having broadcast programs with similar language in the past. He concluded that the forceful presentation of race relations was simply too hot for television, even educational television.[16]

---

was only wounded. (If you shot him off-camera, it didn't matter—he could live or die.)"[17]

The moralistic critics of broadcasting have been much more successful than the esthetic ones. Sex and profanity are rare on radio and TV, and violence is muted. Broadcasting as a result is much less realistic, but no less harmful.

ENTERTAINMENT VALUE

As we have already mentioned, most critics of broadcast entertainment concentrate on the sorts of programs selected, not on the very fact that entertainment monopolizes the bulk of broadcast time.

But implicit in their criticisms is the notion that broadcasting should aim at "higher goals" than mere entertainment. The distinction between High Culture and Mass Culture is not that the former is more entertaining than the latter; for the vast majority of the American viewing public the reverse is true. Rather, High Culture is considered superior to Mass

Culture because of the issues it deals with, the ideas it communicates, and the sensibilities it develops.   In other words, High Culture is better because it is more than *just* entertainment.

Similarly, those who object to obscenity, profanity, and violence in broadcasting do not argue that these three make a program less entertaining.   Instead, they claim that obscene, profane, or violent entertainment—however entertaining it may be—is harmful to public morals.   Once again, their concern is based on a standard other than entertainment.

It is impossible to criticize broadcast entertainment without invoking some such extraneous standard.   In this, at least, broadcast executives are quite right.   Evaluated solely as entertainment, the best entertainment is clearly that which the greatest number of people enjoy the most.   By this measure television provides consistently superlative entertainment.

The positive value of "mere entertainment" deserves more serious attention than it usually receives from critics of the media.   Few societies are as fast-paced, demanding, and exhausting as American society.   In the face of the daily grind of living, the need to relax and unwind is paramount.   Broadcast entertainment serves this need admirably.

Even by the extraneous standards used in judging High Culture, broadcast entertainment has much to be said for it.   The average American finds most of High Culture meaningless and tiresome, difficult to understand and impossible to enjoy.   Whatever it is that intellectuals derive from, say, Shakespeare, the average citizen forced to sit through an evening of "Hamlet" would derive little from the experience.   Perhaps he could be taught to appreciate Shakespeare—but the point is that *he has not been taught* to appreciate Shakespeare.   Yet he does appreciate "Bonanza."   And perhaps he learns from "Bonanza" many of the same humanistic lessons that intellectuals get from "Hamlet."

The authors are reluctant to criticize the "quality" of broadcast entertainment.   But we would criticize its quantity.   Granting that broadcasters do a good job of entertaining the public, we wonder whether they could spare a little additional time and effort for informing the public as well.

The broadcast media have incredible potential for the dissemination of news and information.   To some extent this potential is realized; certainly broadcast news has contributed greatly to the political awareness of the American public.   But the non-entertainment programming on radio and television is often disappointing.   In some ways broadcast news is limited by the nature of the medium; in most ways it is limited only by the policies of broadcasters.

Television is an entertainment medium. The typical TV station offers perhaps three hours of non-entertainment programming a day—roughly 15 percent of the total. Only half of the three hours is devoted to news: an hour at dinner time and a half-hour in the late evening. A little of the remainder is used for documentaries. Most of it goes to religious and agricultural programming in the early morning.

The late evening news is usually a rehash and condensation of the early evening news. And the early evening news is at least a third advertising, sports, and weather. The average TV viewer is lucky if he is offered as much as 40 minutes a day of genuine, original news.

Nevertheless, television news is incredibly powerful. As we have seen (see page 239), the American public relies more on television for its news than any other medium. There are more people watching the network newscasts every night than there are reading all the front pages of all the newspapers in America. No newspaperman in the country even approaches Walter Cronkite in influence.

The power of television was first widely recognized in 1951, with the Kefauver Crime Investigation Committee hearings in New York. *Daily News* reporter Lowell Limpus described the public's response to the televised hearings:

> They're still trying to figure out just how many people dropped everything to camp in front of the TV screens for an entire week or more. They packed bar-rooms and restaurants to watch Virginia Hill. Suburban housewives entertained swarms of neighbors who studied Frank Costello with bated breath. Big department stores set up TV sets for customers who wouldn't buy anything while former Mayor O'Dwyer was on the stand.[18]

The televised Army-McCarthy hearings a couple of years later are widely credited with having put a stop to the demagogic career of Senator Joe McCarthy. The public was able to judge the man and his method for itself. In four years, newspapers had not been able to demolish McCarthy. Television did it in a few weeks.

The power of television news is demonstrated by the power of its opponents. TV newsmen have been attacked from all sides. Vice-President Spiro Agnew accused them of being tools of the liberal Eastern clique. Black radicals and young people accused them of being tools of the Establishment. Everyone senses the power of television—and would dearly love to control it.

The skilled intercutting of words and pictures can heighten the impact of a story far beyond the capacity of the print media. Witness the 1968 Democratic convention in Chicago. On the audio, Mayor Richard Daley denied the existence of police violence; on the video, that violence filled the screen. Many observers felt the combination was unfair and misleading. Many others felt it was an example of superb journalism. Certainly it was powerful. A *New Yorker* critic observed:

> It seems to me quite likely that television will bring forth, sooner or later . . . a man so skilled at manipulating and juxtaposing, in strong individual style, innumerable fragments of visual and aural reality into a sequential mosaic that he will carry forward the present state of instantaneous electronic-image montage to an altogether new level. It will be an extraordinarily compelling and dangerous journalistic art form.[19]

If broadcasters were more interested in power and less interested in profits, there would be grounds for concern. Fortunately or unfortunately, such is not the case. Local station owners have the option of using or not using each network program. This is called giving the show "clearance." And non-entertainment programming has always had serious clearance problems.

In 1968, for example, ABC received clearance from 217 affiliates for the entertainment series "Bewitched"—but only 124 clearances for its evening news. NBC had 222 clearances for "Bonanza"—but only 171 for its documentary "NBC White Paper."[20] Many of the stations that do give clearance to network documentaries tape them for use on Sunday afternoons, or at other outlandish hours. The average station turns down nearly 30 percent of network news and public affairs, scheduling an old movie or a series rerun instead.

Television station managers are ambivalent about news. Surprisingly often, the best news operation in a city is also the strongest—and most profitable—station in that city. Jerome R. Reeves of the Corinthian Broadcasting chain is convinced that "news is the essential element in this medium, the best it has to offer. Once you get the audience aware of this, you have strength . . . the only real link with your community. People come to depend on you and watch you more."[21] A popular news program can help boost ratings for the rest of the night's schedule. And it is pleasing to the FCC at license renewal time.

But a good news operation costs money. NBC, for example, spends $42 million a year to gather the news. It operates a hundred film crews at an annual cost of $90,000 per crew, and spends another $2.5 million a year just on film. In return for this investment, the Huntley-Brinkley show was the network's biggest source of revenue in 1969—bigger than "Laugh-In" or "Saturday Night at the Movies." Advertising time during the show sold for $22,000 a minute, earning the network a cool $34 million a year. Yet NBC still lost money on its news operation. So did CBS and ABC.[22]

Most local stations are unwilling to lose money—even if they build prestige in the process. Nearly 60 percent of all local news departments earn a profit; another 20 percent break even. They manage to do so by keeping costs (and therefore quality) to a minimum. Half the television stations in the country have annual news budgets of less than $100,000.[23]

Television executives are rarely former newsmen. Most often they are promoted out of the sales department; occasionally they come from the entertainment side. They are the nation's most important journalists, but they are not interested in journalism. Nor are they interested in power—though they possess all too much of it. What interests them is profit—and so the news operation must pay its own way.

TV VERSUS NEWSPAPERS

Television news differs from newspaper news in scores of ways. Some of these differences are inevitable results of the nature of broadcasting—but most of them are not.

1. Sensory Involvement. The power of television rests in its capacity to combine voices and moving pictures. Yet that very capacity often turns out to be a disadvantage. TV newsmen are trained to think in terms of good film footage. They avoid at all costs the "stand-upper" or the "talking head"—a reporter simply reading the story without audio-visual aids. The assumption that the viewer wants to see action may or may not be justified, but it is nearly universal. The parallel assumption in radio is that voice actualities are a must. "Get the s.o.b. on the phone" is the motto of most radio news departments.

But how do you get good films or tapes on the new city budget? Or on the President's decision to veto a housing act? Or on the discovery of a new cure for arthritis? Because of its preoccupation with audio-visuals, broadcasting is forced to underplay such stories as these. At best, the newscaster will emphasize some filmable aspect of the event—the political repercussions of the decision instead of the decision itself. Many important stories never get covered on TV because they cannot be effectively photographed.

2. Pseudoevents. The broadcaster's undying allegiance to film footage encourages him to concentrate on pseudoevents (see pp. 147–49). Press conferences, grand openings, conventions and such may not offer much real news—but they guarantee decent footage. By the time a station has covered all these ready-made stories, it has very little time or manpower left for anything else.

Newspapers report events.   Television and radio, by and large, report staged interviews about events.   Michael Arlen of the *New Yorker* carries this to its logical extreme:

> I have this picture of the last great interview: The polar icecaps are melting.   The San Andreas Fault has swallowed up half of California. Tonga has dropped the big egg on Mauritius.   The cities of the plain are leveled.   We switch from Walter Cronkite in End-of-the-World Central to Buzz Joplin, who is standing on a piece of rock south of the Galapagos with the last man on earth, the water rising now just above their chins. Joplin strains himself on tiptoe, lifts his microphone out of the water, and, with a last desperate gallant effort—the culmination of all his years as a TV newsman—places it in front of the survivor's mouth.   "How do you feel, sir?" he asks.   "I mean, being the last man on earth and so forth. Would you give us your personal reaction?"
>
> The last survivor adopts that helpless vacant look, the water already beginning to trickle into his mouth.   "Well, Buzz," he says, gazing wildly into the middle distance, "I feel real good."[24]

3. Speed.   Television and radio can get the news to the public much faster than newspapers.   The bulk of your evening newspaper is written in the morning; the evening newscast includes stories that won't be printed until tomorrow morning.   This makes broadcasting the ideal vehicle for spot news.   Radio is far superior to television in this respect, because TV executives are reluctant to interrupt profitable entertainment programming with a news bulletin.   After all, who sponsors a news bulletin?

4. Time Limitations.   TV news is usually limited—by choice, not necessity—to half an hour at a time.   There is room for perhaps 20 stories at the most, some of which will get no more than 30 seconds.   If you were to set the text of a half-hour newscast in type, it would fill less than half of a newspaper front page.

On big news days, a newspaper can add a few pages to make room. Television can't—a highly profitable show is scheduled right after the news.   It takes a major cataclysm (an election or an assassination) to make a TV station add more news.   When it does so, it loses money.

5. Indexability.   Newspapers can be indexed.   For reporters, this means they can be clipped, filed, and used later as background for a story. For readers, it means they can be browsed through.   Nobody reads a newspaper cover-to-cover.   You turn to the sections that interest you, check the headlines, and read only what you want.

None of this is possible in broadcasting.   Radio and TV newscasts can be taped and stored, but they cannot be indexed for easy access.   Unless a station builds a morgue of newspaper clippings (and very few do), it starts fresh with every story.   As for the viewer, he has no choice but to watch the show "cover-to-cover." That's great for advertisers—it's impossible to skip the commercials. But it is a giant barrier to lengthening the newscast. Who wants to sit through 90 minutes of news just to hear the three or four stories he's interested in?

6. Impermanence. Newspapers can be saved. You can read them at your leisure, clip them, show them to your friends, or post them on your wall. But unless you own a home video-tape machine, broadcasting is a now-or-never proposition. The impermanence of broadcast news probably contributes to its frivolity. Why kill yourself researching a story that will be dead and gone thirty seconds after it starts?

7. Intrusiveness. Broadcasting is intrusive. Even a tape-recorder makes many news sources self-conscious and careful. A camera, a microphone, and a bunch of klieg lights are much, much worse. The appearance of a TV crew alters the nature of any event, from a press conference to a riot. In comparison with broadcasters, print newsmen are almost invisible.

Part of the intrusiveness of broadcasting is the fame of many broadcast newsmen. Few people know what James Reston looks like—but everyone can recognize Walter Cronkite. "During the 1964 campaign," recalls Robert MacNeil, "David Brinkley went to a shopping center in California to watch Nelson Rockefeller on the stump. There was a sizable crowd around Rockefeller but, when Brinkley was spotted, it melted and massed around the bigger attraction, the TV commentator."[25] The same thing can happen to a local "star" newscaster.

8. Competition. One thing you can safely say about radio and TV news: Both are highly competitive. The average city today has only two newspapers, but it has three or four television stations and dozens of radio stations. Newscasts get ratings like everything else on TV, and thousands of dollars may ride on the results. Competition may not always produce a better newscast, but it does keep reporters on their toes.

9. Generalism. Except for the weather and sports people, broadcasting has no news specialists. The typical station is too poor and understaffed to afford a labor writer or a science reporter. The broadcast journalist covers everything.

10. Local News. Most television stations are located in big cities—but their signals reach dozens of smaller cities and towns. The local news of these smaller communities is almost never covered on TV. If you live more than 20 miles from the nearest TV station, you will have to subscribe to a newspaper to get any local news. And for national and international news you will be relying on the networks and the wire services. Very few local stations cover anything but their own cities.

We have detailed ten major differences between broadcast news and newspaper news—mostly to the disadvantage of broadcasting. Some of these differences are inevitable; others can be changed. It is up to broad-casters—and viewers—to determine whether they ought to be changed, and if so how they ought to be changed.

It is probably unfair to judge television news by the same standards applied to newspapers. The media *are* different. Certainly television does a better job of covering the news than radio or movie newsreels did before it. Moreover, two of the most traditional criteria for judging newspapers are speed and accuracy. Television is far superior to the print media on the former, and at least their equal on the latter.

Where television falls down is on the traditional criterion of compre-hensiveness and the relatively recent criterion of interpretation. The first failing is almost inevitable, given the technical limitations of the medium. And the second is improving. Network TV now does an excellent job of reporting *and* interpreting the major national and international stories of the day. In the process, unfortunately, the minor stories get reduced to headlines—or are eliminated entirely. And most local TV news operations give their cities only token attention.

It is impossible to be truly well-informed simply by watching televi-sion news. But even the most avid newspaper reader can gain by adding a little TV news to his diet.

RADIO NEWS

Throughout the 1940s, radio was the most important news medium in America. It nurtured such renowned journalists as Edward R. Murrow, William L. Shirer, and H. V. Kaltenborn, who covered World War Two with honor and distinction. Then came television. In 1951, for the first time, the networks earned more money from TV than from radio. In 1952, for the first time, A. C. Nielsen reported that there were more TV sets than radio sets in use every evening. And by 1956 radio's share of the advertising dollar was down to a meager 5.7 percent.

Today, radio ranks third in entertainment (behind television and movies), and third in news (behind television and newspapers). In order to survive, radio stations have been forced to adopt one or another for-mula—usually music. Today's radio programming is designed for back-ground, not for concentration:

> Radio is the one medium that cannot seize the eye. It is therefore the one mass medium that can serve an active audience: getting up, bath-ing, eating, doing housework, shopping, commuting, picnicking, camping, cooking, going to bed. Radio became a symbol of the competitive deter-

mination of the mass media to occupy any remaining fragment of audience attention. Radio's role became that of a constant companion.[26]

Formula radio may well have saved the medium from near-extinction.

But it had a devastating effect on news quality. The typical radio station styles its news coverage to fit its formula. A hard rock station will adopt a frantic pace, with wire service tickers pecking away in the background. A classical music station will present a sedate, underplayed, two-minute report every hour. Both newcasts are prepared and read by disc jockeys, not trained journalists.

The typical radio station subscribes to only one wire service—the special UPI or AP broadcast wire, which moves the news in neat five-minute packages, ready to read. Every hour the disc jockey rips the copy from the wire and reads it over the air. Local news is pirated from local papers. Larger metropolitan stations may have a news staff of four or five men. But even there the emphasis is on the headlines, the notable and quotable. Even the four major radio networks (ABC, CBS, NBC, and Mutual) carry little more than headlines and features.

As of January, 1970, there were 4,267 AM radio stations and 2,070 FM radio stations in the United States. In entertainment programming they are incredibly diverse. In news programming they are incredibly similar. Melvin Mencher of the Columbia School of Journalism made these observations on a cross-country auto trip:

> A station in a town thirty miles ahead came in, and for the fifth time that day I heard the same state news that had been ripped from the wires most of the day. The first item was the number of traffic fatalities in the state for the year, with a description of the latest death; next an endless rundown on bids on state highway construction; then the weather—temperature, wind velocity, barometric readings for every section of the state.

NEWS ENTERTAINMENT

In 1969 Senator Edward Kennedy was involved in a tragic auto accident, resulting in the death of companion Mary Jo Kopechne. Radio station KIKK in Houston reported the story this way: "Oh, what happened that night of the parteeee. In that lonely island, a two-bedroom cottage where these men without their wives were. . . ." According to Richard Dobbon, the station's news director, that kind of coverage is very popular with his audience. "We say what they want to hear and it sells."

In return for his entertaining approach to news, Dobbon gets "a slight $5 per newscast talent fee" over and above his salary.[27] Such talent fees are not uncommon in broadcast news.

It was like this from Canada through the midwest into the southwest. Local stations sounded alike. Traffic accidents, arrests, judicial actions, deaths—courtesy of the local mortuary—statements by the mayor, the governor, a senator. All of it from the record, as dry and as concealing as dust on the highway. . . .[28]

The best available radio news comes from the handful of big-city stations that have adopted an all-news format—notably WINS in New York and KCBS in San Francisco. Yet even these stations concentrate on voice-actuality pseudoevents, repeated over and over at half-hour intervals by pleasant-voiced performers. The best that can be said about the finest radio news is that it's almost as good as the average television news. Which isn't all that good.

DOCUMENTARIES AND LIVE COVERAGE

The strongest moments in television are its on-the-spot reports of important events. The Kefauver crime investigation . . . the Army-McCarthy hearings . . . the assassination and funeral of President Kennedy . . . the first man on the moon. These are the programs one remembers and talks about years afterward.

But notice that all four stories mentioned above were of such monumental importance that television had no choice but to stop everything and cover them. Even so, there were probably network executives who were reluctant to do so. And beyond doubt the networks lost money on all four.

Ordinary documentaries also lose money—even the ones that are prepared in advance and don't have to pre-empt scheduled shows. TV stations run them because they are prestige-builders, and because they earn credit in the eyes of the FCC. Most stations use as few documentaries as they think they can get away with.

Television excels in noncontroversial documentaries. Underwater photography, African wildlife, the treasures of our art museums—these and hundreds of similar topics have been magnificently handled by one or another network in the last few years. Controversial documentaries are something else. Almost always, they turn out wishy-washy.

Part of this is the government's fault. The fairness doctrine requires broadcasters to present all sides of any controversy they touch at all. Though the fairness doctrine says nothing about presenting all sides "equally" in the same program, many broadcast executives are afraid to produce a hard-hitting documentary. Robert MacNeil tells the story of an NBC documentary on gun control. The first version examined the problem in some detail, then closed with strong support for gun control legislation. After viewing this version, NBC executives ordered that an interview with Frank Orth (head of the National Rifle Association) be added at the end to "balance" the presentation. MacNeil feels that what was finally aired had no guts, no spirit, and no point of view.[29]

Any topic that's worth a documentary is bound to involve some powerful people and institutions. If the documentary is hard-hitting, someone is likely to resent it—and television doesn't like to make enemies. The fairness doctrine is sometimes a reason for avoiding controversy; more often it is an excuse. A few years ago, CBS planned a program on the role of organized religion in the war on poverty. The producers found that many Protestant churches were reluctant to accept federal antipoverty money for fear they might endanger the traditional separation of church and state. At the request of several Protestant groups, the documentary was cancelled. How did these groups know what CBS was up to? CBS had asked them—routinely—if they had any objections to the proposed documentary.[30]

The attitude of many television executives toward documentaries is well expressed by Richard Behrendt, program manager of KRON-TV in San Francisco. A documentary, complains Behrendt, "takes up a great deal of time and money . . . and may hold people up to ridicule." This from a station whose pretax profits in 1968 were $6 million on revenues of $12.1 million.[31]

When television does undertake a controversial documentary, the results can be magnificent. Undoubtedly one of broadcasting's finest moments in 1970 was the CBS documentary "The Selling of the Pentagon." The power of this exposé of Defense Department news management is indicated by the magnitude of the response it produced. The government protested bitterly; the Pentagon demanded and received rebuttal time; a Congressional committee determined to investigate the documentary for bias (see p. 160). CBS undoubtedly knew in advance that the program would stir up a hornet's nest of denials and recriminations. In broadcasting the show, and rebroadcasting it in the midst of the furor, the network showed great (and unaccustomed) courage.

EDITORIALS

In 1941, the Federal Communications Commission outlawed broadcast editorials, ruling that "the broadcaster cannot be an advocate." The Commission changed its mind in 1949, but very few stations took advantage of the opportunity to editorialize. In 1969, less than half the broadcast stations in the country ran even a single editorial. Less than ten percent ran one every day—standard practice on even the poorest newspapers.

When broadcasters do editorialize, they usually stick to noncontroversial topics: "Support Your Local Red Cross" and such. Why? The history of FCC disapproval is part of the answer. So is current government regulation. The fairness doctrine encourages a "yes, but on the other hand" approach in editorials. And the personal attack rule requires stations to give free time to any individual or group criticized in their editorials. Broadcasters who endorse a political candidate must give free time to all his opponents. There are significant hindrances to a strong editorial policy, but they are not the real reason most broadcasters lack such a policy. The real reason is much simpler. Strong editorials make enemies, and broadcasters will do nearly anything to avoid making enemies.

Whatever kind of non-entertainment programming you look at—news, documentaries, or editorials—the conclusion is the same: incredible potential, seldom fulfilled. Perhaps the greatest public service the broadcast media can be expected to perform is to make the viewer aware that there is much more to know than he can ever learn from television and radio.

———————

The quality of broadcast programming is determined by the structure of the broadcast industry. It is determined, in other words, by the power of the networks, by the impotence of the government, and by the overwhelming need to satisfy a mass audience and thus attract advertisers. If broadcasting is to change for the better, its structure must change first. Technological developments make this possible, but political factors make it unlikely.

MONEY

Television is one of the most profitable businesses in the United States. Precise figures are hard to come by, but the average metropolitan TV station returns a profit of nearly 100 percent annually on its tangible investment. A run-of-the-mill successful station can easily take 50 percent of its gross revenues in profits. Consider these numbers for a minute. Suppose a station owns $3 million worth of equipment and has gross revenues of $5 million a year. Its annual profit, according to our calculations, should be at least $2.5 million. No wonder television is sometimes called "a license to print money."

Radio is a riskier proposition. No big-city TV station with a network affiliation loses money—but some network radio stations do. Still, most major radio outlets earn tidy if unexciting profits. In 1970, FM station KCBH in Los Angeles was sold for $1.6 million. Nobody pays that kind of money for an unprofitable station.

Broadcasters earn all their money from advertising. In 1968, advertisers bought $3,163,851,000 worth of time from radio and television stations throughout the country. Roughly two-thirds of this amount was paid to TV stations and networks; the rest went to radio. Local advertising rates range from $2,000 a minute down to $10 a minute, or even less. Network rates go as high as $60,000 a minute, sometimes even higher. Ad rates are calculated in terms of the cost for every thousand viewers or listeners. Radio, naturally, costs less than television. Afternoons are cheaper than evenings, and the most popular shows are of course the most expensive.

Broadcasters are pretty good about passing on some of their prosperity to employees. Beginning broadcast journalists earn about $50 a week more *to start* than newspaper reporters earn after five years on the job. Broadcast engineers and technicians also do better than their print media counterparts. And of course the salaries of television's stars are astronomical. The leading actor in a successful network series earns at least as much as the *publisher* of the average newspaper.

The goal of nearly every broadcaster is to earn money. He can satisfy that goal only by attracting advertisers. And on network television at least, he can attract advertisers only by achieving a mass audience, an audience measured in millions and tens of millions. And how do you capture a mass audience? By programming light entertainment.

It wasn't always that way. In the mid-1930s, half the shows on CBS radio were unsponsored. Listeners were offered drama from the Mercury Theater, music from the New York Philharmonic, news from the Capitol Cloakroom, and information from the American School of the Air. In 1936, CBS presented 311 public-service broadcasts from 27 countries—opera from Moscow, Palm Sunday services from Jerusalem, the 400th anniversary of the death of Erasmus from Rotterdam. NBC, meanwhile, organized the NBC Symphony Orchestra under Arturo Toscanini, and commissioned a series of original operas by American composers. Early television was similarly blessed.

Very little of this remains. Except in emergencies, no program today goes unsponsored. And the sponsor demands two things of his show: that it bore no one, and that it offend no one. Inevitably it won't excite anyone very much either—but that doesn't bother the sponsor. His goal is millions and millions of listless, uncritical viewers. Broadcasters do their best to give him what he wants.

There are three television networks in the United States: CBS, NBC, and ABC. All three operate radio networks as well; the only other radio network of any size is Mutual.

How does a television network work? Its main job is to produce or purchase programming—roughly 100 hours of programming a week. For each program the network must find an advertiser or group of advertisers to foot the bill. Then the network offers the show to local TV stations around the country. It doesn't sell them the program. On the contrary, it pays them to carry it, and even lets them insert some of their own local commercials in the middle. A network will do whatever it has to do to get itself an affiliate in every major city. The more affiliates it has, the more desirable it looks to national advertisers. And national advertising is the network's *only* source of revenue.

Now suppose you were the owner of a television station in, say, Denver. You have 18 hours a day of air time to fill. You could, of course, fill them on your own with local programming. But that costs money—and you're not at all sure you can find enough advertisers to support 18 local hours a day.

Your alternative is to hook up with, say, CBS. The network is offering you its standard agreement. It will supply you with 14 hours a day worth of programs. You can use as much or as little as you want, but for each show you use CBS will pay you so much money. Of course most of the ads during the network shows will be network ads, but you may include a few of your own as well. The advantages of this arrangement are obvious. You won't have to worry about more than four hours a day of your own programming. You'll earn extra money from the network for carrying its shows. And you'll have an easy time convincing local advertisers to sponsor the popular network programs. You have nothing to lose, everything to gain.

The network set-up works to everyone's advantage, so naturally it dominates the industry. The vast majority of the television stations in the country are either owned by or affiliated with one or another network. If there are two stations in town, one is bound to be CBS and the other NBC. If there are three stations, the third will settle for the less profitable ABC affiliation. Only if there are four or more stations in a city will there ever be an "independent."

The independents have it rough. Few can afford to produce more than five or six hours a day of their own programming. The rest they have to buy. Independent stations are the principal customers of the syndicates and independent producers. They buy old movies and serial reruns by the thousands. Occasionally they are allowed to use a network show which the local affiliate has turned down.

As of December 1, 1969, there were 689 commercial TV stations in the

NETWORK ENTERTAINMENT

Three television networks now produce 96 percent of all the entertainment on TV. To this single task they devote the bulk of their resources and talents.

Television entertainment starts with a producer, who tries to guess what next year's mass audience will like based on what this year's mass audience liked. Once he has developed a concept for a series, he takes it to a network executive producer, who decides (guesses) whether or not it will work (sell). If the network gives the go-ahead, the producer begins hiring: a team of writers, a director and an assistant director, a set designer, an art director, a technical director, a lighting director, a wardrobe mistress, cameramen, soundmen, actors and stars. Together they produce a pilot, which the network then tries to sell to potential advertisers.

Once the advertisers are more or less lined up, production begins in earnest. The steps along the way depend on whether the show is videotaped (all at once) or filmed (in separate scenes to be edited and combined later on). In either case, the prime considerations are time and money. An actor complains that a piece of dialogue sounds unnatural—too bad, we've got to shoot it today. A set designer suggests that a scene take place in an attic instead of a cellar, since an adequate attic set has already been built for another show—good idea, we'll save a few thousand dollars that way.

The average hour-long television show is produced in six days at a cost of $200,000–$250,000. A 90-minute feature film, by contrast, may take six months and several million dollars to produce.

United States. Of these, 213 were affiliated with NBC, 192 with CBS, and 159 with ABC. Only 125 stations had no network affiliations. All but a handful of these were UHFs, and many were in financial difficulties.

Network control does its part to help keep television a *mass* medium. Occasionally a local advertiser might be found who was willing to sponsor a minority-interest program, an opera for example. It is much, much harder to find a national advertiser who is willing to do so. And even if one existed, the sponsors of adjacent programs would complain bitterly. An opera would turn off so many viewers that some of them might actually turn off the TV set.

GOVERNMENT

In recent years, the Federal Communications Commission has become more and more concerned about network domination of broadcasting. In 1970 the Commission made its move. It ruled that no station in the top 50 markets could carry more than three hours of network programming during the "prime time" hours of 7 to 11 p.m. For most of the country, 7–7:30 was already local. Now the networks made plans to abandon the 7:30–8 period as well.

According to one FCC staff member, the purpose of the new rule was to encourage minority-interest broadcasting. "The commissioners," he said, "are nostalgic for the good old days of 'Robert Montgomery Presents,' 'The U.S. Steel Hour' and 'The Fireside Theatre,' and are hoping for a renaissance."[32] Since the FCC has no direct power over the networks, it is trying to force greater programming variety by forcing local stations to produce some of their own prime-time shows.

Whether or not the tactic works, it has broadcasters running scared. Not the rule itself—that's a minor burden—but its possible significance for the future. The FCC has traditionally left broadcasters pretty much alone, content to regulate frequencies and rubber-stamp license renewals. Some FCC regulations are annoying (the fairness doctrine for instance), but none of them does any significant harm to profits, so the stations cheerfully abide by them.

In theory, however, the FCC can control broadcasting a lot more closely than it does. And in the late 1960s there were signs it might begin to do so. The new prime-time rule was one such sign. Another was the proposed regulation limiting cross-media ownership. A third was the revocation of the license of WHDH in Boston. A fourth was the more-than-perfunctory renewal hearings conducted for stations KRON in San Francisco, WPIX in New York, KSL in Salt Lake City, and KHJ in Los Angeles. The spectre of government control looms behind every decision made by every radio and television executive today: "Suppose the FCC doesn't like what I have decided."

Not surprisingly, broadcasters are fighting back. And they have powerful friends in Congress to help them fight. Consider, for example, the bill sponsored in the Senate by Rhode Island Democrat John Pastore. The Pastore bill prohibited the FCC from considering any challenge to a broadcast license until after it has determined whether or not the licensee is doing a satisfactory job. This is rather like holding elections for political office only after the incumbent has been impeached. Obviously, the Pastore bill would lead to very little turnover in broadcast licensees.

Representatives of the National Association of Broadcasters defended the bill in the following terms:

> The public's interest lies in the continuance of the station license in the hands of a good operator. Without reasonable assurance that his privilege as a licensee will continue if he gives good performance, the licensee has little incentive to build himself a long-term place in the city of license or to try to improve his facilities. Uncertainty imposes on him

very difficult problems in such practical areas as hiring and training people which are—one hopes—long-term commitments.[33]

There is a lot of validity to this argument. But it overlooks the basic question: Should the FCC guarantee a permanent license to every just-barely-adequate broadcaster, or should it try to pick the best broadcaster for each station?

Recent appointments to the FCC make it highly unlikely that the Commission will pursue the activist stance it adopted in the late 1960s. In January of 1970, the Commission issued a policy statement noting that it would always favor a current licensee over a challenger as long as the former's programming was "substantially attuned to the needs and interests" of his area. The statement added that "as a general matter, the renewal process is not an appropriate way to restructure the broadcasting industry."[34] Since the FCC policy incorporates the basic thrust of the Pastore bill, interest in the bill quickly subsided. But in 1971 a federal court overturned the policy because it was inconsistent with the Communications Act. As the FCC contemplated its appeal, frightened broadcasters turned once again to Senator Pastore for protection.

How little it takes to frighten a broadcaster! At the height of its activism, the FCC never refused to renew more than two or three licenses a year—out of some 2,300 renewal applications. Even that was enough to bring incredible political pressure to bear. As long as Congressmen continue to depend on broadcast coverage for re-election, the likelihood of a truly strong FCC is very, very remote. Fear of the Commission seems to be a powerful force in the minds of many broadcasters. But the Commission itself has done little to alter the structure—or the content—of television and radio.

THE PUBLIC

Broadcasters reply to every criticism of programming with the statement that they are only giving the public what it wants. Are they? The question is hard to answer.

Any survey of public attitudes toward television is likely to reveal the same sorts of criticisms we have been talking about in this chapter. A 1970 Louis Harris poll, for example, found that viewers wanted to see more news, documentaries, and educational programs—and less rock music, quiz shows, soap operas, and mysteries.[35] Is this a true reflection of public opinion, or does it reflect what the public thinks it should think? Probably the latter. There has seldom been a documentary with a higher rating than the average quiz show.

College graduates are the most caustic critics of television programming, and they watch TV at least one-third less than the national average. But when a college grad does tune in, he skips the "quality" programs and settles for the same light entertainment everyone else is watching.[36]

Consider two recent studies. The first one found that only ten percent of the population said there was ever a time when they wanted to watch television but could find nothing on that they cared to watch.[37] The second one found that the total television audience was declining for the first time. Between 1968 and 1969, 36 of the top 50 markets showed drops in the number of viewers.[38] Put the two studies together and they yield an important conclusion. Those who customarily watch TV are happy with what they see. Those who are unhappy with TV simply aren't watching. Television cannot expand its audience beyond current levels unless it appeals to this latter group.

Will broadcasters voluntarily diversify their programming in order to attract the unhappy minority? Not likely. They're doing very nicely, thank you, with the happy majority. They aim to keep it that way.

CHANGES

Back in 1959, FCC Chairman John Doerfer apologized for broadcasting in the following words: "It is an infant industry and it is going through growing pains, the same as the printing press had to do over a period of years. It is a stage."[39]

Broadcasting hasn't changed much since then. Perhaps it is still an infant. Perhaps it is a retarded adolescent. In any case, it often seems unchanging and unchangeable.

If broadcasting ever does change, it will be because technological developments forced it to do so. There are at least six technologies with this capacity:

1. Pay TV.
2. Videotape.
3. FM and UHF.
4. Noncommercial TV.
5. Satellite TV.
6. Cable TV.

We will discuss each in turn.

1. Pay TV. Pay television earns its profits directly from the viewer, not through advertising. It is therefore immune to the "mass market" syndrome; any show can be profitable if those who want to see it are willing to pay enough for the privilege. Broadcasters and movie theater owners are apparently convinced of the potential of this new medium.

For the last 20 years they have waged an aggressive and never-ending battle against it.

Pay TV was first tested in 1951. In 1957 the FCC asserted its power to regulate the new medium, and in 1959 it announced itself ready for a full-scale trial. The experiment was begun in 1962 in Hartford, Connecticut, and lasted for more than six years. Some 5,000 subscribers paid an average of $1.22 a week for a smorgasbord of 87 percent feature films, five percent live sports events, and eight percent cultural programming. In its first three years, pay TV lost over $3.5 million. The Hartford system estimated that it needed at least 20,000 subscribers to break even.[40] It never got close.

Despite the Hartford flop, several pay TV companies are now getting ready to enter the major markets—with the blessings of the FCC. They may hurt ordinary broadcasters some, and may hurt the film industry quite badly. But their programming is bound to be mainly Masscult entertainment, mostly movies and sports. Minority groups, it seems, are not willing to pay enough for special programs geared to their needs. Pay TV, like ordinary TV, is aiming at the mass market.

2. *Video Cassettes.* In 1969, CBS announced the development of an Electronic Video Recording device, which permits an ordinary home television set to be operated like a phonograph or a tape recorder. Purchasers could use blank EVR cartridges to record their favorite shows, or they could buy pre-recorded cartridges to play whenever they wished.

Within months half a dozen companies announced their own competing video cassette systems. A few have trickled onto the market, but most are still being held back while their manufacturers try to make them compatible with each other, so that one company's pre-recorded cassette can be played on another company's machine.

Like pay TV, the pre-recorded video cassette is not dependent on advertising. A "quality television" industry may well develop, somewhat parallel to today's classical record industry. Or it may not.

3. *FM and UHF.* Frequency Modulation (FM) radio is a different area of the spectrum from ordinary Amplitude Modulation (AM) radio. Ultra High Frequency (UHF) television is a different area of the spectrum from ordinary Very High Frequency (VHF) television. The technical differences are unimportant here. What is important is that FM doubles the size of the radio band, while UHF sextuples the space for television stations. By providing for many more stations, both FM and UHF make it possible to diversify broadcast programming.

Neither is a new invention. Both, in fact, date back before World War Two. But for several decades the FCC actively opposed their development, preferring to nurse along the infant AM and VHF media. It wasn't until the 1960s that the Commission changed its mind. In

1961 it permitted FM stations to broadcast in stereo, opening up a new market of music buffs and hi-fi nuts. In 1962 it persuaded Congress to require UHF receivers on all new television sets in interstate commerce. And in 1964, it put strict limits on FM simulcasting, forcing the stations to develop their own programs.

These moves made FM and UHF broadcasting economically feasible. AM broadcasters who had kept their FM affiliates inactive began to see the possibility of profit. VHF stations and networks which had been reluctant to invest in the opposition began to apply for UHF licenses. By 1970 there were 2,461 FM radio stations and 286 UHF television stations on the air.

This tremendous increase in the number of broadcast outlets did not bring about the revolution in programming that the FCC had hoped for. Most FM stations operate on a low budget and broadcast nothing but music; one disc jockey, one engineer, and one ad salesman are all they need.

As for UHF, it has turned out to be a carbon copy of VHF. In 1967 there were 133 commercial UHF stations in operation. Only 44 of them showed a profit, and of these 42 had a network affiliation. Out of 89 non-network stations, only two were operating in the black.[41] Either commercial UHF stations stick to Masscult entertainment, or they lose money.

4. Noncommercial TV. There are currently 182 noncommercial television stations in the country, most of them UHF. The stations are operated by colleges and universities, state and local governments, and various nonprofit civic groups. Some are strictly educational. Others go far beyond the classroom to program political, social, and cultural events of interest. Whatever their content, all 182 stations accept no advertising. They are supported entirely by donations from individuals and grants from companies, foundations, and governments.

The Educational Broadcasting Corporation is the largest of the noncommercial TV "networks." It was born in 1970 out of the merger of National Educational Television (NET) and WNDT, New York's major educational station. Its greatest achievement so far has been Public Broadcast Laboratory, a weekly news program. The Children's Television Workshop, formerly associated with NET but now independent, is responsible for "Sesame Street," the most successful children's show to date.

The Corporation for Public Broadcasting was chartered by Congress in 1967. The ultimate purpose of the bill was to establish a true fourth network of noncommercial stations. So far, however, funds have been scarce. In 1968–1969, the Corporation received $5 million from the Federal government. This was raised to $20 million in 1969–1970—still nothing to compare with the $3 billion annual receipts of commercial broadcasting.

The Corporation for Public Broadcasting simply administers federal funds for non-commercial programming. It is up to each station to decide whether to use the program. John Macy, head of CPB, notes that:

> Our aim is not to compete with the commercial networks in mass audience, with sustained viewing, but rather to provide a diversity of viewing choice and, hopefully, to offer something that is going to be meaningful, stimulating, and entertaining to the people who view it.[42]

The main barriers to educational TV so far have been lack of funds and political pressure to avoid controversial programming.

Educational television has unlimited potential. The stations have already been allotted. Now the money and freedom must be found to do something worthwhile with them.

5. Satellite TV. In 1962, AT&T launched the first experimental communications satellite. Later that year, Congress created COMSAT, a semipublic corporation aimed at developing the potential of communications satellites. INTELSAT, an international consortium with the same purpose, was organized in 1964. AT&T owns 29 percent of COMSAT, the largest single stockholder.[43] It is also the most influential member of INTELSAT.

AT&T, you should recognize, is the company that owns the land lines connecting TV stations into networks. It earns a substantial percentage of its profits from those lines. Quite naturally, then, AT&T is not too enthusiastic about communications satellites—which do the job much more cheaply. As a consequence, the use of satellites has tended to be restricted to international transmissions of news and special events.

In 1970 the FCC finally woke up to this fact and agreed to accept bids from the three networks for their own competing satellite systems. There are two possible plans. One would preserve the local stations and use the satellites only to replace the AT&T land lines. The other calls for direct network to satellite to home transmissions, bypassing the local stations entirely. So far nothing has been done about either.

Bear in mind that both plans tend to increase the power of the three networks. At a minimum, satellites will save the cost of land lines; at best, they'll eliminate the middleman and give the networks a direct line to their viewers. The potential of communications satellites extends far beyond either plan. Instead of three networks, we could now have thirty or more—enough for every kind of minority programming. No one in power is seriously considering this alternative—certainly not the networks or AT&T.

Science writer Arthur C. Clarke and scholar Wilbur Schramm are among those who have seen the real potential of satellites. Writes Clarke:

> The Electronic Blackboard would be of enormous educational value.
> . . . It would teach medicine, agriculture, sanitation and simple manu-

facturing techniques even to primitive peoples.   Later, specially-taped programmes could teach writing to preliterate populations; ultimately the Blackboard could act as the village newspaper and information centre. The social value of such a device can hardly be overestimated; it would change the political and cultural patterns of the whole world.[44]

And Schramm:

The likelihood is that governments, businesses and industrial concerns will have more data than ever before on which to base decisions and less time in which to make them. . . . It is likely that satellite communications will tend to speed up diplomacy just as it will speed up other relationships involving discussions, data handling and decision making.[45]

All this is within our grasp today.   If we never get there, it will be for political and economic reasons, not technological ones.

6. Cable TV.   Cable television is a system for sending a picture from studio to home via a wire or cable, instead of over the air.   It was first developed in the mid-1930s.   For more than a decade, cable was used mainly to connect stations into networks.   By the 1950s it was used also to improve TV reception in rural areas, mountainous terrain, and skyscraper cities.   The subscriber usually paid a hook-up fee of $10 and a monthly rate of $5, in return for which he was guaranteed a perfect picture.   The broadcast industry was delighted.

Then, early in the 1960s, a few cable operators began to import signals from other cities for their clients.   Suddenly local broadcasters were no longer delighted; the cable outfits threatened to steal part of their audience.   And distant broadcasters complained that the cable companies were using their programs without payment.

Enter the FCC.   In 1965, under pressure from the broadcast industry, the Commission declared that it had the right to regulate cable TV.   A year later it established a complete set of highly restrictive rules.   Among other things, cable systems in the top hundred markets were forbidden to import distant signals unless they could prove that no damage would be done to existing stations.

The proponents of cable quickly organized their own lobbying effort. They pointed out the incredible advantages of the new medium:

- Cable can easily carry 20 channels; technically, its capacity extends as high as 84 channels.   Yet cable "stations" take up no space on the overcrowded electromagnetic spectrum.
- Cable can "broadcast" as selectively as needed.   Specialized news and advertising can be programmed for each city, town, neighborhood, or block—even for particular racial or political groups.
- Cable picture quality is uniformly excellent, especially in color.

- Cable is far cheaper than over-the-air broadcasting, sometimes running as little as $5 an hour for an entire channel. This is well within the grasp of school systems, local political candidates, and even ordinary citizens wishing to communicate with their neighbors.
- Cable paves the way for a two-way communications network. It can transmit a facsimile newspaper or a library reference service. It can replace the post office and the telephone. The possibilities are endless.

This is not just propaganda: The possibilities *are* endless. Once an entire country is wired for two-way telecommunications, anything is feasible—from instant political referendums to stay-at-home shopping centers. It all starts with cable.

In 1970, the FCC tentatively reversed its opposition to cable. Out-of-town signals, it proposed, might be imported by cable operators if they paid a set percentage of the gross into a general fund for copyright owners. An additional levy of five percent would be used as a subsidy for educational broadcasting. Cable systems with more than 3,500 subscribers would be required to originate some of their own programming.

Most important, the Commission ordered the three commercial TV networks to get out of the cable business within three years. It also prohibited joint ownership of cable and ordinary TV stations within the same community. And it proposed a further set of rules that would bar joint ownership of cable systems and radio stations, and cable systems and newspapers (as well as limiting the total number of cable systems any one owner could hold).

These provisions were essential to the development of cable, because as of 1970 an estimated 32 percent of all cable systems were owned by broadcast stations and networks. And the attitude of a local station owner toward his own cable system tended to resemble the attitude of AT&T toward its satellite division—why should we cut off our nose to spite our face? With broadcasters and newspapers forced out of the cable business, the major monopolist left will be the telephone company, which currently owns roughly thirty percent of all existing cable systems.

Despite the new regulations, the FCC is not about to let cable endanger the financial health of over-the-air broadcasting. Former Commissioner Rosel H. Hyde admitted as much in 1969. The goal of the Commission, he said, is "to integrate the CATV [cable] operation into the national television structure in a manner which does not undermine the television broadcast service."[46] Bureaucratese translated: Let cable flourish only to the extent that it does no harm to the profits of existing broadcasters.

As of 1970, cable television is still used mainly as an aid to reception. More than 2,300 cable systems are now in operation. They serve a total of some 4.5 million households—roughly eight percent of all American homes. The current investment in cable plant and equipment exceeds $500 million, and annual revenues are in excess of $300 million. All these figures are rising rapidly. Irving Kahn, past president of the TelePrompter Corporation, predicts that within ten years 85 percent of all U.S. television reception will be via cable.[47]

Such a development would change the face of American broadcasting. The change might well be a fantastic boon for the viewer, but for existing broadcasters it would be an unmitigated disaster. If they have anything to say about it, the change will never occur. And through their powerful lobby in Washington, they are likely to have a great deal to say about it.

NOTES

[1] "The Harris Poll," San Francisco *Examiner*, January 19, 1970, p. 50.

[2] *Broadcasting Yearbook*, 1968, p. 22.

[3] *Ibid.*, pp. 22, 24.

[4] Statement at a San Francisco convention of the Association of American Law Schools, San Francisco *Chronicle*, May 9, 1970.

[5] Newton N. Minow, *Equal Time, The Private Broadcaster and the Public Interest* (New York: Atheneum, 1964), chap. 1.

[6] Gary A. Steiner, *The People Look at Television* (New York: Alfred A. Knopf, Inc., 1963), p. 235.

[7] Edward A. Shils in *Culture for the Millions*, Norman Jacobs, ed. (New York: Van Nostrand Reinhold Co., 1961) p. 508.

[8] Dwight Macdonald, quoted in Bernard Rosenberg and David Manning White, eds., *Mass Culture, The Popular Arts in America* (New York: The Free Press, 1957), p. 60.

[9] Alexis de Tocqueville, *Democracy in America* (New York: Vintage Books, 1945), II, pp. 50–54.

[10] Macdonald, quoted in Rosenberg and White, *Mass Culture*, p. 61.

[11] Shils in *Culture for the Millions*, p. 510.

[12] Dwight Newton, "How Permissive Can TV Get?" San Francisco *Sunday Examiner and Chronicle*, February 1, 1970, Sec. B, p. 5.

[13] A. Bandura, D. Ross, and S. A. Ross, "Imitation of Film-Mediated Aggressive Models," *Journal of Abnormal and Social Psychology*, Vol. 66, 1963, pp. 3–11.

[14] R. Walters, E. Thomas, and C. Acker, "Enhancement of Punitive Behavior by Audiovisual Displays," *Science*, Vol. 136, 1962, pp. 872–73.

[15] S. Feshbach, "The Stimulating Versus Cathartic Effects of a Vicarious Aggressive Activity," *Journal of Abnormal and Social Psychology*, Vol. 63, 1961, pp. 381–85.

[16] Malcolm Boyd, "A Play Called *Boy*," and Armand Hunter, "The Case of the Missing Boy," *Television Quarterly*, Fall, 1965, pp. 25–39.

[17] John Stanley, "The Year Many a Villain Was Worded to Death," San Francisco *Sunday Examiner and Chronicle, Datebook*, January 4, 1970, p. 12.

[18] Lowell Limpus, "Television News Comes of Age," *Nieman Reports*, July, 1951, p. 11.

[19] Thomas Whiteside, "Corridor of Mirrors," *Columbia Journalism Review*, Winter, 1968–69, p. 54.

20 Marvin Barrett, ed., *Survey of Broadcast Journalism*, 1968–69 (New York: Grosset & Dunlap, Inc., 1969), p. 14.

21 Albert R. Kroeger, "Television News," *Television Magazine*, February, 1965, pp. 28–29.

22 Sheldon Zalaznick, "The Rich Risky Business of TV News," *Fortune*, May 1, 1969, pp. 92–97.

23 Kroeger, "Television News," p. 30.

24 Michael J. Arlen, *Living-Room War* (New York: The Viking Press, Inc., 1969), pp. 194–95.

25 Robert MacNeil, "The News On TV And How It Is Unmade," *Harper's Magazine*, October, 1968, p. 75.

26 Richard L. Worsnop, "Competing Media," *Editorial Research Reports*, Vol. II, No. 3, July 18, 1969, p. 542.

27 Nicholas von Hoffman, "Surprises in Your Radio News Report," San Francisco *Chronicle*, December 13, 1969, p. 8.

28 Melvin Mencher, "The Roving Listener," *Columbia Journalism Review*, Fall, 1966, pp. 45–46.

29 Robert MacNeil, *The People Machine* (New York: Harper & Row, 1968), Chap. 11.

30 Richard Severo, "What's News at CBS?" *The New Republic*, March 12, 1966, p. 33.

31 "FCC's KRON-TV Quiz: 2 Views," *Variety*, April 22, 1970, p. 35.

32 "Three-Quarter Time," *Newsweek*, May 18, 1970, p. 73.

33 Vincent T. Wasilewski, Remarks before the Federal Communications Bar Association, May 29, 1969, p. 7.

34 "FCC Tries To Keep Up with Technology," *Broadcasting*, December 29, 1969, p. 50.

35 "The Harris Poll," San Francisco *Examiner*, January 19, 1970, p. 50.

36 Steiner, *The People Look at Television*, pp. 159–60, 168, 202.

37 John P. Robinson, "Television and Leisure Time: Yesterday, Today, and (maybe) Tomorrow," *Public Opinion Quarterly*, Summer, 1969, pp. 219–20.

38 "The Mystery of the Missing Audience," *Broadcasting*, February 9, 1970, p. 19.

39 Meyer Weinberg, *TV in America* (New York: Ballantine Books, 1962), p. i.

40 "Coming Soon: Pay-TV," San Francisco *Sunday Examiner and Chronicle*, November 23, 1969, Sec. B, p. 6.

41 Ralph Lee Smith, "The Wired Nation," *The Nation*, May 18, 1970, p. 592.

42 "Future of Non-Commercial TV," *U.S. News and World Report*, December 8, 1969, pp. 94–97.

43 Herbert I. Schiller, *Mass Communications and American Empire* (New York: Augustus M. Kelley, 1969), p. 130.

44 Edward M. Kimbrell, "Communication Satellites II," Freedom of Information Center Report No. 245, Columbia, Mo., July, 1970, p. 7.

45 *Ibid.*, p. 7.

46 Smith, "The Wired Nation," p. 594.

47 *Ibid.*, p. 587.

SUGGESTED READINGS

ARLEN, MICHAEL J., *Living-Room War*. New York: The Viking Press, Inc., 1969.

BARRETT, MARVIN, ed., *Survey of Broadcast Journalism*. New York: Grossett & Dunlap, Inc., 1969, 1970.

LANG, DAVID L., ROBERT K. BAKER, and SANDRA J. BALL, *Mass Media and Violence*. A Report to the National Commission on the Causes and Prevention of Violence. November, 1969. Available from the Government Printing Office, Washington, D.C.

MACNEIL, ROBERT, *The People Machine*. New York: Harper & Row, 1968.

SCHILLER, HERBERT I., *Mass Communications and American Empire*. New York: Augustus M. Kelley, 1969.

SKORNIA, HARRY J., *Television and Society*. New York: McGraw-Hill Paperback, 1965.

———, *Television and the News*. Palo Alto, Calif.: Pacific Books, 1968.

SMITH, RALPH LEE, "The Wired Nation," *The Nation*, May 18, 1970.

STEINER, GARY A., *The People Look at Television*. New York: Alfred A. Knopf, Inc., 1963.

13 Other Media

Most of the nonlocal content in the American mass media comes from the wire services and feature syndicates, especially the Associated Press and United Press International. These two services tell us almost everything we know about events in other states and other countries. Working with skeleton staffs at breakneck speeds, the wire services often provide less than adequate coverage—but without them we would have no coverage at all.

On the night of September 30, 1962, the Associated Press office in Atlanta was the focal point for the hottest news story of the day. Aided by federal troops and assailed by rioting students, James Meredith, a Negro, was enrolling at the University of Mississippi.

Reporter Van Savell was on the phone from the university. Retired Army General Edwin A. Walker, he dictated, had just taken command of the violent crowd, and had personnally led a charge against federal marshals. Savell's dispatch sped over the AP wire to newspapers and broadcast stations from Manhattan to Manila. But in the heat of the moment, Savell had made a mistake. General Walker sued for libel.

Though the General had been present on campus and had addressed a group of students, a Texas jury would decide that he had not "assumed command" or "led a charge of students against federal marshals." Not until 1967 would the U.S. Supreme Court overturn the $500,000 judgment awarded Walker in Texas.

The Supreme Court decided that the libel standards for public figures like General Walker should take into consideration the problems of wire service newsmen. Justice Harlan put it this way:

> The dispatch which concerns us in Walker was news which required immediate dissemination. The Associated Press, received the information from a correspondent who was present at the scene. . . . Considering the necessity for rapid dissemination, nothing in this series of events gives the slightest hint of a severe departure from accepted publishing standards.[1]

In other words, wire services have to work so fast they're bound (and allowed) to make mistakes.

EVERYTHING FOR EVERYBODY

The Associated Press and United Press International are the two major wire services in the United States. AP has 8,500 clients around the world, including 1,750 newspapers and 3,100 broadcast stations in the U.S. alone. UPI is a little smaller. It has 6,000 customers world-wide; 1,600 newspapers and 2,300 broadcast stations in the U.S. For most of their clients, AP and UPI are the principal source of non-local news. For many, they are the only source.

Every minute of every day, somewhere in the world, a wire service client has reached its deadline. As a result, wire reporters are always under pressure to get the story now. As one Midwest editor put it: "AP covers the news in a hell of a hurry, and this is what we expect of it."[2] Speed is the main goal of both AP and UPI. Frequent errors are the result.

The political biases of wire service clients run the gamut from the far left to the far right. To keep everybody happy, the wires must have no biases of their own. "We can't crusade because we have papers of every complexion under the sun," notes Wes Gallagher, general manager of AP. "A crusade that pleases one is an anathema to another."[3] Hence the traditional wire service "cult of objectivity."

But objectivity, like speed, has its drawbacks. Often the facts alone are not enough to make the meaning of a story clear. Sometimes the facts are simply misleading. One longtime Washington staffer recalls: "You said what Joe McCarthy said and you couldn't say it was a goddamn lie."[4] This is still a big problem for wire service reporters. At best, they are permitted to give both sides of the story—but not to tell readers which side they believe is right. Some client somewhere might disagree.

The growth of interpretive journalism hasn't bypassed the wire services entirely. More and more often, reporters are freed from their routine assignments to do in-depth articles on one or another subject. But in the routine stories themselves, interpretation is still taboo. Correspondents are urged to get the facts as quickly and succinctly as possible. News analysis takes time and space, both of which are in short supply. And besides, some client somewhere might disagree.

Objective or not, the wire services have no choice but to color the news. To start with, they choose the news. They decide which events to cover. They decide which stories to put on the national wire and which to use only regionally. And twice a day, they give each client a "news budget," a list of those stories so important he shouldn't go to press without them. If something happens and the Associated Press ignores it, then it might as well not have happened. If the Associated Press declares it's big news, on the other hand, it will make the front page of hundreds of papers across the country.

The wire services have their own sort of bias—the bias of "appropriateness." Critic Murray Kempton recalls the funeral of Pope Pius XII. The scene was a madhouse of confusion, yet the AP and UPI stories depicted only peaceful pilgrims praying for the Pope. Says Kempton:

> Journalism, at least wire service journalism, has as one of its functions the preservation of the social fabric, a certainly decent aspiration. The social fabric requires that some people, like mourners at funerals, be seen at their best and that others, like participants in civic disturbances, be seen at their worst. . . . [T]he focus is on the persons who cry at funerals or who shout at demonstrations. . . .[5]

In an effort to keep its clients happy, a wire service is far more likely to confirm traditional values than to question them.

Anything to keep the clients happy. Out of the AP office in Cranston, Rhode Island, comes the following story. A stalled motorist flagged down a lady driver and asked for a push. When he warned her that his car wouldn't start till it hit 35 miles per hour, she thoughtfully backed up and raced her car into his—at 35 miles per hour. This is a good yarn, and nearly every AP subscriber used it. Only one problem: It's phony. It happened, if it happened at all, a generation ago. Every few years some bored wire reporter invents it all over again for comic relief. To keep the clients happy.

Different clients have different needs, so AP and UPI offer a variety of services. For major metropolitan newspapers there is the national wire, several regional wires, and an assortment of special wires—sports, financial, weather, features, etc. They all operate 24 hours a day. The fee is figured on a sliding scale based on circulation; a big-city paper may pay as much as $5,000 a week for all ten AP wires.

Smaller newspapers don't need that much. Many make do with a single teletype, a mixture of international, national, and regional news, sports, weather, features, and everything else. Still smaller papers may sign up for one wire eight hours a day, period, paying as little as $50 a week for this minimal service. For broadcasters, meanwhile, there is the special broadcast wire, complete with five-minute newscasts, ready to read.

Convenience is the key. The broadcast wire doesn't contain much news, but it doesn't require much work from the disc jockey either. Similarly, both AP and UPI offer their reports on perforated tape, geared for automatic typesetting machines. Notes Norman E. Isaacs of the Louisville *Courier-Journal:* "Most small papers don't seem to give a damn about the quality of wire service copy—as long as the price is kept low and they can get it delivered on tapes."[6]

NOT ENOUGH FOR ANYBODY

The Associated Press was founded in 1848 by six New York newspapers. To this day it remains a cooperative; AP members elect a governing board which tells the operating staff what to do. United Press International, on the other hand, is a private business. It is the product of a 1958 merger of the United Press (founded by E. W. Scripps in 1907) and the International News Service (founded by William Randolph Hearst in 1909). UPI has no members, only customers.

The difference is meaningless. In point of fact, AP and UPI compete for the same clients—newspapers and broadcast stations. Roughly a quarter of the media subscribe to both services, but most settle for one or the other. And so the competition is fierce.

Among newspaper editors, AP is considered better for Washington and international news, and generally more reliable. UPI is thought to have superior coverage of the White House, the Soviet Union, and Latin America, as well as brighter writing. Each strives constantly to outdo the other. "I don't know of two outfits more destructively devoted to the American principle of free-enterprise competition than AP and UPI," says top UPI reporter Louis Cassels. "Competition in news gathering drives expenses up, and competition in selling drives income down."[7] Today, UPI is losing money, and AP finds it increasingly difficult to break even.

The problem is heightened by the existence of a number of supplemental wire services which offer specialized or interpretive news. The three leading supplementals are operated by the New York *Times,* the Chicago *Daily News,* and the Washington *Post* jointly with the Los

Angeles *Times*. Together they have over 600 clients. Most metropolitan newspapers receive a large assortment of supplementals. Here is the San Francisco *Examiner*'s list:

(HHS) Hearst Headline Service
(CDN) Chicago Daily News
(TTS) Toronto Telegram Service
(CST) Chicago Sun-Times
(NWS) Newsweek Service
(WBS) World Book Service
(WNS) Women's News Service
(CQS) Congressional Quarterly Service
(NEA) Newspaper Enterprise Association
(LDE) London Daily Express

Largely because of the competition, both AP and UPI have begun cutting corners. Many of AP's 108 U.S. bureaus are skeleton staffs in cramped quarters with inadequate files. Like UPI's 100 bureaus, they are usually located in newspaper offices. Both services depend largely on local newspapermen to do their reporting for them on a part-time basis. In small towns they use housewives and students, paying a flat rate of $5 an item. The staff shortage is especially acute overseas. War zones aside, there are only 500 American reporters in the entire rest of the world.

Gary Drewes is UPI bureau manager in Pierre, South Dakota. He is also the bureau's entire staff, UPI's man in South Dakota. Seldom leaving his one-room office, Drewes covers all stories, even disasters, by telephone. Every day he checks the water level at five local reservoirs—important news for the regional wire.

Merriman Smith, until his death in 1970, was the chief UPI correspondent at the White House. Affairs of state were his daily concern. He was the man who said "thank you, Mr. President" after every press conference. He had a front-row seat at history in the making. But for every Merriman Smith, there are hundreds like Gary Drewes, checking on reservoirs and waiting for something to happen.

The pride of the wire services are their Washington bureaus, manned by staffs of 150 for AP and 90 for UPI. Even that isn't enough, as Jules Witcover of the Newhouse National News Service explains. Here's how Congressional committees are covered:

> Overworked AP and UPI staffs routinely make collection runs, visiting a number of committee hearings on any given morning, dutifully collecting witness' speech texts, and going back to the House or Senate press gallery to dictate or to grind out several stories. Far from its being digging reporting, it is not even routine reporting. It is skimming. . . .[8]

In Washington, as elsewhere, the wire services do the best they can. There is too much news to cover in too many places. There are too many clients demanding too much for too little money. A great deal of news goes ignored, or poorly covered, or uninterpreted. Even so, AP and UPI move ten times as much copy over the wires as the average client wants to use. It is hard to justify asking for more.

FEATURE SYNDICATES

The first feature syndicates were organized during the Civil War, but they were small-time affairs until the 1880s, when Samuel S. McClure got into the act. McClure offered newspapers all over the country a steady diet of 50,000 words a week—everything from Kipling to cooking. His rationale for syndication remains true to this day:

> A dozen, or twenty, or fifty newspapers—selected so as to avoid conflict in circulation—can thus secure a story for a sum which will be very small for each paper but which will in the aggregate be sufficiently large to secure the best work by the best authors.[9]

Today there are dozens of successful feature syndicates. The largest is King Features, with annual billings of more than $100 million. Syndicate copy is designed for inside pages and Sunday editions, and is often sold in ready-to-print form. Topics are varied, but mostly light—household hints, advice to the lovelorn, astrology, gardening, hobbies, and the like.

The most admirable syndicated features are undoubtedly the political columnists. Men like Walter Lippmann, Drew Pearson, and Westbrook Pegler have had an incalculable influence on the course of American government. Even today, columnists such as Joe Alsop and Jack Anderson offer the best interpretive journalism to be found. Through the syndicates, they offer it in hundreds of newspapers across the country. The syndicated columnist is a powerful man.

But the big money-makers for the syndicates are the comics. A newspaper that pays $50 a week for Joe Alsop, say, may pay as much as $125 a week for Dick Tracy—and many more papers get Tracy than Alsop. The Chicago *Tribune*-New York *Daily News* syndicate earns a fortune without a single public affairs columnist on its payroll. But no large syndicate can survive without comics.

The feature syndicates and the wire services control much of the content of the average newspaper. Ben Bagdikian estimates that, aside from advertising, roughly 30 percent of the average paper is syndicated.[10] Another 40 percent comes from the wire services. Put these two figures together, and you begin to understand why one American newspaper looks so much like another. If the wires and the syndicates do a bad job, it is literally impossible for newspapers to do a good one.

Movies are no longer the immensely profitable mass medium they once were. Television put a stop to that. But the film industry today is probably more creative and more charged with excitement than ever before in its history. Though the movie audience is small, it is heavily concentrated among young people. No other mass medium is as much a part of the youth culture.

HOLLYWOOD AND KIDS

In 1929, 110,000,000 people visited a movie theater every week. In 1968, weekly movie attendance was down to 21,000,000. Many factors contributed to the decline, but television was by far the most important. The recent history of the film industry is the history of its response to television.

The major Hollywood studios responded to the competition of television by producing fewer but more spectacular feature films. Movie theaters moved to the suburbs with the expanding middle class, and rocking-chair seats, wide screens, and stereophonic sound created a film experience that could not be duplicated on the home TV set. The big-budget blockbuster became the typical movie of the 1950s and 1960s.

Occasionally the tactic worked. "The Sound of Music" was the most profitable movie of 1965, perhaps the most profitable movie of the decade. "Funny Girl," "Oliver," and "2001: A Space Odyssey" also made money. But these were flukes. A more representative film was "Dr. Doolittle," which cost Twentieth Century Fox an estimated $18 million loss. On the strength of spectacular flops, five of the major studios reported losses totaling $110 million in 1969. Several others were forced to fold in the late Sixties, and no studio was getting rich.

Rising costs were part of the problem. "I wish 'The Sound of Music' had never been made," remarked one studio production chief. "The industry lost sight of reality and thought that budgets didn't require a ceiling."[11] Star performers demanded as much as a million dollars a film, and the studios willingly paid the price, unable to believe that an Elizabeth Taylor or a Julie Andrews no longer guaranteed a box-office hit. Many films in the 1960s cost as much as $20 million to make; very few of them grossed the $50 million needed to recoup the cost.

But even a $20 million spectacular can make money if enough people want to see it. The big mistake of the film industry was to underestimate the public's satisfaction with television. Faced with the choice of an old movie on TV (for free) or a new movie in town (at three dollars a seat), the typical American preferred to stay home in his easy chair.

There was one exception: young people. A survey commissioned by the Motion Picture Association of America found that:

1. Nearly all movie-goers are under 30.
2. More than half are under 20.
3. Roughly a third are under 15.[12]

Despite these facts, the major studios paid very little attention to teen-agers. Instead, they aimed their films at a middle-class, middle-aged "family" audience—hoping that if box office receipts didn't justify that emphasis, sales to television and foreign markets would.

In the late 1950s and early 1960s, the studios did try to attract the youth market with a series of beach party and Elvis Presley movies. But these films were several years behind the musical pulse of America's teen-agers. In choosing between a Presley movie and a Beatles record, the kids bought the record—and had their own beach party.

Meanwhile, a new generation of filmmakers was graduating from col-lege. Like their fellow students, they were impressed with the potential of the medium, and with the innovative work of the European masters—Truffaut, Godard, Fellini, Antonioni. They were not impressed with Hollywood. "It was frustrating," one young filmmaker explained. "For one reason or another, the industry was unresponsive to personal films. The industry was controlled and dominated by a business industrial men-tality."[13] Instead of seeking jobs with the big studios, many novice film-makers founded their own independent companies. The movies they produced spoke directly to the youth culture.

In a few short years they revolutionized the industry. "The Gradu-ate," "Bonnie and Clyde," "Midnight Cowboy," "Easy Rider," and "Alice's Restaurant" all cost next to nothing to produce (by Hollywood standards). All earned phenomenal profits. The major studios quickly began bank-rolling the independents. If filmmaker Haskell Wexler could bring in "Medium Cool" for under a million dollars for Paramount release, why should Paramount spend over $20 million on a bomb like "Paint Your Wagon"? By the end of the 1960s, the film industry had made up its mind. It bet its future on independent low-budget production and the American youth market.

The box-office failure of a number of "youth" films in 1970 brought this conclusion back into question. So did the success of two almost-spectaculars, "Airport" and "Patton." The run-away best-seller of 1971 was "Love Story." Though produced on a relatively low budget and devoted to the romance of two college students, "Love Story" can hardly be said to have pandered to the youth cult. It pandered to a much broader interest in high-class soap opera.

Was the low-budget, youth-oriented film of the late 1960s a temporary aberration? Or was the big-budget, general-interest film of the early 1970s a passing fad? Only time will tell, but the latter seems more likely than the former. In the face of television, expensive movies will always have trouble making money, and young people are still the most enthusiastic movie market by far. Hollywood is not about to forget these facts again.

SEX AND SUCH

Crucial to the current film revolution is the almost total freedom of moviemakers to say and show what they want. "Midnight Cowboy" featured a male prostitute in the starring role, and the great financial success of "I Am Curious (Yellow)" is attributable only to its explicit sex scenes. In an era when even an Establishment star like Richard Burton can portray a homosexual without loss of stature, movie taboos have all but disappeared.

In 1952, the U.S. Supreme Court ruled that movies are protected by the First Amendment. Films could be censored and banned, but only under specific laws within Constitutional limitations. Throughout the 1950s and 1960s these limitations expanded, and today only a film that is utterly without redeeming social merit is censorable. Local governments are free to harass "dirty" movies—and many do so regularly—but they cannot stop them.

Under pressure from citizens groups like the Legion of Decency, the Motion Picture Producers and Distributors of America had long ago passed the Motion Picture Code. This "voluntary code of self-regulation" prohibited sex, vulgarity, obscenity, and profanity, as well as certain controversial topics. It didn't begin to relax until the mid-1950s. "The Man with the Golden Arm" was refused an MPPDA seal because it depicted narcotics addiction. The film received such praise from the critics that in 1956 the Code was amended to allow discussion of drugs. By 1961, the Code also permitted "restrained, discreet treatment of sexual aberrations in movies."[14]

Foreign filmmakers and American independents ignored even the liberalized Code. And the film-going public (mostly young people) seemed unconcerned that their favorite movies lacked the MPPDA seal. The major studios, desperate for a piece of the action, were forced to adopt a new code. In 1968, the Production Code and Rating Administration was established. It assigned each movie one of four classifications. The 1970 revised ratings are:

G All ages admitted. General audience.
GP All ages admitted. Parental guidance suggested.

R Restricted. Under 17 requires accompanying parent or adult guardian.

X No one under 17 admitted.

In effect, the rating system took the film industry off the self-censorship hook. Henceforth, the industry would simply announce which movies were clean and which were dirty. The rest was up to the public.

But the rating system had some strange side-effects. At the beginning, several studios actually tried for the "X" rating, as a come-on for fans of "adult" fare. A rash of ultra-frank sexploitation films also followed the switch from self-censorship to ratings. Then the reaction set in. Local governments and civic groups began putting pressure on theater owners to carry only "G" and "GP" movies. In 1970, 47 percent of the members of the National Association of Theater Owners had a standing policy of no "X" rated films.[15]

In self-defense, producers start censoring their own movies, struggling for an "R" instead of an "X" or a "GP" instead of an "R." For the same reasons, the Code Administration relaxed its standards. In 1969, "Midnight Cowboy" was rated "X"; in 1970, it was re-rated "R."

The rating system has not brought about the hoped-for death of censorship. Nor has it matured over the past few years; there is something incredibly childish about judging the morality of a movie on the basis of whether or not a nipple shows in reel 3. Nevertheless, the film industry is freer today than ever before, and much of the credit goes to the ratings.

THE REST OF THE BUSINESS

To most people, "film" means entertainment, feature movies shown in movie theaters. Yet there are many other kinds of films—documentaries, newsreels, educational films, industrial films, and so forth.

Fewer than 200 feature films and more than 10,000 non-theatrical films are produced in the United States every year. This does not include the additional thousands of commercials and television programs filmed annually. Producers of non-theatrical movies include government agencies, schools and colleges, hospitals and religious groups, and more than a thousand business corporations. These movies are collected and distributed by some 2,600 American film libraries. Their total budget is in excess of a billion dollars a year.

Motion picture documentaries and newsreels flourished in the 1930s and 1940s. Today, this kind of programming is handled mostly by television—but not exclusively. What was "Woodstock" if not a documentary?

Still, the largest categories of non-entertainment films are the educational and the industrial. The goal of educational movies is to inform (and indoctrinate) young children. The goal of industrial movies is to train (and indoctrinate) employees. Film has proved itself an ideal medium for these purposes.

Even entertainment films are an indoctrination of sorts. Today's movie industry deals explicitly with the fundamental concerns of its principal audience, young people. Its handling of themes such as revolution, alienation, and sex is sometimes insightful and honest; more often it is shameless pandering. Fortunately, the good movies tend to earn more money than the bad ones—but Hollywood keeps producing bad movies in quantity anyhow. All of which raises an important question: Are the "with-it" filmmakers serving the youth culture, or are they molding, co-opting, cheapening, and perverting it?

———————

As a mass medium, books are a failure. Once he finishes his schooling, the average American has very little to do with them. And when he does read a book, he almost always chooses a mass market paperback, the lightest of light entertainment. It is relatively easy to publish a book, and thus exercise some influence over the "reading public." But the general public remains untouched.

BREAKDOWN

The book is the basis for our system of education and the repository of our culture. It is through books that the young learn what they have to learn and the wise teach what they have to teach. To those who are literate, books offer a permanent record of the best and worst in American civilization—and all other civilizations.

The offer is often ignored. The average American reads very few books after leaving school. And the books he reads have very little to say about American civilization or any other. Of course there are books that have changed the world—*Uncle Tom's Cabin,* for example, or Darwin's *Origin of the Species.* But they did it indirectly. Fewer people have read these two since they were published than the number who watched "Bewitched" on TV last night. In the long term, books may well be the most important of the mass media. But in the everyday life of the average citizen, they are by far the least influential.

The best way to understand book publishing is to look at the kinds of books that are published every year. The following table shows the 1969 total sales volume for each kind of book produced in the U.S.[16]

Educational Books:		
Textbooks	$	797,350,000
Reference books		603,050,000
Professional books		286,000,000
General Books:		
Book club books	$	220,000,000
Trade hardbacks		199,000,000
Mass paperbacks		173,000,000
Juvenile books		140,000,000
Religious books		108,000,000
Trade paperbacks		41,000,000
Other books		189,690,000
Total:	$	2,757,090,000

Some of these categories deserve amplification.

Educational Books. It is obvious from the table that educational books—especially textbooks—are by far the biggest segment of the book publishing industry. Educational books account for more than 60 percent of total sales dollars. Textbooks alone account for nearly 30 percent of total sales. This is in part a recent phenomenon—war babies have reached school age, higher education has expanded enormously, and teachers have started using many short texts instead of one long one. But textbooks and other educational books have always been an important and profitable part of the publishing business.

Needless to say, textbooks are read only by students. Reference books (except for encyclopedias and dictionaries) circulate mostly to libraries and specialists; professional books are reserved for doctors, lawyers, scientists, and the like. If you are interested in the effects of books on the average American adult, you must forget about this category.

Mass Paperbacks. Much has been written about the "paperback revolution," and most of it is wrong. For one thing, paperbacks are not a recent invention. As early as 1840, many newspapers earned money on the side by printing paperback "extras" of popular novels. Hardcover publishers did the same thing in the 1870s, specializing in pirated editions of the English classics. They soon ran out of classics, and the International Copyright Law of 1891 put most of the paperback publishers out of business.

They started again in the 1930s. By this time the economics of the industry were clear. Cheap paper-bound books could earn money only if they were published and sold in enormous quantities. In 1939, Robert F. deGraff decided to market his Pocket Book series through newsstands and chain stores instead of book stores. That year he published 34 titles in all, selling 1,508,000 copies. The mass market paperback was born.

The difference between mass paperbacks and "trade" paperbacks is quantity. Trade paperbacks are printed in lots of five or ten thousand. They are sold mostly through the nations 800 full-fledged bookstores and 8,000 variety and stationery stores with book departments. The average price for a trade paperback is $1.95 or so. Mass paperbacks, on the other hand, are printed in lots of 200,000 or more. They are designed to sell for 75¢ to $1.25 in drugstores and supermarkets—a total of 85,000 outlets throughout the United States.

Mass paperbacks are cheap. They sell a lot of copies, but don't earn much money. By the time a publisher is through buying reprint rights and paying wholesalers and distributors, he *has* to sell a lot of copies to earn anything at all. In 1970, paperback sales zoomed past the $200 million mark—but they still account for less than five percent of publishing revenues, and an even smaller percentage of publishing profits. Contrary to popular opinion, paperbacks do not dominate the book business —at least not from the publisher's point of view.

The reader's point of view is another story. Textbooks aside, roughly two-fifths of all the books in the country are paperbacks. The average nonstudent seldom if ever reads a hardcover book.

Book Club Books. The Book-of-the-Month Club was founded in 1926. Members were notified of each month's selection a few weeks in advance; they had the option of turning it down or buying it (by default). In nearly 50 years of operation, the system hasn't changed a bit. The only difference is the number of clubs. Today one may join travel book clubs, mystery book clubs, psychology book clubs, and even dirty book clubs. The 1969 gross income of all the clubs was $220 million, and it is estimated that by 1972 they will distribute 133 million books a year.

Publishers initially feared that book clubs would hurt bookstore sales. They had the same fear about paperbacks—but neither has proved justified. Cass Canfield of Harper & Row notes that "club mail-order operations have created hundreds of thousands of new book-buyers in areas where booksellers are scarce or nonexistent."[17]

Trade Hardbacks. When most people hear the word "book," they immediately think of the trade hardback—the kind of book you find in libraries and bookstores. Most of the 30,000 new titles published in the United States every year are trade hardbacks. Aside from some 3,000 books of fiction, most trade hardbacks deal with information—agriculture, art, biography, business, etc.

Trade hardbacks offer a wealth of culture, information, and entertainment to those who read them. Very few people read them. Fewer than five percent of all trade hardbacks sell more than 5,000 copies before they go out of print. Only 36 million trade hardbacks were sold in 1967. That's one book for every five and a half Americans.

Despite the disappointing taste of most readers, book publishing is a profitable and growing industry. The annual production of new books increased only 40 percent from 1929 to 1959—but from 1959 to 1969 the increase was over 100 percent. Textbooks and paperbacks accounted for the bulk of the gain.

Most publishers earn money, but very few earn a lot of money. Bestsellers are the chancy part of the business. Twenty companies said no to Thomas Wolfe before an editor at Scribner's saw potential in *Look Homeward, Angel*. No one believed that Jacques-Yves Cousteau's *The Silent World* or George Plimpton's *Paper Lion* would sell millions. But bestsellers make up an infinitesimal part of publishing profits. Most of the money is made on textbooks, children's books, and similar specialties. A publisher's income is largely determined by his "backlist"—the number of books that sell small but steady amounts year after year.

Publishing is a very conservative business. An editor reads a manuscript and guesses that it might sell four or five thousand copies, at five dollars a copy. He adds up the expenses of printing and distributing, and calculates that five thousand sales will mean a net of $6,000 or so. On the basis of these figures, he offers the author a contract—ten percent royalty with an advance of $2,000. A year or two later (publishers work slowly) the book comes out. If it sells the expected five thousand copies, the author earns his advance plus an additional $500 in royalties; the publisher earns about $3,000. If it sells almost no copies, the author gets to keep his advance and the publisher loses a few thousand dollars. If by some miracle it sells a million copies, the author gets rich and the publisher gets richer.

But miracles don't often happen. Most books either earn a few thousand dollars or lose a few thousand dollars. It's a slow way—it's no way —to get rich.

Book publishing is simultaneously a tight-knit monopoly and a wide-open field. It takes very little cash to start a small publishing firm. Job-lot printers can be hired to produce the book, and professional wholesalers will distribute it for a percentage of the take. Most of the nation's 6,500 publishers work in precisely this fashion—one or two men producing only three or four books a year.

Then there are the biggies, the New York publishing houses with dozens of editors and hundreds of books on their backlists. It is estimated that 350 publishers are responsible for 90 percent of all book titles. A mere two dozen publishers produce two-thirds of the nation's books. Many of these are giant corporations, listed on the New York Stock Exchange. More than a few of them own interests in television, newspapers, magazines, computers, and other industries. Quite often the publishing arm of these corporations is less profitable than some of the other subsidiaries.

Big companies inevitably earn most of the money in book publishing; they publish most of the books. But anyone can compete with them, and some of the most successful books have been brought out by very small firms, often through the use of jazzy promotion campaigns.

The typical New York publishing house doesn't approve of jazzy promotions. Its goal is simply to produce a few very fine books, a few very popular books, and a lot of very average books, earning a small but steady profit in the process. It is a tribute to the publishing business (one is tempted to call it a profession) that an admirable book can always find a publisher, even if it is clearly fated to lose money. In the long run, the climate of American opinion is greatly influenced by the book industry, because the opinion-leaders and trend-setters are readers. Regrettably, they are the only readers.

NOTES

[1] *Associated Press v. Walker* (388 U.S. 130) in Marc A. Franklin, *The Dynamics of American Law* (Mineola, N.Y.: The Foundation Press, Inc., 1968), p. 652.

[2] A. Kent MacDougall, "Grinding It Out, AP, UPI Fight Fiercely For Front Page Space," *Wall Street Journal*, January 28, 1969, pp. 1, 16.

[3] *Ibid.*, pp. 1, 16.

[4] Jules Witcover, "Washington: The Workhorse Wire Services," *Columbia Journalism Review*, Summer, 1969, p. 10.

[5] Murray Kempton, *New York Post*, April 29, 1969.

[6] MacDougall, "Grinding It Out," pp. 1, 16.

[7] *Ibid.*, pp. 1, 16.

[8] Witcover, "Washington: The Workhorse Wire Services," p. 11.

[9] Ben H. Bagdikian, "Journalism's Wholesalers," *Columbia Journalism Review*, Fall, 1965, p. 27.

[10] *Ibid.*, p. 28.

[11] "The Old Hollywood: They Lost It at the Movies," *Newsweek*, February 2, 1970, p. 66.

[12] Theodore Peterson, Jay W. Jensen, and William L. Rivers, *The Mass Media and Modern Society* (New York: Holt, Rinehart and Winston, Inc., 1965), p. 128.

[13] Richard Houdek, "The New Hollywood," *Performing Arts*, January, 1970, p. 6.

[14] Harold L. Nelson and Dwight L. Teeter, *Law of Mass Communications* (Mineola, N.Y.: The Foundation Press, Inc., 1969), p. 366.

[15] Vincent Canby, "Will a Censor Get the Teenybopper?" San Francisco *Sunday Examiner and Chronicle, Datebook*, March 29, 1970, p. 30.

[16] "Sales of Books Total $2,750 Billion in 1969," Association of American Publishers Press Release, October 8, 1970.

[17] Cass Canfield, *The Publishing Experience* (Philadelphia: University of Pennsylvania Press, 1969), p. 60.

SUGGESTED READINGS

BAGDIKIAN, BEN H., "Journalism's Wholesalers," *Columbia Journalism Review,* Fall, 1965.

KNIGHT, ARTHUR, *The Liveliest Art.* New York: Macmillan, 1957.

MACDOUGALL, A. KENT, "Grinding It Out, AP, UPI, Fight Fiercely For Front Page Space." *Wall Street Journal,* January 28, 1969.

WITCOVER, JULES, "Washington: The Workhorse Wire Services," *Columbia Journalism Review,* Summer, 1969.

14 Advertising and Public Relations

Advertising is the all-important connection between the mass media and the world of commerce. The relationship is symbiotic. Without advertising, neither the media nor the industrial establishment could survive in the form we know them today. Not only the character of the mass media, but the character of American society itself, is determined to a large extent by the institution of advertising.

In 1954 the net profits of Revlon, Inc., a cosmetics company, stood at $1,297,826. In 1955 CBS introduced a new TV quiz program, "The Sixty-Four Thousand Dollar Question." Revlon sponsored the show, as well as its twin: "The Sixty-Four Thousand Dollar Challenge." Both programs were on the air until 1958, when it was proved that they were rigged. During those four years, Revlon's net profits rose to $3,655,950 in 1955, $8,375,502 in 1956, and $9,688,307 in 1958. When a Senate committee asked Martin Revson, owner of Revlon, whether his phenomenal success was due to sponsoring the two shows, he answered musingly: "It helped. It helped."[1]

In 1963 the Clark Oil and Refining Company spent its entire $1.6 million advertising budget on television. Until then, Clark had limped along with annual earnings of $1.5 million or so. The first year following the TV campaign, the company earned $2.1 million. It committed itself permanently to television—and in 1969 Clark Oil earned $13.0 million. Said one Clark executive: "That's really advertising power."[2]

ADVERTISING AND BUSINESS

American business spends over $20 billion a year on advertising, most of it in the mass media. This figure represents only the raw cost of time and space. It does not include the salaries of the nation's 400,000 advertising men, or the expense of preparing and producing the ads. The actual cost of advertising is closer to $40 billion a year—$200 for every man, woman, and child in the country.

What does American business get in return? Increased sales, of course. The "success stories" of Revlon and Clark are two of thousands that could be told. Frederick R. Gamble, former president of the American Association of Advertising Agencies, puts it this way:

> Advertising is the counterpart in distribution of the machine in production. By the use of machines, our production of goods and services has been multiplied. By the use of the mass media, advertising multiplies the selling effort. . . . Reaching many people rapidly at low cost, advertising speeds up sales, turns prospects into customers in large numbers and at high speed. Hence, in a mass-production and high-consumption economy, advertising has the greatest opportunity and the greatest responsibility for finding customers.[3]

The purpose of nearly all advertising is to induce the buyer to purchase something that the seller has to sell—a product, a service, a political candidate, or whatever. A successful ad is an ad that sells—and most ads are successful.

Advertising can boost sales in two ways: by winning a bigger share of the market, or by increasing the size of the market itself (perhaps creating the market to start with). The first technique may be called competitive advertising; it says "Buy our brand of aspirin instead of the brand you're using now." The second is noncompetitive advertising; it says simply "Buy more aspirin." Most ads are a combination. They urge the consumer to switch brands and to buy more.

Business competition is not limited to advertising, of course. A manufacturer or a store may compete by cutting its prices, improving its products, or offering superior service. It is not hard to find examples of ads that are essentially "informational"—telling the public about a genuine competitive edge. But these tactics have limited value. Aspirin is aspirin. It is nearly impossible to make a better aspirin. And price-cutting may lose more in profits than it gains in sales; how many people would switch brands to save a nickel? Competitive ads for aspirin—and many other products—have no real differences to talk about. The competition is not in the products, but in the ads themselves. Meyer Weinberg describes the big-money television advertisers this way:

> Having eschewed competition by cutting prices, the Top Fifty instead go all out to attract the consumer's attention by amusement or entertain-

ment. There is no other way of driving consumers to prefer one sub-stantially identical item over another. Thus advertising agencies special-ize in the manufacture of spurious individuality. . . .[4]

So much for competitive advertising. If the only way a manufacturer could earn a dollar was by stealing it from some other manufacturer, America's gross national product would be at a standstill. Fortunately or unfortunately, this is not the case. Industry grows by creating new consumer needs. Wigs, cigarettes, electric washers, power lawnmowers, toiletries, fur coats, and aluminum cans are not really essential to life, liberty, and the pursuit of happiness. But manufacturers have convinced us that they are. They did it with advertising.

Consider the TV ad budgets of the top twenty advertisers on network television in 1969.

Procter and Gamble	$120,540,700
Bristol-Myers	58,632,900
Colgate-Palmolive	53,709,000
R. J. Reynolds	50,756,000
General Foods	49,642,300
American Home Products	42,144,800
General Motors	40,999,000
Sterling Drug	38,196,000
Warner-Lambert	37,756,900
American Brands	37,278,100
Phillip Morris	32,491,100
Gillette	31,521,300
Ford Motor	30,636,300
Miles Laboratories	30,261,100
General Mills	29,172,000
British-American Tobacco	28,414,000
Lever Brothers	26,846,500
J. B. Williams	26,302,500
Chrysler	26,025,100
Loews Theaters	25,821,700

Aside from wealth, what do these twenty corporations have in com-mon? They all manufacture nonessential goods. The needs they serve are, in the words of John Kenneth Galbraith, "psychological in origin and hence admirably subject to management by appeal to the psyche." Gal-braith goes further. "The individual serves the industrial system," he says, "by consuming its products. On no other matter, religious, political, or moral, is he so elaborately and expensively instructed."[5]

The overarching goal of all advertising is to get the consumer to con-sume. Communications researcher Dallas Smythe recalls an ad in the New York *Times* which filled an entire page with the message: "Buy

Something." Smythe comments: "The popular culture's imperative—'Buy Something'—is the most important educational influence in North America today."[6] Erich Fromm sums it all up in a phrase. American man, he says, is no longer *Homo sapiens,* but *Homo consumens*—Man the consumer.[7]

America is the wealthiest nation in the world. It is also the most wealth-conscious, the most materialistic. Advertising deserves some of the credit and much of the blame.

ADVERTISING AND THE MEDIA

If Big Business as we know it couldn't exist without advertising, neither could the mass media. Television and radio earn all of their money from advertising, which fills some 20 percent of the total air time. Newspapers and magazines earn well over three-quarters of their income from advertising, which occupies roughly 60 percent of the available space. Of all the mass media, only books and movies are completely independent of advertisers.

Newspapers, magazines, television, and radio compete for every advertising dollar. As of 1968, newspapers had 29 percent of the total. Television had 17.5 percent; magazines had 11.5 percent; and radio had 6.5 percent. The other 35.5 percent went to direct mail, billboards, and the like.[8] This division of the spoils is not a constant. The development of radio ate significantly into the percentage shared by newspapers and magazines. The development of television did a lot of damage to radio and magazines.

But as long as advertising continues to grow, there is plenty of money to go around. In 1941, the total cost of all advertising was less than two billion dollars. Today, that figure is over twenty billion dollars. A minute of time on network radio may now cost up to $8,000. A full-page ad in a major newspaper may run as high as $10,000. A full page in a national magazine may sell for more than $60,000. And a minute on network television may go for a phenomenal $100,000 or more. Advertisers willingly pay the going rates, and all four media are earning good money.

ADVERTISING AND THE PUBLIC

The influence of advertising over media content has already been discussed in considerable detail (see Chapter 5). Direct threats and outright bribes are not unknown, but they are far less common than tacit "mutual understandings." The mass media, after all, are completely dependent on advertisers for their profits. They don't have to be threatened or bribed to keep the advertisers happy. It comes naturally.

None of this is inevitable. Take British television, for example. There are two networks, one commercial and the other government-sponsored. On the non-commercial network, no ads are permitted. On the commercial network, advertisers have only one choice—which station to give the ad to. Station managers schedule the ads as they please, and no commercials are permitted in the middle of a program. Unable to choose their show (much less to produce it), British advertisers have next to no influence on British programming.

The American mass media not only adjust their content to meet the needs of individual advertisers. They also adjust their attitudes to promote the interests of the business community as a whole. In an essay entitled "Mass Communication, Popular Taste and Organized Social Action," sociologists Paul Lazarsfeld and Robert Merton put the case this way:

> Since the mass media are supported by great business concerns geared into the current social and economic system, the media contribute to the maintenance of that system. This contribution is not found merely in the effective advertisement of the sponsor's product. It arises, rather, from the typical presence in magazine stories, radio programs and newspaper columns of some element of confirmation, some element of approval of the present structure of society. . . .
>
> Since our commercially sponsored mass media promote a largely unthinking allegiance to our social structure, they cannot be relied upon to work for changes, even minor changes, in that structure. . . . Social objectives are consistently surrendered by the commercialized media when they clash with economic gains.[9]

As we have already said several times, American business spends $20 billion a year on advertising. Naturally, this cost is not absorbed by advertisers in the form of reduced profits. It is passed on to the consumer in the form of increased prices. A bar of soap that sells for 30¢ might cost only 26¢ if Procter and Gamble didn't spend $120 million a year on television. Harry Skornia has computed the cost of television advertising alone to a family with disposable income of $5,000. The annual "tax" for free TV, he found, is $53. It breaks down this way.[10]

Cosmetics and toiletries	$12.00
Patent medicines and drugs	10.00
Car	10.00
Food	6.00
Cigarettes	5.00
Gasoline, oil, tires	3.00
Soaps and detergents	3.00
Other	4.00
	$53.00

A similar computation could be made for radio, newspapers, and magazines.

Defenders of advertising point out, however, that by increasing the demand for consumer goods advertising makes possible the economies of mass production and mass distribution—economies that may be passed on to the consumer. Economists have disagreed for decades as to the net effect of these opposing influences: Advertising both costs us money and saves us money.

Whatever its effect on the economy, the effect of advertising on the media is clear. The content of newspapers, magazines, television, and radio is determined by corporate interests, in an unending effort to turn People into Consumers.

———————

The job of the nation's 400,000 advertising men and 100,000 public-relations men is persuasion. It is a hard job, and they do it well. They also do it ethically, at least according to their own standards. But ethical or not, the professional persuaders are too skillful, and too powerful, to be studied with equanimity.

ADVERTISING MEN

Advertising men face their greatest challenge when introducing a new kind of product, creating a need that does not already exist. Enzyme soaps are a typical case. Developed in the late 1960s, enzyme soaps do essentially the same job as standard detergents, perhaps a little more effectively. But without exception, the companies that manufacture enzyme cleaners also make detergents, and bleaches to boot. Their goal, of course, is to sell the new product while maintaining the sales records of the old ones. How, then, did the Brand X Detergent Company introduce Enzyme X?

The company's first move was to hire a New York advertising agency, one of the big ones geared for national campaigns. Brand X was a major account, so an agency vice-president was assigned the job of account executive. Like most account executives, he had an M.B.A., but had been catapulted to the vice-presidency at the age of 38 by several phenomenally successful campaigns. He was earning in excess of $50,000 a year, and was already planning to quit and start his own agency, perhaps with Brand X as his first big client.

The job of an account executive is to act as liason between the client and the agency's creative people. In this case, the executive planned to make use of the following departments: research, copy, art, layout, production, and media. Selecting one or two men from each department, the account executive put together a planning group that would stay with the account from start to finish.

It was a psychologist from the research department who pointed out the obvious: "We cannot base our advertisements on the superiority of enzymes over detergents, because our client manufactures detergents as well. We must therefore urge the consumers to add the enzyme product to the detergent and bleach they already use, in order to obtain an even cleaner wash than before." Everyone agreed that this appeal was essentially irrational (what is "cleaner than clean"?), but everyone agreed that it could work. The research department verified that women are emotionally attached to their old detergents and will not give them up— but will cheerfully dump an extra ingredient into their wash if convinced that it will give them the cleanest clothes on the block.

Convincing them was, of course, the job of the copy, art, and layout departments. The media department, meanwhile, tentatively decided to stress national women's magazines and daytime TV soap operas. Work began on four different magazine ads and three television commercials, each in 60-second, 40-second, 30-second, and 10-second versions. Since the agency's movie production facilities were already working to capacity, an independent filmmaker was called in to help.

Throughout this period, the account executive was in constant contact with the Brand X advertising department. He obtained their approval for each ad and each commercial. He also got their permission to test-market the product in a dozen communities, trying out various appeals to see how they worked.

According to the research department, these tests produced one unexpected result. Housewives, it seems, were not only willing to add Enzyme X to their wash; they were also willing to use it as a pre-soak before washing. New commercials were designed to stress this additional function.

Now the media department went into action. Using data from the Audit Bureau of Circulations, the media men began deciding which ads to place in which newspapers and magazines, when and how often. Their main criteria were total circulation and total cost—how many readers per dollar could they reach in each publication. But it wasn't that simple. The "enzyme-buying public" was obviously easier to reach in some magazines than in others; even newspapers vary in the number of women readers they attract. Quality and minority-group magazines required ads different from the mass magazines. There were back covers to be considered, and special editions, and regional magazines, and dozens of other factors.

But choosing the print media was child's play compared with placing broadcast commercials. The main tool here was the ratings, prepared by the A. C. Nielsen Company and the American Research Bureau. Broadcasters live and die by the Nielsen and ARB rating reports, simply because advertisers swear by them. In this case, the main candidates for commercials were the daytime network soap operas. Each show was carefully examined in terms of its cost per thousand viewers, its credibility as an advertising vehicle, its popularity with the sorts of people who might buy enzymes, and so forth. Consideration was also given to the possibility of commissioning and sponsoring a special program, but this was rejected. In the end, spot commercials were placed in seven different network serials.

The media department had plenty of help deciding where to place its ads—from the space and time salesmen in the advertising departments of each newspaper, magazine, and broadcast station and network. In theory, this is a cut-and-dried process. The media have their ad rates; the client pays the full rate; the agency remits 85 percent of it and keeps the other 15 percent as its commission. In reality, there's a lot of room for wheeling and dealing—to get the client a lower price and the agency a higher commission.

Media commissions account for about three-quarters of the income of most advertising agencies. The other quarter comes from surveys, production, and similar "expenses," for which the client pays a premium. After covering its own expenses, the average ad agency has a net profit of only four percent of the gross. Madison Avenue is not a cheap address, and advertising men are well paid.

How did the enzyme campaign work out? Like most advertising campaigns, it was a success. Housewives obediently began adding enzyme products to their wash, or using them as pre-soaks; the more impressionable housewives did both. Enzyme X became a big money-maker for the Brand X Detergent Company. After a year or two, the company (and nearly all its competitors) decided to add enzymes to its detergent as well. Properly advertised, this gimmick helped to boost detergent sales without damaging the sales of non-detergent enzymes. By 1971, the cooperative American housewife did her wash in the following manner: first an enzyme pre-soak, then an enzyme detergent supplemented with more of the pre-soak and with bleach. Her clothes were cleaner than cleaner than clean, and detergent-caused eutrophication had become a serious water pollution problem.

Such is the power of advertising.

PUBLIC-RELATIONS MEN

In 1641, Harvard College sent three preachers to England on a "begging mission." At their request, a fund-raising brochure, *New England's First Fruits,* was prepared by the elders of the Massachusetts Bay Colony—the first public-relations pamphlet written in the New World. Press releases, pseudoevents, and the rest of the PR arsenal followed soon after. Though the first professional public-relations firm wasn't founded until 1904, the techniques were already well-established before the American Revolution.

The difference between advertising and public relations is one of methods, not goals. Martin Mayer puts it this way:

> Advertising, whatever its faults, is a relatively open business; its messages appear in paid space or on bought time, and everybody can recognize it as special pleading. Public relations works behind the scenes. . . . The advertising man must know how many people he can reach *with* the media, the public relations man must know how many people he can reach *within* the media.[11]

This is a valid distinction, but advertising and public relations are often so intertwined that it is hard to tell where one leaves off and the other begins. When a political candidate, for instance, puts himself in the hands of the professionals (as candidates customarily do nowadays), he not only gets advertising specialists to write his commercials. He also gets public-relations specialists to write his speeches. The two kinds of specialists work together to build a consistent (if unreal) image of the candidate.

If anything, public relations is a broader field than advertising. Every politician employs a full-time press secretary even after the election, though he may have no further need for an ad agency. Government departments don't advertise much, but they use literally thousands of professional PR people. And every college and every corporation has its own "public-information department" or "public-relations counsel."

Whatever his title and whoever his employer, the public-relations man has but one job: to use the mass media to build a favorable image of, or for, his client. PR techniques run the gamut from handouts to junkets, from press conferences to bribes. They are disscussed fully in Chapter 6.

What concerns us here is public relations as a social force, as a mass medium in its own right. How much do you know about, say, the Bell Telephone system? And where did you learn what you know? You learned a little of it from personal experience. You learned a great deal more from those charming and impressive AT&T ads. And you learned by far the most from the efforts of the Bell PR department. Those efforts range from the little "newsletter" that comes with your bill every month, to planted newspaper articles about Bell's work in minority recruiting. They range from Bell-sponsored science films distributed free to primary schools, to cute magazine fillers about the adventures of a long-distance operator. They range from widely publicized grants to educational TV stations, to county fair exhibits of telephone technology.

There is nothing dishonest about all this. Public-relations men seldom lie. But they do mislead. At best, they distract the public's attention from disagreeable facts and concentrate its attention on agreeable ones—agreeable to the client, that is. The Bell System really does impressive things technologically; it is generous in its support of education; it works hard on minority recruiting; it doubtless has thousands of courteous, helpful operators who love people. But the Bell System is other things as well, things you seldom hear about.

Back in 1909, a telephone company executive complained that people "know us as a monopoly, and that creates hostility at once because the public doesn't like monopolies. They have no opportunity to see us and know us. . . ."[12] Today, Bell is a much richer and more powerful monopoly than it was in 1909. Public resentment is kept at a minimum—thanks to the efforts of a superlative public-relations staff.

There is nothing unusual about Bell Telephone. Every company, union, government, and charity uses the same techniques. Much of what we know about our world comes to us (free of charge) courtesy of the nation's 100,000 public-relations men.

ETHICS

The first advertising agencies were founded in the 1840s. By 1860 there were thirty of them. As middlemen between the advertisers and the publications, they were in an ideal position to cheat both—inflating prices, demanding kickbacks, and so on.

These abuses didn't improve until 1869, when George P. Rowell began publishing the *American Newspaper Directory,* an accurate listing of newspaper circulations and ad rates. Also in 1869, the N. W. Ayer & Son agency was founded to buy space for advertisers on a straight commission basis. Thereafter, it was not so easy for ad agencies to manipulate publishers and advertisers.

But manipulating the public was something else. Many ads at the turn of the century—especially those for patent medicines—were grossly misleading, often outright falsehoods. The public put up with them for a few decades, then began to complain. Several of the more ethical agencies joined in the campaign against misleading advertising. The Better Business Bureau was founded in 1913, the Audit Bureau of Circulations in 1914. The Association of Advertising Clubs developed a model "truth in advertising" law. It was championed by the trade journal *Printers' Ink,* and was soon adopted by several states.

Advertising became more and more sophisticated, with the introduction of mass psychology, copy-testing, and integrated campaigns. The Wheeler-Lea Act of 1938 was designed to outlaw misleading ads for foods, drugs, and cosmetics. But all it could really stop was dishonest ads—and advertisers were learning how to mislead without lying. During World War Two, the Advertising Council was organized to promote rationing, war bonds, and the like. The Council continued to do public-service work after the war, but the propaganda techniques mastered in wartime were soon put to use for corporate clients as well.

Today, every aspect of an ad is carefully calculated for maximum effect—the words, the colors, the tones of voice. Advertisements, and even products, are designed to appeal to subconscious needs and irrational desires. The psychologist is in some ways the most important man in the ad agency. For many years, Marlboro was known as primarily a women's cigarette. An advertising task force (mostly psychologists) was put to work trying to change this unfortunate image. Marlboro is now considered the cigarette for he-men.

Industry spokesmen argue that it is up to the consumer to protect himself against the "hidden persuaders" of advertising. Their commitment to ethics is confined to the bromides and truisms in the Advertising Code of American Business. Even this limited document is more honored in the breach than the observance. One clause of the Code provides that "advertising containing testimonials shall be limited to those of competent witnesses who are reflecting a real and honest choice." The violations of this provision are too numerous to mention.

At best, the advertising industry polices itself to weed out the most blatantly dishonest practitioners. The subtle ones are free to do as they like—so long as they remain sufficiently subtle.

The mass media have historically recognized an obligation to screen advertising, but have seldom met that obligation. There are exceptions. Back at the turn of the century, E. W. Scripps appointed an advertising censor for his newspaper chain. And several papers today, notably the New York *Times* and the St. Louis *Post-Dispatch,* turn away ads that might injure or mislead the reader. But most newspapers do not reject much advertising except on moral or political grounds—from "X" rated movies and left-wing demonstrators, for example.

Both the Radio and the Television Codes contain guidelines on advertising. The broadcaster is urged to "refuse the facilities of his station to an advertiser where he has good reason to doubt the integrity of the advertiser, the truth of the advertising representations, or the compliance of the advertiser with the spirit and purpose of all applicable legal requirements." He is also supposed to turn down an ad whenever he "has good reason to believe [the ad] would be objectionable to a substantial and responsible segment of the community."[13]

In practice, broadcasters obey the second injunction but ignore the first. They refuse to accept ads for hard liquor, fortune-tellers, condoms, or suppositories, because these are offensive to certain groups. But they were completely unbothered by the lethal danger of cigarettes and the blatant misrepresentation in cigarette commercials. They cut out tobacco ads only when Congress forced them to—and they complained bitterly every step of the way.

The only institution actively fighting advertising abuse is the government—notably the Federal Trade Commission. But the FTC is very limited. For one thing, it takes too long. By the time the FTC has decided that a particular TV commercial is illegal, the commercial has long since been junked and a new one put in its place. Moreover, the FTC can act only against outright dishonesty, a comparative rarity. It can order a TV commercial to stop lying, or a newspaper ad to stop disguising itself as editorial copy. But it cannot tell either one to stop playing games with people's minds.

Public relations plays games with people's minds too—and is completely unregulated by any government. Not that PR men are without ethics. Back in 1906, PR pioneer Ivy Lee sent the following "Declaration of Principles" to newspaper publishers:

> This is not a secret news bureau. All our work is done in the open. We aim to supply news. This is not an advertising agency; if you think any of our matter ought properly to go to your business office, do not use it. Our matter is accurate. Further details of any subject will be supplied promptly, and any editor will be assisted most cheerfully in verifying directly any statement of fact. . . . In brief, our plan is frankly and openly, on behalf of business concerns and public institutions, to supply to the press and public of the United States prompt and accurate information concerning subjects which it is of value and interest to the public to know about.[14]

Lee's Declaration of Principles is, in effect, a public-relations handout on behalf of public relations. It forms the basis for the Public Relations Code of the Public Relations Society of America.

Despite these principles, PR is dangerous. Publicists do not often lie, but stretching the truth is an integral part of their business. And unlike advertisers, they do it in secret. Their work does not carry the unspoken "caveat emptor" of paid advertising. With no control by government and very little by the mass media, public-relations men tell us what they want us to know.

Advertising and public relations have been around too long to be eliminated now. The media and the industrial establishment depend on them. Society as we know it could not exist without them. But when you make a list of all the mass media, do not forget to include advertising and PR. And if your list is in order of influence on American civilization, do not forget to put them at the top.

NOTES

[1] Meyer Weinberg, *TV in America* (New York: Ballantine Books, 1962), pp. 46–47.

[2] Lawrence B. Christopher, "Clark Oil Finds Out TV Really Works," *Broadcasting,* March 2, 1970, pp. 42–44.

[3] Theodore Peterson, Jay W. Jensen, and William L. Rivers, *The Mass Media and Modern Society* (New York: Holt, Rinehart and Winston, Inc., 1965), p. 191.

[4] Weinberg, *TV in America,* p. 194.

[5] John Kenneth Galbraith, *The New Industrial State* (Boston: Houghton Mifflin Co., 1967), pp. 37–38, 201.

[6] Dallas Smyth, "Five Myths of Consumership," *The Nation,* January 20, 1969, p. 82.

[7] Erich Fromm, *Escape from Freedom* (New York: Farrar & Rinehart, Inc., 1941).

[8] "Ad Volume Increased 6.3% in 1968," *Marketing/Communications,* February, 1969, p. 60.

[9] Bernard Rosenberg and David Manning White, eds., *Mass Culture, The Popular Arts in America* (New York: The Free Press, 1957), pp. 465–66.

[10] Harry J. Skornia, *Television and Society* (New York: McGraw-Hill Book Company, 1965), p. 96.

[11] Martin Mayer, quoted in Peterson, Jensen, and Rivers, *Mass Media and Modern Society,* p. 191.

[12] *Ibid.,* p. 195.

[13] Radio and Television Codes.

[14] Sherman Morse, "An Awakening in Wall Street," *American Magazine,* September, 1906, p. 460.

SUGGESTED READINGS

CUTLIP, SCOTT M., and ALLEN H. CENTER, *Effective Public Relations.* Englewood Cliffs, N.J.: Prentice-Hall, Inc., 1970.

DELLA FEMINA, JERRY, *From Those Wonderful Folks Who Gave You Pearl Harbor.* New York: Pocket Books, 1970.

McGINNISS, JOE, *The Selling of the President 1968.* New York: Trident Press, 1969.

PACKARD, VANCE, *The Hidden Persuaders.* New York: Pocket Books, 1957.

PART FOUR
COVERAGE

We come now to the last section of the book, "Coverage." In earlier sections we talked about the structure and functions of the media. We detailed their history. We traced the patterns of media control by various groups and individuals, from governments to publishers. We examined each medium in turn to see what made it unique. Now, finally, it is time to turn to content. In a sense, the first three-quarters of the book was intended to show why the media perform the way they do. This section is intended to evaluate the performance itself.

Some 320 pages ago, we listed four functions of the mass media—to inform, to entertain, to influence, and to make money. It should be obvious by now that the authors consider the first of these functions by far the most important. In the chapters that follow, therefore, we will be interested in only one question: How good a job do the mass media do of informing the public? We will not attempt to judge media performance in the areas of entertainment, persuasion, and profit.

Before evaluating the quality of news coverage, it is essential to consider standards of evaluation. Nothing is good or bad in itself; it is good or bad with respect to some standard. The following are the most important of the many standards that have been proposed and used by the media and media critics.

1. Profitability. The American mass media are, for the most part, privately owned and privately financed. Unless they earn a profit, they will fail. And a newspaper or broadcast station in imminent danger of failure is unlikely to spend much money improving its news operation. A mass medium that earns a lot of money may still do a poor job of covering the news. But a medium that loses money almost always does a poor job.

2. Audience Satisfaction. Like profitability, audience satisfaction is a necessary but not a sufficient condition for media quality. If nobody reads a newspaper article it can accomplish nothing—but many articles are well read and still accomplish nothing.

3. Accuracy. An inaccurate news story is always, without exception, a poor news story. Most editors and reporters know this, and strive mightily to spell the man's name right, even if they do not fully understand what he is saying.

4. Objectivity. Nearly all responsible journalists aim at objectivity, and quite often they fail. When the home team wins 6–4, it has "thumped" the opposition. When the home team loses 6–4, it has been "edged." Words have connotations as well as denotations; they imply more than they say. As long as reporters must work with words, complete objectivity is impossible. And even an "objective" reporter must decide whom to interview, what to ask, and which facts to include in his story. Fairness is a reasonable standard to ask of newsmen. Literal objectivity is not.

5. Advocacy. Underground editors and other committed journalists often complain that where one side is right and the other is wrong, objectivity is a false god. Was objectivity a good thing in the 1950s, when it forced the media to be "fair" to the self-serving allegations of Senator Joseph McCarthy? Journalists whose goal is advocacy, who wish to convince their readers of some point of view, have little use for objectivity.

6. Unusualness. Most editors urge their reporters to find stories that are distinctive, dramatic, or in some way unusual. If overused, this standard becomes more a definition of sensationalism than of news. If the media ignore what is typical and stress what is weird, they inevitably present us with a weird picture of the world. Nonetheless, "man bites dog" is still a bigger story than "dog bites man."

7. Relevance. Relevant news is important news. What kinds of stories are most relevant?—those that are local, timely, and directly useful to the audience. This standard, too, is sometimes overemphasized. The most local, timely, and useful stories around, after all, are the supermarket ads.

8. Completeness. The New York *Times* is the most complete news-paper in the country. Does that make it the best newspaper? For historical research, yes; for headline-skimming, no. A three-hour TV news show is hardly three times as good as a one-hour show, especially if you're waiting for a particular story. When we demand completeness, what we are really asking for is a sample of the news that is adequately large and appropriately varied. We are talking about selection.

9. Independence. However a medium selects its news, its judgments should be its own, and should not be influenced by outside pressures. If a newspaper kills a story because a big advertiser insists on it, then it is a poor newspaper—not because it killed the story (maybe it didn't deserve to run), but because it deferred to the wishes of an advertiser. Independence is absolutely essential for good journalism.

10. Propriety. The mass media have an obligation to keep within the bounds of propriety and good taste. But what are those bounds? Some businessmen think it's in poor taste to report declining sales figures. Some revolutionaries think it's in good taste to report do-it-yourself bomb-making techniques. Most editors disagree—on both counts.

11. Comprehensibility. As the world grows more complicated, it be-becomes less and less adequate for newsmen to stick to the facts in their reporting. The facts of Vietnam, the facts of inflation, the facts of racial and student unrest, are not the entire story of these events. Interpretation is essential to put the facts into a meaningful context, to make them comprehensible to the reader or viewer.

12. Uniqueness. Democracy is predicated on the assumption that all kinds of news and opinion are available to the public, competing in the free market of ideas. The trouble with this assumption is that most of the media today are not ideological competitors. They all say pretty much the same things, and that isn't healthy. We therefore propose the standard of uniqueness. Any mass medium that is significantly different from its competitors is by definition better than one that is undifferentiated. New York City is better off with both the *Times* and the *Daily News* than it would be with two papers like the *Times*. Offbeat media should be cherished.

We have listed a dozen standards. We could list a hundred, but this isn't the place for it. The point to be stressed here is that judgments of quality are meaningless without explicit criteria. Go ahead and criticize the mass media; you're as qualified as anyone else. But first make sure you know what your standards are.

15 Coverage
of Government

In theory, the mass media serve the public as independent watchdogs over government activities. In practice, this adversary relationship is difficult to maintain. Factors like friendship, news management, and secrecy make it hard. Routine makes it nearly impossible. The overworked Washington press corps and the even more overworked City Hall reporters have all they can do to report the activities of government. There is little manpower left over to investigate or criticize.

The heroic, hard-drinking "typical" newspaperman of the movies has a lot of flaws, but in at least one way he is ideal. His attitude toward government officials is magnificently suspicious and uncompromising. Inevitably, he winds up the third reel with a crusading exposé on the abuse of public trust by a public official—and to hell with the repercussions.

Critic William L. Rivers has a name for this attitude. He calls it "the adversary relationship," and he considers it the basis for all good coverage of government.[1] Every government official, Rivers explains, has a job to do—passing laws, running a federal agency, or whatever. Reporters also have a job to do—informing the public about everything that goes on within the government. Sometimes the reporter's job and the official's job coincide; they work together and everybody's happy. But sometimes their jobs come into conflict. Either the official wants to publish something that the reporter considers inaccurate or unnewsworthy, or the reporter wants to publish something that the official would prefer to keep secret. That's when the adversary relationship comes into play.

If the reporter goes along with the official's view on what should and should not be printed, then he is no longer a good reporter. He has abdicated his responsibility to act as the public's watchdog in Washington, or in City Hall. A good reporter, by definition, does not take official statements at face value. He refuses to protect the image of officeholders. He persists in asking embarrassing questions, and fights for the answers. He is, in short, an adversary.

The adversary relationship doesn't mean simply that reporters and government officials should get mad at each other occasionally. It means that they should both respect the inevitability—even the desirability—of conflict. Officials often have good reasons for hiding or distorting the truth, at least temporarily. Newsmen have good reasons for seeking the truth and releasing it to the public. For the adversary relationship to function properly, each must accept as valid the goals of the other. A government official who tells all is as bad as one who lies perpetually. A newsman who prints every piece of dirt is as bad as one who censors himself constantly.

It is worth stressing that the adversary relationship is a peculiarly American notion of the proper attitude of the media vis-à-vis the government. Throughout most of the world and most of history, the job of the media has been to publish whatever the government wants published. A good reporter in Seventeenth Century England or Twentieth Century Russia is defined as a reporter who gets the official line right and repeats it effectively.

Only in libertarian societies are the mass media a sort of "fourth branch of government," assigned the task of checking up on the other three branches. And only in a democracy must a good reporter be a hard-headed, two-fisted son-of-a-bitch—the kind of guy you might make a movie about.

BARRIERS TO ADVERSARITY

In the real world, as opposed to movies and theories, the adversary relationship has a tough time surviving. Many of the reasons for this will come up later in the chapter, but we will list some of the more important ones now.

1. Friendship. Most government reporters are specialists; they cover the Justice Department or City Hall or the Pentagon full-time. Specialization has many advantages, but one big disadvantage: The reporter is likely to become a close personal friend of his news sources. "The more you go out to dinner," said Drew Pearson, "the more friends you make and the more you diminish the number of people you can write about without qualms of conscience or rebukes from your wife."[2]   Friendly reporters seldom write embarrassing articles about their friends.

2. Sympathy.   Closely related to friendship is the sympathy that often develops between a reporter and his major sources. It is good for a newsman to understand the official's point of view, but if he understands it too well for too long he may come to accept it. It is for this reason that most New York newspapers impose a mid-season shuffle on the reporters who cover the Yankees and the Mets. Such a shuffle would do wonders for Washington coverage.

3. Dependence.   Government reporters depend on their sources for everything from front-page scoops to last-paragraph quotes. They are understandably reluctant to do anything to offend them. For years the Senate press corps overlooked the growing financial fortunes of Bobby Baker, a $19,000-a-year Senate employee. It was an outsider who got wind of the story, pursued it, and turned it into a national scandal. The Senate regulars viewed Baker as a vital source of information; they viewed the exposé as a nuisance.

4. Alliance.   Many a reporter starts out covering a government official and winds up working for him—unofficially. Washington is full of such part-time officials. They draft bills, guide press conferences, suggest handouts, and otherwise join in the process of governing. Their reporting, of course, suffers.

5. Complexity.   There was a time when most reporters understood (or thought they understood) most news. No longer. Today a government reporter must deal with more than politics. He must write about the intricacies of space flight, inflation, the arms race, air pollution, and hundreds of similar topics. To make sense of these issues, he relies heavily on the help of government experts. It is hard to be aggressive and independent in covering a story you don't understand to start with.

THE GROUND RULES

When a news source agrees to talk to a reporter, it is the source, not the reporter, who decides the rules of the game. Over the years, a number of interview "conventions" have developed in Washington—and have been widely copied on the local level. If he wants his interview, a reporter is obliged to obey these conventions.

Direct quotation. This is the most open (and still the most common) of the categories. The reporter may quote the source verbatim and by name, with no restrictions.

Not for direct quotation. Interviews in this category may be attributed to their source, but must be paraphrased instead of quoted. Prior to television, many Presidents held "not for direct quotation" press conferences; if their statements backfired they could always claim that wasn't quite what they meant. Lesser officials still resort to this convention for the same reason.

Not for attribution. This convention permits the reporter to quote his source directly, but not by name. Instead, he must attribute the remarks to "a reliable official," or "a State Department spokesman," or "persons close to the President." The "not for attribution" interview is an ideal way to launch a trial balloon or a leak (see p. 146). Those in the know can usually figure out who opened his mouth, but the public is kept completely in the dark.

Background. A reporter at a backgrounder may print everything he hears, but he dare not even imply that he *has* a source, much less give the source's name. This convention is often used by lower-level government employees who want to attack a policy without losing their jobs, and by higher-level officials who want to test public reaction to an undeclared policy. Official Washington is often as ignorant as the public of the source of a backgrounder.

Off the record. This is the convention of greatest secrecy. Reporters at "off the record" briefings may not publish what they hear, even anonymously. Officials use this device to keep newsmen up to date on developing stories. They also use it to plug leaks. One reporter emerged from an exclusive interview with President Theodore Roosevelt and told his colleagues: "I've just seen the President. He told me everything I knew already, and all that I was preparing to write—but he pledged me to secrecy on every fact I had, and now I can't write the blooming story."[3]

The value of the interview conventions is obvious. They offer the conscientious government official a middle ground between complete openness and complete secrecy. It is fair to say that many important stories would never reach the public at all if it were not for the conventions.

Their danger is just as obvious. Take backgrounders, for example. Alfred Friendly, managing editor of the Washington *Post,* points out that backgrounders are useful "when a person of considerable importance or delicate position is discussing a matter in circumstances in which his name cannot be used for reasons of public policy or personal vulnerability." Fair enough. But Friendly adds that backgrounders are also used "by persons who want to sink a knife or do a job without risking their own position or facing the consequences to themselves."[4] The other interview conventions are similarly useful—and similarly abused.

6. Secrecy. Government secrecy has already been discussed in considerable detail (see Chapter 6). All we need say here is that a reporter who tries to dig for the truth is very likely to run into an endless series of classified documents and closemouthed sources.

7. News Management. A large fraction of the public-relations men in the country are employed by government. Their job (see Chapter 6 and Chapter 14) is to manage the news in the best interests of their employer. A PR man is like a dam. The reporter who uses him as an information source saves a lot of time and effort. But it is the PR man who manages the flow of news; he can drown the reporter with facts or make him die of thirst. And behind the dam, he may be hiding the dirtiest water of all.

THE WASHINGTON PRESS CORPS

Washington D.C. is the news capital of the world, the Mecca for every ambitious political journalist. At this moment, there are more than 2,000 full-time reporters at work in Washington—the largest, most talented, and most experienced press corps anywhere.

It wasn't always that way. The first Washington correspondent reached the city in 1822. He was Nathaniel Carter of the New York *Statesman and Evening Advertiser,* and his job was to supply readers with "the latest intelligence of every description which can be obtained at the seat of government."[5] Carter was soon joined by others, but it wasn't until the Civil War that Washington became a really important source of news. By 1867 there were 49 correspondents listed in the Congressional Press Galleries.

As the government grew, so did the press corps. And so did the importance of news from Washington. Elmer E. Cornwell Jr. has analyzed six weeks worth of front pages from two newspapers (the New York *Times* and the Providence *Journal*) for every year from 1885 to 1957. Cornwell's sample for 1885 yielded 447 column inches of news about Congress and the President. By 1909 the figure had increased to 508 column inches. By 1925, it was up to 1,235 column inches. And in 1933, the height of the Depression, it reached an incredible 1,914 column inches.[6]

Today's figure is probably somewhat lower—but not much. Two thousand reporters can cover a lot of news.

The size of the Washington press corps is a mixed blessing. Public officials couldn't grant personal interviews to 2,000 men even if they wanted to. Instead, they resort to mass press conferences—with batteries of microphones, shouted questions, and very little dialogue. In this impersonal, hurried environment, news management is much, much easier.

Even 2,000 men may not be enough. The vast majority of American newspapers and broadcast stations have no reporter in Washington. Of course the larger newspaper chains have their own Washington bureaus, as do the three broadcast networks. So do the newsmagazines, and several hundred of the top newspapers. Even so, most of the mass media depend on just two sources for all their Washington news: the Associated Press and United Press International.

AP, with 150 reporters, and UPI with 90, do their best to staff every executive department, subcommittee hearing, and diplomatic reception in Washington. Not surprisingly, they fail—there is simply too much to cover. The major events of the day get covered well enough, but the minor ones are rewritten from press releases, or ignored entirely. In 1959, AP had six reporters assigned to the Senate and five to the House of Representatives. But only one man was available to cover the Treasury Department, the Commerce Department, and the Federal Reserve Board. Inevitably, he missed a lot of stories, and seldom had time to dig beneath the surface of any. "When I went to Washington," recalls a former AP bureau chief, "I had seventeen men. When I left I had seventy-seven. And the whole time I was there, I was one man short."[7]

Besides covering the news for those media without their own Washington correspondents, the wire services also backstop the media that have their own men. A newspaper with one or two Washington reporters wants more for its investment than a duplication of the wires. The Podunk *Gazette's* Washington correspondent may spend his days covering one big story in detail. Or he may concentrate on items of local interest, like the activities of Podunk's Congressman. He may even be asked to arrange invitations to prestigious parties for his publisher's friends when they come to visit. Whatever he does, he spends very little time at the Treasury Department, the Commerce Department, and the Federal Reserve Board. That kind of news is left to the wires.

What is the Washington press corps? It is dozens of men sweating it out in the White House press room, and one visit a year to the Federal Maritime Administration. It is CBS at a news conference, UPI rewriting a handout, *Newsweek* looking for color, and the New York *Times* on the trail of an exposé. It is a newspaper stringer interviewing a hometown businessman, invited to testify about the threat of cotton imports. It is an industrial lobbyist masquerading as a reporter for a trade magazine. It is a syndicated columnist telling the country what it ought to think about Cambodia. It is a Cambodian reporter telling his countrymen what they ought to think about Washington. It is a documentary film crew recording the nightlife at a fashionable party.

It is 2,000 newsmen covering the news capital of the world—doing the best job they can, a better job than we have any right to expect, but still a sorely inadequate job.

The two most thoroughly covered buildings in Washington are the White House and the Capitol. Literally hundreds of reporters are assigned the job of telling the country what the President and Congress are up to. Despite the vast amount of coverage that results, there are serious problems and gaps. News about the President is managed by the President's staff. News about Congress gets lost in the shuffle.

THE PRESIDENT AND THE PRESS

The President and Congress are engaged in a constant battle for newspaper space and broadcast times, each hoping to influence the public more than the other. Reporters have traditionally been quick to take advantage of this conflict, playing off one against the other in search of the best possible story. Reporters still play this game, but less successfully than ever before. Since the Roosevelt administration in the 1930s, the President has been the acknowledged winner of the battle. The White House is universally accepted as the most important news source in Washington, the nation, and the world. Congress must settle for second-best.

The American President is the most public of Chief Executives. His every action, word, and gesture is scrutinized, reported, and discussed by hundreds of journalists. This total lack of privacy must be a personal annoyance to the President, as well as interfering with his political and diplomatic flexibility. But it is also very valuable to him. To the extent that the President can influence what is written about him, he thereby influences public opinion. The President needs the press—and uses the press—to help him rally support for his programs, opposition for his enemies, and respect for his office. The history of President-press relations is the history of Presidential efforts to control the media.

For the first hundred years of American history, Presidents controlled the press by sponsoring their own newspapers. President John Adams offered the official Federalist party line in the *Gazette of the United States*. President Thomas Jefferson did the same for the Republicans in the *National Intelligencer*. Each administration supported its party papers with government advertising and joblot printing contracts. Opposition papers had to scrounge for private funds.

This state of affairs continued until 1860, when President-elect Lincoln refused to establish an official newspaper. Instead, he utilized the Government Printing Office, thus ending the use of printing contracts as hidden subsidies. Suddenly the President was on his own in his relations with reporters. During the Civil War, Henry Villard of the Associated Press became the first newsman assigned to cover the President full-time. A few years later, in the wake of Lincoln's assassination, Andrew

Johnson became the first President to be formally interviewed by an independent, unaligned reporter.

After the Civil War, Congress grew in importance and the Presidency declined. Press relations were casual. One reporter won a five dollar bet by ringing up President Grover Cleveland on the new telephone to ask if there was any news. Cleveland reportedly answered the phone himself, and told the reporter he could safely go to bed.

In the 1880s, public interest in the President began to rise again. The stage was set for a man who could capitalize on that interest to wrest control of the government from Congress. That man was Theodore Roosevelt.

Roosevelt was the first President to realize that he could manipulate the media to mold the public. He set up permanent White House quarters for the press. He permitted several reporters to interview him every day while he was being shaved. He ordered his secretary, William Loeb Jr., to act as press liaison. He invented the tactic of releasing news on Sunday to take advantage of the wide-open Monday-morning front page. Comments Elmer E. Cornwell Jr.: "T.R. did not just provide bully entertainment for an enthralled public, but dramatized the potential of the office for affecting the course of public policy by means of a dynamic relationship with the electorate via the mass media."[8]

Roosevelt knew how to take the press off the scent of an embarrassing story. When T.R. backed a Panamanian revolution against Colombia in an effort to get the Canal Zone, the opposition press began to growl. So the President immediately ordered all military men in Washington to get out and run in the park as part of a physical fitness program. The hilarious misadventures of pot-bellied generals and admirals kept the press corps busy for a week—by which time it had forgotten all about the Canal Zone.

Presidential press relations after Roosevelt are characterized by three tactics: the press conference, the press secretary, and direct use of the broadcast media.

THE PRESS CONFERENCE

The Presidential press conference was invented by Woodrow Wilson as a way of giving every reporter a chance and still leaving time in the day for other matters. At first it worked out very well for everybody. Though Wilson held a few "background" discussions to explain his views on pending legislation, most of his press conferences were on the record. They were scheduled twice a week and were open to all accredited reporters.

Franklin Roosevelt made great use of Wilson's invention, holding over 900 press conferences in his thirteen years in office. Unlike Wilson,

F.D.R. refused to be quoted directly. But he was unfailingly frank and open with reporters, often devoting an entire conference to a single topic. At this point, the press conference was still a convenience for both the reporter and the President.

Then came Truman. Faced with an increasingly huge press corps, including more and more foreign journalists, Truman gradually abandoned Roosevelt's easygoing press conference style. He stopped doing much backgrounding, stopped concentrating on a single topic in each conference, and stopped chatting informally with reporters before and after. Everything became much more formal. A reporter would rise, state his question, and sit; the President would carefully recite his answer, then turn to the next reporter.

The crowning blow came in 1951, when Truman began taping his press conferences for release to radio. Forced to weigh every word for its possible effects, Truman made the conferences even less lively, less useful than before. He ignored the information needs of the press and public, and concentrated on making a good performance. The press conference was becoming a tool of news management.

Two new wrinkles were added in the Eisenhower years. First, Ike began using the first few minutes of each half-hour conference to read a prepared statement, encouraging reporters to stress that statement in their articles. Second, Eisenhower had his press secretary, James Hagerty, arrange for friendly reporters to ask the questions the President wanted to answer. Both the prepared statement and the planted question have since become press conference staples.

The Kennedy administration was the first to permit live television broadcasts of press conferences, and this too has become standard procedure. Television has reduced the reporter to a participant in a stage show. It is not unusual to see newspapermen at press conferences not bothering to take notes; many readers will see the thing on TV anyhow, and a complete transcript will be available minutes after the end. It is also quite common for reporters to ask pointless questions simply in order to be seen on TV asking a question.

Woodrow Wilson scheduled his press conferences regularly, but no President since Truman has felt obliged to do so. Truman, by the way, averaged 3.8 press conferences per month. Eisenhower held 2.0 per month, and Kennedy held 1.8 per month.[9] In his first two years in office, President Nixon held precisely thirteen press conferences.

Today, press conferences are scheduled at the President's pleasure, and are conducted according to the President's rules. The ingredients are now pretty well standardized: a big room, hundreds of reporters, dozens of cameras and microphones, a prepared statement, several planted questions with prepared answers, and perhaps four or five spontaneous questions with no discussion and no follow-up. Little wonder Tom

Wicker of the New York *Times* calls the press conference "more an instrument of Presidential power than a useful tool of the press."[10]

THE PRESS SECRETARY

While President Wilson conducted his twice-weekly press conferences, Joseph P. Tumulty (Wilson's advisor) held daily briefings for reporters. From that time on, Presidents came to rely more and more on their press secretaries.

So did reporters. From 1933 to 1945, President Roosevelt's press secretaries were never once quoted in the media. Truman's press secretaries were quoted only once. But James Hagerty, Eisenhower's press secretary, was named hundreds of times as a source of news about the President.[11] And the names of later press secretaries—Pierre Salinger, George Christian, Bill Moyers, Ron Ziegler—were as well known to the public as those of the more prominent Senators and cabinet officials.

As the number of Presidential press conferences has declined, the importance of the press secretary has soared. Nixon was the first President to split the job in half. Herb Klein, the White House Director of Communications, coordinates the PR effort, while press secretary Ron Ziegler meets with reporters almost hourly to answer questions and issue releases. The average White House correspondent writes at least a story a day. Yet he is lucky if he sees the President once a month. The bulk of the news about Nixon comes, not from Nixon, but from Ziegler and Klein.

The job of the press secretary is a tricky one. He dare not antagonize the press corps or justify charges of a "credibility gap." So he tries to be genuinely useful. He answers factual questions, helps set up interviews with Presidential assistants, and even uses his influence to get important stories released on time. But his first allegiance is, of course, to the President.

The most talented press secretary of our time was probably James Hagerty. One of his favorite tricks was to release good news from the White House, bad news from anyplace else. A State Department triumph, for example, would always be announced by the President himself; a State Department flop would be announced by the State Department.

Hagerty always held back a few middling stories—the appointment of a new ambassador, say—for the inevitable day when Eisenhower would take off on a golfing trip. Russell Baker explains the ploy:

> If editors demanded a Presidential story a day, it follows that reporters will be found to satisfy them one way or another. On days when there is no news, they will poke around darkened rooms, look under the carpet, or start staring at the west wall and adding two and two in news stories. When that sort of thing happens, the White House is in trouble.

Hagerty prevented this by seeing to it that there was rarely a newsless day. If there was no news, he made a little.[12]

There is nothing especially evil about these techniques. But they *are* news management. The press secretary *is* the President's man.

LIVE AND IN COLOR

Franklin Roosevelt was the first President to demand a chunk of broadcast time to speak directly to the public without a reporter in the middle. Roosevelt averaged only two or three radio "fireside chats" a year—yet their effect on public confidence and support was substantial.

By the Eisenhower years, television was available for the same purpose. Yet both Eisenhower and Kennedy used TV only for emergencies, such as the Cuban missile crisis of 1961. Presidents Johnson and Nixon adopted a different approach. Both men resorted to television regularly to circumvent the questions and interpretations of the press corps. Nixon, for example, took to the air 25 times in his first 22 months in office. In January of 1970, he became the first President ever to deliver a routine veto message (an HEW appropriations bill) live and in color.

Historian Clinton Rossiter claims that immeasurable power has flowed from Congress to the President because of the latter's ability to reach the people directly via television.[13] Certainly no other government official can command such use of the public air waves. In the summer of 1970, several antiwar Congressmen sought a remedy to this Presidential monopoly. They petitioned the Federal Communications Commission for reply time to the President under the fairness doctrine. The networks granted the time before the FCC could act—leaving the issue unresolved.

If Congress has grounds for griping about Presidential TV appearances, so does the press corps. When the President goes directly to the public, he runs the show. It is hard for a reporter to be an adversary when he isn't even there.

Presidents are so accustomed to running the broadcast show that they do so even when it isn't their show. In 1967, President Johnson submitted to an interview with the three network White House correspondents. Several times during the videotaping, Johnson stopped the questioning and asked for a playback, to see how he was coming across. Later, the President issued a steady stream of instructions on which parts should be edited out and which should be left in. CBS and ABC protested. At first, they were told that Johnson was worried about national security; then the White House admitted that some of his statements were politically sensitive. When the interview was finally broadcast, only CBS told its viewers that it had been edited under White House supervision.[14]

QUESTION PERIOD

Four days a week, from 2:30 to 3:30, the British House of Commons comes alive. Every important government official, including the Prime Minister, is expected to be on hand to answer whatever questions the Members of Parliament may care to ask.

The rules are quite formal. Questions must be submitted in writing at least two days in advance, to give each Minister a chance to prepare. A Member is limited to three questions, plus "supplementaries" or follow-ups. Members may not make speeches, ask hypothetical questions, slander individuals, or raise broad policy issues that cannot be answered quickly. Aside from that, anything goes.

It is an appealing system. On the very day Sir Anthony Eden ordered the Suez invasion in 1956, he had to stand for questions about the policy. An American President, by contrast, would have been unavailable for comment, or at best would have appeared on television with a prepared speech. It seems strange to us to have Members of Parliament performing the adversary function which in this country is reserved for newsmen. But the system works. The debate is lively and informative—and widely reported in the press. Parliament gets more unmanaged information out of the Prime Minister in a week than American journalists can extract from the President in a month.

PRESIDENTIAL COVERAGE

The President of the United States receives more attention from more newsmen than any other person in the world. Unfortunately, it is the President himself who controls that attention, who decides what is to be covered and what is to be hidden or ignored. Through press conferences, press secretaries, and television appearances, the President is in an ideal position to manage the news.

Within these constraints, the President receives superlative news coverage. Almost every item on his daily schedule is turned into a news story of some sort. Almost every political move is carefully examined and dissected. Almost every statement, however trivial, is recorded for posterity. Almost every legislative proposal is reported in depth. There is very little that the American public does not know about its President— except what the President does not want it to know.

On December 8, 1969, President Richard Nixon held one of his infrequent televised press conferences. The following morning, Tom Wicker of the New York *Times* catalogued the President's misstatements of fact during the conference. Nixon stated that U.S. Marines in Vietnam had built over 250,000 churches, pagodas, and temples; in reality, they had built 117 churches and 251 schools. Nixon stated that it would cost the government $70 to $80 billion a year to guarantee a minimum annual income of $5,400; in reality, that cost would run about $20 billion a year. Nixon stated that there were no American combat troops in Laos; in reality, there were Air Force bombers, CIA agents, and Army personnel to support the native forces.[15] Some of these discrepancies may result from differing interpretations of the facts. Others must be errors, if not lies, on the part of the President.

The point is this. Only the small minority who read Tom Wicker's column had a chance to consider these discrepancies. The vast majority who watched the press conference on TV knew nothing about them. Such is the power of Presidential news management.

But there is another point. The New York *Times* did, after all, print the Wicker column, and syndicated it to other newspapers across the country. The adversary relationship may be fighting a losing battle against Presidential news management—but it hasn't lost yet.

CONGRESS AND THE PRESS

The United States has only one President—but it has 535 Congressmen. This simple fact has several important implications. For one thing, it makes it extremely difficult for a Congressman to manage the news as the President does. For another, it puts every Congressman in competition with every other Congressman for the limited amount of available publicity. And Congressmen *need* publicity. They need it to get re-elected in their districts; they need it to gain stature as possible candidates for higher office; they need it to bring their views to the attention of the President and the party leaders. The Capitol Hill reporter, unlike the White House correspondent, is operating in a buyer's market for news.

This is not to say that Senators and Representatives have no use for public-relations men. Nearly every Congressman, in fact, has a press secretary of one sort or another. But it's a different job. The President's press secretary does his best to manage the news. A Congressional press secretary struggles merely to get into the news. One Senator summed it up this way: "Remember, there is only one evil thing the press can do to you—it may not mention you."[16]

Congressmen are so desperate for media attention that they often tailor their activities to the apparent preferences of reporters. James Reston comments:

> The influence of reporters on the conduct of individual members of the House and Senate, particularly the House, is much greater than is

generally realized. For example, if reporters tend to play up the spectacular charges or statements of extremists on Capitol Hill and to play down or ignore the careful, analytical speeches of the more moderate and responsible members—as, unfortunately, they do most of the time—this inevitably has its influence on many other members, particularly new members. . . . [T]he new Congressman often draws the obvious conclusion and begins spouting nonsense to attract attention.[17]

Congressmen need the media at least as much as the media need Congressmen.

The days when reporters were unwelcome on Capitol Hill are long gone. The House of Representatives opened its doors to newsmen in 1789; the Senate followed suit in 1795. There were occasional squabbles in the early 1800s, but by 1841 the right of reporters to roam freely through the Capitol was well established.

Except for some slight discrimination against the black and underground press, any legitimate newsman from any country may apply for a Congressional press card. Once admitted, he is treated like visiting royalty. The press gallery hovers directly over the presiding officer's desk in both Houses, providing a box-seat view of the proceedings. Wire service reporters have special muted telephones within the chambers themselves. Pages are available for newsmen who wish to summon Congressmen from their seats for interviews or off-the-record consultations. And few Congressmen ignore such a summons.

Behind the press gallery, reporters have an extensive suite of rooms for work and relaxation, with staff assistants whose salaries are paid by the government. Every possible piece of equipment—from typewriters to reference books to swank leather couches—is provided for the convenience of the press. Symbolic of the easy access of newsmen to Congressional news is a sign over one of the elevators in the House wing of the Capitol. It reads: "Reserved for Members and the Press."[18]

Broadcasters are more limited than the print media in their coverage of Congress. Only on special occasions, such as a State of the Union address, are cameras permitted on the floor. Nevertheless, there is very little going on in Congress that reporters don't know about—even if they can't take pictures of it.

Although the Capitol press corps knows just about all there is to know about Congress, the public does not. There are several categories of Congressional news that are seldom if ever adequately covered:

1. The serious, uninflammatory policy speeches of Congressmen, especially members of the House.
2. The content of important laws that are passed without controversy.
3. The political deals and hypocrisies of Congressmen, who say one thing in their speeches and another in their votes.

CONGRESSIONAL COMMITTEES

The most important vehicle for Congressional news management is the committee, where the real work of Congress is accomplished. It is in committee that bills are written and political deals are consummated, with everything neatly settled before the floor show begins. Such committee sessions take place behind closed doors; the press is seldom invited.

Congressional investigating committees, on the other hand, not only invite the press; they stage the whole show with the press in mind. In theory, Congressional investigations are supposed to collect information for use in the legislative process. In practice, the main purpose of many investigations is publicity. The late Senator Joseph McCarthy built his reputation as a fearsome hunter of Communists primarily through his activities as chairman of the Senate Permanent Investigating Subcommittee. The committee investigation is the closest Congress can come to the news management potential of a Presidential press conference.

---

4. The activities of lobbyists and their influence on Congressional action.
5. The personal peccadilloes of Congressmen—arrests, sexual assaults, drunkenness, marital problems, etc.

Some of these lapses can be attributed to broad media problems that have nothing to do with Congress—the emphasis on action and controversy instead of underlying issues, for example. But most of the failures of the Capitol press corps are a direct result of the peculiar relationship that develops between Congressmen and reporters. It is a relationship characterized by mutual dependence and mutual esteem.

After a few years on the Hill, a Congressional correspondent is likely to develop close friendships with his main news sources. He jokes with them, parties with them, literally lives with them day in and day out. He may even work with them—helping them to draft bills, then following through with the necessary publicity. It is not wholly unknown to find reporters at the Capitol who hold down part-time jobs as press secretary to some Congressman. Not surprisingly, veteran Congressional reporters eventually start thinking like Congressmen.

The Capitol press corps does a fine job of covering the sensational but nonadversary side of Congress. No really big bill gets passed or defeated without an endless series of articles on who intends to vote which way for what reasons. The political jockeying of Republicans and Democrats is dutifully reported nearly every day. The opinions and activities of Congressional leaders are followed almost as closely as those of the President himself.

But when all is said and done, the public learns little about Congress that Congress doesn't want it to learn. The typical Congressman fights to get his name into the papers, not to keep it out. If his speeches are moderate, his committee work sound, his votes sensible, and his bills less than earth-shaking, he is very likely to go unnoticed. There are 535 Congressmen, but only one President.

Each arm of the government presents its own special problems for newsmen. The problems associated with the President and Congress have already been discussed. Supreme Court coverage is plagued by the quest for speed. Coverage of the executive agencies suffers from a dire shortage of manpower in the face of bushels of press releases. Reporters covering state government are lacking in specialized training. Friendships and "civic boosterism" hinder aggressive coverage of local government.

THE SUPREME COURT

Monday is Supreme Court day. At precisely 10 a.m., the Court goes into session, the week's opinions are read aloud, and printed copies are distributed. By noon it's all over for another week.

There are few news beats more clearly defined than this one. Reporters are not allowed to interview the Justices. They write their stories from court-supplied background material, briefs, and the printed opinions, period. This is such a difficult assignment that no more than 35 or 40 newsmen appear regularly enough to rate term passes. The vast majority of the print and broadcast media rely exclusively on the wire services for their Court news.

The hallmark of wire service reporting is speed. On decision day, AP has three men assigned to the Court. One man sits in the courtroom, collects the written opinions, and shoots them via pneumatic tube to his colleagues below. The other two have the job of wading through thousands of words of legal jargon. They must identify the case, determine the decision, pinpoint the majority and minority opinions, select the quotes, and fill in the background—all in a matter of minutes. As always, AP tries frantically to beat UPI with the first bulletin. If a dissenting opinion gets muddled in the process, that's only to be expected.

There are some kinds of news where speed is a sensible goal—but it is doubtful that the Supreme Court is one of them. Most cases are pending for years before the Court reaches a decision; one would think the public could wait a few minutes more to find out what the decision was. It

takes a trained lawyer hours of careful checking to figure out the significance of a judicial opinion. Wire service reporters do the job in minutes.

Not surprisingly, they often make mistakes. In 1962, AP reported that
the Supreme Court had ruled that "a state or city may not interfere in
any fashion with peaceful racial integration demonstrations in public
places of business." This was simply wrong. The Court had actually
decided that a city which officially supported segregation could not prosecute Negroes for seeking service in privately owned stores. The decision
applied only to those areas where segregation was official policy.[19] Such
errors and misinterpretations are quite frequent.

AP General Manager Wes Gallagher has proposed that the Supreme
Court lock its doors on decision day—with the press corps inside. Half an
hour or so later, the doors would be opened, and everyone would be released at the same time. So far the Court has refused to go along. The
wire services would like to be forced to spend some time studying the
decisions. But neither is willing to do so voluntarily, and let the other
get the story on the teletype first.

The Supreme Court does not manage the news. It employs only one
press officer, who discusses the impact of various decisions with reporters
if they ask. If coverage of the Court is inadequate—and it is—the media
have no one to blame but themselves.

THE EXECUTIVE AGENCIES

More than ninety percent of the federal bureaucracy in Washington is
made up of the personnel of executive agencies—from the State Department and the Defense Department all the way down to the Food and
Drug Administration and the Civil Aeronautics Board. The job of these
agencies is to put into operation the policies dictated by the President
and Congress.

An overwhelming amount of news is generated each day by the executive agencies. Reporting that news aggressively and independently
would be a hard job for the entire Washington press corps. And the entire Washington press corps isn't available. Except for the Pentagon and
the State Department, agency assignments are the least glamorous of all.
The media count on the wire services for just about all their agency news.
And the wire services count on a handful of overworked reporters.

In manpower terms alone, the press is beaten before it begins. A
UPI reporter, say, assigned to cover the Departments of Labor, Commerce, and Agriculture, may get as many as 40 handouts a day from the
three departments. He has time to rewrite ten of them—if he doesn't
waste any time on additional research. Every telephone call to get more
information on one story means ignoring another story entirely. A really

careful look at one story means forgetting the whole rest of the day's events.

A second impediment to investigative coverage is the attitude of most civil servants toward the press. While Congressmen and Presidents seek out publicity, most agency employees wouldn't mind if they never saw their names in print. They are polite and friendly with reporters, but suspicious and closemouthed. A few years ago, consumer affairs writer Trudy Lieberman of the Detroit *Free Press* asked the Agriculture Department for the names of manufacturers whose hot dogs exceeded the government limit of 30 percent fat. It took many weeks (and the combined efforts of Herb Klein, the American Society of Newspaper Editors, the Freedom of Information Center, and a formal appeal) to pry the list loose.[20]

Occasionally a disgruntled civil servant will tell reporters (often anonymously) about some agency action of which he disapproves. And even more occasionally a stubborn newsman will dig to the bottom of an agency story. But only the most important executive departments rate investigative coverage more than once or twice a year. The typical executive agency is lucky to get routine coverage.

According to one researcher, 22 percent of all news coming out of Washington can be traced to handouts from the executive agencies.[21] That still leaves hundreds of handouts that are never made into news stories at all. As for investigative reporting, newsmen covering the agencies simply haven't got the time.

STATE GOVERNMENT

In many ways, news coverage of state government is like coverage of Congress. According to a Rutgers University seminar of leading state legislators, statehouse reporters tend to focus on the superficial side of government. They are preoccupied with scandal, and unduly attracted to the antics of publicity-minded celebrities.[22]

Moreover, state government reporters are even more likely than Congressional correspondents to begin thinking like their sources. Most state capitals are small towns, physically and emotionally. Officials and reporters work together and play together; they eat at the same restaurants, drink at the same bars, and live in the same hotels. The following admission from an Oregon newsman is probably typical of the views of his colleagues:

> I wouldn't report it if a member were drunk all session . . . so long as he was doing a good job for the state. I wouldn't report it, I mean, unless . . . somebody else would, so it would become general knowl-

edge anyway. Or if I knew a legislator was getting his liquor from the dog-race lobbyists, I wouldn't write that up . . . I'd have to tell all the good about him—all the good things he's done—if I told the bad.[23]

In the past, access to information has been a major problem in the coverage of state government. This excuse is no longer adequate. Most states now have "freedom of information" laws guaranteeing reporters the right to look at official documents and attend official meetings. More than half the states permit newsmen to sit in on legislative committee hearings. And at least 14 states allow live broadcasts of legislative sessions. It is perfectly clear that the press corps knows what's going on in state government. If the public seldom finds out, reporters have only themselves to blame.

Cozying up to news sources is a big piece of the problem—but it is not the biggest piece. The fundamental reason for poor coverage of state government is manpower, pure and simple. Editors just don't believe the state capital is all that important. They send their best political reporters to Washington or to City Hall. They staff the statehouse with cynical old-timers who couldn't make it and inexperienced youngsters who have yet to try. And not *too* many of those. The New York *Times* has over thirty men in Washington—but only four men in Albany. Most New York papers get along with one man in Albany, or depend entirely on the wire services.

State government coverage combines the worst aspects of coverage of Congress and of the federal executive agencies. As with Congress, reporters are reluctant to offend their sources. As with the executive agencies, reporters are too busy to look into anything carefully. So exposés are rare, and even routine reporting is spotty.

LOCAL GOVERNMENT

In the summer of 1969, the Cincinnati *Enquirer* ran a series of articles entitled "The Movers and the Shakers." The series outlined precisely who ran the city and why, and was highly critical of many of the Republican friends of *Enquirer* publisher Francis Dale. What turned Dale into an anti-Establishment muckraker? It seems he was annoyed at his country-club cronies for refusing to back him as the Republican candidate for governor of Ohio. He authorized the series to get even.[24]

Some such ulterior motive is often at the root of what little hard-hitting local journalism there is.

On the whole, the mass media are not particularly interested in municipal government. One typical study of daily newspapers in Iowa found that several papers allotted more space to the Drew Pearson column every day than they gave to City Hall. Very little local government news ever made the front page, and such important offices as City Clerk, City Attorney, City Treasurer, and City Engineer were almost completely ignored. Even the editorials on local issues were devoid of facts.[25] The only municipal agency that is *always* fully covered is the Police Department.

Bad though it is, newspaper coverage of City Hall is exemplary compared to the job done by the rest of the media. The wire services, which backstop everyone else in Washington and the state capital, are almost useless on the local level. As a rule they are content to rewrite the front page of the best paper in town.

And the broadcast media are content to rewrite the wire services. Few if any stations have a large enough staff to cover City Hall on a regular basis. They show up—cameras, microphones, and all—for scheduled press conferences, period. Even in cities that permit TV cameras in City Council meetings and the like, it takes a major controversy to attract the interest of broadcasters. Except for educational stations, televising a routine meeting is out of the question. Even sending a crew for a few minutes of news footage is a rare investment of time and manpower.

In 1968, the newspapers of San Francisco went out on strike. During the blackout, only three or four newsmen showed up each morning for Mayor Joseph Alioto's press briefing. And *they* were from the struck newspapers! Despite the strike, nobody from the city's radio and TV stations attended the conference on a regular basis. Hadley Roff, Alioto's press secretary at the time, notes that "the electronic media continued to act simply in response to our alarms. When we told them something big was coming up, they responded. Otherwise, nothing."[26]

When municipal government is covered, the coverage is often unbearably dull. Stuart A. Dunham of the Camden (N.J.) *Courier-Post* describes it as "a vast gray monotony, lit only occasionally by a spark of interest." News about City Hall, he says, is inevitably written "in the terms of procedure and in the language of city ordinances."[27] Readers naturally shy away from such articles—and editors respond by cutting down the size of the City Hall bureau.

LOCAL ADVERSARITY

What is lacking in local government coverage (aside from enthusiastic reporters with enough space to tell the story right) is a sense of the adversary relationship. A study of 88 newspapers in Minnesota revealed the startling fact that most editors saw themselves as promoters of civic virtue. Few thought they ought to serve as "watchdogs" over government, and only two discussed the regular reporting of local controversy.

Most wanted to put their best foot forward—and the best foot of their communities.[28]

In 1961, Robert Judd investigated the attitudes of West Coast reporters toward government officials. The reporters, he found, were content to act as "passive gatekeepers" between the officials and their editors. They emphatically denied the existence—or desirability—of any sort of adversary relationship.[29] No doubt the officials were in complete agreement.

Civic Boosterism is the name of the game. In 1968, *McCall's* magazine ran an article on the quality of American drinking water. The article named 102 cities whose water supplies were rated as only "provisionally approved" by the U.S. Public Health Service. For newspapers in those 102 cities, it was a big story. Eighty percent of the papers covered it, and half of them ran two or more articles on the subject.

But how did they cover it? Only one paper in five contacted the Public Health Service for comment. Only one in five discussed the matter with local water pollution experts. And a grand total of two reporters got in touch with the *McCall's* author for clarification.

Four-fifths of the papers built their articles around the reactions of local waterworks officials—the sources least likely to admit a problem. The Topeka (Kansas) *Daily Capital* was typical of this approach. It left unchallenged this statement from the local superintendent of utilities: "For this guy to pick on our water supply, I am inclined to think he doesn't know what is going on. . . . I just can't see how some guy can come out and say something like this. This is the same water I drink, that I give my wife and kids—even my dog." The vast majority of the papers responded to the *McCall's* article as an insult to their cities. They set out to discredit the article—not to examine the issue.[30]

Throughout most of the world, the mass media are considered essentially a tool of the government. The United States is nearly unique in the role it assigns to the media: not only to tell the public what government officials are saying, but also to tell the public what government officials are doing—even if the officials would rather the public didn't know. The media in America are expected to inform the people so that the people can select and instruct the officials.

Perhaps this is too much to expect. Limited by news management, friendship with sources, civic boosterism, understaffing, and other factors, it is hard enough for the media to do an adequate job of routine reporting. Independent and aggressive journalism often is out of the question. Too frequently, the public's watchdog winds up thumping its tail to the government's music.

But until the media are released from this responsibility, they must live up to it. Walter Lippmann said it thus:

> The tension between elected officials and the working press is not a deplorable inconvenience. . . . It is at the very heart of the American

system of government. For in the absence of this tension it may be perfectly possible for an elected official to . . . manipulate the press and prevent it from making an independent audit of the conduct of affairs.[31]

Perhaps the standard is impossibly high. The American media have met it better than those of any other country in the world. But they have failed nonetheless.

News coverage of political campaigns is spotty. The media recognize elections as perhaps the most important of all recurring stories. But despite massive coverage, there are glaring omissions, and underlying issues

---

A MAVERICK GOES UNDER

To find the adversary relationship in a local context, you have to look at the mavericks—underground papers, urban weeklies, and an occasional courageous editor.

Gene Wirges of the Morrilton (Arkansas) *Democrat* was such an editor. In the fall of 1960, Wirges noticed that local candidates supported by the Conway County Democratic "machine" always won their races on the strength of the absentee ballots. In one typical election, a reform school-board candidate led the "live" votes by a margin of 200 to 132—but the absentee votes went 143 to 9 for the machine candidate, making him a winner. Wirges suspected fraud. He began looking closely at the Conway County government, and he published what he found. An otherwise placid weekly, the *Democrat* became an investigative tiger.

Harrassment began in June of 1961. First the prosecuting attorney announced that charges would be filed against Wirges for double-mortgaging his paper. Wirges was able to prove his innocence. Then the state government charged that he was $600 behind in his unemployment insurance payments. A deputy sheriff immediately posted a notice that the paper would be sold at public auction to cover the debt. Wirges got in touch with the state employment office, and the auction was postponed. Next, the machine organized an advertiser boycott of the *Democrat,* and urged the paper's reporters to resign. Wirges did without advertisers and reporters.

What finally nailed him was two libel suits, brought by members of the machine, and tried before a machine judge. The County Clerk sued for $100,000 and was awarded $75,000. A County Judge sued for $200,000 and was awarded the full $200,000.

Both verdicts would probably have been overturned by a higher court, but Wirges couldn't afford the appeal. On November 26, 1963, the *Democrat* was sold to pay the libel judgments.[32]

---

are seldom adequately discussed. The average American learns more about the candidates through campaign advertisements than he does through the news.

PUBLIC OPINION

The American government pays more attention to public opinion than any other government in the world. It always has. Back in 1837, European visitor Harriet Martinu wrote that "the worship of Opinion is, at this day, the established religion of the United States."[33] Many visitors since have made the same observation.

Every American politician, however independent he may secretly be, justifies his actions on the basis of public opinion. He may do his best first to manipulate public opinion so that it supports his views. But if he cannot change the public, he will usually change his own views. At the very least, he will keep them hidden. It is extremely rare for an American political figure to declare: "Most people disagree, but *I* believe thus-and-such!"

The mass media are crucial to this entire process. It is through the media that a government official tries to sway public opinion. It is through the media that he learns whether or not he has succeeded. And it is through the media that the public finds out where he stands, or at least where he says he stands. The greatest amount of communication of this sort takes place around election time, as the public prepares to pick its government.

Though public opinion is King in America, it often seems a blind King. In 1970, one California Congressman easily won re-election to his tenth consecutive term. A poll taken just before the election revealed that after 18 years fewer than half the voters knew his name. Findings like this one may call into question the viability of democracy as a system of government. Certainly they call into question the adequacy of the performance of the mass media.

PICKING THE CANDIDATES

Long before the campaign begins, the media are busy picking the candidates, acting as a combination "handicapper" and "scout." Some politicians are ignored or rejected. Others are identified for the public as political "comers."

Political satirist Russell Baker calls the media "The Great Mentioner." It was The Great Mentioner that first suggested George Romney as an ideal Republican Presidential candidate for 1968. And it was The Great

Mentioner that ruled Romney out of the race after he claimed he had been "brainwashed" by the U.S. military in Vietnam. Similarly, the Presidential aspirations of Senator Edward Kennedy have risen and fallen twice as The Great Mentioner gave or withheld approval.

Then come the two nominating conventions, when the politicians get to choose among the candidates the media have anointed. The conventions are television's Roman Circus. CBS and NBC spend over $5 million apiece on convention coverage, only a third of which is recouped through commercials. They take the loss willingly to pyramid the prestige of their entire news operations. The average TV viewer spends a total of 15 hours watching the two conventions—a very impressive hunk of time.

It's as impressive to the politicians as it is to the networks. Convention time is the politicians' greatest single opportunity to attract the attention and approval of the voters. Not surprisingly, they gear the spectacle to meet the needs of television. They put their best foot forward—and the foot has pancake makeup on it. One critic comments:

> Actually, television is in a trap at a political convention. If it agreed just to point its cameras at the surface of events in the hall, the politicians would press their opportunity to put on a self-serving show. When television plunges in to try to find such real news as subsurface deals and dissent, its legions stir up commotion, and the coverage is often illusory anyway. The real decision-making is almost always hidden from the cameras. What we see for the most part is television covering the public version of private arrangements.[34]

There is little doubt that this criticism is accurate. And yet, television convention watchers do get occasional glimpses of the realities of politics. And when the party machine breaks down, as it did in 1968 at the Democratic convention in Chicago, the glimpses are likely to be more than occasional. The selection of Presidential candidates is not a wholly public procedure, and probably it never will be. But it is a great deal more public than the selection of state and local candidates—largely because state and local conventions are not covered by television.

COVERING THE CAMPAIGN

The mass media are not the most important influence on voting decisions. Family background, economic status, geographical location, and other demographic factors are far better predictors of an individual's vote than what he reads in the papers or sees on TV. But most elections are decided by a small "swing vote" which is able to overcome demographics and change its mind during the campaign. And swing voters are greatly influenced by the media.

Even the average voter may be significantly affected by media content. A 1969 study found that 70 percent of American adults make regular use of television for information on candidates and campaigns; 50 percent use newspapers and 25 percent turn to magazines.[35] An earlier study, completed in 1960, revealed that four-fifths of all Americans learned more about national election campaigns from newspapers and television than from interpersonal conversation.[36] It is still quite likely that most Americans are more influenced by their friends than by the media when it comes to political opinions and attitudes (see p. 5), but political information appears to come largely from the media.

Traditionally, the media have been as unfair in election coverage as they thought they could get away with. In 1952, for example, several researchers found that newspapers that supported Eisenhower on their editorial page tended to give him more and better coverage on their news pages as well. Papers that supported Stevenson were equally biased in favor of their candidate. Since there were many more Republican than Democratic papers, this raised a serious ethical problem.

The problem is much less important today. Guido H. Stempel studied campaign coverage in 15 metropolitan dailies for 1960 and 1964, and found that both parties were given roughly equal news space.[37] The same was true in 1968; even third party candidate George Wallace was treated fairly.[38] Of course there are still some publishers left who let their editorial bias show on their news pages (see p. 100 for an especially flagrant example). Campaign coverage is probably less fair in the smaller papers than in the bigger ones, and less fair in local races than in national ones. But bias is no longer the biggest problem in campaign coverage.

Of course the editorial endorsements themselves are biased; they're meant to be. And Republican candidates still have a near-monopoly on newspaper endorsements. These can be enormously influential in small, relatively unpublicized elections. Between 1948 and 1962, California newspapers endorsed the winning candidate in local elections 84 percent of the time. They picked the winning state senator 65 percent of the time, and the winning state assemblyman 63 percent of the time.[39]

But the more news coverage a particular election receives, the less difference it makes who gets the publisher's endorsement. Today, television is by far the most important source of election news—and the vast majority of TV stations don't endorse any candidate at all. As long as the news coverage is fair and extensive, we can safely ignore the influence of endorsements. And for major races, at least, most election news coverage today is both fair and extensive.

Unfortunately, it is also pretty poor. Rarely does a newspaper article or a television program undertake to compare the qualifications of the candidates or their views on the issues of the campaign. Broadcasters claim that the equal time rule (see p. 198) makes this difficult or impos-

THE CAMPAIGN TRAIL

The conditions of campaign coverage haven't changed much in the last century or two. The following is a tongue-in-cheek excerpt from "Rules of the Road," written by a group of reporters and found among the papers of William Jennings Bryan after the election of 1896.[40]

> *Working Hours.* Nature requiring a certain amount of rest for the recuperation of the faculties, twenty-one hours is fixed as a working day for members of this party. To insure the enforcement of this regulation the Associated Correspondents agree that no record shall be made of speech, reception, bon-fire, salute, or any other occurrence between the hours of 1:30 a.m. and 4:30 a.m. No walking delegate shall have power to abrogate this regulation.
>
> *Home Offices.* Home offices shall be treated with the consideration due their isolated position, and a chain of communication shall be kept up which will insure hearing from the cashier once in a while. Inquiries from news editors regarding lost dispatches, reminders that the Sunday paper goes to press yesterday afternoon, and requests to interview Bryan on the charge that he robbed his grandmother's orchard, shall be answered by letter the day after the election.
>
> *Creature Comforts.* All members of this party shall be entitled to three triangular meals a day, subject to appetites of local reception committeemen. Sandwiches from railway eating houses shall be used as mortars for the cannon from which salutes are fired. Campaign cigars shall be smoked only on the open prairies.
>
> *Straw Votes.* To discourage the straw vote fiend, the poll of the correspondents shall be reported as follows:

> To supporters of Bryan—
> McKinley and Hobart   .   .   .   16
> Bryan and Sewall   1
> To supporters of McKinley—
> Bryan and Sewall   16
> McKinley and Hobart   .   .   .   1

sible to do. Newspapermen have no such excuse; they simply don't bother.

Instead of examining the underlying issues, the media cover election campaigns the way they cover sporting events. Candidate X gains a few points by attracting the support of a certain labor union. Candidate Y recovers by claiming his opponent is soft on the crime issue, and pulls ahead with an aggressive speech at a Rotary luncheon. Candidate X gets back into the game by swimming in a polluted river to dramatize his devotion to the environment. And so on, right up to election day. The media dutifully report charges and counter-charges, proposals and counter-proposals, pseudoevents and more pseudoevents. The public learns more about the imaginations of the competing campaign managers than it does about the qualifications and intentions of the candidates.

It is almost as if the newspaper reader and the television viewer were not voters at all, but rather disinterested observers of the political process. The media offer us an incredibly detailed blow-by-blow account of the campaign. They keep us right up-to-the-minute on who's winning and how. But they tell us almost nothing about who ought to win, about how the world might change if one candidate won instead of the other. As amateur political scientists, we can learn a lot from the media. As voters, we can learn little.

The clearest sign of this emphasis on who-will-win instead of who-should-win is the media's preoccupation with pre-election polls. Polls tell us absolutely nothing about the candidates, and theoretically they should be of zero interest to voters. Yet the public demands to know who's ahead, and the media cheerfully comply.

The accuracy of a poll depends on the size of the sample, the wording of the questions, and dozens of other factors. The media offer us few clues. In 1966, the New York *Times* ran a story entitled "Which Poll Do You Read?" The article discussed two polls on the New York gubernatorial race between Nelson Rockefeller and Frank D. O'Connor. The Daily News Straw Poll gave O'Connor 41.7 percent of the vote to Rockefeller's 38.4 percent. The Oliver Quayle Poll had Rockefeller ahead 40 percent to 27 percent. The *Times* said nothing about sampling procedure, polling techniques, or which pollster was likely to be right.[41] Nor did it concern itself with the larger question: Why should a voter think about who's ahead in deciding whom to vote for?

POLITICAL ADVERTISING

For many people the main source of "news" about political candidates is not the news at all. It is political advertising, especially television advertising. This use of broadcasting is a fairly recent development. The following chart shows the total amount of money spent on radio and TV time in every Presidential campaign since 1952.

1952	$ 6,100,000
1956	9,500,000
1960	13,700,000
1964	34,600,000
1968	58,900,000

These figures do not include production costs, or state and local races, or newspaper and magazine advertising.

The typical political ad is a 30-second or one-minute TV spot inserted between two popular entertainment programs. It is designed and produced by a professional advertising agency. The candidate has a veto power, but he doesn't use it very often if he wants to win. After all, in the business of packaging and marketing products the ad agencies are pros. The candidate (the product) is a mere amateur, and acts accordingly. He does what he's told.

A classic case of political advertising was the 1966 re-election bid of New York Governor Nelson Rockefeller. The incumbent, Rockefeller was extremely unpopular with the electorate, and early polls indicated that literally any Democrat could defeat him. Frank D. O'Connor was picked for the job.

Rocky won the election (by 400,000 votes) on the strength of a massive media campaign. He spent well over $2 million on television ads alone. On WNBC in New York City, Rockefeller ran 208 commercials at a cost of $237,000; O'Connor bought 23 ads on this station, spending only $41,000. It was that way throughout the state. In the rural city of Watertown, the Rockefeller campaign spent $3,067 on 99 TV spots; O'Connor spent $1,307 on a mere 18 spots.

Jack Tinker & Partners (of Alka-Seltzer fame) designed the commercials. Rockefeller's face and voice were seldom used. A typical early ad featured a talking fish in an underwater news interview. The reporter asks the fish about the Governor's Pure Waters Program. The fish says that things are still pretty smelly, but thanks to Rocky they're getting better. "I would say, uh, next to a fish. . . . I'd say he's the best Gov. . . ."

Later the campaign took a nasty turn. One script read: "Frank O'Connor, the man who led the fight against the New York State Thruway, is running for governor. Get in your car. Drive down to the polls, and vote." Actually, O'Connor had fought for a free thruway against Rockefeller's plan for a tollroad. But the O'Connor campaign lacked the money to clear up the record.[42]

The Rockefeller-O'Connor race raises two obvious, important, and unanswered questions. First, what does it mean for democracy when only the wealthiest candidates (or those with wealthy supporters) are able to mount an effective "modern" campaign? And second, what does it mean for democracy when political candidates are sold to the public like Alka-Seltzer?

Of course there is another side to the argument. It is said, with some justice, that television advertising is the only way an unknown candidate can reach the public and defeat a well-established incumbent. In 1970, John Tunney successfully challenged George Murphy for a California

Senate seat largely on the strength of his ads. Cleveland industrialist Howard Metzenbaum beat astronaut John Glenn for Ohio's Democratic Senatorial nomination in much the same way. And in Pennsylvania, a complete unknown named Milton Shapp spent four years, two campaigns, and millions of dollars advertising his way to the Governor's Mansion.

Though it is too early to tell for sure, it seems likely that political advertising has made it easier for unknowns to challenge incumbents, and has lessened the dependence of all candidates on the party machine. These are highly desirable results.

But the cost is high too. John Tunney may in fact be a better man than George Murphy—but you couldn't prove it by his ads. A typical Tunney commercial showed a handsome figure walking down a deserted California beach, accompanied by a pretty blond wife and four children. A close-up reveals the candidate himself, complete with a mop of Kennedy-like hair and a trace of a Boston accent. He speaks: "We can fly to the moon, we can split the atom, we can build great cities. But we cannot build the ocean or the sky. These are gifts. . . . My vote and voice will be with the protection of this great state of ours." A slogan flashes across the screen: "You need a fighter in your corner. John Tunney is a fighter." (John Tunney's father Gene is the former heavyweight boxing champion of the world.)

In recent years, an increasing number of politicians have expressed concern over the growth of campaign advertising. This culminated in 1970 with a new law limiting campaign expenses to seven cents per voter or $20,000, whichever is more. The bill was vetoed by President Nixon —perhaps because Republicans tend to have more money to spend than Democrats. Some such limitation is likely to be passed again within the next few years, but at best it will affect only the amount of political advertising, not its style or content.

Only a popular "backlash" can put a stop to superficial and misleading political ads. Such a backlash may now be in the offing. You can see it in the enthusiastic public response to *The Selling of the President,* a cynical account by Joe McGinniss of the 1968 Nixon campaign. You can see it also in the 1970 election results. In Illinois, incumbent Ralph Smith outspent his opponent Adlai Stevenson III two-to-one, but lost nonetheless. In Arkansas, Governor Winthrop Rockefeller was defeated for re-election by unknown Dale Bumpers, who ran his campaign on a considerably smaller budget. And in Florida, Democrat Lawton Chiles won a Senate seat by walking up and down the state in the old-time political fashion. Chiles spent only $30,000 on media advertising, a fraction of his opponent's expenditures.[43]

It is at least possible that the campaign style of the 1970s will deemphasize slick political advertising. But most experienced politicians are betting against it. As long as the media continue to do an inadequate job of campaign reporting, political ads will probably continue to dominate the election scene. Candidates will continue to be merchandized like Alka-Seltzer, and may the wealthier man win.

ELECTION NIGHT

The broadcast media devote an incredible amount of money and time to election night coverage. The networks let out all the stops, hiring every computer programmer and news analyst in sight. Local broadcasters do the same thing on a smaller scale. No expense is spared to make sure that viewers are told who won and who lost at the earliest possible second. A great deal of network prestige rides on the question of which one makes the important predictions first.

There is little to criticize in this election night performance (now that they wait for the California polls to close before telling us who won the Presidential race). Voters are provided with accurate, detailed, up-to-the-minute information. Only Michael Arlen of the *New Yorker* has found grounds for complaint:

> I do feel considerable sympathy, though, for campaign workers who slave like navvies for months and months, are finally assembled in the ballroom of the Hotel Van Meter with their hopeful smiles and their new hairdoes and all those ribbons and paper cups, and are then told by Walter Cronkite twenty minutes after they get there that on the basis of 167 votes in the Upper Lompoc District their candidate has just fallen in the dust and everything is over.[44]

Of the thousands upon thousands of news stories about national and local government, the best-covered story of them all may well be election night. This in itself tells us something important about the mass media. They are at their best with the concrete details of a dramatic competition, where they can impartially record the battle and impartially announce the winner. No story involves less news management than the results of an election. No story is less influenced by friendships with news sources, or by civic boosterism. No story, in short, makes so few demands for independence, integrity, and the adversary relationship. That is why the media do such a good job with election results.

NOTES

[1] William L. Rivers, *The Adversaries* (Boston: Beacon Press, 1970).

[2] Leo C. Rosten, *The Washington Correspondents* (New York: Harcourt, Brace and Company, 1937), p. 249.

[3] "Politicians and the Press," *Saturday Evening Post*, August 18, 1923, p. 72.

4 Alfred Friendly, "Attribution of News," *Nieman Reports,* July, 1958, p. 12.

5 Douglass Cater, *The Fourth Branch of Government* (New York: Vintage Books, 1959), p. 78.

6 Elmer E. Cornwell Jr., "Presidential News: The Expanding Public Image," *Journalism Quarterly,* Summer, 1959, p. 278.

7 William L. Rivers, *The Opinionmakers* (Boston: Beacon Press, 1965), pp. 22–23.

8 Elmer E. Cornwell, Jr., *Presidential Leadership of Public Opinion* (Bloomington, Ind.: Indiana University Press, 1965), p. 14.

9 *Ibid.,* pp. 178–94.

10 Tom Wicker in *The New York Times,* September 8, 1963, quoted in James E. Pollard, "The Kennedy Administration and the Press," *Journalism Quarterly,* Winter, 1964, p. 14.

11 Cornwell, *Presidential Leadership,* p. 220.

12 Rivers, *The Opinionmakers,* p. 144.

13 Clinton Rossiter, *The American Presidency* (New York: Harcourt Brace Jovanovich, Inc., 1956), p. 114.

14 Robert MacNeil, *The People Machine* (New York: Harper & Row, 1968), pp. 316–17.

15 Tom Wicker, "Critique of Nixon's Reporting," San Francisco *Chronicle,* December 11, 1969, p. 1.

16 "Politicians and the Press," p. 76.

17 James Reston, *The Artillery of the Press* (New York: Harper Colophon Books, 1966), p. 73.

18 George Barnes Galloway, *The Legislative Process in Congress* (New York: Crowell, 1953), p. 222.

19 Wallace Carroll, "Essence, Not Angle," *Columbia Journalism Review,* Summer, 1965, p. 5.

20 *Archibald Newsletter,* Number 5, August, 1970 (Columbia, Mo.: An irregular attachment to Freedom of Information Center Reports), pp. 2–3.

21 Edward M. Glick, "Press-Government Relationships," *Journalism Quarterly,* Spring, 1966, pp. 53–54.

22 Tom Littlewood, "The Trials of Statehouse Journalism," *Saturday Review,* December 10, 1966, p. 82.

23 John F. Valleau, "Oregon Legislative Reporting: The Newsmen and Their Methods," *Journalism Quarterly,* Spring, 1952, p. 167.

24 Rivers, *The Adversaries,* p. 120.

25 Bernard Stern, "Local Government News," *Journalism Quarterly,* Spring, 1950, pp. 152–54.

26 David M. Rubin, "Politics and a Newspaper Strike," Unpublished paper, Stanford University Department of Communication, March 17, 1968, p. 6.

27 Stuart A. Dunham, "Local News Coverage: A Vast, Gray, Dull, Monotony," ASNE (American Society of Newspaper Editors) *Bulletin,* May, 1966, p. 3.

28 Clarice N. Olien, George A. Donohue, and Phillip J. Tichenor, "The Community Editor's Power and the Reporting of Conflict," *Journalism Quarterly,* Summer, 1968, p. 250.

29 Robert P. Judd, "The Newspaper Reporter in a Suburban City," *Journalism Quarterly,* Winter, 1961, pp. 40–42.

30 David M. Rubin and Stephen Landers, "National Exposure and Local Cover-Up: A Case Study," *Columbia Journalism Review,* Summer, 1969, pp. 17–22.

31 Raymond L. Bancroft, ed., *City Hall and the Press* (Washington: National League of Cities, 1967), p. iv.

32 Roy Reed, "How to Lynch a Newspaper," *The Atlantic,* November, 1964, pp.

59–63; and Ben H. Bagdikian, "Death in Silence," *Columbia Journalism Review,* Spring, 1964, pp. 36–37.

[33] Seymour Martin Lipset, *The First New Nation* (Garden City, N.Y.: Anchor Books, 1967), p. 123.

[34] Charles McDowell, Jr., "Carnival of Excess, TV at the Conventions," *Atlantic Monthly,* July, 1968, p. 43.

[35] Serena Wade and Wilbur Schramm, "The Mass Media as Sources of Public Affairs, Science and Health Knowledge," *Public Opinion Quarterly,* Summer, 1969, p. 198.

[36] Dan Nimmo, *The Political Persuaders* (Englewood Cliffs, N.J.: Prentice-Hall, Inc., 1970), p. 113.

[37] Guido H. Stempel III, "The Prestige Press in Two Presidential Elections," *Journalism Quarterly,* Winter, 1965, p. 21.

[38] ———, "The Prestige Press Meets the Third Party Challenge," *Journalism Quarterly,* Winter, 1969, p. 701.

[39] James E. Gregg, "Newspaper Editorial Endorsements and California Elections, 1948–62," *Journalism Quarterly,* Autumn, 1965, pp. 532–38.

[40] Ralph M. Goldman, "Stumping the Country: 'Rules of the Road,' 1896," *Journalism Quarterly,* Summer, 1952, pp. 303–6.

[41] Gerhart D. Wiebe, "The New York *Times* and Public Opinion Research: A Criticism," *Journalism Quarterly,* Winter, 1967, p. 656.

[42] James M. Perry, *The New Politics* (New York: Clarkson N. Potter, Inc., 1968), pp. 107–37.

[43] "Punctured Image," *Newsweek,* November 16, 1970, p. 77.

[44] Michael J. Arlen, *Living-Room War* (New York: The Viking Press, Inc., 1969), p. 19.

SUGGESTED READINGS

Cornwell, Elmer E. Jr., *Presidential Leadership of Public Opinion.* Bloomington, Ind.: Indiana University Press, 1965.

Nimmo, Dan, *The Political Persuaders.* Englewood Cliffs, N.J.: Prentice-Hall, Inc., 1970.

Reed, Roy, "How to Lynch a Newspaper," *The Atlantic,* November, 1964.

Rivers, William L., *The Opinionmakers.* Boston: Beacon Press, 1965.

———, *The Adversaries.* Boston: Beacon Press, 1970.

Rubin, David M., and Stephen Landers, "National Exposure and Local Cover-Up: A Case Study," *Columbia Journalism Review,* Summer, 1969.

Siebert, Fred S., Theodore Peterson, and Wilbur Schramm, *Four Theories of the Press.* Urbana, Ill.: University of Illinois Press, 1963.

16 Coverage of Crimes and Demonstrations

The favorite topic of the mass media, bar none, is crime—violent crime. The emphasis they place on it is at best a waste of space; at worst it may do significant harm. The only kind of crime story that deserves the intensive coverage it gets is the riot or civil disturbance—because it is more than simply a crime. Unfortunately, riots (and even noncriminal peaceful protests) are too often treated as simple crimes, with little or no attention to grievances and underlying issues.

America has always been profoundly interested in violence and lawlessness—a holdover, perhaps, from its revolutionary and frontier beginnings. Nowhere is this preoccupation more clearly reflected than in the content of the nation's mass media.

Much of the crime and violence in the media is fictional. Radio and television have grown rich on the exploits of Western and detective heroes, on shows like *The Shadow, The Lone Ranger, Gunsmoke,* and *The Untouchables.* The film industry, paperback books, and comic books are equally dependent on crime, preferably laced with sex and torture. And a whole genre of American magazines is devoted to tales of triple murders and the like.

The news media also know a subject that will "sell" when they see one—and violent crime is the biggest seller of them all. It always has been. The first specialized reporter in American journalism, hired in

1833, covered the police beat. The most typical article in the yellow press at the turn of the century was the crime story, with headlines like "Death Rides the Blast," "Love and Cold Poison," "Screaming for Mercy," and "Baptized in Blood." The tabloid papers of the 1920s followed the same tradition. They are still at it today. So are many standard-size newspapers, though their headlines may be smaller. Even the New York *Times* cannot resist a juicy murder now and then.

In 1954, Cleveland police announced that osteopath Sam Sheppard was being held on charges of bludgeoning his pretty wife Marilyn to death. The wire services played the story big, and newspapers across the country gave it smash display. Herbert H. Krauch of the Los Angeles *Herald & Express* (2,000 miles from Cleveland) exulted: "It's been a long time since there's been a murder trial this good."[1]

The average American newspaper or broadcast station may or may not cover a new city ordinance or a school bond issue. But a bank robbery, an assault, or (gulp—hold the presses) a rape/murder is sure to get extensive play.

It is hard to justify this kind of coverage in terms of the intrinsic importance of crime news. Perhaps if the media reported the sociology of crime, or white collar crime, or organized crime, such attention might be warranted. But a barroom brawl simply isn't as important to the community as a school bond issue.

Editors, however, believe that crime news sells newspapers—and they are probably right. In 1956, two sisters were raped and murdered in Chicago, boosting newspaper circulation figures by 50,000 copies. A year later, a rapist ran amuck in San Francisco, and circulation went up by a similar margin.[2] No school bond issue ever accomplished that.

There is another reason for lavishing time and space on crime news: It is ridiculously easy to cover. A reporter sits at a desk in the police station. He listens to the police radio and chats with his friends on the force. Every once in a while he phones the smaller stations in the area, and checks the blotter. Then he calls the newsroom and dictates the gruesome facts to a rewrite man, who puts them into English. The reporter himself needn't even know how to write.

This technique for handling crime news results in several abuses. Since the reporter works hand-in-glove with the police, crime stories inevitably favor the official point of view. On a minor story, the reporter is unlikely to see the arrested person at all; the man's protestations of innocence or charges of police brutality therefore go unreported. Moreover, a newsman who confines his research to the police blotter will never learn much about the underlying causes of crime, or even the motive for a particular crime. Many criminal acts today are a reflection of social unrest, of racial discrimination or political repression. Such factors are far too seldom adequately covered by the media.

IDENTIFYING THE ACCUSED

The identification of accused or convicted criminals is an unsettled ethical problem for the mass media. Until a decade ago, it was customary for the media to include the race of the suspect in every crime story. Today this practice is frowned on, sometimes on the grounds that race is irrelevant, sometimes on the grounds that its relevance, though genuine, is subject to misinterpretation by a fearful white middle class. But even today most newspapers give the names and addresses of suspects, making a tentative racial identification possible if the reader wants to work at it.

A related controversy centers around the names of juvenile offenders. Some editors argue that a young person is more likely to "go straight" if he is not publicly identified as a criminal; they therefore withhold the names. Others believe that readers have a right to know the names of criminals in their midst, and that the embarrassment of publicity may actually aid in their redemption. Government officials also disagree on this point. In some states all juvenile records are confidential. Other states leave it up to the editor, and still others let the judge decide for each particular case.

The entertainment approach to crime news and the dependence on police sources also result in far greater coverage of arrests than of trials. News of an arrest is both absorbing and easy to get. News of a trial requires a lot more work on the reporter's part, and it is of interest to readers only if the case is especially important or especially juicy. And when a man is acquitted or charges are dropped, that's hardly news at all.

At a minimum, most crime news is a waste of time, space, and manpower. It does the suspect harm (see Chapter 7), and society no good. It may even do society harm. As early as 1801, observers were already protesting the excesses of media sensationalism:

> Some of the shocking articles in the paper raise simple, very simple wonder; some terror; and some horror and disgust. . . . Do they not shock tender minds and addle shallow brains? They make a thousand old maids and ten thousand booby boys afraid to go to bed alone.[3]

Much has been written about the effects of media violence on the American psyche (see Pages 275–77). It is hard to assess how much damage crime news actually does—but certainly it does little good.

There are exceptions, of course. The assassination of President Kennedy was a "crime" story, but no one would argue that it didn't deserve the intensive coverage it received. The same may be said for the alleged crimes of Jack Ruby, Sacco and Vanzetti, and Lt. William Calley. Even the celebrated Charles Manson case may be defended on grounds of social significance. But the clearest example of a genuinely important crime story is a riot.

A RIOT BEGINS

It was Sunday, July 23, 1967. The Detroit *Free Press* had only a skeleton staff in the office when reports of looting and arson in the black section of town began filtering in. Police reporter Red Griffith told the newsroom the demonstrations had begun with a police raid the night before. Griffith also reported that the violence was spreading rapidly—despite police claims that it was under control. One *Free Press* reporter had already been struck by a bottle and sent to the hospital.

The deadline for Monday morning's first edition was fast approaching. Tom De Lisle, the youngest reporter on the staff, was toying with the lead for his rundown on the worst damage areas. "Can I call it a riot?" he asked assistant city editor Wayne King. Determined not to contribute to the trouble, King said no. Shortly afterward, Michigan Governor George Romney called out the national guard, making the riot condition official. Even so, the word "riot" appeared only three times on the front page of Monday morning's paper.[4]

This was only the first of thousands of journalistic decisions that faced the *Free Press* during the next four days of uncontrolled violence. The paper acquitted itself well, and its coverage of Detroit's unrest has since been hailed as a model for American journalism.

The practical problems of riot coverage are enormous. Among the ones that turned up at the *Free Press* were the following:

Supplies. During a riot, the media may find a sudden need for such items as gas masks, helicopters, and two-way radios. These must be stockpiled in advance. The disruption of supply lines during a civil disturbance makes them impossible to obtain. It's hard enough then to keep up with the need for paper, ink, food, and the like.

Coordination. At the height of the Detroit riot, the *Free Press* had fifty reporters out in the field. Careful coordination is needed to keep track of them all, to keep them from roaming freely and to make sure that every angle gets covered.

Danger. Newsmen and cameramen covering a civil disorder are likely to be attacked by either side—or both. The Walker Report documented scores of cases of police violence against reporters during the demonstrations outside the Democratic nominating convention in Chicago in 1968. And rioters, of course, are naturally resentful and fearful of newsmen.

Identification. Reporters on rooftops look like snipers. Reporters in ties and jackets look like government agents. Reporters who drive too fast look like they're running away. Reporters who drive too slow look like they're looters. Identifying oneself as a newsman in the middle of a riot can be very difficult.

These are all serious problems. But it is not the practicalities that make riot coverage one of the hardest jobs in journalism.

RUMORS AND BLACKOUTS

"The truth, the whole truth, and nothing but the truth" isn't a bad motto for the mass media—but it is a very difficult motto to live up to in covering a riot. Nine times out of ten, the media get their first word of a civil disturbance from one of two sources: the police radio or the wire services. Both are more concerned with speed than with accuracy. And both are notoriously unreliable in a crisis, mixing fact and rumor in about equal proportion.

In Tampa, Florida, for example, a deputy sheriff died in the early stages of a disturbance. AP and UPI immediately bulletined the news that he had been killed by rioters. Half an hour later reporters discovered that the man had suffered a heart attack.[5] In 1969, the Third World Liberation Front organized a student strike on the Berkeley campus of the University of California. Mike Culbert, editor of the Berkeley *Gazette,* notes that "the wire services didn't know what was going on. The early leads in the first days of the strike were atrocious. At one point AP was taking down my *speculation* on what was happening and moving it as the early lead."[6]

Not that newspapers and broadcast stations have a much better record on riot rumors. During the Watts riot of 1965, radio station KTLA sent a reporter aloft in a helicoptor. In the space of a few hours the man told his audience that the Shrine Auditorium was on fire, that communists were directing the uprising, and that the Minute Men were about to invade the ghetto. All were unsubstantiated rumors, and all turned out to be false. The reporter hedged his statements with phrases like "police believe" and "it is thought that"—but few listeners noticed the qualifiers.[7]

KTLA and Watts are not unique. In Detroit, a radio station broadcast a rumor that blacks were planning to invade the suburbs that night. In Cincinnati, several newspapers reported that a group of white youths had a bazooka in their possession. The invasion never materialized, and the bazooka turned out to be inoperable. A false rumor that police had killed a black cab driver in Newark is believed to have triggered that riot, and an unfounded report of the killing of a seven-year-old boy fanned a disturbance in Plainfield, New Jersey.

As the media have grown more experienced with civil disruption, they have become more cautious about publishing unproved rumors. Some editors and broadcasters have gone even further. They habitually withhold the established facts of explosive incidents, in the hope that those incidents will not escalate into full-fledged riots.

News blackouts of this sort have a long history in the South. In the early 1960s, one Southern city established an interracial commission to desegregate its lunch counters. An agreement was negotiated, the media kept mum, and the sit-ins proceeded without violence. Says one member of the commission: "I am convinced that if these matters had received normal news treatment, the alarm would have sounded among the Ku Klux Klan and the redneck types, and that they would have been there with their baseball bats and ax handles; extremists among the Negroes would have responded in kind."[8]

The blackout argument seemed most persuasive during the summer of 1967, when a rash of urban riots appeared to be feeding on each other's publicity. Detroit might not have happened, it was said, if the fury of Newark had not been reported so fully in the media. Editors in many cities drew up secret agreements to keep quiet about their own ghetto unrest. Some of these agreements may still be in effect.

It is probably true that early publicity about a minor incident can help it grow to major proportions. People hear on the radio about a scuffle a few blocks away. They head on down to see what's going on, and pretty soon it isn't a scuffle any more; it's a riot. Nevertheless, a news blackout sets a very dangerous precedent. Word-of-mouth rumors are likely to be even less accurate than the mass media. And if serious grievances

---

CREATING THE NEWS

It is hard for the media to cover a riot without affecting its course in one way or another. Marked press cars, tape recorders, spotlights, and cameras all act as lightning rods for the sparks of a disturbance. They attract on-lookers and alter the behavior of participants. Both rioters and policemen have been known to "perform" for the press.

Perhaps the media can't help influencing the news—but they don't have to manufacture it. During the Newark riot, a New York newspaper photographer was witnessed urging and finally convincing a young Negro boy to throw a rock for the benefit of the camera. In Chicago a few years later, a TV camera crew was observed leading two "hippie" girls into an area filled with national guardsmen. As the camera started rolling, one of the girls cried on cue: "Don't beat me! Don't beat me!" Virtually all the media have rules against this sort of thing, but rules tend to be forgotten during a riot.

have festered to the point of a riot, the people have a right to know about it.

Otis Chandler of the Los Angeles *Times* has written of "the social value of truth; whether or not truth hurts, whether or not truth is inflammatory."[9] When the media refuse to publish the facts of civil disruption, they do the public as much damage as when they rush to publish unfounded rumors. Truth is what's needed—the whole truth and nothing but the truth.

BALANCE AND BACKGROUND

"The whole truth" about a riot includes a lot more than what happened and how much damage was done. In particular, it includes the "background" of the riot. Why did a group of people suddenly explode? What were their grievances, and how legitimate were they? What could the community have done to attack the underlying issues and prevent the outburst? What can the community do now to keep the same thing from happening again?

Ideally, of course, these questions should be discussed by the media long before any riot. Every civil disturbance is proof that some problem has gone unattended, and usually this means the media have failed to expose the problem for the community to see. The riot itself is a desperate form of communication. When people are able to air their grievances effectively in a peaceful manner, they do not riot.

Once the riot begins, it is up to the media to make up for lost time and begin reporting the issues. It shouldn't take a riot to make editors aware of this responsibility, but sometimes it does. The very least we can expect is decent coverage of the underlying issues during and after the explosion.

Quite often we don't even get that. Which reporter does your local city editor pick to cover a violent disruption or even a peaceful demonstration on campus? The education writer, who knows (or should know) the issues? Or the police reporter, who knows how to keep tabs on the number of arrests? Most of the time it's the police reporter—and the resulting article reflects his special expertise. City Editor Roy Grimm of the Oakland *Tribune* admits that "perhaps we take too much of the police beat approach to these things, and get too involved in the running battle."[10]

The problem is largely a matter of sources. In the middle of a full-scale riot, it is hard enough for a reporter to figure out who speaks for the police. And he *knows* the police. He has worked closely with them for years, and has built up a relationship of mutual trust and cooperation. By contrast, the reporter is likely to have no sources at all (let alone cooperative ones) among the rioters—the blacks, students, radicals, or whatever. So he lets his police sources do the job for him. And his story turns out like a play-by-play account of a ball game: all action and no motivation.

And no inaction either. The media, like the police, are interested primarily in what's happening. They don't much care why, and they don't much care how limited the action is. A single incident of violence in a long, peaceful demonstration is fated to be the only incident that makes the evening news. "By focusing on a handful of violent activists," admits Frank Stanton of CBS, "we may give the impression that that's the way it is all over. This is the danger in all kinds of demonstrations. Our tendency is to try to go where the action is."[11]

Professor Nathan Blumberg of the University of Montana uses the adjective "orthodox" to describe the attitude of the media toward civil disturbances and peaceful protest demonstrations. He gives as an example the 1968 antiwar march on the Pentagon. The smallest crowd estimates came from police and military sources, and these were the ones the media used. Students and hippies were a minority among the demonstrators, yet the media made it seem that they were the only people there. The Army claimed that it was the demonstrators themselves who fired tear gas into the crowd, and the media let the lie go unchallenged until days after the event.

In nearly every demonstration or civil disturbance (Chicago in 1968 was an obvious exception), the "orthodox" media rely on official sources for most of their information. They stress action and violence, and ignore the underlying issues. "Perhaps it is too much to expect," Blumberg concludes, "that a press with an undeniable stake in the economic and political system would report fairly on those who are fundamentally dissatisfied with the status quo."[12]

In the early 1960s, the mass media began learning how to cover demonstrations and protest marches. In the middle 1960s, they had to start all over again, learning how to cover ghetto riots. In the late 1960s it was campus rebellions instead. And now a fourth kind of civil disturbance is upon us: the hit-and-run, unfocused "guerilla" attack on the Establishment. Once again the media are painfully learning the ropes.

As revolutionary tactics change, old lessons become valueless and new ones must be learned. But some problems remain constant. The mass media still publish inflammatory rumors. They still withhold facts. They still stage news events. They still emphasize action. They still ignore underlying issues. They still rely heavily on official sources. And they still present an essentially "orthodox" viewpoint on dissent and dissenters.

The mass media will have a lot to say about whether there will be a revolution in this country, and whether it will be peaceful or violent.

OVERKILL

Important though civil disturbances are, it is doubtful that they deserve as much coverage as they receive. In late 1968 and early 1969, San Francisco State College was the scene of a major student rebellion. The San Francisco *Chronicle*'s file on the story, some staffers jokingly claim, is thicker than its morgue for World War Two. In one three-week period, the *Chronicle* carried 1,531 column inches on the events at S.F. State. The Vietnam war, by contrast, was allotted only 388 inches.[13]

If the *Chronicle* had devoted all that space to exploring the issues behind student unrest, we would have no complaint. But as always, the stress was on action. A good demonstration is almost as effective as a good murder for selling newspapers. But who wants to read a list of grievances or demands? Bloody heads add spice to a TV news show, but who wants to watch films of students quietly attending class? San Francisco's media had hold of a top-notch story. No one dared to drop it and give the competition an edge.

Much will depend on what the media choose to call a revolution, and what they choose to say or not say about the revolutionaries.

NOTES

1 "The Case of Dr. Sam," *Time,* November 22, 1954, p. 88.

2 John Lofton, "Trial by Fury—A Projection of the Public Mood" (mimeo of draft for chapter from *Justice and the Press*), pp. 13–14.

3 *Ibid.,* p. 5.

4 *Reporting the Detroit Riot* (New York: American Newspaper Publishers Association, 1968), pp. 3–4.

5 National Advisory Commission on Civil Disorders (Kerner Commission), *Report of the National Advisory Commission on Civil Disorders* (New York: Bantam Books, Inc., 1968), p. 373.

6 William L. Rivers and David M. Rubin, *A Region's Press: Anatomy of Newspapers in the San Francisco Bay Area* (Berkeley, Calif.: Institute of Governmental Studies, University of California, Berkeley, 1971), p. 125.

7 William L. Rivers, "Jim Crow Journalism," *Seminar,* March, 1968, p. 16.

8 *Ibid.,* p. 12.

9 Otis Chandler, "The Greater Responsibility," *Seminar,* March, 1968, p. 7.

10 Rivers and Rubin, *A Region's Press,* p. 122.

11 Letter from CBS President Frank Stanton to Pennsylvania Senator Hugh Scott, August 9, 1967, p. 3.

12 Nathan B. Blumberg, "A Study of the Orthodox Press: The Reporting of Dissent," *Montana Journalism Review,* 1968, pp. 7–9.

13 Rivers and Rubin, *A Region's Press,* pp. 112–13, 164.

BLUMBERG, NATHAN B., "A Study of the Orthodox Press: The Reporting of Dissent," *Montana Journalism Review*, 1968.

NATIONAL ADVISORY COMMISSION ON CIVIL DISORDERS (KERNER COMMISSION), *Report of the National Advisory Commission on Civil Disorders*. New York: Bantam Books, 1968.

Reporting the Detroit Riot. New York: American Newspaper Publishers Association, 1968.

WALKER, DANIEL, *Rights in Conflict*. New York: The New American Library Inc., 1968. Report submitted to the National Commission on the Causes and Prevention of Violence.

17 Coverage of War and National Security

Covering wars—hot and cold, declared and undeclared—is perhaps the most difficult assignment the media face. War news is of consuming interest to the American public, but it is hard to collect and even harder to interpret. Government censorship and self-censorship are ever-present problems. Some news is censored in the interests of national security; much more news is censored for lesser reasons, such as national face-saving.

For more than a year, James Reston of the New York *Times* knew that the United States was flying high-altitude spy planes (U-2s) over the Soviet Union. His paper did not report the fact. Then, in 1960, a U-2 was shot down and its pilot captured. President Eisenhower denied everything. The *Times*, which knew the denials were lies, printed them without comment. Only after the President finally admitted the truth did the *Times* finally publish the truth.

Reston believes that this was a correct judgment. He agrees that it is contrary to the traditional journalistic ethic, but he adds: "In this time of half-war and half-peace that old principle of publish-and-be-damned, while very romantic, bold and hairy, can often damage the national interest."[1]

No doubt there are times when American military adventures should not be reported by the mass media. Equally clearly, there are times when it is vitally important that those adventures be reported. The problem is telling one from the other.

NATIONAL SECURITY?

Consider two other instances when the *Times* neglected to report what it knew—the Bay of Pigs invasion of 1961 and the Cuban missile crisis of 1962.

Tad Szulc's article on the planned invasion was already dummied into the front page of the *Times,* under a four-column headline. But managing editor Turner Catledge and publisher Orvil Dreyfoos had grave reservations. They feared that the story might give Castro the warning he needed to repel the invasion, thus endangering the lives of the CIA-supported invaders and damaging the national security of the United States. After much heated debate, the article was toned down. References to the CIA and to the "imminence" of the invasion were dropped, and the whole thing was run under a single-column headline. There were no immediate repercussions.

When the invasion took place, it was a total failure, a serious blow to U.S. prestige. A month later President Kennedy confided to Catledge: "If you had printed more about the operation you would have saved us from a colossal mistake."

The Cuban missile crisis was another kettle of fish. The *Times* Washington bureau knew that there were Russian missiles inside Cuba, and that Kennedy was planning to do something about them. The President telephoned Dreyfoos and asked him to hold off on the story. Dreyfoos agreed. The result was a spectacularly successful blockade, a triumph for American diplomacy (which badly needed a triumph). Kennedy, at least, gave the *Times* part of the credit for that success.[2]

The Cuban crises of 1961 and 1962 illustrate two important points. First, it is extremely difficult for the media to know when they should kill a story for reasons of national security. The *Times* made a bad mistake in 1961, but showed extraordinary wisdom in 1962—by doing precisely the same thing. Second, when faced with this sort of dilemma, the media have typically killed the story. With the benefit of hindsight, we can find hundreds of articles that should have been published and weren't. There are many fewer cases of published articles that did serious damage to national security.

American journalists have traditionally drawn a hard-and-fast line between wartime and peacetime. When the nation is at war, censorship has been accepted without argument. But in time of peace, newsmen have viewed the public's right to know as the paramount consideration in deciding what to publish. An informed public, after all, is a cornerstone of democracy. How then can the truth be detrimental to the national interest?

This once-unquestioned distinction is now permanently muddled. Modern warfare is no longer a matter of clear-cut enemies and established battle fronts. The next formal, declared war the United States fights will probably be the world's last. The undeclared conflict in Southeast Asia is a war. The on-going struggle against the "communist menace" is a war. The occasional "peace-keeping action" in Latin America or the Middle East is a war. The stockpiling of missiles and atomic bombs is a war. In these terms, the United States has been constantly at war since the 1940s, and will remain at war for the foreseeable future. Does this mean that wartime standards of self-censorship should go forever unopposed? Perhaps so.

Douglass Cater lists four kinds of stories that should not be reported (even in "peacetime") because of national security:

1. Advance disclosures of the U.S. government's position on issues to be negotiated at the international conference table.
2. Leaks on security matters which include the built-in bias of those who did the leaking.
3. Technical data of little interest to the ordinary reader but of immense value to the "enemy."
4. The clandestine operations of our government, both diplomatic and military.[3]

By and large, the American media abide by these standards. As we shall see later, the fact that they do so contributed significantly to the increasing American involvement in Vietnam in the late 1960s.

GOVERNMENT CENSORSHIP

More often than not, the media are not directly faced with the question of whether to print or not to print. The government makes that choice for them. Sometimes it does so by putting tremendous pressure on reporters and editors. Sometimes it does so by forbidding publication of certain facts. And sometimes it simply lies. Assistant Secretary of Defense Arthur Sylvester, himself a former reporter, defended these tactics at the time of the Cuban missile crisis: "I think the inherent right of the government to lie—to lie to save itself when faced with nuclear disaster—is basic, *basic*."[4]

That right is apparently also assumed by the government when faced with something less than nuclear disaster. Consider the American involvement in the Dominican Republic in 1965. Reporter Martin Goodman recalls the period:

The central issue of public policy from the start, of course, was whether the United States was justified in intervening.

The first public justification offered was the need to save the lives and property of American and other foreign citizens. But privately, from the beginning, United States embassy officials indicated the real reason was the fear of Communist involvement in the rebellion. The official attempts to document this charge were at the heart of the controversy between the government and the press. . . .

United States embassy officials on April 29 showed several reporters a list of fifty-three known Communists allegedly involved. This was the opening of what came to be a numbers game. . . .

There were many discrepancies. Some of those listed were not Communists. Two had been jailed more than a week before the revolt began. Six had not been in the country, and at least four had not been in Santo Domingo. . . .

There were other questions of fact. Time and again the government spokesmen denied things that the reporters had seen.

Most of these outside incidents can be lumped under the question of whether or not the U.S. was neutral in its intervention. The official spokesmen, both political and military, said it was. Against this were the personal observations of scores of reporters, and much evidence dramatically captured by television cameras. . . .[5]

Politically sophisticated Americans have come to expect lies and news management from the Departments of Defense and State. So have the media—but they print them nonetheless.

HISTORY OF CENSORSHIP

The history of wartime censorship and news management is as old as the history of war itself. In this country it starts with the Revolution. Loyalist newspapers were persecuted throughout the war, and many were forced to stop publishing altogether. Patriot papers fared just as badly in Tory-held territory.

Almost immediately after the Revolution, Major General Arthur St. Clair and his troops were slaughtered by Indians. A Congressional committee convened to study the disaster, and asked President Washington to furnish the relevant documents. Washington refused, claiming that disclosure of the calamity would injure the prestige of the new nation. The refusal stuck. Thus, as early as 1792, the right of the government to withhold information for reasons of national security was established. And so was the difficulty of distinguishing between wartime and peacetime.

Coverage of the War of 1812 was casual, and based mostly on official reports. Censorship was thus unnecessary. Much the same thing was true during the Mexican-American War. News reports were colorful and heavily pro-American; the government felt no need to interefere. But the Civil War was a different story. It was the most heavily reported war up to that point in American history, and by far the most divisive.

In July of 1861, the Union Army issued an order forbidding telegraph companies to send reports on military affairs. The goal of this measure was to restrict the communications of spies and to prevent the Confederacy from learning about troop movements and the like through Northern newspapers. For several months the ban was extended to non-military reporting as well, but Congress objected and the earlier rule was reinstated. Even this was a serious infringement on freedom of the press, but the Supreme Court was in no mood to defend the First Amendment at the expense of the war effort.

In order to transmit news by telegraph, reporters were required to submit their stories for government censorship. In theory only information of military value to the enemy was to be excised, but many field commanders used their censorship power to eliminate unfavorable publicity as well. Reporters who wrote glowingly about their favorite generals were free to work without restriction. Those who were more critical of military tactics found themselves out in the cold; a few were actually accused of treason.

Critical newspapers were similarly harrassed. The federal government temporarily shut down the New York *World*, the *Journal of Commerce*, and the Chicago *Times* for publishing stories deemed detrimental to the war effort. Confederate soldiers dealt even more harshly with the *North Carolina Standard* and other "union-screamers." None of these papers supported the enemy, but any criticism seems periously close to treason in time of war.

The Spanish-American War was so short and so successful that censorship never got off the ground. Strangely enough, there was need for it. The yellow press gleefully printed any news it could find, including news of troop movements and strategy planning. Commented *The Journalist:* "We gave the Spaniards no use for spies, for our yellow journals became themselves the spies of Spain."[6] Sensationalism was at its height; William Randolph Hearst sailed his own yacht to war, and actually captured a few hapless Spanish sailors off the coast of Cuba. Hi-jinks and hoaxes inevitably impeded the war effort, but the confident U.S. military voiced no serious objections. It was a fun war.

World War One was not fun. Censorship and news management were merciless. Reporters had to be accredited by the Allied forces, and needed special permission to move from one location to another. Every dispatch from the front was ruthlessly censored in the interests of troop morale and domestic enthusiasm, as well as national security.

Back home, meanwhile, the government's Committee on Public Information was organized under George Creel. During the course of the war, the C.P.I. set up standards of voluntary press censorship and issued more than 6,000 press releases, many heavily larded with patriotic propaganda. The press observed the voluntary codes, and many American newspapers printed all 6,000 of Creel's releases.

Just to make sure, the government nationalized the infant radio industry, calling a halt to all wireless experimentation. It also passed the Espionage Act, the Trading-with-the-Enemy Act, and the Sedition Act, all of which limited the kinds of news and opinion the mass media were permitted to publish. The Sedition Act was by far the most expansive of the three. It prohibited "any disloyal, profane, scurrilous, or abusive language about the form of government of the United States, or the Constitution, military or naval forces, flag, or the uniform of the army or navy of the United States." More than 75 Socialist and German-language publications were prosecuted or threatened under these acts.

But World War One was The War To End All Wars, and very few reporters or editors objected to government censorship. Raymond S. Tompkins comments:

> The censorship irked them and they hated it at first, but gradually they grew used to it and wrote what they could, working up all the "human interest stuff" available and learning quickly that the censors loved it and almost invariably passed it—provided it said nothing about the drinking, stealing and rugged *amours* of the *soldat Américain.* . . . Dragooned into thinking about and observing the war in terms of what would get printed he [the correspondent] went on exuding larger and larger gobs of slush, to the continual delight of the appreciative censor, the supreme satisfaction of his managing editor and the glory of the paper that had sent him.[7]

In World War Two, voluntary self-censorship was instituted once again. The government issued codes urging the media to censor their reports of shipping, planes, troops, fortifications, armaments, war production, and even the weather. The program was largely successful. No American paper reported the German submarine blockade of 1942. Radar and the atomic bomb were both developed in absolute secrecy, though there were reporters and editors in the know.

The C.P.I. was revived in the form of the Office of War Information, and once again patriotic press releases filled the media. The same agency examined all communications entering or leaving the United States, and deleted whatever it thought was detrimental to the national interest. In one case this included the word "God-damned" in an Ernie Pyle dispatch. Like its predecessors, World War Two had its share of unreported stories.

The Espionage Act was still in force. Though it was used sparingly, America's few pro-Nazi media were soon suppressed.

The Korean conflict was America's first full-fledged undeclared foreign war, and the first generally unpopular war in the Twentieth Century. The government censors soon became less concerned with national security than with troop morale and military prestige. In 1950, AP's Tom Lambert and UP's Peter Kalischer were forced to return to Tokyo for "reorientation." And the Eighth Army announced that "criticism of Command decisions or of the conduct of Allied soldiers on the battlefield will not be tolerated."[8]

The censorship grew worse after General MacArthur's drive into North Korea brought the Chinese Communists into the war. In the face of intense criticism, MacArthur authorized censorship of all dispatches that might injure military morale or embarrass the U.S. government. Only after President Truman removed MacArthur from command was some measure of freedom of the press restored.

Then came Vietnam.

VIETNAM AND THE MEDIA

The story of the U.S. commitment in Southeast Asia begins as early as 1961. By then, it was already American policy to camouflage the shortcomings of the Diem regime. As one U.S. "adviser" put it: "Bad news hurts morale."[9]

He didn't say *whose* morale—and it's a pertinent question, since at that point U.S. officials claimed there were no Americans fighting in Vietnam. When an American aircraft carrier was observed in action on the Saigon River, a U.S. information officer merely said, "I don't see any aircraft carrier."[10] In 1962, the State Department sent a secret cable to Saigon:

> CORRESPONDENTS SHOULD NOT BE TAKEN ON MISSIONS WHOSE NATURE IS SUCH THAT UNDESIRABLE DISPATCHES WOULD BE HIGHLY PROBABLE. . . . WE RECOGNIZE IT NATURAL THAT AMERICAN NEWSMEN WILL CONCENTRATE ON ACTIVITIES OF AMERICANS. IT IS NOT—REPEAT NOT—IN OUR INTEREST, HOWEVER, TO HAVE STORIES INDICATING THAT AMERICANS ARE LEADING AND DIRECTING COMBAT MISSIONS AGAINST VIET CONG.[11]

As the war intensified throughout 1963, this policy could not hold up. A band of young newsmen (Neil Sheehan of UPI, Malcolm Browne of AP, David Halberstam of the New York *Times*, Charles Mohr of *Time*) reported again and again that Americans were indeed fighting in Vietnam—and losing.

Such articles were not popular back home. President Kennedy suggested that the *Times* replace Halberstam. Mme. Ngo Dinh Nhu, in the midst of a good-will tour of the U.S., commented that the reporter "should be barbecued and I would be glad to supply the fluid and the match."[12] The *Times* resisted both proposals, and Halberstam remained in Vietnam. Charles Mohr was not so fortunate. *Time* freely altered the sense of his dispatches, and eventually published a special article charging the Saigon press corps with "helping to compound the very confusion that it should be untangling for its readers at home."[13] Mohr immediately quit his job in protest, and later moved to the *Times* himself.

Halberstam and Mohr were part of a small minority. Most of the reporters in Southeast Asia acted more as mailmen than as newsmen. They faithfully delivered to their readers the messages of U.S. diplomatic and military sources. Many depended heavily on the daily government briefings and propaganda sessions—the famous "Saigon Follies." Some never got out into the field at all.

Dependence on official sources was, in fact, the great sin of the media throughout the mid-1960s. Consider the following statements from Defense Secretary Robert McNamara:

> 1962: "There is no plan for introducing combat forces into South Vietnam."
> 1963: "We have every reason to believe that [United States military] plans will be successful in 1964."
> 1964: "Reliance on military pressure upon the North would not be a proper response."
> 1965: "We have stopped losing the war."
> 1967: "Substantial progress has been achieved on virtually all fronts—political, economic, and military."[14]

Some of these statements were errors in judgment. Some were probably outright lies. In either case, the vast majority of reporters in Vietnam knew better—but very few of them bothered to set the record straight.

In November of 1967, the government undertook a supreme effort to reassure the American people about Vietnam. Ambassador Ellsworth Bunker and General William Westmoreland were put on public display. Westmoreland described the situation as "very, very encouraging;" Bunker spoke of "steady progress" and declared that two-thirds of South Vietnam was now under control. A scant two months later came the highly successful Tet offensive against the South.

The media had quoted Westmoreland and Bunker verbatim. They never forgave President Johnson for making them (as well as himself) look foolish. Though the government's "credibility gap" had opened long before, it was only after Tet that the gap was mentioned frequently in the press. From 1968 on, coverage of the war in Southeast Asia grew more and more aggressive, independent, and critical.

To read the American press before Tet, U.S. forces in Vietnam had no deserters, no racial conflict, no drug problem, and no crimes or atrocities. It is a comment on the Saigon press corps that even after Tet, when many "unreportable" stories were beginning to receive coverage, the news of the My Lai massacre first broke as a result of the independent efforts of Seymour Hersh, a free-lance writer working out of Washington.

Vietnam was an undeclared war, and so outright censorship played only a minor role. The underground press was free even to support North Vietnam without federal prosecution. Individual correspondents were free to write what they pleased. To be sure, uncritical reporters had an easier time hitching rides to the front, and found their sources more cooperative when they got there. Harrassment of the most bitter war critics was common. But on the whole, the government had little use for censorship in Vietnam. It lied instead. It lied to the reporters, and it lied to the public.

And when (as frequently happened) the lies of the authorities were contradicted by events in the field, an embargo was placed on all reporting of those events. The most flagrant embargo came during the invasion of Laos in 1971. For six days, the media were forbidden to report any events taking place on the Laos-Vietnam border. Afterward, the Associated Press wrote:

> The U.S. Command in South Vietnam has placed an embargo on certain news from the northern part of the country. Embargoes are nothing new in Vietnam, but available information indicates the one imposed last week is the strictest yet seen. . . .
>
> In this case, officials informed newsmen of the embargo but prohibited them from mentioning it and did not brief them until later—thus, in effect, placing an embargo on the embargo. . . .[15]

The embargo quite clearly had nothing to do with national security. Its goal was to forestall public protest against widening the war. But the Nixon administration claimed that the national security was at stake, and without exception the media went along with the embargo. Though opposed to the war, they were unwilling to second-guess the President on a question of national security. Bay of Pigs all over again.

Later in 1971, a former Defense Department consultant delivered to the New York *Times* a top secret government report on U.S. Vietnam policymaking throughout the 1960s. The report documented the war's "credibility gap" in fantastic detail, revealing many discrepancies between official policies and official statements. Despite its top secret status, the *Times* decided to publish the report. A temporary injunction forbidding publication was fought before the Supreme Court, which granted the *Times* the right to publish (see pp. 153–54, 173).

The significance of the Pentagon Papers (as the report came to be called) is twofold. On the one hand, the incident represents an unsuccessful government attempt at precensorship of the press—a hallmark of authoritarian control. Perhaps more important, it represents a decision by the nation's foremost newspaper to reveal the wartime secrets of the government. The *Times* determined to its own satisfaction that the Pentagon Papers contained little or nothing damaging to American national security. Although the Pentagon hotly disputed this conclusion, the *Times* stood firm on its opinion and published the report. The lesson of Bay of Pigs was beginning to take hold.

BROADCASTING AND WAR

Next to moonshots, wars are probably the most exciting, dramatic, "colorful" stories to be found. They are hard to capture in paragraphs of cold type, but ideally suited to the capabilities of radio and television.

World War Two was radio's finest hour. The entire country thrilled and chilled as Edward R. Murrow and his colleagues reported, live, the air blitz over London, the invasion of France, and other critical moments in the fighting:

> This is Edward Murrow speaking from Vienna. It's now nearly 2:30 in the morning and Herr Hitler has not yet arrived. No one seems to know just when he will get here, but most people expect him sometime after ten o'clock tomorrow morning. . . .
>
> Young storm troopers are riding about the streets, riding about in trucks and vehicles of all sorts, singing and tossing oranges out to the crowd. Nearly every principal building has its armed guard, including the one from which I am speaking. . . . There's a certain air of expectancy about the city, everyone waiting and wondering where and at what time Herr Hitler will arrive.[16]

Television's war was Vietnam—the first time in history mothers have watched their sons suffer and die on the six o'clock news. Not that there was much suffering and dying to be seen. In the interests of decency and propriety, the networks have managed to present a uniquely antiseptic picture of modern warfare. We see flag-draped coffins loaded onto helicopters with all due pomp and ceremony—not headless G.I.s in plastic bags. Michael J. Arlen comments:

> I can't say I completely agree with people who think that when battle scenes are brought into the living room the hazards of war are necessarily made "real" to the civilian audience. It seems to me that by the same process they are also made less "real"—diminished, in part, by the physical size of the television screen, which, for all the industry's advances, still shows one a picture of men three inches tall shooting at other men

three inches tall, and trivialized, or at least tamed, by the enveloping cozy alarums of the household.[17]

It is difficult to say whether television has helped or hindered the continuation of the war. On the one hand, it has made public the horrors of war; on the other hand, it has turned those horrors into exciting adventure stories. Only one thing is certain: Television *has* simplified the war in the mind of the public. Complex issues and conflicting claims are next to impossible to capture on film.

Until the Tet offensive, the broadcast media (like the rest of the press) docilely accepted the official version of events in Vietnam. On many occasions filmclips that seemed to contradict that version were simply dropped from the nightly news. And documentaries were uniformly patriotic, with perhaps a three-minute interview with Senator Fulbright to acknowledge the existence of "responsible dissent."

All that changed after Tet. The following excerpt from the CBS Evening News of June 27, 1970, is in many ways typical of Vietnam broadcast reporting today. The Cambodian invasion has just ended, a party is under way, and Morely Safer is interviewing a young American soldier on his way out:

> Safer: What was the morale like in the field among the men?
> Soldier: It was pretty bad. These clothes, I've had these clothes on for about 40 days now. We can't get clothes. We can't—mail is slow, it's pretty bad. There were a lot of people killed, and a lot of people were sad. Why, this at the end, you know? We're supposed to forget about it, something like that.
> Safer: A lot of men smoking marijuana. Was that common in your outfit?
> Soldier: Pretty common, I'd say. Just about everybody I know smokes marijuana in my outfit. There is nothing else to do.
> Safer: But the beer flows on and the band plays on and the girls are sympathetic and cheerful in that sweet, hometown way. . . . This attempt by the Army to put a nice neat World War II finish to the war in Cambodia makes for very good, very appealing propaganda pictures, but as one tanker asked me as we arrived here back at Katum, who's paying for all those ghosts we left behind? Morely Safer, CBS News, at Katum on the Cambodian border.[18]

If you oppose the war and distrust the government, this is interpretive reporting at its finest. But even those who support the war and the government must admit that at long last television has begun to speak its mind. The official view of the war in Vietnam has been too hard to swallow too many times for too long. Reluctantly, hesitantly, with agonizing slowness, the mass media have regained a little of their independence.

THE WORKING LIFE

For ambitious young reporters, war has always been the quickest route to fame. But it is also the most professionally demanding and physically dangerous assignment available.

Vietnam is no exception. In the last decade, hundreds of American newsmen have been wounded in Southeast Asia, and at least six have died. Charles Mohr, now of the New York *Times,* reports:

> There may be no inherent journalistic virtue in getting shot at (and there is even less to be said for getting hit), but with an estimated 230,000 Vietcong now scattered around South Vietnam it is difficult to avoid, even if a correspondent is trying hard to be cautious. If the correspondent is doing his job right it is impossible to avoid. . . .
>
> I spend a lot of my time running. Near Danang I ran so far away from a grenade after the pin had popped that only one fragment hit me in the leg. Near Kontum author Bernard Fall and I found ourselves in a mild road ambush and raced each other to a ditch where I fell into a nice hole concealed by bushes while Fall had to flatten himself on the hard bare ground. . . .
>
> No sensible reporter deludes himself that he is being heroic in this war. The heroics are reserved for the troops who do not enjoy the supreme privilege that any reporter can exercise at any time. That is the chance to say, "I'd love to stay, fellas, but I've got to get back to Saigon and file."[19]

NOTES

[1] James Reston, *The Artillery of the Press* (New York: Harper Colophon Books, 1966), pp. 20–21.

[2] William McGaffin and Erwin Knoll, *Anything But the Truth* (New York: G. P. Putnam's Sons, 1968), pp. 205–9.

[3] Douglass Cater, "News and the Nation's Security," *Montana Journalism Review,* 1961, pp. 2–3.

[4] William L. Rivers, *The Opinionmakers* (Boston: Beacon Press, 1965), p. 129.

[5] Martin Goodman, "Numbers Game," *Columbia Journalism Review,* Summer, 1965, pp. 16–18.

[6] Frank Luther Mott, *American Journalism,* 3rd ed. (New York: The Macmillan Co., 1962), p. 536.

[7] Joseph J. Mathews, *Reporting the Wars* (Minneapolis: University of Minnesota Press, 1957), pp. 157–58.

[8] Mott, *American Journalism,* p. 853.

[9] Stanley Karnow, "The Newsmen's War in Vietnam," *Nieman Reports,* December, 1963, p. 4.

[10] *Ibid.,* p. 6.

[11] McGaffin and Knoll, *Anything But the Truth,* p. 79.

[12] Gay Talese, *The Kingdom and the Power* (New York: World Publishing Co., 1969), pp. 466–67.

[13] Karnow, "The Newsmen's War in Vietnam," p. 3.

[14] Bruce Ladd, *Crisis in Credibility* (New York: The New American Library Inc., 1969), pp. 167–68.

[15] Associated Press, February 5, 1971.

[16] Erik Barnouw, *The Golden Web* (New York: Oxford University Press, 1968), pp. 77–78.

[17] Michael J. Arlen, *Living Room War* (New York: Viking Press, 1969), p. 8.

[18] Marvin Barrett, ed., *Survey of Broadcast Journalism, 1969–1970* (New York: Grossett & Dunlap, Inc., 1970), pp. 145–46.

[19] Ruth Adler, ed., *The Working Press* (New York: Bantam Books, Inc., 1966), pp. 80–81.

SUGGESTED READINGS

ADLER, RUTH, ed., *The Working Press.* New York: Bantam Books, Inc., 1966.

CATER, DOUGLASS, "News and the Nation's Security," *Montana Journalism Review,* 1961.

LADD, BRUCE, *Crisis in Credibility.* New York: The New American Library Inc., 1968.

McGAFFIN, WILLIAM, and ERWIN KNOLL, *Anything But the Truth.* New York: G. P. Putnam's Sons, 1968.

MATHEWS, JOSEPH J., *Reporting the Wars.* Minneapolis: University of Minnesota Press, 1967.

RESTON, JAMES, *The Artillery of the Press.* New York: Harper Colophon Books, 1966.

18   Coverage of Race

As long as there has been an America, there have been racial and ethnic minorities which the American mass media ignored or mistreated. Chief among these today are the blacks. In recent years the media have improved greatly in their coverage of blacks, but they still have a long, long way to go. Public indifference to the plight of the black community is both reflected and exacerbated by media performance.

In July of 1967, in the middle of a long, hot summer of ghetto riots, President Lyndon B. Johnson appointed the National Advisory Commission on Civil Disorders. Headed by Governor Otto Kerner of Illinois, the Commission was charged with the task of determining why blacks were rioting in the streets. Its final report placed a good deal of the blame on the mass media:

> The media report and write from the standpoint of a white man's world. The ills of the ghetto, the difficulties of life there, the Negro's burning sense of grievance, are seldom conveyed. Slights and indignities are part of the Negro's daily life, and many of them come from what he now calls "the white press"—a press that repeatedly, if unconsciously, reflects the biases, the paternalism, the indifference of white America.[1]

The Kerner Commission argued forcefully that the media alternately ignore and abuse the black man. White readers are not forced to come to grips with the problems of the ghetto and their own bigotry. Blacks are afforded little opportunity to make known their grievances and life-style. Two separate and unequal communities are thus perpetuated, with no communication between them. Unable to make themselves heard in any other way, blacks take to the street. Uninformed about the realities of ghetto life, whites are surprised. And so are the media, which ought to have known better.

THE ETHNIC PRESS

Minority ethnic groups have always been discriminated against in this country—though no other discrimination has been so long or so virulent as that against the blacks. Denied access to the majority media, these groups have traditionally organized their own. Though they could not speak to the WASPs, they could at least speak to each other.

The first foreign-language newspaper in America, the Philadelphia *Zeitung,* was founded in 1732. By 1914, the height of American immigration, there were more than 1,300 foreign-language publications in the country. The German press led the list, followed by the French, Italian, Japanese, Polish, Yiddish, and Scandinavian. War, depression, and as-similation soon took their toll. In 1970, according to *Editor & Publisher,* there were only 232 regularly published foreign-language newspapers in the United States.

The foreign-language media exist for the unassimilated, for ghetto groups that are still not a part of mainstream America. Today, this means primarily the Spanish-speaking—the Puerto Ricans in the East, the Mexi-can-Americans in the West. *El Diario,* for example, is a Spanish-lan-guage tabloid daily in New York City. Its more than 76,000 readers make it the largest foreign-language publication in the country.

How is *El Diario* different from other New York City newspapers? One 1968 analysis found the following:

> *El Diario* showed 50% Latin orientation on its front page, 46% on its "important" news pages, 78% in its inside news space, and 75% of its sports space. In addition, *El Diario,* on occasion, added a Latin slant to its coverage of essentially nonethnic news items. . . .
>
> What this means quite simply is that the Puerto Rican butcher, baker and taxi driver in New York City is reading, more often than not, differ-ent news than that read by his New York *Daily News*-reading counter-part. He, a member of the minority, is not reading much of the news read by the majority of New York City newspaper readers.[2]

Black people speak English. Unlike many Mexican-Americans and Puerto Ricans, they can read the white media. But they find so little there of relevance to their lives that they support a second, independent system of black media as well.

The first Negro newspaper in America was *Freedom's Journal,* founded in New York in 1827. More than twenty others, mostly devoted to the slavery issue, were established before the Civil War. Untypical but indicative was the case of one Willie A. Hodges, who in 1847 sought to have his opinions published in the New York *Sun.* He was told that if he wanted to see his ideas in print he would have to print them himself. So he did, in a newspaper he called the *Ram's Horn.*[3]

From 1850 to 1970, nearly 3,000 Negro publications were founded in the United States. Most were short-lived, but some survived for generations, exercising a tremendous influence on the development of the black community. Among the most successful were the Chicago *Defender* (1905), the New York *Amsterdam News* (1909), the Pittsburgh *Courier* (1910), and the Norfolk *Journal and Guide* (1911). Like most black papers, these four emerged from the inner-city ghetto. But they were really national newspapers, available at ghetto newsstands across the country.

Thomas W. Young of the *Journal and Guide* explains the influence of these papers during the early 1900s:

> By the turn of the century, second-class citizenship had become a hard reality for the Negro. . . . As the grievances against this status began to mount, it was the Negro press that aired them and thus became the chief vocal agency for the protest. These newspapers were more than just protest organs. Because news of Negro progress and aspirations was effectively quarantined by the general press, Negro newspapers became also the chroniclers of contemporary life and activities in their segregated world. . . . Even while waging that battle, many Negro newspapers developed into substantial, successful commercial ventures.[4]

In 1945, the Pittsburgh *Courier* boasted a circulation of 250,000. The Chicago *Defender* (202,000) and the Baltimore *Afro-American* (137,000) were close behind. Whites and blacks alike considered the editors of these papers to be the leaders of the Negro community. Presidents Roosevelt and Truman read the papers almost as faithfully as the typical ghetto black. Gunnar Myrdal could justly comment in his book, *An American Dilemma,* that "the Negro press . . . is rightly characterized as the greatest single power in the Negro race."[5]

Today, the *Courier*'s circulation has dropped to 60,000; the *Defender* and the *Afro-American* are similarly impoverished. Presidents no longer pay them much attention, and neither does the ghetto.

What happened? Economics are part of the answer. Rising costs have forced most black newspapers to abandon their national editions and curtail even their home editions. Competition is another piece of the problem, especially competition from black-oriented radio stations. But more important than either of these is the failure of the Negro press to keep pace with the black revolution.

John Murphy, publisher of the *Afro-American,* explains: "Newspapers are small businesses and publishers are businessmen. Surely you'd have to describe black publishers as conservatives, I suppose. In earlier years, black newspapers were spearheads of protest. Today we're much more informational." The publisher of the *Amsterdam News,* C. B. Powell, agrees. "We have not kept up with the black revolution," he admits. "But you've got to realize that we don't see our role as leaders. We are not out to revolutionize. When the *Amsterdam News* sees issues that are too revolutionary, we speak out against them."[6]

It is not that the black press has turned suddenly conservative. Rather, black newspapers have changed very little over the past few decades. They still feature crime and sensationalism on page one, black sports and black society on the inside pages. Meanwhile, the "movement" around them has been changing constantly—from civil rights and freedom someday to Black Power and Freedom Now! Black publishers are at best ambivalent about the change. A young black reporter in Chicago comments:

> Look, man, you get tired of brothers and sisters bugging you on the street because your paper isn't with The Movement. You know, one day our paper looks like it might be getting with it and the next day it sounds like the *Trib* [the highly conservative, white, Chicago *Tribune*].[7]

Little wonder, then, that the two best read black newspapers in the country today are *Muhammad Speaks* (400,000+) and the *Black Panther* (110,000). Both stand in the forefront of the black revolution.

Establishment black magazines face the same sorts of problems. *Ebony, Jet, Star,* and the like have all been forced to radicalize their content in order to retain their circulation. Still, they tend to shy away from politics, leaning instead toward the cultural "Black is Beautiful" side of the revolution. Only the massive influx of black-oriented consumer advertising has kept them afloat.

The medium that is most successful in speaking to the black community today is black radio. With rare exceptions, that medium does not speak *for* the black community. Jerry Buck, AP's television-radio writer, says that there are now some 530 radio stations in the country that program "the soul sound." Only nine of them are black-owned.[8] In the typical ghetto radio station, only the disc jockeys and the janitors are black.

New York *Times* writer Fred Ferretti (who found 16 black-owned stations) describes the programming of one of them:

.A black disc jockey—paid far less than white counterparts on larger stations, and with less chance of advancement—may play an Aretha Franklin record, then in "down home" accents assert that the record undoubtedly "made your liver quiver and your knees freeze." Then he will segue into a frantic plug for a Top Forty rock number before playing the record—deafeningly. On the hour, news will consist of a piece of wire copy ripped from a teletype and read verbatim by the same disc jockey. Required public service time will be filled mainly by pseudo-evangelist hours. And commercial sponsors will be sought willy-nilly, without sifting the "dollar-down, dollar-a-week forever" entrepreneurs from the non-deceptive advertisers.[9]

It seems almost unnecessary to add that this sort of programming is of little if any use to the black community.

The real tragedy of the black media is that they exist at all—that the white media have been unable or unwilling to meet the needs of black people. Almost as tragic is the fact that even the black media have failed to meet black needs. Black radio is owned by whites; black newspapers are run by conservatives. Only the revolutionary journals of propaganda speak directly and relevantly to their audience.

COVERING THE REVOLUTION

The history of white coverage of blacks prior to 1954 can be summarized in a word: Nothing. From time to time a movie or radio drama would feature a black character (almost always stereotyped as a bumbling, laughable menial). And newspapers and magazines carried their share of hard news about black criminals and features about black athletes. That was it for the Negro.

Then, in 1954, the Supreme Court announced its school desegregation decision and the modern civil rights movement was born. As far as the white media were concerned, it was a virgin birth—the movement came out of nowhere, with no hint of long-standing grievances. Arthur B. Bertelson of the St. Louis *Post-Dispatch* describes the rude awakening:

> At first, we self-consciously proffered tidbits with a heavy coating of soothing syrup. We dredged up sticky little features about those few Negroes who had made it. . . . In our news columns, God forgive us, we quoted those "leaders" who counseled the Negro community to be patient, that we were all good fellows, that all would be well before they knew it.
>
> When it became obvious that [the civil rights movement] wasn't going to assimilate this kind of pap, some of us began to try a little harder and discovered that what was required was a steady diet of raw—and, more often than not, unpalatable—truth.[10]

The "truth" as served up by the nation's newspapers and TV stations told of blacks valiantly struggling for their freedom from southern oppressors. Reporters on the so-called "seg beat" were sent south for months at a time. They were horrified by what they saw, and their sense of outrage permeated their stories.

After a burst of gunfire stitched holes in a University of Mississippi doorsill, *Newsweek* reporter Karl Fleming turned to a companion and said, "You know, if I were Meredith, I wouldn't go to school with these bastards."[11] Millions of *Newsweek* readers experienced the same revulsion. So did anyone who watched television or read a newspaper.

From *Brown v. Board of Education* in 1954 to the Watts riot of 1965, the civil rights movement was centered in the South. The northern media (which means the national media) did a commendable job of covering that movement. It was an easy story to cover—the heroes and villains clearly identified, the whole mess conveniently far away. Throughout the decade, those very same media managed to ignore completely the festering sores of their own local ghettos. Civil rights reporters invaded Mississippi and Alabama by the hundreds, but only an occasional crime writer bothered to visit Harlem, Watts, or Hough.

The southern media didn't have it so easy. The violence was in their own backyard; the challenge was to their own way of life. On the whole, they acquitted themselves well. Ted Poston, now a reporter for the New York *Post*, writes:

> There have always been, and there still are, some fine and courageous Southern papers. As a native Kentuckian, I was reared from my earliest days on the Louisville *Courier-Journal*. As a college student, Pullman porter, and dining-car waiter, I received a valuable adjunct to my education through the Nashville *Tennessean*, the Atlanta *Constitution*, the St. Louis *Post-Dispatch*, and other pillars of liberal journalism in the South.[12]

Ralph E. McGill of the *Constitution* and Harry S. Ashmore of the Little Rock (Ark.) *Gazette* both won Pulitzer Prizes for their coverage of southern racial unrest.

After the Watts riot of 1965, the focus of the story moved north. And the media discovered all over again that black people were big news. Newspapers and broadcasters moved mountains in a frantic effort to cover the endless succession of riots, demonstrations, and confrontations that characterized the late 1960s. The job they did was less than perfect (see Chapter 16), but in a casualties-and-damage sense it was better than adequate.

To be sure, racial conflicts have not always received fair and ample treatment in the media. Local radical leaders are sometimes blacked out by local papers and stations. Peaceful demonstrations are ignored, or are made to look violent. Police sources are taken at their word, even when directly contradicted by ghetto witnesses. And confrontations of tremendous significance are downplayed or misplayed. In 1968, three black students were shot and killed by police in Orangeburg, South Carolina. The media barely mentioned the incident. Two years later, when four white students were killed at Kent State University, the story filled front pages for days.

Nevertheless, media coverage of the facts of racial unrest has been magnificent in comparison with coverage of the grievances that underlie that unrest. As the Kerner Commission report stressed again and again: "The Commission's major concern with the news media is not in riot reporting as such, but in the failure to report adequately on race relations and ghetto problems. . . ."[13]

COVERING THE BLACK MAN

There are three criticisms frequently voiced about media coverage (and noncoverage) of the black man. First, the media have failed to make clear to white readers the problems, frustrations, and tensions of the ghetto. Second, the media frequently exhibit bias or racism in their approach to black news. And third, the media have ignored the everyday life of the black man, the "good news" that comes out of the ghetto.

PROFESSIONAL STANDARDS

In the wake of Watts, the University of Missouri invited 75 newsmen to a conference to propose guidelines for racial news coverage. Among the major recommendations were these:[14]

1. Probe the areas of discontent. Dig beneath the surface both before and after a crisis, and examine proposed solutions to problems.
2. Stay with the story. Concentrate on thorough follow-up of developments after the first day's headlines.
3. Include interpretation, whenever necessary, to explain to a predominantly white readership *why* an incident occurred.
4. Assign the best reporters to the police beat.
5. Time news stories so as to avoid stoking the fires of prejudice. For example, it might be advisable to wait until a Negro family had settled down in a white neighborhood before carrying a story about the move.
6. Distinguish between the authentic and the "phony" Negro leader. Exercise caution in giving advance publicity to professional bigots and hatemongers of all races.
7. Increase the number of Negroes in all departments of the news media, with particular emphasis on the reportorial staff.

We have said enough already about the first criticism.   As a rule, the media are much better at covering a crisis after it arrives than they are at seeing it on the way.   The racial crisis of the 1960s was no exception. As long as the black community kept its suffering and anger to itself, the media were content to leave well enough alone.   Only after the inevitable explosion did they suddenly wake to the issue of race.   And even then, they concentrated on the explosion itself, devoting far less time and space to the underlying grievances.

The charge of racism is a hard one to document.   In 1968, black militants in Oakland, California, organized a boycott of a white-owned ghetto shopping center.   In response, the Oakland *Tribune* printed a cartoon of a gloved hand pointing a pistol at the reader. "What would *you* do in a case like this?" asked the caption.   "Think it over carefully because soon you may have to decide whether you want to run a business with a gun to your head or close up shop." Two black reporters resigned in protest, charging *Tribune* publisher William Knowland with racism.[15]   At best, the cartoon seems a rather extreme response to the time-honored pressure tactic of a boycott.

Oakland, by the way, will soon have a black majority, as white middle-class residents flee to the suburbs.   The *Tribune* may well flee right along with them, expanding its suburban coverage and cutting down on inner-city reporting.   The Detroit *News*, among other papers, has already taken this step.   The reasons may well be economic; advertisers are most interested in the wealthy suburbs.   But from the viewpoint of the ghetto resident, at least, it looks like racism.

More often than not, racism in the news media is unconscious and indirect.   Robert E. Smith of *Newsday* offers a few examples:[16]

- The New York *Times*, in an article on President Johnson's farewell to a group of high-ranking black government officials, carefully referred to "the well-dressed Negro officials and their wives."
- Under a photo of two Negro baseball stars, the Detroit *News* ran the caption: "Here Come de Tigers!"
- An ABC network documentary forgot at least ten percent of its audience when it had the narrator intone: "We don't know what it's really like to grow up as a black."
- A *Newsday* article on three black members of a prestigious government committee noted with some wonder that they were "well-educated, articulate, and middle class."
- In the wake of a disturbance, the Tampa *Tribune* headlined the startling fact that "Sunday Night Racial Rioting Had At Least One Negro Hero."

Smith adds that the media often refer to black racism as "reverse discrimination."   It is reverse, of course, only from the white point of view. Similarly, a frequent media response to racial unrest is a plea for a "return to normal," which to the black man presumably means a return to poverty and frustration.   On a more trivial level, Smith points out that reporters refer to black athletes by their first names far more often than white athletes. This is, perhaps, a genteel and well-intentioned sort of racism, but it is racism nonetheless.

The third criticism is in many ways the most important. It is almost a prerequisite for white acceptance of blacks that the everyday reality of black living, the good and the bad, be made clear to white readers. It is also essential to black self-acceptance (and black pride) that this everyday reality be portrayed by the media. As the Kerner Commission put it: "It would be a contribution of inestimable importance to race relations in the United States simply to treat ordinary news about Negroes as news of other groups is now treated."[17] The Commission went on to specify the need for black content in newspapers, magazines, movies, radio, television, and advertising.

The print media have made the least progress of all. Even today, northern newspapers seldom carry much in the way of black club news, black society, black engagements and marriages, even black obituaries. Some southern papers still reserve this material for special segregated "Black Star" editions. And when a black civic group plans a dance, say, or opens a youth club, it is extremely unlikely to get much publicity from the white press. The same goes for magazines. On April 19, 1968, *Life* gave tremendous play to the murder and funeral of Dr. Martin Luther King. The King story featured the only black faces to be found anywhere on the pages of that issue.

The blackout of "good" Negro news sometimes goes even further. For many years the Jackson *Daily News* Relays were the most publicized

---

CHICANOS IN THE MEDIA

There are 5.6 million Mexican-Americans in the United States; the two million who live in California comprise that state's largest minority. There have been Chicano entertainers and movie stars—Dolores Del Rio and Ramon Novarro, Anthony Quinn and Ricardo Montalban, Trini Lopez and Vikki Carr. But for the most part, the media image of Mexican-Americans has been less than positive. Says TV critic Dwight Newton: "On movie screens, and later television screens, they were pictured as loiterers, loafers, cowhands, revolutionaries, assassins, bad guys."[18] And in the news, of course, they were ignored.

Little wonder, then, that the Chicano organization Nosotros (founded by Montalban) objected strenuously to the corn chip advertising campaign featuring the "Frito Bandito." Most stations self-righteously resisted the pressure, until eventually it was the advertiser, not the media, that decided to abandon the character.

Since the Los Angeles disruptions of 1970 and 1971, Chicanos are beginning to get some serious attention in the news media. Does it take a disruption to capture that attention? Apparently it does.

---

track-and-field meet in Mississippi. In 1968, the relays were reluctantly integrated. In 1969, black athletes won many events, but their pictures were not printed in the *Daily News*. In 1970, rather than face the dilemma again, the paper canceled the meet entirely.

Film and broadcasting have a somewhat better record. From "Gone With the Wind" to "Guess Who's Coming to Dinner" is a big step. And "Cotton Comes to Harlem," a spoof of white stereotypes about ghetto life, is a bigger step still. The same change is reflected on television—from black menial to black superhero to black ordinary guy. In 1970, actor Bill Cosby, formerly of "I Spy" (a superhero show), inaugurated his own comedy series, in which he played an average schmo who just happened to be black. It was a big step for television.

MINORITY EMPLOYMENT

One of the most obvious signs of racism in the media—and one of the most important reasons that racism has survived so long—is the ludicrously small number of black reporters. The Kerner Commission hit this point hard:

> The journalistic profession has been shockingly backward in seeking out, hiring, training, and promoting Negroes. Fewer than 5 percent of the people employed by the news business in editorial jobs in the United States today are Negroes. Fewer than 1 percent of editors and supervisors are Negroes, and most of them work for Negro-owned organizations. . . . News organizations must employ enough Negroes in positions of significant responsibility to establish an effective link to Negro actions and ideas and to meet legitimate employment expectations.[19]

Spurred on by the Commission, the mass media have spent the last few years searching frantically for black newsmen. Not surprisingly, they found few blacks with both the interest and the training; no one had ever bothered to encourage the former or provide the latter. At a recent convention of the California Newspaper Publishers Association, one talented black college junior was extended half a dozen firm job offers, while his white counterparts were informed that money was tight and jobs were scarce. The black student was forced to turn down all his offers; he had already accepted one from a Northern California television station.

This frenzy of recruiting activity raises several questions. First, is it legitimate or is it tokenism? There is reason to suspect the latter. For one thing, the very media that have scurried to hire a black or two have been extremely reluctant to support large-scale journalism training programs for blacks. And they have hesitated to place their black employees in policy-making positions.

Consider the following incident. Ben Gilbert, then city editor of the Washington *Post*, received a telephone call from a New York *Times* executive. How many blacks had the *Post* hired, he wanted to know, and where did it find so many? Gilbert told him that the *Post* had twelve, and then asked how many blacks the *Times* employed. "Three," came the response, "but we won't lower our standards."[20] This sort of dialogue makes it very difficult to believe that media employment of blacks is anything but tokenism.

An even more vital question is this one: What should black reporters be doing once they're hired? When the Washington *Post* hired its first black reporter in 1952, it was careful to assign him only nonracial stories, where his presence and copy would stir up no controversy. But during the riots of the late 1960s, many newspapers found that their white reporters were ineffective (and even unsafe) in the ghetto. When these papers got around to hiring their first black, they naturally assigned him to the "civil rights" beat.

Most black reporters today devote a significant percentage of their time to black news. Many are glad to do so; that's where the action is, and that's where they can make the greatest contribution. But others object to this form of segregation. Says one veteran: "I would want to be hired as a newsman, not as a Negro. . . . I want to feel that if the civil rights problem ended in the morning, I'd still have a job to do. . . . On the job, I try to be a mirror. I talk to somebody and he starts talking about niggers. I don't correct him. I take it down. I just want to be sure I spell it right."[21]

Ideally, of course, black reporters ought to be covering all kinds of stories, including racial ones. But ours is not an ideal world. The biggest contribution a black newsman can make today is to help his paper do what it should have been doing long ago—covering the black community completely, fairly, and sensitively. Again and again, white reporters have proved themselves unable or unwilling to do this. Given the incredible gravity of racial conflict, we cannot help feeling that black newsmen are most desperately needed in the ghetto.

NOTES

[1] National Advisory Commission on Civil Disorders (Kerner Commission), *Report of the National Advisory Commission on Civil Disorders* (New York: Bantam Books, Inc., 1968), p. 366.

[2] David Sachsman, "Two New York Newspapers," unpublished paper, Stanford University, 1968, p. 11.

[3] Jack Lyle, ed., *The Black American and the Press* (Los Angeles: The Ward Ritchie Press, 1968), p. 3.

[4] Thomas W. Young, "Voice of Protest, Prophet of Change," in *Race and the*

News Media, ed. Paul L. Fisher and Ralph L. Lowenstein (New York: Anti-Defamation League of B'nai B'rith, 1967), pp. 127–28.

⁵ L. F. Palmer, Jr., "The Black Press in Transition," *Columbia Journalism Review,* Spring, 1970, p. 31.

⁶ *Ibid.,* pp. 33–34.

⁷ *Ibid.,* p. 34.

⁸ Jerry Buck, "Blacks Own Few Radio Stations," Palo Alto (Calif.) *Times* (AP), April 8, 1970, p. 21.

⁹ Fred Ferretti, "The White Captivity of Black Radio," *Columbia Journalism Review,* Summer, 1970, p. 35.

¹⁰ Arthur B. Bertelson, "Keeper of a Monster," in *Race and the News Media,* ed. Fisher and Lowenstein, pp. 61–62.

¹¹ Ray Jenkins, "Open Season in Alabama," *Nieman Reports,* March, 1965, p. 8.

¹² Ted Poston, "The American Negro and Newspaper Myths," in *Race and the News Media,* ed. Fisher and Lowenstein, p. 64.

¹³ *Report of the National Advisory Commission on Civil Disorders,* p. 382.

¹⁴ Fisher and Lowenstein, eds., *Race and the News Media,* pp. 9–10.

¹⁵ "Is Oakland There?" *Newsweek,* May 18, 1970, p. 100.

¹⁶ Robert E. Smith, "They Still Write It White," *Columbia Journalism Review,* Spring, 1969, pp. 36–38.

¹⁷ *Report of the National Advisory Commission on Civil Disorders,* p. 385.

¹⁸ Dwight Newton, "A Minority Seldom Seen," San Francisco *Sunday Examiner and Chronicle,* Feb. 14, 1971, Sec. B, p. 4.

¹⁹ *Report of the National Advisory Commission on Civil Disorders,* pp. 384–85.

²⁰ Jules Witcover, "Washington's White Press Corps," *Columbia Journalism Review,* Winter, 1969–1970, p. 44.

²¹ *Ibid.,* p. 46.

SUGGESTED READINGS

FERRETTI, FRED, "The White Captivity of Black Radio," *Columbia Journalism Review,* Summer, 1970.

FISHER, PAUL L., and RALPH L. LOWENSTEIN, eds., *Race and the News Media.* New York: Anti-Defamation League of B'nai B'rith, 1967.

GREENBERG, BRADLEY, and BRENDA DERVIN, "Mass Communication Among the Urban Poor," *Public Opinion Quarterly,* Summer, 1970.

LYLE, JACK, ed., *The Black American and the Press.* Los Angeles: The Ward Ritchie Press, 1968.

NATIONAL ADVISORY COMMISSION ON CIVIL DISORDERS (KERNER COMMISSION), *Report of the National Advisory Commission on Civil Disorders.* New York: Bantam Books, Inc., 1968.

PALMER, L. F., JR., "The Black Press in Transition," *Columbia Journalism Review,* Spring, 1970.

WITCOVER, JULES, "Washington's White Press Corps," *Columbia Journalism Review,* Winter, 1969–1970.

19   Coverage
of Specialized News

The front pages of American newspapers are filled with news of national and local government, of crime and violence, of wars and racial problems. Little room (and little time) is left for more specialized kinds of news. In areas like foreign affairs, science, environment, consumer protection, education, and labor, only the most sensational stories are likely to reach the public. Often these are not the most important ones.

Different topics become "important" in the mass media for different reasons. Some are well covered because of their obvious and direct impact on the audience—urban riots, for example. Others, such as minor crimes and human-interest features, receive extensive treatment because the audience finds them absorbing, because they are easy to cover, or because they are traditional media staples.

A topic that embodies all these sources of appeal is bound to monopolize the front page. A battle, for example, is exciting to read about and clearly important to know about; it is a traditional news item and a relatively easy one to report. Battles are likely to be well-covered.

The reverse is also true. Topics that are new to the media, or difficult to report, or dull to read about, or hard to relate to, inevitably receive short shrift in our news. Such topics, unfortunately, are often very important.

When editors compare notes on readership, they often disagree on which kinds of news are the most popular—sports, comics, the front page, or what. But when it comes to the least popular kind of news, they are unanimous. Foreign affairs takes the palm, hands down.

As evidence of audience apathy, editors may point to any of a number of studies. A typical one, conducted in 1953, found that the average adult read only twelve column inches of foreign news a day, spending roughly two minutes and 20 seconds doing so. When the readers were asked if they'd like to see more international news in the papers, only eight percent answered yes. Fourteen percent had no opinion, and 78 percent said definitely not.[1]

Little wonder that most editors have cut their foreign news to the bone. There are exceptions, of course. The New York *Times* gives 22 percent of its news hole to international affairs, and the *Christian Science Monitor* devotes 37 percent of its space to foreign news. But the figure for the average daily paper is less than eight percent. And the figure for most broadcast news operations is lower still.

Besides public indifference, editors have another good reason for downplaying foreign news: It is difficult and expensive to cover. A good foreign correspondent needs special training in the culture, politics, and language of the country (or more likely the countries) he is to cover. But trained men command higher salaries—not to mention the added costs of food, lodging, and "hardship pay" for an American forced to live and work overseas. Just to make matters worse, the host country may impose severe restrictions on where the reporter may travel and whom he may interview. His stories may be censored to the point of uselessness; he and his family may even be kicked out of the country entirely. It seems a lot of trouble to go to for an article that nobody will read anyhow.

War zones aside, there are fewer than 500 full-time American newsmen abroad. The wire services have the largest foreign staffs, and supply the vast majority of the international news in the American media. Only a half dozen newspapers (notably the New York *Times*) have more than one or two men overseas. So do the three television networks and a handful of magazines. The typical local newspaper or broadcast station, of course, has no foreign staff at all.

On the whole, American foreign correspondents are topnotch reporters, skilled and experienced in their trade. The swashbuckling loner of movie fame has pretty much disappeared, to be replaced by the organization newsmen. Leo Bogart notes that the modern overseas reporter "works as part of a bureau team, and he is rooted to his station by long residence, an established family life, and a comfortable income."[2]

Nevertheless, 500 men spread over an entire world make a thin network. True, they are aided by hundreds of part-timers, freelancers, and foreign nationals working as stringers. But on the other hand, they are heavily concentrated in Western Europe, and spend most of their time reporting the same stories. England, France, and Germany are reasonably well covered. Not so Ethiopia, Finland, and Guyana.

Nearly all the foreign news that reaches the American public falls into one of three categories. In order of importance, these are: the political, the sensational, and the colorful.

Political news is the most common largely because it is the easiest to gather. Government officials are happy to explain their viewpoint, and to supplement the explanation with handouts and other documents (many of them already translated into English). Local newspaper reports, which often reflect official government thinking, are another important source. The opposition stance, of course, is harder to find and more dangerous to report. Many reporters are content to make do without it.

Sensational news is popular with reporters because it is popular with readers. "For the A wire," writes a former AP bureau chief in Colombia, "I file earthquakes, student riots, general strikes, assassination attempts, and plane crashes. These I send 'urgent' if a reasonable number of peo-

---

CHAUVINISM

Four-fifths of all U.S. foreign correspondents, according to one study, believe their reports should not be influenced by American foreign policy.[3] This is an admirable stance—but also a somewhat naive one. Reporters are people, and so they inevitably carry a built-in nationalistic bias. So do editors and publishers—and for that matter so do readers. The bias is expressed in the kinds of countries reporters get assigned to, in the kinds of stories they choose to write, and in the kinds of information they include in the stories. There is no more reason to trust an American newsman writing about Cuba than a Cuban newsman writing about America.

In a classic study of the New York *Times,* Walter Lippmann and Charles Merz documented this bias with respect to the Russian Revolution. Most Americans, and hence most American reporters, wanted Bolshevism to fail. Between 1917 and 1919, therefore, the *Times* reported no less than 91 times that the new Soviet government was about to fall. The authors termed this "a case of seeing not what was, but what men wished to see."[4] The Lippmann-Merz conclusion is as valid today as it was in 1919.

Even if reporters were able to shed their free-world bias, few editors or readers would appreciate the change. A reporter who learned "to float free and almost denationalize himself," writes Christopher Rand, "would be rushed home to be reindoctrinated."[5]

---

ple have been killed. For the regional and secondary news wires I include items about coffee, oil—Texas is most interested—and banditry."[6]

Colorful news is prized for its human-interest value, though it may give little insight into the people it describes. Typical topics include Japanese geishas and African hitchhikers. Often these items have a strong American angle: "Hot Dogs Big Hit in Iran" or "Bolivians Find New Uses for Saran Wrap."

SCIENCE AND MEDICINE

A survey conducted in 1958 revealed the startling fact that 37 percent of newspaper readers read all the medical news available to them, and 42 percent wanted more. For non-medical science news both figures stood at 28 percent—considerably higher than the percentages for crime news, national politics, and other "popular" topics.[7]

So what happened? Did editors immediately increase the amount of science and medical news in their papers? They did not. The average newspaper today devotes just under five percent of its news hole to science and health. So did the average newspaper in 1958. The average broadcast station, by the way, allots an even smaller piece of its news time to science and medicine. The weekly news magazines do considerably better, but for really complete information you have to read a few specialized publications—*Scientific American, Psychology Today, Popular Science, Science Digest, Today's Health,* etc.

Why have editors ignored what looks like a public mandate for more science news? Money is part of the answer. A skilled science writer must have at least a little training in science; such men are hard to find and expensive to hire. Most metropolitan papers already have one science writer (as do the wire services, the news magazines, and the TV networks). They are reluctant to look for another.

But there is a more fundamental answer. Editors simply don't believe the public really wants more science news. The science that now appears in the papers, they point out, is a very special kind of science: the sensational, the colorful, the halfway-political, plus an occasional monumentally important discovery. Of course the readers like that kind of stuff. But would they really go for the more everyday scientific advances? Most editors think not.

The national space effort was the big science story of the 1960s. It was handled, not as a complex scientific project, nor even as a controversial political one, but rather as an exercise in chauvinism and fantasy. The National Aeronautics and Space Administration was the only available source of information, and its experts literally taught science writers the ABCs of space. NASA's press releases and "information kits" were always voluminous, always enthusiastic, and always careful to conceal any and all problems. The U.S. space effort was the subject of more fan writing and less investigative reporting than the baseball World Series.

Then came the Apollo fire. In January, 1967, three astronauts died during a routine test of their capsule. James A. Skardon wrote in the *Columbia Journalism Review:*

> The Apollo fire brought reality with shocking suddenness. It destroyed the fairy-tale aspects of the space program, riddled the carefully contrived NASA success image, and exposed the performance of NASA, its prime contractors, and the press itself to public examination.[8]

Hindsight tells us that Skardon was over-optimistic. The tragic incident was soon forgotten, NASA lived through the scandal, and the public lost interest in space exploration only after the first Americans set foot on the moon. Mission accomplished.

This show-business approach to science news is more the rule than the exception. When Dr. Christiaan Barnard of Cape Town became the first surgeon to perform a successful heart transplant, the mass media turned him into an instant celebrity. The medical and legal complications of the story were almost ignored, as was the fact that 20 surgical teams around the world were ready to perform the same operation. *Time* gleefully put Dr. Barnard on its cover, and reported that his daughter was a champion water-skier. CBS brought him to America to appear on "Face the Nation," and NBC was shocked to learn that he would not allow it to film the next operation. Instead, NBC paid thousands of dollars for exclusive rights to the life story of Philip Blaiberg, Dr. Barnard's second patient.[9]

Nearly all front-page science and health stories share this sensational, uncritical approach. Inside stories usually resort to a light human-interest angle instead. Veteran science writer Frank Carey lists some of the stories he has covered:

> Scientists found that even the mighty dinosaurs had rheumatoid arthritis . . . Researchers came close to isolating the sex-lure chemical by which the female German cockroach calls her boy-friend to a date . . . Proof was established at long last that women are broader in the derriere than men . . . Gout sufferers could take heart in the finding that their ailment apparently is a hallmark of genius . . . Wise men at a famous laboratory ran a six-day cocktail party for mice and found that, as with men, there are "social drinkers" and teetotallers among them, not to mention a few real souses. . . .[10]

While men like Carey are busy with these items, many genuinely significant (but unromantic) science stories go completely unreported.

In June of 1969, ABC commentator Edward P. Morgan addressed a journalism conference at Stanford University. "In the 1950s," he mused, "reporters covered the cold war in depth, but they missed completely the civil rights movement and the racial crisis of the 1960s. What crisis of the 1970s, I wonder, are the mass media failing to report now?" Morgan then answered his own question: environmental deterioration.

All that's changed now. Some time in 1969, the news media suddenly discovered the environment. Maybe it was the Santa Barbara oil spill and the sight of seabirds covered with goo. Perhaps it was the sudden environmental interest of major political figures like Senator Edmund Muskie and President Richard Nixon. Possibly editors across the country finally got fed up with commuter traffic, smog, junkyards, and skyscrapers. Whatever the reasons, there is no doubt that after decades of neglect the subject of the environment was suddenly glamorous.

There are at least six reasons why the media ignored the environment for so long, and why they still cover it more poorly than they might.

1. Until very recently there has been no environmental group powerful enough to fight for press coverage. The popular image of the Sierra Club or Audubon Society member is that of an ineffectual, fluttery birdwatcher. Only in the last year or two have strong local pressure groups developed, capable of making environmental news and forcing the media to cover it.

2. The short-run economic interests of the media favor unbridled industrial growth and environmental exploitation. On the one hand, advertisers dislike articles on the need for pollution control (especially if they name the polluters). And on the other hand, growth—however uncontrolled—means more readers and higher advertising rates. It takes a courageous publisher or broadcaster to bite the hand that feeds him.

3. The environmental story is seldom a visible one. Air and water pollution, DDT and mercury poisoning, the population explosion—these are all stories that build up slowly, imperceptibly, from day to day. There is no specific news event, no press conference, no handout, on which to hang the story. A reporter cannot interview a lake and ask if it's dying; until the lake is dead, in fact, there is seldom *anyone* to interview.

4. For reporters with little background in chemistry, biology, and the like, the environmental story is next to impossible to cover. Without special training, reporters are at the mercy of their sources, who often have good reason to hide the truth. As Roberta Hornig of the Washington *Star* has said, "every story is like taking a college course."[11]

5. Unless it is approached with imagination and flair, an environmental article can be deathly dull—full of facts and figures, chemicals and

ECO–PORNOGRAPHY

The environmental bandwagon is as appealing to advertisers as it is to reporters and editors. In 1970, the Standard Oil Company of California claimed that its F-310 gasoline additive would dramatically cut air pollution. The Pacific Gas and Electric Company claimed that its nuclear power plants would provide "a balance of ecology and energy." And Potlatch Forests Inc. claimed that it spent millions to stop its paper plant from polluting the Clearwater River. Literally thousands of ads and commercials have expressed the advertiser's sudden environmental responsibility.

Many of these advertisements are so misleading that Thomas Turner terms them "eco-pornography."[12] The F-310 campaign was declared fraudulent by the Federal Trade Commission. The PG&E ads forgot to mention that nuclear power plants cause thermal pollution. And Potlatch proved its concern for the Clearwater River with photos taken upstream of the plant; downstream was an ecological disaster.

Eco-pornography not only misleads the public. It also exhausts the public's interest in environmental problems. Advertising executive Jerry Mander writes: "People's eyes are already beginning to glaze at the sight of still more jargon about saving the world. It's awfully hard to outshout roughly a billion dollars of advertising money."[13]

---

gadgets, measurements and more measurements. Many editors made it a policy not to run such stories on their front page—or not to run them at all.

6. Environmental news is inherently interdisciplinary. A good ecology reporter must master not only the scientific technicalities of his beat, but also its political, social, cultural, and economic ramifications. A science writer can't handle it on his own; neither can a business writer or a political writer.

Environmental news coverage in 1970 was as extensive as one could reasonably expect. Will environmental news coverage in 1975, say, be equally extensive? Perhaps not. In December of 1970, NBC newsman John Chancellor told a Stanford University audience that, in his opinion, media interest in the environment had already peaked and was on the decline. As if to prove the point, NBC cancelled its environmental documentary series, "In Which We Live," after eleven weeks.

If ecology does turn out to be just a fad for the news media, it may well be (as one bumper-sticker put it) "The Last Fad." The quality of our environment and perhaps our very survival are at stake.

CONSUMERS

Americans devote a good portion of their lives to the art of consuming. One might think, therefore, that the mass media would take a lively interest in consumer news. One might think wrong.

Most of the main reasons for media inattention to the consumer protection story are already familiar to us. First, there is no powerful consumer's lobby to fight for coverage. Second, advertisers prefer to retain their monopoly on consumer information. Third, the plight of the consumer has only recently reached "crisis" proportions, forcing the media to take notice.

There is a fourth reason of equal importance: The federal government often prefers to "protect" the manufacturer instead of the consumer. Until recently, the Federal Trade Commission maintained a notoriously cozy relationship with the companies it was supposed to regulate. And the other agencies of government have traditionally followed suit.

In one famous case, Consumers Union asked the Veterans Administration to release the results of its tests on hearing aids. CU planned to run the findings in its influential magazine, *Consumer Reports*. The VA turned down the request on the grounds that it wished to avoid publicizing the trade secrets of the hearing aid manufacturers. Consumers Union took the case to court, and eventually won the right to the data. CU President Colston E. Warne commented: "It is abundantly clear that a search of Government files would reveal a considerable body of information about the performance of available goods and services on the American market. . . . The need today is to unlock that information."[14]

It is true that the government is often reluctant to release consumer information that might embarrass manufacturers. But it is also true that very few publishers and broadcasters have followed the lead of *Consumer Reports* and sought that information in court.

What little consumer news does reach the media is frequently ignored or underplayed. The Washington *Post* has traditionally consigned consumer news to the women's section; the New York *Times* often puts it on the financial pages. When Ralph Nader's book *Unsafe at Any Speed* (a critical attack on the automobile industry) was offered to the nation's press for serialization, 700 newspapers turned it down.[15] More often than not, advertiser pressure is the cause of the omission. On the CBS evening news, Walter Cronkite read an item stating that many pharmaceutical products were actually useless—but he didn't say *which* products. One was mouthwash; the CBS news was sponsored that evening by Scope mouthwash.

By the end of the 1960s, consumer protection was too big a political issue for the media to ignore. Supermarket boycotts, stockholders' uprisings, and the like were news events that simply had to be covered. The same was true of the actions and pronouncements of government officials, who did their best to capitalize on the wave of consumerism. The circulation figures of *Consumer Reports* tell the story. Founded in 1936, the magazine finally reached a circulation of a million in 1966. By 1970 it had climbed to nearly 1,900,000—and it was still climbing.

Consumer news has a long way to go, but it is a great deal better today than it was three or four years ago. Unfortunately, it took a crisis in public confidence to make it that way. For decades, the media were content to ignore the plight of the consumer. Only when consumer affairs became an undeniable political issue—when they could ignore it no longer—did they show a sudden interest.

EDUCATION AND LABOR

Most educators would agree that education reporters need every bit as much specialized training as science reporters. Most labor experts would say the same for labor reporters. Most editors think they're both wrong —for different reasons.

Labor news simply isn't popular enough to justify a specialist. According to one study in the 1950s, labor news filled less than two percent of the average newspaper, and was read by only 17 percent of the readers.[16] The figures are certainly not higher today; in all probability they have declined. In any event the number of specialized labor editors has gone down. In 1951, there were 154 of them listed in the *Editor & Publisher Yearbook.* In 1967, there were only 12.

Education, on the other hand, has quite obviously increased in importance since the 1950s, when it filled only 1.4 percent of the average paper and was read by only 16.6 percent of the readers.[17] And the number of education editors has risen also. Out of 52 major metropolitan newspapers, only ten had an education specialist in 1945. By 1966, 49 of them did.[18] Education is a typically "soft" beat. It generates a lot of news, and therefore deserves its own full-time reporter. But very few editors believe that reporter requires any special training.

Untrained reporters in both fields are ill-equipped to handle the technicalities of their subjects—pension fund manipulations and curriculum developments, cost-of-living raises and the theory of permissivism. Fortunately, they are seldom asked to do that kind of story anyhow. The public's interest in labor and education is severely limited. People like to read stories about controversy in the schools and crisis on the picket lines. That is mainly what they get.

Former Secretary of Labor W. Willard Wirtz notes that in his field "good news, reversing the adage, is no news." Wirtz continues: "A strike is invariably the subject of extended coverage, with pictures, and usually with accompanying editorials. The peaceful signing of a new collective bargaining agreement, even in a major industry, is at best a one-day story, usually on an inside page."[19] Similarly, in education, college riots receive sensational front-page coverage, while colleges that have found peaceful solutions to their problems are rarely covered at all.

———————

Certain favored kinds of specialized news are not required to compete for space and time with political stories and the like. Instead, they are organized into special sections of a newspaper, magazine, or broadcast news program, and are granted regular allotments of space and manpower. Usually these special sections are extremely popular, though the news they offer is often substandard.

BUSINESS

The mass media in America pay an impressive amount of attention to the world of business and finance. The average daily newspaper allots at least three or four pages a day to this subject—more than it gives to foreign affairs, science, environment, consumers, education, and labor combined. Almost every paper has a business editor, and the average metropolitan daily employs a business staff of half a dozen men or more. Broadcasting, meanwhile, devotes several minutes a night to news of commerce and finance—more time than it gives to any other specialized topic except sports and weather. And there are more magazines devoted exclusively to business than to any other special interest.

Why all this attention? True, there are nearly 30,000,000 stockholders in the United States, most of whom like to check the listings every day or two. But there are 76,000,000 union members in the country, and still labor news is scarce.

There are at least four explanations. First, business news has a long tradition in the mass media. The first American newspapers were begun to meet the needs of the merchant community for news of ship arrivals and the like. Though the percentage of businessmen among their readers has declined, most papers have never lost their early allegiance to the world of commerce. Second, the audience for business news, though small, is very dedicated. Many readers buy an afternoon paper solely in order to check on the stock market—information they cannot get from broadcast news. Third, media owners are businessmen themselves, and therefore sympathetic to the information needs of the business community.

The fourth reason is probably the most important: Business news is cheap and easy to gather. The biggest chunk of the business section is-of course the stock tables. These come direct from AP or UPI by high-speed wire, ready to be inserted into the paper. For offset papers no typesetting is required, much less editing. National business and economic stories also come via wire. Papers that need more of this sort of news than AP and UPI provide can subscribe to the special Dow Jones and Reuters business wires. As for local business and financial news, that comes in "over the transom"—press releases by the bushel from all the firms in town. A business reporter can work for years without ever leaving his desk. Some do. Many more leave their desks only to attend lavish press luncheons, boozy retirement banquets, and free junkets to new factories in exotic places.

Good business reporting, of course, is by no means cheap or easy. For one thing, corporate information policies are far more secretive than those of government. The law permits private corporations to hide what-

---

BUSINESS PUFFERY

The biggest problem in most business reporting is puffery—free publicity for local corporations masquerading as legitimate news. The Wilmington (Del.) *News-Journal* is one of the few newspapers in the country with an explicit policy on the subject:

> *Personnel Changes.* Appointments, promotions, resignations, etc., are news up—or down—to a point, depending on how important the job is. . . .
>
> *New Businesses.* A new business or a change in ownership is news. So is a major expansion of an established firm, or a major remodeling project. Let's not get sucked in, however, by somebody who's just added another showcase or finally put a badly needed coat of paint on the walls. . . .
>
> *Business Anniversaries.* The fact that a firm has been in business for x number of years hardly excites our readers. . . . We will not report such anniversaries except on special occasions—such as a 50th, 75th, or 100th anniversary. . . .
>
> *Company Awards.* If a company could get newspaper coverage of awards it makes or prizes it gives its own employees, there would be no limit on the number of plaques, scrolls, certificates, and gold keys gathering dust in Wilmington households. So let's help fight the dust menace by covering only very special awards within a company—a recognition of 50 years of service, for example—or genuine honors bestowed by professional organizations embracing more than a single company. . . .[20]

Try these standards out on your own local paper and see what you find. You will probably be disappointed. Most people are when they take a close look at business news.

---

ever facts they want to hide; it allows them to close their meetings—even "public" stockholder meetings—to the press. Moreover, corporate PR departments do not share the ethic of open access to news. Most government officials understand that an investigative reporter is doing his job and doing it well. Company officials, by contrast, are likely to consider him a discourteous snoop. It is a paradoxical truth that the public is told more about the most trivial federal agencies than about industrial behemoths like Standard Oil and General Motors.

Even if a business reporter could get the information he needed, he would have great difficulty imparting it to his readers. Few subjects are as complex and hard to understand as the intricacies of corporate finance —or for that matter government finance. Suppose U.S. Steel announces a six percent price hike. It takes an unusually well-trained business reporter to calculate the effects of the move, and to decide whether or not it is inflationary. And it takes an unusually gifted writer to translate these conclusions into language a layman can understand. It can't be done in a 40-second TV spot, or even a 500-word article. But will the audience wade through anything longer?

Good business reporting, then, is extremely difficult. You can find it, daily, in the *Wall Street Journal,* a newspaper so comprehensive that many non-businessmen read it for information; so elegant that many others read it for pleasure. You can find it, somewhat less frequently, in the weekly news magazines, which do their best to chart complex trends in simple words. You cannot find it in the average newspaper or broadcast news program.

TRAVEL AND REAL ESTATE

The vast bulk of travel and real-estate news seems to be pure pap, designed only to fill the space between advertisements. Perhaps this is unfair. But it is certainly the case that real-estate brokers, airlines, and resorts advertise generously, and find a perfect environment for their ads in the uniformly enthusiastic and uncritical content of the travel and real-estate sections. And it can hardly be a coincidence that the "news" in these sections so often features the very same places as the ads.

Even the best newspapers regularly fall into these traps. Stanford N. Sesser offers some evidence on the New York *Times:*

> A *Times* travel article on Haiti spoke of "an optimistic spirit" among the Haitian people, who "give the impression that even though they lack the material abundance of some parts of the world, they share the pride that comes with independence." Not only is this description directly contradicted by articles on Haiti in the *Times'* regular news columns, but

the travel story also fails to point out that dollars spent by visitors to Haiti go into the pocket of [now deceased] dictator Francois Duvalier, who desperately needs hard currency to prop up his repressive regime.[21]

Perhaps you feel a travel story has no business talking about dictators and repressive regimes anyhow. But it could at least talk about poor accommodations, overcrowded airplanes, rude customs officials, or the fact that some idyllic vacation isle has just been destroyed by a hurricane. You won't find those stories, either, in the travel section of your local paper. Nor will you find them on radio or television, or in specialized magazines like *Holiday* and *Travel News.*

Real-estate news is more of the same—rewritten press releases designed to persuade the reader and please the advertiser. Ads and commercials for the Potomac Electric Power Company always feature the words "It's Flameless!" One day not too long ago, the Washington *Post* ran a two-page ad for the company. Ferdinand Kuhn comments:

> This time the shinplaster of pseudo-news, fore and aft, was as thick as a featherbed. On that single day the paper printed 145 column inches, almost seven columns, not labeled as advertising, about the delights of electrified home life.
> It told of the joys of electric heating, cooling, floodlighting, and gadgetry unlimited, including an electrically warmed birdbath. . . . When a story dealt with electric heating, the writer was careful to include the adjective "flameless." . . . Again, I suppose, any resemblance to a paid commercial in these news columns was purely coincidental.[22]

These sins are more culpable on the real-estate pages than in the travel section, for real-estate news includes (or should include) a number of genuinely important stories. The quality of urban life is inextricably tied to the amount and kind of new housing that is built. The issues are complex, requiring expertise in such diverse fields as architecture, economics, ecology, and sociology. Perhaps we can forgive the travel section for ignoring the problems of vacationers. But we cannot forgive the real-estate section for ignoring the dangers of unplanned growth.

RELIGION

The newspaper religion section is not unlike the travel and real-estate pages, on a smaller scale. It usually runs a page or two on Friday or Saturday, and is filled with a host of small advertisements from all sorts and sizes of churches. The remaining space is given over to puffery— sermon topics, youth group plans, Sunday school courses, fund-raising campaigns, and the like. The section is not a big money-maker (often the ads are run without charge).   Rather, it is a gift to the churches, a sort of homey, popular, innocuous newspaper tithe.

The wire services move several solid religion articles a week, often controversial ones, but they seldom find their way to the religion section. Instead, they must fight for space on the regular news pages.   Usually they lose the fight and are left out altogether.   The sins of the religion section are thus those of omission, not commission.

Broadcasting, meanwhile, devotes nearly an hour a day to religion. The time is divided between early morning sermonettes and Sunday afternoon discussion groups—always very dignified and seldom very con- troversial.   In rural areas a surprising number of radio stations (and more than a few TV stations) are in the hands of broadcast evangelists, who preach their version of the Gospel and collect contributions.

The best religious news is to be found in the periodical press (and one daily newspaper, the *Christian Science Monitor*).   *Time* and *Newsweek* run searching analyses of religious trends in every issue.   So do the "lay journals" like *Commonweal* and *Commentary*.   And there are literally thousands of local and denominational religious magazines for those with more specialized interests.   Outside of magazines, however, there is very little hard news on religion to be found in the mass media.

SPORTS

Spectator sports are probably America's foremost recreational activity. And since most spectators can't get to the game in person, they rely in- stead on the mass media.   Every sporting event of any significance at all is carried live on radio or television.   The networks bid in the millions of dollars for the rights to the most important games.   Newspapers allot more space to sports than to any other specialized topic (except perhaps the women's pages), and males turn to the sports pages more than to any other section.   Broadcast news programs are even more overbalanced in favor of sports, devoting up to one-third the available time to that single topic.   And the specialized sporting magazines, led by *Sports Illus- trated,* are among the most profitable in the country.

With all that time and space, we have a right to expect sports news as detailed and comprehensive as news of the government.   In a sense, that's what we get.   Certainly every game, every injury, and every trade receives wide attention in the media.   But it is one-sided attention.   If the man was traded because he couldn't get along with his teammates, we are unlikely to be told about it.   If the injury resulted from simmering racial conflicts among the players, we are unlikely to be told about it. And if the game was poorly played and deadly dull, we are unlikely to be told about it. The sports pages, like the travel, real-estate, and religion pages, present a uniformly positive and enthusiastic picture of the world they cover.

Sportswriters are, first and foremost, fans. As Leonard Shecter has put it: "The man who covers a baseball team year after year spends a good deal more time with the management of the ball club than with his own editors; indeed, with his own wife. He becomes, if he is interested enough in his job to want to keep it, more involved with the fortunes of the team than that of his newspaper."[23]

There's nothing so terrible about this as long as it is confined to the amateur level. Who can quarrel with a local paper that refers to the town's star Little Leaguer as a pint-sized Ted Williams, and makes excuses for the 0–23 record of the high school basketball team? But professional athletics—and much of college athletics—is big business. Working to fill a 60,000-seat stadium is not the same thing as helping to support the Little League. On that level the fans have a right to know why seat prices were raised, or why the coach kept his star halfback on the bench. And nonfans have a right to know about illegal recruiting, racial unrest, and the like. If a professional boxing match was a rotten fight, we should be told. If it was fixed, we should be told that too.

ENTERTAINMENT

Herbert Kupferberg likes to tell the story of a young reporter who was sent to interview Van Cliburn when the famous pianist arrived in town to play a Tchaikovsky concerto with the local orchestra.

BROADCAST SPORTS

A newspaper sportswriter may get a few gifts and bribes from the team he covers, but at least it's the paper that pays his salary. Television sportscasters, on the other hand, often get their money directly from the team. And television itself has a strong economic interest in the continued popularity of the sporting events it programs. Little wonder, then, that TV announcers-commentators have more in common with promoters than with other newsmen.

Typical of broadcast sports is ABC's Chris Schenkel, who even "sidesteps naming the player who commits an atrocious personal foul when it is obvious to all in the stadium."[24] But don't despair. ABC also has Howard Cosell, always ready to jump in with scandals, rumors, and instant critiques of the players and the team. No one knows how he gets away with it, but perhaps he is the start of a new trend.

The reporter begins the interview by saying: "Mr. Cliburn, there are two questions I would like to ask you at the very start: How do you spell Tchaikovsky, and what is a concerto?"[25]

The story may be apocryphal, but Kupferberg's point is obvious. The average newspaper pays so little attention to the arts that it does not bother to hire a reporter who understands them.

Yet the average newspaper does have an entertainment section, averaging several pages a day and often dozens of pages on Sundays. Entertainment magazines, from *TV Guide* to *Screen Romances* to *Rolling Stone,* are enormously popular. And entertainers are by far the most frequent guests on radio and TV interview shows.

This is by now a familiar paradox. The mass media devote a great deal of time and space to entertainment, but they publish almost no solid entertainment news. What they do publish can be divided into four categories: service items, press releases, human-interest features, and reviews.

Roughly half the entertainment content of the media is strictly service —radio and TV logs, movie listings, and such. This material is of real value to readers. It is also of real value to the entertainment industry, which shows its appreciation by advertising generously. Interspersed among the ads and the logs are PR releases, touting the virtues of this or that extravaganza. Finally, the editor tosses in a couple of wire service features or locally written human-interest pieces. It takes a real expert to tell this stuff from the PR. It is all light, readable, and invariably glowing.

The reviews are the only entertainment articles that try to be independent. On the whole they succeed. Many a movie theater owner has complained bitterly (and fruitlessly) about unfavorable reviews. But some reviewers still feel an obligation to be kind, and some are susceptible to the subtle bribe of endless free tickets. The Little Theater, meanwhile, is every bit as sacrosanct as the Little League.

WOMEN

To a greater extent than most people realize, women have their own "separate but equal" mass media. Their magazines are among the top sellers in the country—*McCall's, Family Circle, Better Homes and Gardens, Ladies' Home Journal, Redbook.* From ten in the morning to four in the afternoon women absolutely own television. And in newspapers they have the women's section, often called the "family life" section.

What's in it? Here are the most common topics according to one recent survey: club news, food preparation, homemaking, recipes, beauty tips, weddings and engagements, fashion, society, decorating.[26] In addition, many editors put their etiquette and advice columns (always the most popular columns in the paper) in the women's section. And if the publisher can afford to use color anywhere, this is where he'll use it—food and fashion in full color.

The content of the women's section hasn't changed much since the 1880s, and apparently most women like it the way it is. Certainly the advertisers like it that way—a fact that many critics have noted but few have objected to. Consider, for example, the following piece of mild criticism:

> So far as food is concerned, most of the "coverage" consists of recipes. In some instances, the recipes are tied in with the foods being advertised in that day's paper. This is done particularly on Thursdays, when food advertising is heavy before the traditional shopping day, Friday. This is fine, but it isn't enough.[27]

Pandering to advertisers is not, of course, the worst sin of the mass media. It isn't even the worst sin of the women's section. Far more serious is the general inattention to serious issues of special interest to women: the dangers of certain food additives, the ecological consequences of detergents, the fight against sexual discrimination. Today, at long last, some metropolitan dailies are beginning to use these stories on the women's pages. They still have a long way to go.

All these special departments—women, entertainment, sports, religion, travel, real estate, and business—have several things in common. First, they are all accorded a great deal more space than they would get if they had to compete for it on the general news pages. Second, they are all popular with specific groups of readers and ignored by everyone else. Third, they are all geared to keep advertisers happy, and to that end they shy away from controversial or investigative reporting. And fourth, they are all getting away with it.

The journalistic ethic may have been designed with political news in mind, but it should not be limited to political news. Even a stamp-and-coin reporter has an obligation to be honest, aggressive, accurate, and independent. It's time he began living up to it.

NOTES

[1] Bernard C. Cohen, "The Press, The Public and Foreign Policy," in *Reader In Public Opinion and Communication* (2nd ed.), ed. Bernard Berelson and Morris Janowitz (New York: The Free Press, 1966), pp. 134–35, 142.

[2] Leo Bogart, "The Overseas Newsman: A 1967 Profile Study," *Journalism Quarterly*, Summer, 1968, p. 305.

[3] Frederick T. C. Yu and John Luter, "The Foreign Correspondent and His Work," *Columbia Journalism Review*, Spring, 1964, pp. 5–12.

[4] Walter Lippmann and Charles Merz, "A Test of the News," *The New Republic,* August 4, 1920, pp. 1–42.

[5] James R. Whelan, "The Agencies and the Issues," *Nieman Reports,* December, 1967, pp. 8–9.

[6] Peter Barnes, "The Wire Services in Latin America," *Nieman Reports,* March, 1964, p. 5.

[7] Chilton R. Bush, ed., *News Research for Better Newspapers* (New York: American Newspaper Publishers Association Foundation, 1967), II, pp. 37–38.

[8] James A. Skardon, "The Apollo Story: What the Watchdogs Missed," *Columbia Journalism Review,* Fall, 1967, p. 13.

[9] Hillier Krieghbaum, "Dr. Barnard as a Human Pseudo-event," *Columbia Journalism Review,* Summer, 1968, pp. 24–25.

[10] Frank Carey, "A Quarter Century of Science Reporting," *Nieman Reports,* June, 1966, p. 8.

[11] "Eco-Journalism," *Newsweek,* February 1, 1971, p. 43.

[12] Garrett De Bell, ed., *The Environmental Handbook* (New York: Ballantine Books, 1970), p. 265.

[13] Jerry Mander, "Six Months and Nearly a Billion Dollars Later, Advertising Owns Ecology," *Scanlan's,* June, 1970, p. 55.

[14] "The Consumer's Right to Know," *Consumer Reports,* October, 1968, p. 553.

[15] Arthur E. Rowse, "Consumer News: A Mixed Report," *Columbia Journalism Review,* Spring, 1967, pp. 30–31.

[16] Charles E. Swanson, "What They Read in 130 Daily Newspapers," *Journalism Quarterly,* Fall, 1955, p. 417.

[17] *Ibid.,* p. 417.

[18] C. T. Duncan, "The 'Education Beat' on 52 Major Newspapers," *Journalism Quarterly,* Summer, 1966, pp. 336–38.

[19] Sam Zagoria, "Equal Breaks for Labor News," *Columbia Journalism Review,* Fall, 1967, p. 44.

[20] Curtis D. MacDougall, *Interpretive Reporting,* 5th ed. (New York: The Macmillan Co., 1968), pp. 433–35.

[21] Stanford N. Sesser, "The Fantasy World of Travel Sections," *Columbia Journalism Review,* Spring, 1970, p. 46.

[22] Ferdinand Kuhn, "Blighted Areas of Our Press," *Columbia Journalism Review,* Summer, 1966, p. 8.

[23] Leonard Shecter, *The Jocks* (New York: Paperback Library, 1969), p. 23.

[24] Frank Deford, "TV Talk," *Sports Illustrated,* December 14, 1970, p. 13.

[25] Herbert Kupferberg, "The Art of Covering the Arts," *Nieman Reports,* March, 1965, p. 3.

[26] Chilton R. Bush, ed., *News Research for Better Newspapers* (New York: American Newspaper Publishers Association Foundation, 1969), IV, pp. 28–29.

[27] Sister M. Seraphim, "The Women's Section," *Nieman Reports,* March, 1964, p. 13.

SUGGESTED READINGS

CLAY, GRADY, "The State of Urban Design Reporting," *Nieman Reports,* March, 1966.

DIAMOND, EDWIN, "The Dark Side of Moonshot Coverage," *Columbia Journalism Review,* Fall, 1969.

LEAR, JOHN, "The Trouble with Science Writing," *Columbia Journalism Review*, Summer, 1970.

LOEB, GERALD M., "Flaws in Financial Reporting," *Columbia Journalism Review*, Spring, 1966.

RUBIN, DAVID M. and DAVID P. SACHS, *Mass Media and the Environment: The Press Discovers the Environment.* Report prepared for the National Science Foundation (GZ-1777) and available through Department of Genetics, Instrumentation Research Lab, Stanford Medical Center, Stanford, California.

SERAPHIM, SISTER M., "The Women's Section," *Nieman Reports*, March, 1964.

SESSER, STANFORD N., "The Fantasy World of Travel Sections," *Columbia Journalism Review*, Spring, 1970.

SHECTER, LEONARD, *The Jocks.* New York: Paperback Library, 1969.

SKARDON, JAMES A., "The Apollo Story: What the Watchdogs Missed," *Columbia Journalism Review*, Fall, 1967.

ZAGORIA, SAM, "Equal Breaks for Labor News," *Columbia Journalism Review*, Fall, 1967.

Epilogue

For the most part, this book has been highly critical of the American mass media—for two reasons. First, the media deserve and need criticism. Second, it is vitally important that future journalists (and future community leaders in all occupations) be aware of what's wrong with the media and how they must change to better serve the public.

But it is equally important to preserve a sense of perspective. With all their flaws, the American media are probably both the most independent and the most responsible media in the world. The same television system that produces soap operas by the gross has also given us Walter Cronkite and "The Selling of the Pentagon." The same newspaper system that coddles the establishment and mindlessly attacks dissidents also includes the New York *Times* and the *Christian Science Monitor*. The same magazine system that peddles *True Romances* also peddles *Harper's*.

The best of modern American journalism is unmatched anywhere else in history or in the world today. The rest of modern American journalism must be helped to live up to those high standards.

Index